THE
GNOSIS
OF KALI YUGA

BEING A SUMMARY OF THE UNIVERSAL SCIENCE FOR THE
AWAKENING OF CONSCIOUSNESS AS EXPRESSED THROUGH
THE ESOTERIC DOCTRINE OF MAJOR WORLD RELIGIONS

BY

Aaron G. L. Adoni

I WARN THEE, WHOSOEVER THOU ART, OH, THOU WHO WISHEST TO PROBE THE ARCANES OF NATURE, IF THOU DOST NOT FIND WITHIN THYSELF THAT WHICH THOU SEEKEST, NEITHER SHALT THOU BE ABLE TO FIND IT WITHOUT. IF THOU IGNOREST THE EXCELLENCIES OF THINE OWN HOUSE, HOW DOST THOU INTEND TO FIND OTHER EXCELLENCIES? WITHIN THEE IS HIDDEN THE TREASURE OF TREASURES. OH, MAN, KNOW THYSELF, THUS THOU SHALT KNOW THE UNIVERSE AND THE GODS!

– INSCRIBED UPON THE TEMPLE OF DELPHI

OM TAT SAT.

Table of Contents

1. Preface VII
2. Gnosticism 1
3. Kalkian Ignorance 13
4. Gnosis & Happiness 25
5. Reevaluating Social Norms 37
6. Religion & Sexuality 53
7. The Mind & the Ego 67
8. Psychological Gymnastics 83
9. Return and Recurrence of the Ego 93
10. The Tree of Gnosis 105
11. Meditation Fundamentals 119
12. The Fourth Way & the Human Machine 137
13. Seeing the Emptiness 161
14. Sexual Transmutation 175
15. Pure & Empirical Knowledge 197
16. The Liberation of Good & Evil 209
17. Legion, Human, Christ 225
18. The Brain, Mind, and Sleep 237
19. Soteriology: Salvation has Requirements 253
20. Tantrism 279
21. Indecision 303
22. Rudimentary Kabbalah 321
23. Alchemy: Liquid Fire, Igneous Water 361
24. The Two Types of Intoxication 375
25. Comprehension & Elimination 391
26. Conclusions 411

The Philosopher's Stone

Preface

ALTHOUGH we are often enamored with thoughts of how cultured, educated, and modern the developed world has become in the last century, it is abundantly clear that within the areas of religion and spirituality, the most terrible ignorance and fanaticism reigns.

People today are generally materialistic. Generally, though, we do not want to admit it. Nevertheless, the basis, or center of gravity, that the majority of us hang our actions upon is how it will affect the corporal world, and secondly, how others will perceive it. Our psychology, our whole life, revolves around the material, sensual world, and thus, if we have nothing else, then indeed materialism is all that we have to base our actions upon.

Therefore, we are materialists - not from a philosophical or ideological viewpoint - but from a practical one. Yet, few will admit it, because few have ever taken a moment to think about who they are. We lackadaisically boast so much of our self-cognizance, but in reality we are only cognizant in a materialistic sense: we know what we physically look like. From a psychological standpoint however, we are just a like dog, which upon gazing into a mirror, has absolutely no conception of the nature of the image being reflected. In other words, we do not know who we are. This humanity cannot accurately describe its very own psychological self-image!

Incredibly, in most people this important fact is passed over with outright denial, or even worse, boredom. People believe very much in their self-sapience, even though they are completely and totally wrong. This is what some call *complex ignorance*, which in this case means we do not even know that we do not know anything about ourselves. If we, as a culture, at least knew how ignorant we are, in other words if we were only *simply ignorant*, then things would be generally good, but this is not the case at all.

There appears to be something lacking in today's individual. There is a certain type of complacency, and severe indifference, when it comes to these matters of life and death. Throughout history many philosophers have stuffed man's head full with too many theories, and the charlatans have played too many tricks, leaving the masses suffering mystical indigestion.

"There is nothing new to postulate, all the metaphysical theories have been defeated, and all the so-called super-transcendent sacrosanct religious leaders are nothing more than mythomaniacs...," the learned one says. And for the unlearned? Well, they have been taught by the elders and scribes of society to think like them, to act like them, and to believe like them. So, being that the blind is following the blind, together all of us have fallen into the abyss.

Between the two covers of this book, a very pure form of Gnosis is taught. Many learned ones will disagree, because the nomenclature used herein will proceed beyond the usual Aramaic and Greek, and without any fear, also introduce the reader to Sanskrit, Nahuatl, and Tibetan vocabulary. This may upset some people who believe to be erudite in these matters. These learned ones, the "scribes," the "elders," do not actually know Gnosis, and therefore believe it to be something it is not. This is because their associations of Gnosis are invariably locked within certain appearances, and academic study of Gnosticism is founded in historical, empirical and forensic analysis of ancient documents.

As far as academia goes, this is fine, as they are simply performing their vocation, but it is unfortunate for someone considering themselves "Gnostic" to be informed by academics. Yet, this is the way it has become, because, as it will be stated in this work, today's intelligentsia has become the new priestly cast that the layman puts his faith in. Hence, although Gnosis cannot be accurately understood using the aforementioned avenues of study, for most people today it has become a false foundation of their understanding of it.

Subsequently, what constitutes proper "Gnosticism" today has been formulated by classes of people who have – *by definition* –

no requirement in attaining actual gnosis: academia, historians, or heresiologists. In fact, the word itself, *Gnosticism*, was chosen by modern scholars to describe certain historical religious sects even though the ancient sects in question never actually used this word to describe themselves. They instead always referred to their teachings simply as *Gnosis*. Of course this has caused some confusion, and therefore, in the pursuit of clarity, a simple and practical definition is found in the introductory chapter.

An important distinction must be made between materialistic science, and what we can call Gnostic science. Materialistic science bases its premise on materialistic empirical observation of phenomena. If such observation of phenomena is repeatable to all those who possess the sensual faculties to also observe it, the results are understood to be objective. This means that the causes and effects are deemed identical regardless of the subject (person) observing them.

Gnostic science, which is the methodology of gnosis, is different. Where materialistic science uses the functionalisms of the sensory organs as its foundation, the Gnostic science makes use of the functionalisms of the consciousness as it foundation. The Gnostic science does not admit the definition of *objective* that materialistic science does. The Gnostic science only views objectivity to exist outside of subjective perception. The fact that two subjects, two people, view the world identically through their sensory organs is not enough for Gnostic science to state that their observations are objective.

Materialistic science is always evolving, always changing and always contradicting itself. Yet, materialistic science can be practiced by anyone with good sensory organs, and is necessarily communicated through uncompromised literalism. The Gnostic science, which is the source of all religions, is the study of that which never changes (the Truth), and that which is ultimately incommunicable. Therefore, because the Truth can never be communicated *per se*, the Gnostic science must express its transcendental values through various subjective manners, such as parables, myths, allegories, analogies, poetic verse, rituals, koans, similes, metaphors, music, art, dance, and all other forms of symbolism. This is the chief purpose of the world's various religious forms, practices, and customs.

Gnostic science is only verifiable through experience, never through the intellect, and due to the nature of its values, is necessarily distorted when expressed to others, and the more literal the expression, the more distorted the values become. Herein lays the problem, because the Gnostic science must be experienced, yet it can only be practiced by someone who knows how to awaken the consciousness. Hence, the primary goal of this work is to help someone teach themselves, if only at an introductory level, how to awaken their own consciousness.

> Gnosis is lived upon facts, withers away in abstractions and is difficult to find even in the noblest of thoughts.
>
> – Samael Aun Weor, *The Revolution of the Dialectic*

Due to the fact that practically no one knows or accepts the reality of Gnosis, the majority of heralded experts on these matters may not find this work serious or noteworthy. However, if their consciousness was awakened just a bit, and if they were able to achieve *theopneusty*, or the ability to understand the scriptures, then things would be different. Then, instead of using comparison, rational deduction, and carbon dating to understand Gnosticism, they would use the awakened consciousness. It is obvious that theopneusty lies outside the materialistic sciences and lies entirely within the Gnostic sciences.

The learned ones, even if they are very sincere and devout, even the ones calling themselves Gnostic, Catholic, or Protestant, believe they are *pneumatic* (spiritual), but in reality they are just another type of *hylicist* (materialist). They believe the transition from hylic to a pneumatic is as easy as reading a book, listening to a sermon, attending or performing liturgical works, memorizing scripture, reciting prayers, receiving holy titles from holy men, attending venerable intuitions, etc., etc. All of that is rooted in this world, is ephemeral, and of little consequence in terms of legitimate Gnosticism.

On future pages it will be shown modern "man" does not possess his soul or psyche. As such, he is strictly hylic, and he can be no more than that, no matter what he achieves in this world or what he believes what will come about in the next. Only when he possesses a soul, when he develops his soul, his psyche or *psuchikon*, can he be classified as *psychic* under the Gnostic Valentinian and Pauline schools. Understand that this is not the modern "psychic," no, but the ancient and original, which means *"one who possesses a soul,"* or in other words, *"one who is a master of his psyche."* What it means to possess a soul is unknown in this world today, but it shall become clearer as the reader progresses through the chapters herein, as they are written in a progressive fashion, each one developing upon the previous.

Today, every believer, believers with names like Orthodox, Pagan, Hassidic, Sunni, Jain, Sikh, or even Gnostic, thinks that because he reads and agrees with the ancient scriptures that he is therefore a pneumatic, a spiritual one, but in reality he is yet to even reach the level of psychic! He does not even have a soul! This, of course, is very interesting, because to cross the threshold of hylic to psychic is relatively easy, yet, to achieve the most elevated classification (which every believer already believes to be) is much more difficult. To be born again as *pneumatikos* is something terribly divine, something that cannot be achieved simply by attending rituals and studying parchments.

> Marvel not that I said unto thee, Ye must be born again.
>
> The wind bloweth where it listeth, and thou hearest the sound thereof, but canst not tell whence it cometh, and whither it goeth: so is every one that is born of the Spirit.
>
> Nicodemus answered and said unto him, How can these things be?
>
> Jesus answered and said unto him, Art thou a master of Israel, and knowest not these things?
>
> Verily, verily, I say unto thee, We speak that we do know, and testify that we have seen; and ye receive not our witness.
>
> If I have told you earthly things, and ye believe not, how shall ye believe, if I tell you of heavenly things?
>
> – John 3:7-12

What is that which is pneumatic? Materialists only know its corporal counterpart, the air we breathe, but its hidden mystery is the Spirit: the wind which blows, but we, who are yet To Be, do not know where it comes from or where it is going...

Are you surprised about this? Are you still unaware that you are asleep and do not possess a soul? Are you unaware how you must give birth to your soul? And if you do not know this, how can you call yourself knowledgeable?

The world has yet to understand what it means to receive the witness, and to speak the testimony, because indeed these are Gnostic teachings and the Gnostic teachings are not yet known to the world. Therefore, dear reader, continue forth and uncover how to receive what the Masters of Israel called DAATH, but which was later deemed appropriate to be converted into the Gentile tongue, and be called GNOSIS.

THE AUTHOR

Gnosticism

> For the crime of having accompanied Jesus Christ in the holy land, and because of having celebrated our rituals within Rome's catacombs, we, the Gnostics, faced the lions in the circus of Rome. Then later, in time, we were burnt alive in the flames of the Roman Catholic inquisition. Previously, we were the mystical Essenes of Palestine. So, we are not improvising opportunist doctrines. We were hidden for twenty centuries, but now we are returning once again to the street in order to carry on our shoulders the old, rough, and heavy cross.
>
> Paul of Tarsus took our doctrine to Rome. Yes, he was a Gnostic Nazarene.
>
> Jesus-Christ taught our doctrine in secrecy to his seventy disciples.
>
> The Sethians, Peratae, Carpocratians, Nazarenes and Essenes were Gnostics. The Egyptian and Aztec mysteries, the mysteries of Rome, Troy, Carthage, of Eleusis, India, of the Druids, Pythagoreans, Kambirs, of Mithra and Persia, etc., are in their depth that which we call Gnosis or Gnosticism.
>
> We are now once again opening the ancient Gnostic Sanctuaries, which were closed with the arrival of the Dark Age. Thus, we are now opening the authentic Initiatic Colleges.
>
> – Samael Aun Weor, *The Major Mysteries*

The root of Gnosticism is *gnosis*, which is a Greek word meaning *knowledge*. Gnosis is a very special type of knowledge. Gnosis is that which one must acquire in order to free one's self from suffering, to be liberated or to reach salvation. A *Gnostic*, from a general standpoint, is one who is not only searching for, but also receiving gnosis. A Gnostic's mode of life therefore, from both a practical and philosophical point of view, must be considered *Gnosticism*. I think this is a very sensible method to define these terms.

What we can say, in general, is that the proper understanding of Gnosticism can only be found when one has acquired at least some degree of gnosis. This much is self-evident, is it not? The true essence of Gnosticism cannot be uncovered simply by reading ancient manuscripts and dusty parchments, or by reading the many interpretations of others who have read them. Intellectual pursuit, like nostrils leading a man to his meal, can direct and guide one towards the bread of wisdom, but if one wants to know the contents of the food itself, olfaction is not just inadequate, but absurd. Likewise, it does not matter how many years of earnest and sincere intellectual, conceptual, or philosophical refinements have been obtained regarding Gnosticism, a Gnostic it will not make, because that quality of discipline cannot result in the actual obtainment of gnosis.

Gnosticism is *esoteric*, meaning *hidden* or *kept within the interior*. In other words, gnosis is found within one's own consciousness, and as a corollary to this magnificent fact, it is obvious the quality of discipline required for the actual obtainment of gnosis is related with consciousness. Unfortunately we often confuse consciousness with the intellect or intelligence of a person, and believe that those who possess powerful intellectual abilities possess a great degree of consciousness. It is important to understand that this notion is false.

Due to likewise factors, many of the ideas concerning Gnosticism that are floating around today are inaccurate. They are formulated by people who may study Gnosticism, but who are ultimately not Gnostic. Scholars understand Gnosticism as a somewhat vague and often contradictory collection of beliefs that wildly vary depending upon the time and place. In reality the essence of Gnosticism is very clear, precise, and direct. Yet it is also profound, and often thickly veiled in symbolism and allegory, which makes it difficult to comprehend.

The principles of Gnosticism can be expressed through the lexicon and symbolism of any tradition, leading many scholars to consider Gnosticism *syncretic*. Syncretism is the method of melding seemingly unrelated doctrines, and the usual mode of thinking is to believe that Gnostics borrowed all the theological ideas around them, mixed them together, and made a new type of hodgepodge religion. Of course, the reality is quite the opposite: Gnosis is the very core of all religious pursuit, and therefore it can appear under the guise of any religious form. The exterior, literal viewpoints can only see contradiction and confusion, but the interior, esoteric views see the values of gnosis. Those who have the eyes to see can witness these values glowing in all authentic traditions with terrific clarity.

In conclusion, instead of Gnosticism being defined through its transcendent immutable ideals, it has been defined in essence by nothing more than some religious movements that existed within a small locality and historical period. Just about any eccentric religious movement, simply because it happened to exist around two thousand years ago in Mesopotamia or Egypt, is considered Gnostic when in reality many of these systems were not. Some of these groups, even though they use familiar concepts and words, in reality had nothing at all to do with true Gnosticism, for they are anathematic to the teachings of Christ. The modern definition of Gnosticism prevails simply due to the fact that authentic Gnosticism was held in the strictest secrecy for the last twenty centuries. In such a vacuum of public authority profound ignorance prevailed.

Many "experts" treat Gnosticism as a historical artifact; they believe that its existence was destroyed for the most part by the fifth century. Indeed the original sects did vanish. Yet, the values of Gnosticism were carried on, under the names of different groups, sects, and orders. They all held the common thread of the esoteric doctrine of gnosis and a secret link to Christ.

Generally speaking, a Gnostic is anti-sectarian, with one critical exception: while it is true that there is only one path to God, this path can be traversed in two directions. Remember Jacob's Ladder, where Angels were not only ascending, but descending as well. So it is important to note that throughout history not all these ancient so-called "Gnostic" sects were alike: some were using the knowledge in a negative way, and other groups made use of the knowledge in a positive way. Some traditions call these the Left Hand Path and the Right Hand Path. The Bible is refers to these as the sheep and the goats:

> And He will set the sheep on His right hand, but the goats on the left... Then He will also say to those on the left hand, 'Depart from Me, you cursed, into the everlasting fire prepared for the devil and his angels'...
>
> – Matthew 25: 33, 41

From the academic viewpoint, these two sides are sometimes viewed as ascetic forms of Gnosticism and hedonistic forms of Gnosticism. It is plainly evident that Gnosticism and its antithesis are very concerned with sexuality. Some sects preached the strictest chastity and purity, and other sects that taught defilement and debauchery. This is pointed out clearly in chapter 147 of *The Pistis Sophia*, where Jesus denounces the hedonistic sexual acts purported by other false sects. These other sects are the false Gnostic sects. The false Gnostic sects practice the same doctrine of the Nicholaitans mentioned in the second chapter of Revelation.

Modern pseudo-Gnostic groups, some from the "left," and some from "right," want to castrate the teachings of *The Pistis Sophia*. They want to use the parts they adore and love, and throw away the parts that contradict their own ideas of Gnosticism. They believe that Gnosticism is a free-for-all where one can do whatever one pleases, and indeed, even some believe that this is the very essence of Gnosticism.

Of course, everyone is free to possess their own viewpoints. Therefore, we must state that the man we call Jesus is the supreme Patriarch of the Gnostic Church. This Church is open and accessible to those devout aspirants who awaken their consciousness, because it exists within the *Three Amens*, the Divine Trinity that palpitates throughout space, and finds its physical exponent within the soul of the man who self-realizes them.

Jesus taught the methods to acquire gnosis, but when he delivered his doctrine it was not proper at that time to teach everything publicly, thus the esoteric teachings of Jesus are found in the ancient Coptic text *The Pistis Sophia*. The time has now arrived to teach everything publicly, and this is evidenced by all the Gnostic scriptures that have been found throughout the last two hundred years. The Pistis Sophia is the Gnostic Bible and the words of the Adorable Savior of the World.

> *The Pistis Sophia* contains all the words of the adorable Savior of the world. It was written by the Apostles. Thus, all the Esoteric-Christic instructions that Jesus Christ gave to his disciples on the Mount of the Olives and other holy places is written within this book. This book had been conserved in secret for many centuries. In this book, the Adorable One left an extraordinary, formidable body of doctrine.
>
> – Samael Aun Weor, *The Pistis Sophia Unveiled*

Modern Christianity can be traced back to St. Paul, when his sect of Gnosticism was selected as the major source for what became the New Testament. Contrary to popular belief, Paul's teachings are pure Gnosticism. Unfortunately, without understanding Gnosticism, his writings lack their true depth. The literal interpretations purported today of Paul's writings are not the complete teachings of Christ.

During the times of Jesus there were many men of great wisdom living in the area. Today we can call these people Initiates, Masters, or Gnostics. Whatever the name, these people knew very well about the upcoming birth of Jesus and they prepared the area by teaching their knowledge, forming many of the Gnostic sects. However, some of these people ended up betraying the divine plan because, due to jealously, they did not wish to divulge the wisdom to the masses. So, there was of course a great struggle, and in the end darkness fell over the Earth for many centuries. We know these times as the Dark Ages. It was during these times that the Initiatic Colleges closed their doors and humanity was left to drift upon the waters of its own Machiavellian current.

> Jesus did not found the Roman Catholic Church; Jesus founded the Gnostic Church. The Gnostic Church existed in the times of Saint Augustine. This is the Church which was known by Jeronimo, Empedocles, Saint Thomas, Marcion de Ponto, Clement of Alexandria, Tertulian, Saint Ambrosio, Harpocrates and all of the first Fathers of the Church. In that epoch, the Church was named the Catholic Gnostic Church.
>
> The Roman Catholic Church in its present form was not founded by Jesus. This Roman Church is a deviation or corruption, a fallen

branch of the holy Gnosticism. The Roman Catholic Church is a cadaver...

In this present time, the Roman Catholic Church has totally lost the tradition. That is why we see that in this Roman Church the fire of the temple is lit by acolyte boys, an action that is not only an absurdity, but more over, a very grave sacrilege and an insult to life itself...

– Samael Aun Weor, *The Perfect Matrimony*

The Initiatic Colleges were the schools of authentic esotericism. They were found at the heart of all the great religions. These schools existed for the few, the elite, those who proved worthy, those of unquestionable humility, sanctity, and charity. These schools existed in Egypt, Mexico, Peru, Greece, Chaldea, Rome, Phoenicia, as well as in the heart of India, China, the lands of the Druids, Persia, etc., etc. They educated the chosen ones, and as a consequence when these schools flourished, civilization advanced, yet when they closed, civilization lost its secret guides and darkness covered the Earth.

To you it has been given to know the secrets of the kingdom of God; but for others they are in parables, so that seeing they may not see, and hearing they may not hear.

– Luke 8:10

But we speak the wisdom of God in a mystery, even the esoteric wisdom...

– St. Paul, 1 Corinthians 2:7

Esotericism, or the esoteric philosophy, is really one and same as that which we call Gnosis or Gnosticism. Weaving its way through philosophical, religious, artistic and scientific doctrine, the esoteric philosophy is the common golden thread uniting all divine wisdom. It is everywhere, yet, so hidden that few people even consider its very existence. The concealment has been so complete that its existence has all but been completely forgotten. Many "authoritative" voices express extreme skepticism and contempt towards the very idea of something so profound, yet so unknown. Nevertheless this is the way it is.

It seems that the best way to hide something is to speak through symbolism. In this way a single message contains multiple meanings: those who are prepared to hear the superior WORD will hear it, and those who are not prepared will find a lesser meaning. Different beings need different nourishment, and in this way the one who needs meat, will find meat, and the one who needs milk, will find milk. Milk is easy to ingest, yet meat provides the real nourishment.

The esoteric philosophy is the superior teachings of religion. Yet, these teachings give spiritual "indigestion" for those not ready for them: it is too much, too direct, too radical, too harsh, or too difficult. For these reasons Paul, the great Gnostic Hierophant stated the following:

> I gave you milk to drink, not solid food; for you were not yet able to receive it. Indeed, even now you are not yet able.
> – 1 Corinthians 3:2

Now we can understand a bit clearer as to why Jesus spoke in parables, and why some were given the secrets and some not.

Jesus is the savior of this wretched Earth. He arrived during the Age of Pisces and thus we find the symbol of the fish related to Christ, and his first teaching was turning water into wine. This act of transmutation is authentic Alchemy, a pillar of Esoteric Christianity, and it represents a process that must transpire within both our mundane and "ultra" physiology.

Terribly, the purity of Christianity was vastly diluted, and the spirit of Christ's hidden doctrine survived only on the fringe of civilization. Things began to change with the Renaissance, where enlightened men began to rediscover the ancient forgotten manuscripts which revived literature and philosophy. Likewise, art and music began to flourish. Esoteric societies slowly came out from total repose. Religious freedoms were becoming a reality, and eventually culminated in many religious groups populating the Americas.

Authors such as Eliphas Levi wrote publicly about various esoteric topics as early as the 17th Century. Esoteric societies continued to spread. Historically we find portions of the esoteric philosophy within the Knight Templars, Alchemy, Freemasonry,

Rosicrucianism, sects of Sufism, tantric Buddhism, the Kabbalah, Himalayan ashrams, etc. Each center was a small beacon of light that few people had the access or power to find.

However, things took a radical change by the late 1800^s, as it was at this time that a first introduction to "The New Age Doctrine" was given to the world by H. P. Blavatsky, calling her movement Theosophy, which means "intuitive insight into the nature of God." Theosophy had its share of initiates, however, even before their deaths, politics and schisms degenerated the teachings. Many people studied the doctrine from a purely theoretical point of view. They believed, and many continue to believe to this day that through their theories they will perfect themselves.

Rudolf Steiner addressed this with books of practical esotericism in his school of Anthroposophy. G. I. Gurdjieff, also tired of so many theories, started a school of self-development in which he taught The Doctrine of the Many "I's" which he learned in Tibet. Before degenerating, the Order of the Golden Dawn produced many prolific writers such as Dion Fortune. Max Heindel delivered to us *Rosicrucian Cosmo-Conception*; Mainly P. Hall wrote a library of wisdom, including the *Secret Teachings of All Ages*.

Western authors who denounce eastern wisdom and its praxis as unsuitable for westerners are mistaken in this area. Any validity this argument may have held in the past has vanished. Human culture has globalized and we must embrace this modern fact. J. Krishnamurti, after dissolving the Order of the Star of the East, promulgated a doctrine that is absolutely practical and full of wisdom. Likewise, many Yogis of the orient began delivering their doctrine to the West. For example, it is good to study the practical yoga of Swami Sivananda, Swami Vivekananda, and Paramahansa Yogananda.

> If this inner doctrine were always concealed from the masses, for whom a simpler code had been devised, is it not highly probable that the exponents of every aspect of modern civilization – philosophic, ethical, religious, and scientific – are ignorant of the

true meaning of the very theories and tenets on which their beliefs are founded? Do the arts and sciences that the race has inherited from older nations conceal beneath their fair exterior a mystery so great that only the most illumined intellect can grasp its import? *Such is undoubtedly the case.*

– Manly Palmer Hall

In Christianity, too, especially as far as its central point, the Mystery of Golgotha, is concerned, we must make a distinction between exoteric conceptions and esoteric knowledge. An exoteric contemplation of Christianity, accessible to all the world, is contained in the Gospels. Side by side with this exoteric contemplation, there has always been an esoteric Christianity for those who were willing - as I have said before - to prepare their hearts and minds in an adequate way for the reception of an esoteric Christianity.

– Rudolf Steiner

Behind the veil of all the hieratic and mystical allegories of ancient doctrines, behind the darkness and strange ordeals of all initiations, under the seal of all sacred writings, in the ruins of Nineveh or Thebes, on the crumbling stones of old temples and on the blackened visage of the Assyrian or Egyptian sphinx, in the monstrous or marvelous paintings which interpret to the faithful of India the inspired pages of the Vedas, in the cryptic emblems of our old books on alchemy, in the ceremonies practiced at reception by all secret societies, there are found indications of a doctrine which is everywhere carefully concealed.

– Eliphas Lévi, *Dogme et Rituel de la Haute Magie*

All of these authors and movements worked in their own way to divulge parts of the esoteric philosophy to the public as part of a larger plan to eventually reemerge the totality of Gnosticism to the public and reestablish the Initiatic Colleges for all of humanity. Therefore, these individuals kept away from the highest secrets of the esoteric philosophy for they were only preparations for the future teacher mentioned in various esoteric literatures. The name of this teacher is *Samael Aun Weor*. He is responsible for unveiling the full mysteries of the esoteric philosophy to the public. Obviously some people contest this fact, yet, it is incontrovertible that the breadth and depth of the teachings publicly exposed by Samael Aun Weor is unmatched by any other contemporary teacher.

In a similar way that the esoteric teachings took a great jump in publicity two hundred years ago, the teachings that have been given since 1950 by Samael Aun Weor exist upon a still superior octave: the clarity and power of these teachings is unparalleled, as it will be demonstrated.

> Since Gnostic studies have progressed extraordinarily in recent times, no educated person would fall today as in the past, into the simplistic error of associating the flow of Gnosis with some exclusive spiritual latitude.
>
> Although it is true that in any Gnostic system we must take into account its Eastern Hellenistic elements, including Persia, Mesopotamia, Syria, India, Palestine, Egypt, etc, we must never ignore the Gnostic principles visible in the sublime religious cults of the Indo-American Nahuas, Toltecs, Aztecs, Zapotecs, Mayas, Chibchas, Incas, Quechuas, etc.
>
> Speaking quite frankly and straightforward, we will state: Gnosis is a very natural function of the Consciousness, a *Perennis et Universalis* Philosophy.
>
> Unquestionably, Gnosis is the enlightened knowledge of the Divine Mysteries, which are reserved for a certain elite.
>
> The word 'Gnosticism' encloses within its grammatical structure the idea of systems or methods dedicated to the study of Gnosis.
>
> 'Gnosticism' implies a coherent, clear and precise series of fundamental elements that can be verified through direct mystical experience:
>
> - Damnation, from a scientific and philosophic point of view.
> - The Adam and Eve of the Hebraic Genesis
> - The Original Sin and the fall from Paradise
> - The Mystery of Nahua Lucifer
> - The Death of the Myself
> - The Creative Powers
> - The essence of the Salvator Salvandus
> - The Sexual Mysteries
> - The Intimate Christ

- The Igneous Serpent of our magical powers
- The Descent into Hell
- The Return to Eden
- The Gift of Mephistopheles

Only the Gnostic doctrines that entail the abovementioned Ontological, Theological and Anthropological bases are part of genuine Gnosticism.

— Samael Aun Weor, *The Secret Doctrine of Anahuac*

KALKIAN IGNORANCE

> Unquestionably, the Kalkian personalities are victims of self-deceit. They believe that they have achieved everything when indeed they have achieved nothing and what is worse is that they have lost their sense of veneration. They have forgotten the true and authentic religiosity. They have also lost their humility before the Creator Logos. This is what the Kalkian personalities are.
>
> When one comes to this world, one brings within the essence all the data (which is deposited by nature) that one needs for the inner Self-realization of the Being. But, what happens? One is put into schools, where one is receives a false education and much advice and precepts which are futile. In the end, one creates a false consciousness. The true consciousness within, with the deposited data which one needs to follow the footsteps, to follow the path, to arrive at the Liberation of the Being, remains at the bottom, sadly categorized with the name of subconsciousness. Have you ever seen anything more absurd?
>
> We have to become sincere with ourselves, to recognize that our false consciousness is the one which they have formed for us; the one which was created with all their theories learned in elementary and secondary schools, in college, etc., and through so many other ways (such as with the examples of our elders and the prejudices of this society in which we live). Therefore, it is not the true consciousness.
>
> We must eliminate everything which is false within us. We must completely eliminate, definitely eradicate, that false consciousness (which is based on what we have been told, on school precepts, on college lessons, etc.) so that only the true consciousness, the Superlative Consciousness of the Being, remains within us; that is what matters.
>
> – Samael Aun Weor, *The Revolution of the Dialectic*

We are currently in the epoch denoted by the Indian sages as *Kali Yuga*. There are four major *yugas* (ages), and like the four seasons they cycle incessantly. Satya Yuga is the Golden Age, Treta Yuga is the Silver Age, Dvapara Yuga is the Bronze Age, and Kali Yuga is the Iron Age. It is during the Kali Yuga that the most terrifying forms of ignorance and suffering flourish. As a result of all this ignorance, children today are educated in false ways and end up forming a very strong Kalkian personality.

Everyone today has a Kalkian personality, yet some are stronger than others. Principle characteristics of the Kalkian personality are extreme self-sufficiency, unbearable arrogance, an overestimation of the intellect's supremacy, contempt for ancient wisdom and culture, and a misunderstanding or total underestimation of religious pursuit. This is often coupled with either massive sexual indulgence, or, if the temperament is of another type, terrible sexual repression.

In daily life few people will ever consciously consider themselves as "self-sufficient," but this is exactly part of the problem. We ignore all the factors that allow us to exist, to live and breathe, and we end up believing as if we have total control and dominance over our own lives. But the truth is we have very little control. We cannot even control our own thoughts and feelings, let alone our lives as a whole.

There are a few who feel something is wrong with both society and their mode of living. It is these who are trying to undercover something more about life. They attempt to reevaluate their concepts, their morals, their education, religion, their way of living, etc., in hopes of finding something resembling that which we call the truth. They sense the absurd nature of the Kalkian personality, and they want to discover something more substantial. They feel a certain disquietude within their soul. They possess a conflict that they are trying to resolve, and often this conflict is very terrible and difficult.

On other hand, the very strong Kalkian personalities are extremely proud of our current "modern" society and believe that our contemporary wisdom is unsurpassed. They are champions of modern life and state that today we need different values, a different way for different times. There is a tendency to have a certain type of messiah-like complex in regards to the sapience of modern science and medicine. Today, this learned class of individuals (scientists) is looked upon in the same way the priestly caste was viewed in the past. In their good judgment, today's "wise men" look at animals mating with many different partners and encourage or justify society's desire to emulate this behavior. This and a thousand other ridiculous ideas of the sort are advocated and promoted to not only adults, but to the children as well.

The Kalkian personality is not concerned with actual spiritual pursuit because the Kalkian personality wishes humanity to become animalistic. The Kalkian personality has no true concern for what we can call *human virtue*. The evidence is found in our daily lives and in particular the popular forms of media which promote violence, hatred, revenge, anger, lust, and every other animalistic quality.

There is a degree of truth in saying that today we need new values, but in most cases it is these same "modern" values that impede the reception of the comprehension of the world's religious doctrine. This, of course, causes us to viciously spiral into denser forms of ignorance. The new values we need come about by destroying the Kalkian personality, not by strengthening it.

The Kalkian personality is terribly complex and reactionary. It has come to the point that our personalities have become so complex and fragile that even small inconveniences can cause us insurmountable anguish and irritation. There always seems to be something that is bothering us, and as a result we do not have the freedom to be happy. All the tribulations of daily life that appear to incessantly whip us like a tyrannical nemesis – always impeding our otherwise thought-to-be perfect plan of life – is evidence enough of our state of disrepair. Our thought-to-be perfect way of living is really anything but.

The Kalkian personality believes that the outside world is what impedes its true freedom, its happiness, and getting what it wants. In reality, our nemesis is not the outside world. The nemesis of life is one's own action.

Nemesis is the goddess of retribution. In Buddhism this is called karma, and in Christianity it is called The Law. One's retribution is always equal to one's action. You reap what you sow. You may already know this, but have you yet to take the time to actually comprehend it?

A common mistake of today's society is its perpetual failure to realize mistakes on a personal level. Society is made of individuals, but every individual blames society and circumstance for their faults, failures, sufferings, and stress. We continue to believe we know a better way than the others, we believe we know more than anyone or anything, and yet our lives are filled with mistakes, pain, and misfortune. Could this be due to our own ignorance? Could this be due to our own action, which is guided by our knowledge of life (or lack of)? Do we not know that the superior man always criticizes himself and not others?

We wish to believe that others make our life painful, but this is true only on the most superficial of levels. The horrors that exist in the world are nothing more than the reflections of our internal world, our mind. The true cause of suffering, when viewed with profound depth, is one's own quality of mind, and the actions which are invoked from it.

Terrible fear prevents many people from studying their own mind, and this is certainly regrettable. Solemnly, we must state that these people are not yet mature enough to study this doctrine. Some people cannot withstand the sight of their own lives when they actually take a look at it. If you are feeling sad, depressed, if you are always making mistakes and cannot change your position in life, it can be difficult to accept that the causes and conditions for those circumstances in life are due to your own action. For this reason many people leave this teaching: it is too much for them.

The Kalkian personality is alive and well within religion too. The Kalkian religious personality is a total hypocrite; he accuses others of the same crimes he commits. He thinks that if he just believes in his religion, or attends his local church or temple, then he is saved. In Buddhism, instead of simply believing, the Kalkian Buddhist advocates just repeating (like a machine) a certain mantra daily in order to be liberated. Thus, the same principle, spiritual laziness, manifests differently according to the religion.

The Kalkian personality also fashions the robes of esotericism. Many modern esoteric movements were undermined by the ignorance of the Kalkian personality. For example, the biggest enemy of the worldwide Theosophical movement was the Theosophists themselves. They instilled great fear in those wishing to pursue the esoteric philosophy by stating that it was too dangerous, or that eventually humanity will evolve into perfection without any conscious efforts at all. The Kalkian personality gossips about what it has never experienced firsthand and slanders those which it has never met. In the end, a circus is made of out of very serious matters.

Eventually, these Kalkian pseudo-esotericists promoted their degenerated views into what is now commonly considered "New Age" doctrine. This false New Age doctrine includes the side street psychics, the mediums and channelers of all sorts, the incipient and superstitious forms of Astrology, Numerology, Tarot reading, Hypnosis, etc., etc. Some of these studies have their proper place, but they do not resemble what is found today in many book stores. The genuine New Age doctrine is found, for example, in all the authors mentioned in the previous chapter.

The New Age is in reference to the Age of Aquarius. Today's personality is often scoffs at these terms precisely due to the fanatical and ignorant application of them by the Kalkian pseudo-esotericists. No matter how boisterous one's laughter becomes when the subject of Astrology is mentioned, it will not stop the Aquarian current from entering the atmosphere of our planet and radically transforming society. The Aquarian current is totally *Dionysian*. Remember Dionysus, the God of wine. This is the same wine of Christ. It is the same principle, but under a different name.

The Aquarian-Dionysian influence was the secret progenitor of the 1960's cultural revolution that threw out antiquated taboos and dogmas as well as provided the prolific thirst for the everyday man to transcend his mundane and miserable reality. The problem occurred when – because this aforementioned influence was too strong for this very psychologically weak humanity – the major populace ended up polarizing the Aquarian-Dionysian influence in a *negative* fashion.

Sex is the cornerstone of Aquarian culture because Aquarius rules over the sexual-endocrine glands. Thus, when this massive influence of Aquarius agitated the sexually potent youth of the 1960s, the outcome was an intense desire for revolution, and especially a sexual revolution. Thus, from a transformation of the "hip" ones – the Hipsters and the Beatniks – the Hippie movement resulted, but, as it was stated, this movement (and all of the movements it birthed) is decisively negative.

The positive polarity of the Aquarian current influenced the crystallization of the global Gnostic Movements. All the same principles are found in the Gnostic Movements but polarized in a positive fashion. While the Hippie squanders his sexual potential with so-called "free love," the Gnostic frees himself from desire by transmuting his sexual potency. When the Hippie is experiencing nature through the inferno of drugs, the Gnostic is experiencing the ultra of nature in the heights of meditation.

> Specifically, we will state: psychedelia is the antithesis of meditation. The inferno of drugs is within the interior of the planetary organism on which we live, under the very epidermis of the terrestrial crust.
>
> Hallucinatory mushrooms, L.S.D., pills, marijuana, etc., evidently intensify the vibratory capacity of the subjective powers, but it is ostensible that they could never originate the awakening of the consciousness.
>
> Psychedelic drugs fundamentally alter the sexual genes and this is already scientifically demonstrated. The birth of monstrous children is evidence of the sequence of such negative, genetic mutations.

Meditation and psychedelia are incompatible, opposite, and antagonistic. They can never be mixed.

Unquestionably, these two factors of the Dionysian inebriation refer to and indicate psychological rebellion.

Gnostics and Hippies were annoyed with the vain intellectualism of Mammon[1]. They were bored with so many theories. They arrived at the conclusion that the mind, as an instrument of investigation, is abundantly miserable...

Zen? Jnana Yoga? These are superlative. Faculties of cognition that are infinitely superior to the mind exist in a latent state within us. We can experience that which is the Reality, that which is not of time, in a direct way, by means of these faculties.

Unfortunately, the Hippie Movement preferred the inferno of drugs. Indubitably, they defined themselves perversely.

We, the Gnostics, plainly disappointed with the stubborn intellectualism of Mammon, drink the wine of meditation from the cup of perfect concentration.

Radical and in depth psychological changes are urgent when we are disappointed with the scoundrels of the mind.

To return to the original point of departure is what is wise. Only thus is a radical transformation possible.

Sexology? Bless my soul, oh God, and hail Mary! This theme horrifies the puritans...

It is written in the sacred scriptures with words of fire that sex is a stumbling stone and a rock of offense...

The evidence stands out; we are not the offspring of any theory, school, or sect.

In the crude root of our existence, we only find the coitus of a man and a woman...

We were born nude; somebody cut our umbilical cord; we cried, and then we searched for the maternal breast...

Clothing? Schools? Theories? Erudition? Money, etc.? All of these came later on, as an addition.

Beliefs of all types exist everywhere. However, the unique force that can transform us in an integral and unitotal way is the force

---

[1] *No one can serve two masters; for either he will hate the one and love the other, or else he will be loyal to the one and despise the other. You cannot serve God and mammon.* – Matthew 6:24

that placed us on the carpet of existence. I am referring to the creative energy of the first instant, to the sexual potency.

The delightful love, the erotic enjoyment, is by logical sequence the greatest joy...

To know how to wisely copulate is indispensable when a definitive psychological change is sincerely longed for.

The Hippies forebode all of this when they revolted against Mammon, but they erred in their way. They did not know how to synchronize themselves with the positive pole of Dionysus.

We, the Gnostics, are different; we know how to enjoy. To transmute and sublimate the libido is enjoyable for us. This is not a crime.

The Hippie Movement and subsequent cultures resolutely march on the devolving, descending path of infrasexuality.

The universal, international, Christian, Gnostic movements victoriously progress on the ascendant, revolutionary path of suprasexuality.

– Samael Aun Weor, *The Three Mountains*

It is important to discern the negative teachings from the positive teachings. The majority of what is popularly considered "occultism" or "New Age" is a negative crystallization of Aquarius. Nevertheless, both teachings use the same terminology, the same concepts, and similar methods, and as a result many are fooled. It is almost without exception that the most popular esoteric books are negative. They offer something for nothing, they are the equivalent of "fast-food" for the soul: easy to consume, but ultimately provide no sustenance for the soul to grow in a positive fashion.

Those who choose to manipulate others, who lie and gain power in unruly manner, those who attempt to "attract" the things they desire in life, walk down the left hand path, even if they do not know it. Any attempt to impose one's will upon another person or group of people, any method of ruling over another's mind or will, any attempt to force one's situation in their favor at the expense of others, is one who walks upon the left hand path, even if they are not conscious of the expense they force others to pay. These *lefteous* doctrines often adorn themselves with beautiful theories and spiritual appearances that confuse and deceive their adherents. The sign of the left hand path is the five pointed star, with the superior point downwards.

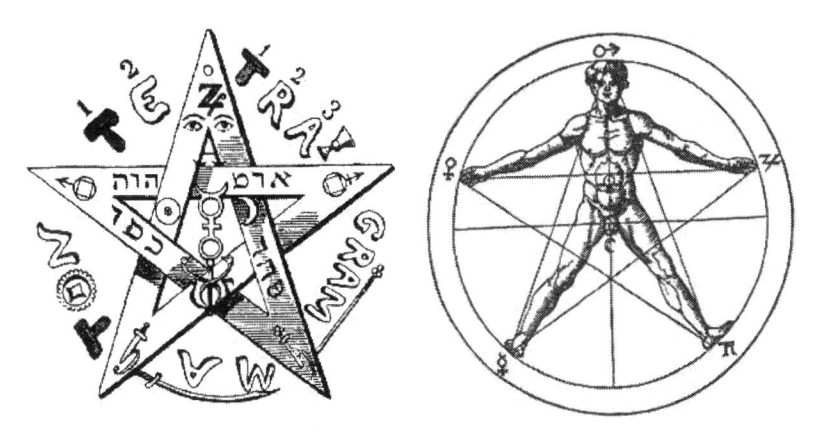

The upright pentagram.

Those who choose love and compassion for all beings walk on the right hand path. They only wish to perform the will of god, nothing more or less. They state that the path to god is difficult, that it is impossible to get something for nothing, and that it is a lie to state that there is some trick or method to take a short cut to happiness and ultimate freedom. As always, the symbols between the two paths are similar: the symbol of the right hand path is the five pointed star facing upwards, symbolizing man's ascent into Heaven.

The similarity between the one who venerates the divine and the one who venerates their desire has led most people into confusion. One states, "We shall live under the cross." The other, "We shall carry the cross." The difference appears subtle, but their meanings are antithetical, for to carry the cross is the live the drama of the cross, but to live under the cross is to be the unjustly accuser of the righteous one.

Kalkian puritanical-hypocritical religious personalities are outraged by the mere sight of the pentagram. They ignore that the flag of the United States of America contains fifty pentagrams on it, and if they were to do the research, would also know that medieval Christians used the pentagram to represent the five wounds of Christ. All of the fear surrounding occultism is based in ignorance.

When Pilate placed Jesus in front of the crowd, he offered them the choice between Jesus the Christ, and another man named Barabbas Jesus. Matthew 27:17, from its original unedited Greek reads: "...*whom will ye that I release unto you? Jesus Barabbas or Jesus which is called Christ?*"

Who is Barabbas? Barabbas can be understood as Bar Abbas, which in Aramaic means "son of the father." Therefore, before the crowd stood Jesus Christ, Son of the Father, and Barabbas Jesus, which is also the "son of the father." As we already know, the crowd frees the criminal and crucifies the innocent.

Barabbas Jesus represents the inverted pentagram, and Jesus Christ represents the upright pentagram. From an exoteric point of view, this represented certain factions which worked against the Lord, as it was explained in the previous chapter. From an esoteric point of view, the crowd represents the impulses in one's body, the emotions in one's heart, and the thoughts in one's head, which, when left without guidance, betrays the inner Lord. In daily life we mistake the two Sons of the Father. Jesus is the upright son, the Redeemer, yet, Barabbas is the fallen son, the sinner.

All our psychological conflict without exception externalizes not only in our physical reality, but within our sentiments, our reasoning, and our volitions. Fortunately, we can take advantage of these processes when we make the conscious decision to observe and resolve them. Life is the refection of who we are, and it provides a full length mirror within which we can view and solve our problems.

Every person looks to solve their troubles, yet, we all continue to suffer them. So few people liberate themselves from even the commonest afflictions of life, therefore, what is necessary is something not commonly understood. If the path to liberation was commonly understood, then the common man would have accomplished it. Something radical must be done.

Our lives tumble in the winds of life like leaves that have fallen from its tree. We ignore that we do not know who we are and even firmly believe we have self-knowledge (gnosis). Contemplate a little: Do you think you know who you are? We should investigate these matters, and when we do, what is found is that our self-knowledge is nothing more than an identity: a name, a job, a sum of likes and dislikes, a nationality, an education, a social status, etc., but that is not who one is. All of that is a personality. Who are you if all your material items, your family, your job, and your physical body are taken away? After pondering this, who are you? What is the meaning of your being? Obviously, society tells us that we are what our personality is, but in reality the personality has no existence. What we know of ourselves is an illusion.

When one fundamentally acknowledges the grand deception of the lives we live, one is moved from within the depths of their own constitution with the yearning to find that which is real. For this reason he will begin the true search for the Secret Path found at the heart of every religion. Every religion has its system upon the Secret Path, but you must know the ciphers in order to see it. The ciphers that form the basic keys of religion have been completely hidden from the uninitiated until a relatively recent time.

Ignorance is darkness. Consciousness is light. When the light shines in the darkness, the darkness does not understand it. With the right effort though, one can make their own light and extinguish ignorance for good.

GNOSIS & HAPPINESS

> The Sufis and the whirling Dervishes' secret science is within Gnosis; the secret doctrine of Buddhism and Taoism is within Gnosis; the Nordic people's sacred magic is within Gnosis; Hermes', Buddha's, Confucius', Mohammed's, Quetzalcoatl's, etc., wisdom is within Gnosis; Christ's doctrine is the essential Gnosis.
>
> – Samael Aun Weor

Being misunderstood at its root, both critics and misguided supporters of Gnosticism often believe that what constitutes gnosis are simply communicable secrets passed from mouth to ear, rituals performed, etc., and possessing this knowledge, or enacting some secret sacrament alone would provide salvation. This is not so.

The secret knowledge, gnosis, is something individual. Everyone has their own gnosis, given to them from that which is called God or divinity, and only one's own gnosis can save one's self. The Gnostics certainly did have secrets of an intellectual type, and rituals such as the Mass, but they were merely a means, an assistance, in order to reach the goal. Actual gnosis is something living and could never be found in the dead letter of any book or sermon. Yet, what books and teachings can do is point towards gnosis and aid those searching for it.

Gnosis is defined as both the knowledge gained through experience and the method or science to achieve it. Unfortunately, academia has no way of recovering the science of gnosis strictly from crumbling parchments, and without the science, there can be no way to acquire the knowledge. Likewise, without gnosis there can be no understanding of Gnosticism.

What is written in the Nag Hammadi, the Dead Sea Scrolls, the Gospel of Judas, etc., reveal many clues and hints, but they rarely provide anything that can be correctly interpreted without previously being exposed to the ciphers that hide their profound inner meanings. As a result, scholars can only depend upon the theories based off their *ideas* of Gnosticism. Thankfully, as it was stated previously, the actual science has been passed through the various esoteric sects throughout the ages and was revived in the 20th Century by Samael Aun Weor.

> Mexican codices, Egyptian papyri, Assyrian bricks, Dead Sea scrolls, strange parchments, as well as certain very ancient Temples, sacred monoliths, old hieroglyphs, pyramids, millenary sepulchers, etc, offer in their symbolic depth a Gnostic sense that definitively escapes literal interpretation and which has never had an exclusively intellectual explanatory value.
>
> Lamentably, speculative rationalism, instead of enriching the Gnostic language, impoverishes it, since Gnostic matters (whether they be written or allegorized in any artistic form) are always directed to the Being.
>
> Thus, it is in this extremely interesting Quasi-Philosophic and Quasi-Mythological language of Gnosis that a series of extraordinary invariants appear: symbols with a transcendental Esoteric content, which silently say much.
>
> Divines and Humans know very well that silence is the eloquence of wisdom.
>
> The characteristics that clearly specify the Gnostic Myth and which mutually complement each other are the following:
> 1. Supreme Divinity.
> 2. Emanation and fall of the Pleroma.
> 3. Architect Demiurge.
> 4. Pneuma in the World.
> 5. Dualism.
> 6. Savior.
> 7. Return.
>
> – Samael Aun Weor, *The Secret Doctrine of Anahuac*

Gnosis is self-knowledge, but it is not ordinary knowledge and it is not simply knowledge of the personality. To know who you are as a personality is fine but that knowledge is worthless at the end of the day. There is something beyond what one normally considers their self to be. This "transcendent self" is so radically different from our ordinary conceptions of self that in Buddhism it is taught as *no-self*.

A man without gnosis is blind to the causes and conditions of his life. In his journey of terrestrial existence, he wanders from one destination to the next. An education, a marriage, a home, these are all destinations on the voyage life. At times he rests, and later he moves on: a new job, the birth of a child, a death in the family, etc. Throughout his journey our traveler gains information about his life, but this does not mean he has acquired gnosis in the strictest sense of the word.

Throughout life we learn many things, but that knowledge is not gnosis, because usually it is just mundane worldly knowledge. Experience in this society is good, this is how we live from day to day, how to deal with investments, how to repair our car and home, how to take care of our family and interact with society, etc. Everything here is not only useful, but necessary, yet it is all related to the personality and of the modern times. Therefore, it is not inner knowledge, it is not true knowledge.

Fortunately it is within this same life that gnosis is waiting to be found. We just need to accustom ourselves to find it. In order to access this special knowledge, we need a "shock" or an "active pressure" upon the consciousness. We need to activate something within that is currently dormant, sleeping. Gnosis cannot be found in a mechanical or blind way. So, if a man travels on life's journey without knowing where he came from or where he is going, blindly following the tides of time, he will quickly find himself dead with little or no true knowledge of life at all.

Sometimes we are given exceptional circumstances that activate our consciousness, allowing us to perceive the greater truths in life, even if it is only for a brief time: an epiphany. For example, when a loved one dies unexpectedly or when a child is born. Events like this cause some people to begin to experience the world in a different manner because it causes the consciousness to be shocked into awakening in some way. Consciousness is the root of perception, and awakening the consciousness allows one to perceive the nature of reality in a more piercing or direct manner.

In the case of death, this shock is not pleasant. Nevertheless, there is tremendous value in understanding the nature of death. It is only after witnessing death that many people seriously contemplate life. Others do not change one iota in their ways of life until they witness the birth of their child. It is only at this moment, shocked by the majestic reality present before them of their newborn do they tremble at awesome creative potential of the human organism. Thus, it is in these ways that they grow up, lose their childish ways and become responsible adults.

It is horrifying that, as a result of a shock of the consciousness, some people let personal crisis become a theme song that they always carry with them; as a result their lives become more terrible. Instead of taking advantage of their situation as leverage to change their life, they become a pig that rolls in its own psychological despair, giving nothing but the mud of their misery as payment to those who keep their company.

If life can give us events that change our understanding of life, we can take the next logical step and conclude that it is possible to provide the consciousness an intentional activation in order to acquire gnosis. By doing this we take a willful comprehension of the causes and conditions of life. This is how we can begin to obtain control of our life, and it can be done in many ways according to ancient tradition. In history we can equate it to terms such as: religious devotion, meditation, or self-observation.

Everyone travels the journey of terrestrial life. Yet, there is another journey that few travel. It is not a journey of external circumstances, but rather of one's state of being. Although everyone changes throughout life few people actually travel this other path. This is the path up Jacob's ladder. Each rung represents a "level of being." The higher rungs are higher levels of being, such as the level of a saint, a prophet, or an angel. The lower rungs pertain to lower levels of being and consequently greater degrees of ignorance and suffering. The true purpose of life is to acquire ever higher levels of being. The greater the level of being one has the greater degree of freedom and happiness one experiences.

In general, society does not teach how to acquire inner knowledge. What it teaches is how to become rich, how to become respected, to be famous, to become a believer, how to conquer and gain power in this society. Some indeed do accomplish all of that. They achieve it all, yet they are not content with life, they are not happy in a true sense. The worthlessness of our modern culture's message is self evident, yet so pervasive that few people even take a moment to question it.

Every individual believes they know how to live in the best way, and upon investigation we find that the root cause of all our action in life is to gain happiness. Contemplate this for a little bit. We act in the way we believe will give us what we want, and what we want, ultimately, is happiness.

But what exactly is happiness? Is happiness getting what we want? Surely, it cannot be, because there are innumerable cases when we do get exactly what we strive for, but we still find ourselves looking for happiness, for something to satisfy us.

Is happiness a promotion at work? The respect of your family, your peers, or boss? Is it the plaques and diplomas that rest upon your wall, perhaps covered with the dust of so many yesterdays? Is it the joy of seeing your child? What if your child grows up to resent you? Where, then, is happiness? Where is happiness when life assaults you with too many unfavorable circumstances?

Some will answer that indeed happiness is one more of these things... the simple pleasures of life... but, for everyone who has experienced it all, all the "happiness" of life, what is their current psychological mood? Do they get angry? Do they get sad? Do they get cranky? Are they frustrated? Do they lie, cheat, or steal? Are they afraid of their inevitable death? Are they sexually content in every possible way?

We must conclude that happiness is indeed very elusive. Where does it come from? Where does it go?

There is a common assumption that happiness is found in the world, "out there," somewhere in the world. The reality is that happiness is a state of mind. Happiness is not a place or any type of circumstantial arising. Happiness is an intrinsic property of the universe. The problem is that our states of mind rely on the events of life. Our mind is a slave of the sustenance of temporal sensation. A true illuminated and happy person finds that happiness from within, regardless of what is occurring in the external stage of the world. A crystal clear mind of illumination does not nourish itself from the events of the world because it craves nothing.

How many times have we gotten that promotion, that raise? Surely, it feels good... but has it ever provided contentment? What provides financial contentment is not a raise, but a state of mind that lacks greed, pride, and fear. As long as one remains greedy, there will never be financial contentment. So long as one is afraid of loosing their "things," they will always want more. As long as one is too proud to own things of lesser value, they will always need to spend more. Money does not make one greedy, it is the mind. Life does not make one sad, rather it is the quality of mind.

Today's success is something defined along the lines of an education, a family, a house, and two cars. This is common in the western world particularly. Yet, having all of this "success" we still find ourselves discontent. So? Now we want a boat and a bigger house, and even more money, something more, *something*. That something cannot be bought, sold, stolen, or cheated – and when one tries to do so they only end up stealing and cheating their own birthright of gnosis. Remember Esau who sold his birthright for a bowl of porridge...

What we do not realize is that the cause of suffering and happiness lies within existence itself. Ignoring this fact we submerge ourselves into hobbies or useless activities in order to avoid the things we do not wish to know of within ourselves; in other words, we ignore, or refuse to admit that we, individually, are the cause of our own state in life. Does such an idea seem too outlandish? We can be quick to take offense at this notion, and yet, who rightfully and obviously receives proper recognition for the numerous accomplishments in one's life? Indeed, it is all too easy for "I," "me," and "myself" to take credit for all that which is good, yet, how interesting is it that the failures one experiences always have long and complicated reasoning behind them?

What is necessary in order to find genuine happiness is to know the truth about ourselves. What is true and what is not true has nothing to do with an argument we form in our mind. This is an important fact to understand, because we all form a very elaborate theory in our heads to justify the state of our lives. We think, "If only people could treat me with the respect I deserve... If only my coworker was not so stupid... If only the world treated me perfectly... *then*, I would be happy." This type of thinking is deceitful and incredibly harmful, nevertheless we choose to believe it because it is the argument we want to believe. We construct very elaborate arguments to appease our self-illusions. In other words, *we believe what we want to believe*, but we pretend it is the objective truth. Ultimately, every logical argument can be refuted with an equally constructed counter-argument. An argument in itself means nothing.

The mind has the dusty fragrance of a library containing endless aisles of books. In this library we can read our many books (memories), but just as reading a book on riding a bicycle has little to do with the experience of actually riding one, accepting or rejecting theory has no bearing on its reality. True reality strikes us not from the mind, but from beyond the mind, because the mind does not have the capacity to know the truth. Perceptions are not reality. We experience reality not through ordinary thought or emotion, but something superior. We need to open up this superior aspect of ourselves because this gives us direct experience of the superior worlds, of the "ultra." This is what is called Heaven or Nirvana.

Obviously, we need to begin with an intellectual, theoretical idea of the esoteric philosophy. Through the reading of this book one can gain a theory, however, that is of no consequence without direct experience. No book or form of logic can provide direct experience. Gnosis is direct, living experiential knowledge. Gnosis is self-knowledge. The mind has already been pushed to its limits. We all know the benefits of the mind, and for this reason I do not need to write about educating the mind. We are already in this very modern society reaching the breaking point of intellectualism. The problem is that we use the mind too much. We are out of balance and as an outcome, the birth the materialistic dialectic, fanatical skepticism, sexual perversion, and a range of mental illnesses are occurring. Therefore, we need to equilibrate ourselves emotionally, physically, and intellectually. We need to regain psychosomatic equilibration.

There are countless theories on God, and the vast majority of spiritual groups are simply proliferating beliefs. However, what is necessary is direct experience. The real goal of this work is for the reader to directly experience the awakening of consciousness. The awaking of consciousness is the absolute antithesis of our present state of mind. Religion tells us to awaken, but we continue to sleep within our false mental representations and mechanical associations. If we want to awaken we need to alter every aspect of our lives, because society is teaching us how to sleep, not how to awaken. To awaken means to see the truth about ourselves, and thus to see the truth in the world around us, but this is no insignificant task. In reality, it is very difficult and requires tremendous willpower.

> Bull-like, noble, a hero, a great sage, and a conqueror, he who is motionless of mind, washed clean and awakened – that is what I call a brahmin.
>
> – Buddha
>
> Love not sleep, lest thou come to poverty; open thine eyes, and thou shalt be satisfied with bread.
>
> – Proverbs 20:13

Due to our sleeping consciousness, we are unaware of the superior aspects of our Being. We know nothing about our true self. We now erroneously assume we are a personality and are consequently identified with something that has no real existence. Therefore, when we awaken, we come to know what we truly are and we come to know about the universe. To know the external world one must know the internal world, because the exterior arrives through the interior. This is why when one comes to know the interior, they come to know the exterior, and likewise those who never explore their own inner psychological country will never gain true knowledge.

It is clear that our interior is a frightful area to situate our attention upon, namely because we never spend any time observing our interior. We rarely, if ever, take the time to contemplate the secret interior impulses of our actions. We ignore our dreams at night to the point of amnesia. Our minds often race at a million miles an hour, and many only find relaxation through the consumption of alcohol or drugs. All of this is evidence of escapism.

It is quite evident that we are smothering our insecurities in vain attempts to remove them. We "escape" through whatever means necessary, because, ultimately, we are afraid of the monster in our dreams, we are afraid to actually look at the mess we have created, we do not want to know what we have made ourselves into. When we unleash that monster, and a fit of rage surges forth, we later state, "I did not act like myself..." Well, if that wasn't you, then who was it? It is that which you try so diligently to ignore, to escape.

Let us now manifestly understand that few people possess the courage to stand in full attention within the darkness of their own creation. Rare is the one who can make out the Path to the Light through the dense, dark labyrinth of their own conditioning. Who actually wants to look in the mirror and see who they really are? Who wants to know how they are seen by others? Who wishes to take responsibility for all the hateful things they have done? Begin to observe life and one will find that very few people want to know who they truly are. People rather live as who they wish to be, who they dream of being.

One can catch their voice saying things like, "When it comes to cleaning the house, I'm a real fanatic... but that's ok." Within this absurd affirmation is a speck of gnosis, a little tiny bit of self-knowledge. To simply justify our fanaticism because we like our fanaticism and we have no desire to remove it will never lead to understanding our fanaticism. Thus our knowledge remains hidden. But to look at it squarely, front and center, without evasion or prevarication, to actually probe the reason behind action: that is something that gives us self-knowledge. You may not know this yet, but self-knowledge is the key to life and death and happiness itself. But, to even grasp this latter fact, one must first have gnosis of finding gnosis! So, just for now take my word for it: self-knowledge is summit and key of all knowledge.

The state of dream is a state of ignorance. We dream constantly, and we are therefore ignorant. All day we dream of being correct, superior, justified... We think with unknowing arrogance, "That driver just cut me off and almost caused a car accident... how could he be so stupid? Why are these people ruining my day?" Once again, this rather odd behavior is seen as normal. In reality it is not normal at all. Perhaps it is normal for a child to cry in front of spilt milk, yet what kind of normal adult would get angry at another person? What is normal in this world is abnormality.

Society itself is greatly infected with a disease that causes this abnormal behavior. The name of the disease is called "ego." It is not of a physical nature, but rather of a psychological nature, and as a result our psychological degradation is quite profound. We are very, very sick, so sick that it takes a large dose of highly concentrated medicine to get better. Being that our illness is of a psychological nature, it is obvious that this medicine is also psychological.

The medicine is gnosis. Sometimes medicine does not taste good. Sometimes, to get better, one has to go through a lot of pain, a lot of crisis, just as a patient needs to go through physical ordeals, like surgery, in order to ultimately be cured. The reader will now understand why Buddha has been known for over 2500 years to be The Great Healer. Jesus healed people of leprosy, yet today this is easy, any doctor can cure leprosy. But who can cure themselves of psychological leprosy? The esoteric significance of Jesus healing the leprous is purely of a psychological nature.

> The pleasure that appears as poison in the beginning, but is like nectar in the end, comes by the grace of Self-knowledge, and is in the mode of goodness.
>
> – The Bhagavad Gita 18.37

The truth is we like to get angry, otherwise, why would we be angry? Have we ever examined our anger? Of course our anger likes to be angry! The answer is to remove our anger through *comprehending it*, to destroy even the shadow of it, not to justify it through reasoning or condemn it through repression. To annihilate one's anger is not something many wish to do, because, they think "that is a part of me, that is who I am, that makes me unique." That is a true statement, but the question then becomes: Why do we like to hold on to our sufferings, why do we want anger to be a part of "who I am?"

If we were to spend just a small amount of time observing it, we would quickly conclude that our psychological country is a mess. It is a land of destitution where various desires fight as war lords to gain dominance and to reign as king. When one particular "lord" becomes governor, we personify that desire: we become identified with it. In that moment, we are that desire, we act in accordance with it – that is until another arrives and takes control. This is how we change our minds, how we say one thing and do another, how we feel one way today and another way tomorrow. Thus, in the same way a puppet is under the influence of the strings that suspend him, so are we subservient to different, contradictory and quasi-autonomous psychological constitutions of our own creation.

If we continue to observe this land, we will discover with astonishment the tangible actions that create and destroy these particular "war lords." This is precisely what we are after in the esoteric philosophy, because if we know how to stop acting in ways that cause suffering and to begin acting in ways that produce happiness, then we can at least have a choice in life.

The "self" is the suffering, the "self" is the arrogance, it is the pride, it is the ignorance, and therefore it is the "self" that must die. That may sound unrealistic, but that statement is more real than any of the lies we live by. It is the essential truth that religion teaches.

Have you transformed your life into everlasting happiness? Have you transformed your life in to conscious happiness? Do you have control over your happiness? Do you really know what happiness is? My friend, we have to awaken, and only then do we have a choice in life. Happiness has nothing to do with sensation, it is not pleasure, and it is not a feeling as it is normally understood. We learn to smile at work and for the camera, but that is not happiness. Happiness is not something to be learned or forced.

Happiness is a joy of existing close to the glory of God, and God is not a person. He is an intelligence, he is love, *he is happiness*. This is how we must understand happiness. It is a deceitful notion that happiness is something to do with sensuality, hording money, "making my parents proud," or one million other ridiculous ideas of the sort.

We have no conception of true happiness. Some people hear about Nirvana and think, "What will I do if I attain nirvana? Enlightenment seems boring... meditation looks dull..." This manner of thinking exemplifies of our incorrect understanding of happiness. We commonly believe happiness has to do with sensation, thus an activity such as meditation – an activity which has little to do with sensation – seems anything but happy. Nevertheless, when meditation is practiced correctly, it brings about experiences that cannot be described in words, which is true joy. Therefore, it is imperative to transvalue our concept of happiness.

It is important to understand that these are not fantastic ideas that simply manifest because we believe in them. We are speaking of the great events that occur due to great sacrifices, triumphs, and efforts. Many people who are searching for "something," are searching for a new set of beliefs. What is better is direct experience, because no belief leads to happiness.

Reevaluating Social Norms

> All things, all circumstance that occur outside ourselves, on the stage of this world, are exclusively the reflection of what we carry within.
>
> With good reason then, we can solemnly declare that the 'exterior is the reflection of the interior.'
>
> When someone changes internally and if that change is radical, then circumstances, life and the external also change.
>
> – Samael Aun Weor, *Revolutionary Psychology*

Do you ever take a second out of the day to notice your psychological state? Do you ever, just for a second, observe the life you live so dramatically? For example, simply notice the various men and women going about their days. It is very interesting to observe all the passionate emotions, the idle chatter heard by the citizens as they pass from every direction, hustling from here to there... Is it possible to walk down the street paying attention to the outside world while inside remaining in perfect silence, observing both our interior state and the state of our exterior world?

How strange it is to forget all the temporary problems of the day, and honestly reflect on the fact that you *are alive and experiencing*. It is very novel to seriously contemplate these matters. What will become obvious to us, as we take a walk and notice the world, is that everyone around us is completely unaware of the fact that they are *alive* and *exist* within the moment. Honestly, it is quite rare to find someone who is within a supreme moment of quietude actually living life within that very moment. It is much more normal to find everyone busy in their heads, busy with the memories of the past, busy with the troubles of now, busy with the future troubles, fantasizing about this or that great thing that will occur, or simply frantic, chaotic, confused...

What does it mean to start living within the moment of now? It means to discontinue thinking for just a moment and to start seeing the world around you. Nine out of ten thoughts we have are wasteful or harmful to ourselves and others. The natural and peaceful state of the mind is silence. It is important to stop mechanical thought and daydreaming. These things are pollutants of the mind, yet we are so conditioned to polluting our mind, that may seem quite impossible to stop thinking even for a moment. But it is possible, with the right effort. One must strive to be aware of the self at all times, and to do this, one must remain internally quiet. One must become aware of the self, because this is where knowledge hides.

The next time you are taking a walk, or sitting on the couch, or at work, notice everything around you, notice yourself. View your internal environment as a hawk views the various fish in the waters below. Look inside yourself in a natural and relaxed manner. Watch, internally stationary, as thoughts and feelings manifest in your psychological space. Suddenly, something arrives: a thought, an idea, an emotion. Where did it come from? Then, it is gone and another takes its place. Why?

Consider *who* is the one manifesting the thoughts that enter into you. Observe how a thought appears, and then just as quickly it is gone. Through this practice one must begin to see that the state of the mind is always changing, it is never permanent. One must also discover the secret interior impulses of the manifestation and elaboration of thought. Profound truths lie within, and they are found with the simple technique of *self-observation*.

Self-observation does not mean you have to open your eyes really wide and act like some type of robot. Rather, what it means is to simply be aware of the internal and external. It is a natural state of being, although at first it may seem anything but natural. This is because the nature of our mind is degenerate. In reality this practice performed correctly does not conflict with any activity of life, however it at first may seem overwhelming, difficult and even impossible during our daily routine. In time, the ability to observe the exterior and the interior simultaneously will become easier, natural even, and eventually one will understand what it really means "To Be" rather than to merely exist.

Simply become aware of the current moment. Become aware of what you are thinking and what you are feeling. One may notice at this point a psychological separation from the physical body. In other words, we will become unidentified with our physical presence as the totality of our presence. Normally, we are entirely identified with our physical body, but if one truly becomes aware, a realization will arrive that the physical body is just a suit of flesh and bones that accepts the sensations of the physical world.

Observe what is going on inside, your current mental state. There is almost always something we are tense about, observe this. Observe how physical tension is the result of psychological tension. As you observe, notice what occurs seemingly independent of physical sensation, and what occurs interdependent of sensation.

When one observes their own self, they modify that very self into observer and observed. The question then becomes: If one is observing the self, then who is the observer? This is part of the question we must answer.

When we begin to look at ourselves with tremendous sincerity we open the doors of self-knowledge, and this is something more valuable than all the currency in the world. We shall begin to earnestly comprehend why it is incongruent to think, for example "I am good looking." This is because it is not the psychological "I" itself that is good looking, but rather the physical body, that when seen through the sense of sight, produces this "I am good looking" attitude. The "I am good looking" is actually a *result*. The "I am good looking" is the result of viewing the physical body with *vanity*. Anyone who observes this fact will realize that there is no way that the "I am good looking" is the physical body, because it is a thought. The observer will realize it is just absurd to think that, and yet, we think upon these lines within every moment of our life because we are mistaken.

The "I" is not the physical body, although the "I" often believes otherwise because it is identified with the body. It, the "I am good looking" (or whatever attitude of that likeness) thinks it is flesh and bones, but in reality this "attitude" is not flesh, but something else. It is a type of energy, but it not physical energy. The "I," the "who I am," is *sleeping* because although the "I" is a psychological element (something not physical), it dreams, in this case, that it is physical.

Although it, the "I," contains a multitude of contradiction and faults, it becomes angry when others make mistakes. This is because the "I" plays a movie in the mind that it is fascinated with. This movie is a piece of propaganda that it both produced and watches; it is a lie that has been repeated since the inception of its creator.

The content of this movie, in many cases, states that others are the cause of "my" misfortunes. The name of this move, in this example, is entitled, "The Drama of the Victim." In this movie we see ourselves victimized by others, we become fascinated with being the one who has been given the short straw. We sing a sad song in our heads, and perhaps the protagonist (the "I"), dreaming, plans his ultimate revenge, because he is fascinated with "getting even."

There are other movies. One is called, "The Drama of the Hero." This movie is played in our heads when we are planning and thinking about our eventual rise to fame and fortune, when we come out "on top."

We play the former title in our heads when we have a "bad" day, and we play the latter movie when had a "good" day. Some are more fascinated with being the maltreated one, and others are more fascinated with being the hero, nevertheless, everyone is fascinated with an idea in their heads. Some are fascinated with being a "martyr," for always sacrificing for others, but because they are fascinated with the idea of it, they actually make other people's lives more difficult. The catalogue of titles is endless.

Begin to observe these things, because it is one thing to intellectually understand and accept this notion, and it is another to actually see it in our lives.

The ego is not something intrinsic. The "I," the self, or the ego is the result or outcome of actions. One such action is the repetition of these deceitful notions that constantly repeated in our minds and hearts. Although the "I" is a result, that result causes new actions, and therefore the strengthening of the "I" becomes an autonomous system. The system, the machinery of the "I," incessantly self-complicates and self-elaborates its own subjective ideas. These ideas unconsciously modify our perception, which as a result change our behavior to be in tune not with reality, but our false perceptions of reality. Thus, the consequence of all of this is one's life leading into persistent suffering, complications and pain. Eventually the state of this machine forms a vicious cycle so strong that it is impossible for one to get out of it. Fortunately, through God's mercy, there is a definitive end to this machine in what is called "Hell," which will be discussed in more detail at a later time.

One of these lies that incessantly repeats itself is entitled, "I am a good person." This is possibly the worst lie of all. We say, "I am a good mother," "I am a good student," "I am a good worker," "I am a good boss." Whatever we do, whatever we are, we always believe in our goodness. Of course, we know that we do the wrong things occasionally, but we always justify our action with some argument that appeases us.

Good is a subjective, relative term that is ultimately meaningless. Measure yourself against absolute perfection, and nothing else, this is what the religious avatars have told us. Nevertheless, we want to always think the best of ourselves, and to do so we find some arbitrary and subjective definition of "good" that we label ourselves as. By doing so we can feel good about ourselves, and we do this because on some unconscious level we believe this is the best way to live. We believe that to feel good about one's self is the conduct of happiness, but it is not. It is patently evident this type of conduct does not produce true happiness. No matter how well we think of ourselves, no matter how much we ignore what we do not like about ourselves, not matter how elaborate our reasoning and justifications become, we still have problems in life.

Thinking bad of ourselves is depression. Therefore, that is also a mistaken method. What is necessary is to not be fascinated with *any* idea of ourselves. Do not "believe" to be either a good or bad person. Actions speak the truth of what one is. What you believe yourself to be has no bearing on who you are. This is because the mind, the self, is always changing. The mind is impermanent, yet our ideas believe otherwise. Therefore, to get caught in an idea of who you are is a total a waste of time. It is a delusion, a cause of suffering, but we love to think well of ourselves because it feels "good."

The idea of "good" is meaningless, because if you observe what feels "good" and what the consequences of those actions bring, you will arrive at the conclusion that what is good is not always good. Even if you think of yourself as neither a good nor bad person, that is still an idea of yourself. Therefore, this is something difficult to understand, and more difficult to enact. To not have an idea of yourself, you must stop dreaming about who you are. You must stop thinking of yourself; you must stop playing the movies in your head. You must remove your egotism. The mind must become serene with transcendent silence.

What is necessary is to observe ourselves. Let us observe that we are not the *body*, but instead the *consciousness* inside of a vehicle called the physical body. This is a wonderful thing because it is a way to become unidentified with our ideas of ourselves. It is a way to step outside the box, so to speak. We can look at our own ideas as an observer and realize how incorrect we are. In similar fashion we can see how these sleeping "I" identifications project in other people.

If we begin to live in the state of now, opposed to the state of the future (daydreaming) or the past (memories), we will find that everyone is very, very busy; we will find that everyone is very, very emotional and passionate about his or her beliefs and morals. Everyone has his or her ideologies. Everyone has their opinions about what kind of person they are. Everyone lives by his or her own personal philosophy. Everyone is identified with the ideas that play incessantly in their heads. What we will rarely find a man who is living within the moment of now. We will never (or, extremely rarely) find anyone who is actually alive. All we find are people who sleep. They sleep and dream of the future. They sleep and dream of the past. They sleep within their own world and completely ignore reality. We are these people. We are asleep, we are dreamers, we always dream of anything but the current moment. We are never in the current moment. We worry about the future. We get emotional about the past. We are never in the now.

What is the purpose of existence? This question is so difficult precisely because we are "asleep." We are sleeping, dreaming, instead of *being*. Think about dreams for a moment: While dreaming one never realizes how absurd the dream is until one awakens from it.

Unfortunately we do not pay attention to existence. The question of life is of course a profound question worthy of a definitive answer. Why then is it so elusive? How can we not understand the reason for our being? We do not know the answers because we are too busy to even ask them. We are so busy with everything that we do not even have time to think why we have things to be busy about. How can we ever expect to question these things if we do not even realize we are too busy? Most forms of external busyness are forms of internal (psychological) laziness.

What is very interesting to notice is that life is simple. When we become busy and frantic, it is not because life is inherently too intricate, but rather because life has become a reflection of our internal complexities. If there is within our minds a lot of chaos, confusion, frustration, pride, arrogance, etc., etc., what else will appear but the effects of those internal causes played out in our everyday life? Everyday life is the exact outcome of what we carry inside, that which we call the self.

For example, we may have a lot of pride and vanity concerning our new car we purchased. Suddenly, someone puts an imperfection on the paint job. This hurts our pride and vanity. It hurts us because in the past we *crystallized* certain *psychological aggregates* within our psychological country that have mistaken values. When these aggregates ("I's") are stimulated with the sensations of our car being scratched, they, the "war lords" of our interior world, rise up to take control.

Certain parts of the "I" become hurt, and we are identified with that hurt. When we are identified with our pride, vanity and envy, etc., then we become hurt by that. But if these parts of our psychology did not exist as such, then who could be hurt? If they did not exist, then there is no "I" to feel these negative emotions.

These psychological constitutions, or egos, have generic names such as "envy," "pride," "anger," "lust," etc. They entrap our consciousness and modify the perception of the consciousness in accordance with the subjectivism of that particular ego. The ego is not one but many. The Gnostic Basilides called these diverse psychological constitutions "appendages" that we must fight against. Valentinus likens man's psyche to a Trojan horse that contains within it many demons to be slain. Understanding The Doctrine of Many "I's" is the foundation of Gnostic psychology.

The consciousness is put to sleep by our psychological aggregates that entrap it. But, if we observe our pride and vanity, what will arise is the understanding that the observer is not the observed. In other words, we become unidentified with our pride and vanity, and then they no longer hurt us. We see the sensations arise, and we see how our vanity wishes to act, we observe its interior actions, but we understand that its actions are based upon lies and illusions. This gives us a choice to act correctly, to act in regards to reality, in regards to love and compassion.

Ultimately, to remove the hurt and pain we feel in our hearts, it is necessary to remove the causes of that hurt and pain. Therefore, it is not enough to simply observe our pride and vanity, it is necessary to comprehend them integrally, in order accomplish their execution. It is necessary, through our self-observation, to gather the evidence of everyday life, to judge our defects in front of the court of our own solemn consciousness, and then send them to death when found guilty of causing pain in our lives and the lives of others.

The true martyr is not simply the one who dies physically for God. This has occurred in history but it is only a reflection of something more profound. The true martyr is the one who dies psychologically for God. It is a million times more difficult to psychologically die than it is to physically die. Everyday people destroy their physical bodies in attempts to escape their problems, but they ignore that the problems of life are psychological and therefore only psychological death and can remove them.

Why does it is seem normal for us to have anger when an imperfection is found on our automobile? Why is it that when we find a psychological imperfection, we justify it and have no concern of removing it? I submit it is because we do not understand the cause of our suffering. I submit that, in fact, we are so confused that we actually love our suffering and few would ever attempt to remove it. We truly believe the conduct of suffering is the conduct of happiness.

It is one thing to observe our faults. It is another to remove them. The former is necessary to achieve the latter. To remove them is to remove the merchants from temple, it is to kill the non-believers, it is to walk on the waters of life, to become consumed by the plumbed serpent of sapience and to live the Seven Days of Genesis.

We begin with observation, we continue with comprehension, and we conclude with elimination. This is the path of self-realization, the awakening of consciousness, the meaning of the life. If we were to remove every impurity of ourselves, then we would reach the summit of Mount Olympus and solemnly prostrate at the feet of God. God is infinite abundance and infinite happiness. That is true happiness. The happiness people think they have is a lie, it is not true happiness. It has nothing to do with our pride and vanity, our anger, our lust, or any other inhuman element we carry in us. God molded man in his image, yet the qualities of God are everything we are not. Therefore, we are not human, but inhuman. This is why it is written, "Be perfect, even as your Father in Heaven is perfect."

We are slaves to our own environment, and what is worse, is we do not even know it. It hurts our pride to admit this, because our pride likes who we are. Many people sleep within their suffering. They will not even look for happiness because they believe they have already found it. It is very strange to see misery easily confused for happiness. Often I hear people tell me that they are "generally happy." Later, perhaps in the same day, I notice they are expressing some negative emotion, they are angry, hurt, afraid, and it is easy to see that they are not happy. But they always ignore this fact. Often I hear people respond to this doctrine affirming that they are not psychologically asleep. Later, they forget where they placed their car keys. This is the result of psychological sleep!

It has come to the point that what we consider happiness to be simply the lack of material or physical suffering. We think, "I am not sick, I have no money problems, I have friends and a family, I am not suffering anything... therefore I am happy." What a hoax! One who is happy does not need to consider that fact for a single moment. Inevitably, we all suffer, and to some extent or another, we are always suffering on some level of unconsciousness. When you have a problem, there is suffering. Where there is anger there is suffering. Where there is sadness there is suffering. Where there is resentment, jealously, anguish, there is suffering. Let us now comprehend what and why Buddha said: Life itself is suffering. But, remember also that he said there is a way to extinguish this suffering.

The truth is there is nothing but contradiction, confusion and ignorance within man's psychology. One part, one "I" wishes to achieve a goal, marriage, while a different "I" wishes something that contradicts the first: fornication with someone its lusts after. Meanwhile a third psychological aspect, some other "I" claims that it is happy and that it is not suffering conflict. When we wait ten minutes and observe again, we find an entirely new set of "I" centers expressing themselves. Now an "I" of boredom has surfaced. Another "I" is dreaming of the past. This is something interesting to contemplate.

The repercussions of our actions crystallize within our psychology, in either a regenerative or degenerative fashion. Materialism and atheism are the outcomes of a degenerate mind. Materialism is the notion that matter arises before anything else and it concludes that all phenomena can be explained within Euclid's three dimensions. The modern person does not think that he is materialistic, but I must say his actions speak louder than his thoughts. It is another deception. This society is very materialistic because that is all it knows and all it can perceive.

Humanity is imprisoned within a three dimensional psychology because of degeneration. Our senses have degenerated because of our actions. We are wasteful in our minds, we destroy our emotional center, and we abuse the temple of our soul (the physical body). This degeneration has been occurring for many lives, and slowly we have become blind to God. Nevertheless, even if it sounds impossible, within the third dimension there are other dimensions, vibrating at specific frequencies that travel faster than the speed of light. We cannot perceive them because they are beyond our sensorial threshold. With certain techniques and much practice one can open the superior senses that break the nominal spacio-temporal barrier much like a jet breaks the sound barrier.

The incipient understanding of physics has yet to make "scientific sense" of the superior dimensions. Regardless, Yogis, Arhats, and wise men throughout the ages have experienced these dimensions consciously. There is nothing profound in stating that worlds exist beyond what is known to the common degenerate mind. The esoteric philosophy states that our senses are atrophied (degenerated), and the one who knows the keys to rejuvenate (regenerate) them will know the interior (superior) dimensions, not through theory, but through consciously living within them.

It took many lifetimes for our superior facilitates to close their doors of perception, but through the right effort they can open again, like a flower blooming in fertile soil. When this flower blossoms, immaculate beauty flows within one's soul and infinite plentitude irradiates from within and out to the world. It is a glorious thing to awaken the consciousness. What is necessary, in order for this flower to blossom, is to work with the sun, with the rain, and with the dirt. This is the Sulfur, Mercury, and the Earth of the Alchemists.

Today's man who cannot even recognize his own sleeping consciousness finds it impossible to experience the subtle interior worlds. This man of course concludes that such worlds do not exist. They say, "If these things exist, then there would be proof!" The proof he is looking for escapes his perception, that is all. In the end nothing can satisfy the skepticism of a degenerate mind. Someone trying to appease the skeptic is a fool. Today's materialistic "civilized" and "educated" man does not like blind belief, but he has no problem believing in many theories that he has never witnessed.

Even so, we cannot function without beliefs. From the incipient, inconclusive knowledge we are educated with, we have no way of truly knowing anything. No one teaches how to think, only what to think. Therefore, our options are to either believe or not believe what we are told to think.

We can have scientific beliefs or we can have religious beliefs. There are absurd beliefs, and there are more reasonable beliefs. Some beliefs are just short extensions of simple observation; other beliefs require more imagination. All beliefs are motivated by various factors, mostly unconscious. This is something we must observe in ourselves.

There is something else called faith. Faith is not belief. Religious fanatics and atheists alike make ill use of the term faith to mean religious belief, or, a belief that has no basis in fact. Faith is actually something different. Faith is not the courage to believe in that which we do not know. That is just a type of ignorance. Contemplate this: The one who has faith does not believe in God, because he knows God. Faith has to do with experiencing a level of objective consciousness. Faith is direct experience. Faith is testimony. If you give your faith of something you are giving your testimony, your experience.

There are three levels of mind. The most dense and educated level of the mind is the *sensorial mind*. This is the mind that takes information from the physical senses and labels, organizes and reorganizes what it perceives. The sensorial mind knows nothing beyond the first three dimensions. It is a dense, unintelligent mind. This mind is the basis of all skeptics. For a skeptic, if cannot be demonstrated in the physical world, it is not "real."

Beyond the sensorial mind is the *mystical mind*, or *intermediate mind*. The mystical mind interpolates and extrapolates sensory data to form abstract concepts. Within the mystical mind lies belief. The mystical mind is the basis of all believers, both in the realm of science and religion. The mystical mind is what differentiates the Christian, the Muslim, the Buddhist, the atheist, the Daoist and every other sect of belief. It is the same with the theories of academia. Everyone has their belief in a particular set of theories. The mystical mind is a house in which we psychologically live. When a psychological tempest comes, we take shelter in our house of the mystical mind. In other words, when we are faced with a harsh crisis, with the unknown, we revert to our beliefs to explain the unknown factors producing that crisis.

Sometimes a large storm destroys the mystical house. When our beliefs do not match our reality, something strange can occur, the atheist becomes a Theosophist... the Christian becomes agnostic, the Hindu becomes Islamic. The cause of such change could be a simple event, a flash of insight, a dream, a misinterpretation, an authentic vision, terrible emotional crisis and pain... really, it could be anything. What we must conclude is that the mystical house of beliefs can be destroyed by any arbitrary event which leads one to find a new house to view life from. I know a man who was a Christian preacher, and later he became a Buddhist. Now he studies the Buddhists scriptures in the same way he studied the Bible. Usually, when one changes their mystical house they believe to have found the "truth," but usually it is just another viewpoint of belief.

Fortunately, there is something beyond the mystical mind and this referred to as the *inner mind*. This is the superior mind, the solar mind, or the objective mind. The objective mind has direct knowledge; this mind does not take knowledge from perception. An experience within the objective mind births true faith. A mustard seed of faith can move mountains, as Jesus said. This means that if we could experience the Truth, even for one moment, it is enough to extend faith into the infinite. If the truth is known for one moment, then in a sense everything is known. What is important is to open the inner mind, but to do so we must use the inferior minds in the right way. We have to dominate the inferior minds like a rider who controls the animals he sits upon. This is the only way to reach our destination.

Belief is necessary in our everyday life. If we wish to get to the top floor of a building, we must first believe that the steps in front of us will lead us there. We may be wrong, or we may be right. What is important to understand is that if one simply rejects the steps, then nothing can occur. Conversely, if one out right accepted the steps without further analysis, error can also occur.

The correct interim state before we know something is to observe without immediately accepting or rejecting. It is said that one must believe while at the same time not believe. The degenerate mind does not know how to do this because this state is achieved when the mind becomes passive and silent. We must believe in order to act, we must not believe in order to properly observe and reevaluate the current situation. If the current situation is not reflecting our belief, then we must reevaluate.

We need a reserved belief. We need to take in the things we do not have direct knowledge of while neither immediately accepting it nor rejecting it. We need to believe at the same time as not believing. As it turns out, this is something terribly difficult for one to do. Often this is referred to as "having an open mind."

Religion & Sexuality

> Indeed, sexual energy is without a doubt the most subtle and powerful energy normally produced and transported through the human organism. Everything that a human being is, including the three spheres of thought, feeling and will, is none other than the exact outcome of distinct modifications of sexual energy.
>
> The control and storage of sexual energy is certainly difficult due to the tremendously subtle and powerful nature of this energy. In addition, its presence represents a source of immense power that can result in a true catastrophe if one does not know how to handle it. […]
>
> When man and woman unite sexually in the perfect matrimony, they are truly ineffable Gods in those voluptuous moments. Man and woman united sexually form a divine androgynous being, a male-female Elohim, a terrifically divine Divinity. The two halves, separated since the dawn of life are united for one instant in order to create. This is ineffable… sublime… this is a thing of paradise…
>
> <div style="text-align:right">– Samael Aun Weor, <i>The Perfect Matrimony</i></div>

Life, death, and sex are the three fundamental properties of existence. Life is the *affirmation*. Death is the *denial*. Sex, in its proper approach, is the communion of all that life is within in a single moment: a *reconciliation* of former two. With this in mind it worthy to dive into these topics in order to discover their existent inter-relationships.

Life, in its physical component, begins with the union of the sperm and ovum, and ends with our final exhalation in our mortal vehicle. We do not see any value in death because, living totally within the personality, we do not know what lies beyond its death. Our society, which we have said is materialistic, cannot understand the true meaning of death because it does not know that which is not physically material. When the physical body is reduced to dust, the only thing we have left is our belief about religion, a certain specific metaphysical philosophy, or there lack of. Unfortunately this type of information is meaningless at the end of the day.

Death is a terribly difficult subject to comprehend, and as a result it is normal to ignore this topic. Instead of understanding death, we wish to extend life. There should be no fear of death, because what really constitutes the Being has nothing to do with the personality. The personality is afraid of death because it will die. The Being, the true self, does not die.

Meanwhile, sex is a topic people dive into very quickly without ever understanding it. Tragically, sexuality has absolutely nothing to with what people believe it is. Sex is anterior to the carnal passions people associate with it. It is, in reality, much more than physical intercourse. Intercourse is the inferior pole of human sexuality. Sex, itself, is the mediating force that manifests between two opposing forces.

We invent a range of technologies in a struggle to sustain and improve life, but this is in vain because we ignore the processes of death. Death itself is a process of beauty, because if the seed does not die, then the tree is not born. If the egg and sperm did not die, the child could not exist.

So if we wish a tree to be born, then without a question we must take a seed from that tree and let it grow. The seed is the connection of life and death. The seed is in a master synthesis, Christ. The seed exists only to die, so its creation can be born. How great it would be if we could all comprehend the value of the seed.

In ancient Egypt, Osiris was carried with heavy analogs towards agriculture because they understood the value of the seed. Osiris-Ra is Christ: every year the crops live, die, and resurrect. That is the Cosmic Drama that resounds itself in every corner of space. The Drama of Christmas was celebrated within countless sects before Christianity, including Pagan and Egyptian mysteries. It is the celebration of the return of the Sun. The spiritual Sun is Christ, Osiris. This is the internal sun, the midnight sun. Intellectual ignoramuses laugh at the ancient cultures for worshiping the sun, yet they attend Church every Sunday.

> Brethren, I speak after the manner of men; Though it be but a man's covenant, yet if it be confirmed, no man disannulleth, or addeth thereto.
>
> Now to Abraham and his seed were the promises made. He saith not, And to seeds, as of many; but as of one, **And to thy seed, which is Christ.**
>
> – Galatians 3:15, 16

The common interpretation of Galatians 3:15 is that Christ was part of the linage of offspring connected to Abraham. This is true in its own extent yet it totally ignores the true value of Christ Principle. The Christ Principle lives in everyone because it palpitates in every atom of space.

Everything that is born is subject to death because they are tied together; one is not complete without the other. Death, in the most complete sense, is simply the movement of energy from one form to another. When the seed dies, the tree is born.

Creation, in all its glory, is always the outcome of sexual energy. To create is a sexual problem. If an architect wishes to build a house, he must first create it in his mind, he must make a blueprint. That takes creative energy. We could also say it takes sexual energy, because creativity and sexuality are one and the same.

Creativity is sexuality. When we understand this, we begin to understand what sex actually is. With this in mind, perhaps it would not seem so absurd to say that imagination is fueled through sexual energy, because imagination is a creative act. In consequence, the quality of our sexual energy is reflected in the quality of our creative facilities, whether it be in the field of business, leisure, or the pursuit of spiritual truths.

To understand the mysteries of life and death, we need a fertile mind because certain concepts are difficult to understand without a mind that is very creative, in other words, full of sexual potency. A mind will run on different qualities of fuel, but it is better for it to run on fuel that has been purified. Sexual energy that is impure, that to say, mixed with lust, is a type of energy that damages the mind, it results in its degeneration. Likewise, immaculate sexual energy has the capacity to regenerate the mind.

Popular media informs us that we will be happier once our most secret sexual desires are indulged. We are foolish to believe this, but we do not question it: it is easy and it feels good, to question it would just ruin the "fun." It also feels good to eat ice cream, but we know very well that to indulge in sweets is dangerous to our health. Unfortunately, the consequences of sexual behavior are not rooted in our biology, but in our psychology (the soul), and therefore materialistic scientific investigation has no district in these matters.

Without knowing or understanding the true consequences, the drugs that "improve" our sexual life continue to proliferate as if it is Ambrosia. We wish to be *sex-gods*, but the truth is we do not even know what sex is. Society thinks sex is pleasure, when in fact sex is creation. God is the creator and sex is his movement of creation.

Really, few people understand sex. It is generally thought that the contraceptive pill, the condom and spermicidal chemicals all have been advancements in society due to the fact that have given us sexual "freedom." Some people believe that contraceptives define us a modern, rational people. I have spoken with people who believe this. Unfortunately, we do not see anything after death. We do not see what occurs when one abuses the sexual energy. All we know about sexual energy is its uses related with pleasure and procreation. We know that this energy can be used to create children and if we do not want to create children than we "must" use contraceptives. This is an interesting argument because the idea of sexual continence is completely rejected.

Approaching this subject, often I have heard, "*We are animals with desires just like any other animal. Continence is an antiquated practice imposed on people out of fear and ignorance.*" Well, it is true that we are animals, but what is lost in that logic is that we are special animals. We are the most highly refined animal. We are the animal that can consciously know the Divine. There are ancient and contemporary teachers that state very clearly that the sexual energy is the vitality of both the body and the soul. This is nothing groundbreaking, the only ignorance of the matter is our attempts to ignore the great potential the sexual energy contains.

Sex is the universal epicenter. It is the center of every social gathering (knowingly or not). It is beginning of every life. Sexuality is the cornerstone of existence, sexuality is vitality, it is life itself, and thus, it is the cornerstone of spirituality. Proper sexuality can revolutionize the world.

To understand the religions of the world correctly, not as they are degenerately taught today, but in their true transcendental aspects, we must experience and live the truths, we must intimately know the sublime realities as they were written. And, although this sounds a little extravagant, a little exceptional, to experience these things is a possibility that lies sleeping at the center of our existence. This is something to be known personally. Proper sexuality when lived produces vitality. Not just physical vitality, but emotional and mental and spiritual vitality. It brings life into what is only today known as existence. God created using the sexual forces, the very same which are available to man. If God were to fornicate like an animal, nothing would exist. The Divine itself would cease to exist.

Animal sexuality is one thing, and human sexuality is another. We evolved under animal sexuality, however what is necessary in order to become a Man is to enact the conduct of human sexuality. This is how the intellectual animal creates himself into a true man. Sexual energy is important to use wisely. To waste it is something terribly foolish. On the other hand, the sexual energy is something that cannot be bottled up either.

Let us now contemplate the following lines from the Bible:

> And if any man's seed of copulation go out from him, then he shall wash all his flesh in water, and be unclean until the even. And every garment, and every skin, whereon is the seed of copulation, shall be washed with water, and be unclean until the even.

The woman also with whom man shall lie with seed of copulation, they shall both bathe themselves in water, and be unclean until the even.

– Leviticus 15: 16 - 18

He that is wounded in the stones, or that his privy member cut off, shall not enter unto the congregation of the Lord.

– Deuteronomy 23:1

Whosoever is born of God doth not commit sin; for his **seed** remaineth in him: and he cannot sin, because he is born of God.

– 1 John 3:9

Jesus answered, "I tell you the truth, no one can enter the kingdom of God unless he is born of **water** and the Spirit. Flesh gives birth to flesh, but the Spirit gives birth to spirit. You should not be surprised at my saying, 'You must be born again.' The wind blows wherever it pleases. You hear its sound, but you cannot tell where it comes from or where it is going. So it is with everyone born of the Spirit."

– John 3:5 - 8

Passages such as the previous are frequently unknown, ignored, or misunderstood. Leviticus 15 is particularly important here. In the Latin, the whole chapter of Leviticus concerns itself about the importance of not expelling the semen from the body, not just the few verses found in modern translation. It repeatedly uses the phrase *fluxum seminis*, but today's Bibles translate this in accordance with the extrications of bodily fluids in general, such as blood, mucus, puss, etc. In this way they have mistranslated and hidden the original teaching.

For example, verse two is mistranslated as, "when any man hath a running issue out of his flesh, because of his issue he is unclean," yet it should be, "when any man has an issue of *semen* out of his flesh, because of his issue he is unclean." This goes unnoticed and uncared for because people today know nothing about the true nature of sexuality and religion.

Most people believe that being "born again" is solved through baptism or by becoming spiritually devout. To become a spiritual person, to revolutionize one's life and to serve the divine is something marvelous, yet this is not how one is born again.

Changing the way one thinks is not to be born again. Believing does not give birth. Who has ever seen a child born out of a belief?

What does give birth is the *water*. Water throughout all culture symbolizes fertility, birth, the eternal mother, and the womb. This is why a woman's "water" breaks when she is to give birth. The water gives birth to everything: it is the first thing mentioned in the book of Genesis, itself being a treatise on the creative (sexual) power of God. Likewise, the "water" of man is his sexual potency: the sexual energy. A man's physical representation of his water is the semen. Jesus states that one must be born of the Water and the Spirit in order to be born again and to be received in Heaven. The Spirit of God hovers over the waters during Creation.

> In the beginning God created the heavens and the earth. The earth was without form, and void; and darkness was on the face of the deep. And the **Spirit of God** was hovering over the face of the **waters**.
>
> – Genesis 1:1, 2

Within the waters is where the Genesis of *any* Creation takes place. The Book of Genesis tells the allegorical story of not just The Creation, but the creation of anything. There is Creation within the birth and development of a child, a Creation within the birth and development of a planet, a star, and even a soul. To give birth and to develop the soul is to be "born again."

The Spirit of God (*Ruach Elohim*) is always hovering over the waters. Within man, waters are related with his semen, sperm, and all the hormones of the endocrine system. Within a woman it is the same, yet it is obvious that instead of sperm, she has ovum. When the word semen in both this book and any religious text is used it is not in the exclusive context of men, it is in regards to the creative energy in both sexes.

The Ruach Elohim, the Sprit of God, is directly related with the "waters" of the biological organism. It is exactly these "waters" that we are going to refer to as the sexual energy. When man and woman sexually unite, then the Spirit of God becomes active within them. This is how the Spirit of God hovers over the face of the (sexual) waters prior to a new creation. Yet, this new creation can be the creation of a new child, or an inner creation of a spiritual nature.

In Hebrew, the language of the Old Testament, the word for God is Elohim, yet the Spirit of God is Ruach Elohim. Let us understand the difference between God and the Spirit of God. The Spirit of God lives within us, yet, because we have not been born of God, God Himself does not live within us. Only when we properly make use of the Spirit of God do we live all of the mysteries of Genesis and are truly "born again." When we elaborate the Spirit of God, then all the infinite potential of God Itself manifests and one is converted into a saint, a Deva, a Buddha, etc.

We have to understand that to be born again is absolutely, incontrovertibly, a sexual problem. This is why the seed remains within the one who is born of God (1 John 3:9); to be born of God is to be born again, and to be born of God, one must make use of that which gives birth. Nothing is born without sex. John 3:9 also tells us that sinning is fundamentally related with sex. This is because the original sin is the abuse of sex. When Eve ate the fruit of Good and Evil, she was performing the sexual act with Adam outside the commandments of God. This is why it is stated that the "fruit" was nice to the senses. Sex always looks delicious to the senses.

The topic of sex is multifaceted and sophisticated, so do not yet draw any premature conclusions about what is being said regarding the sexual issue. All that is being pointed at now is that sexuality plays a fundamental role in religion that has been ignored and forgotten about. It will take time for the reader to comprehend the true nature of sexuality and religion, therefore a good portion of the remainder of this book is devoted precisely to sex.

To the experts, the know-it-alls, what we are stating here concerning the sexual nature of religion is absurd and unacceptable. Yet, this is due to massive ignorance. In the past, this knowledge was hidden for various reasons, both righteous and wicked. Today, everyone has forgotten the true roots of religion: those who at one point suppressed the knowledge did not use it, and over time they forgot it as well. Jesus attempted to restore the knowledge (gnosis), yet he was betrayed and true Gnostic Christianity was destroyed. Thus, today, it is the blind leading the blind, and now both are falling into the ditch.

> Hear the Word of Jehovah, ye children of Israel: for Jehovah hath a controversy with the inhabitants of the land, because there is no truth, nor mercy, nor knowledge (gnosis) of God in the land.
>
> By swearing, and lying, and killing, and stealing, and committing adultery, they break out, and blood touches blood.
>
> My people are destroyed for lack of knowledge (gnosis): because thou hast rejected knowledge (gnosis), I will also reject thee, that thou shall be no priest to me: seeing thou hast forgotten the law of thy God, I will also forget thy children.
>
> As they were increased, so they sinned against me: therefore will I change their glory into shame.
>
> Whoredom and wine and new wine take away the heart. My people ask counsel at their stocks, and their staff declared unto them: for the spirit of whoredom hath caused them to err, and they have gone a whoring from under their (Inner) God.
>
> — Hosea 4: 1, 2, 6, 7, 11, 12
>
> Woe unto you, Doctors of the Law! For ye have taken away the key of knowledge (gnosis): ye entered not in yourselves, and them that were entering in ye hindered.
>
> — Luke 11:52
>
> But we speak the wisdom of God in a mystery, even the **hidden** *(esoteric)* wisdom, which God ordained before the world unto our glory:
>
> Which none of the princes *(intellectuals, pontiffs, the false authorities of religion)* of this world knew: for had they known it, they would not have crucified the Lord of glory *(in their own hearts, minds, and actions)*. [...]
>
> But the natural man receiveth not the things of the **Spirit of God**: for they are foolishness unto him: neither can he know them, because they are spiritually discerned.
>
> — 1 Corinthians 2:7-14

Paul, the author of Corinthians, was a master of the Jewish esotericism known as the Kabbalah. When he wrote about the Spirit of God, he was referring to the Ruach Elohim. The natural man needs to become the spiritual man. The men who do not know the esoteric wisdom, the gnosis, are those who do not have the Spirit of God within them.

In this regard, society it seems has three answers in regards to sex:

1) We deny or reject sexuality.
2) We use sexuality in the creation of physical bodies.
3) We use sexuality to for pleasure (the creation of desire).

The first option is used by many so called spiritual types. The latter options are used by the average man and woman. The third option is used in an exclusive manner by hedonists and "modern, rational" people.

This is yet another interesting topic because a growing majority believes that contraceptives allow sexual freedom. This is false because in reality contraceptives deny the right of sexual expression (creation). Contraception is the antithesis of sexual freedom because in reality it does not free sex, but rather it bottles sex up within the confines of what society wants it to be. This creates a lot of karmic repercussions.

Society desperately wants sex to be pleasure and nothing more. Contraceptives are the rejection of sexuality, because sexuality is not pleasure, but rather creation. Pleasure can come from sexuality - sex can *create* pleasure, but sex is not pleasure itself. To use sex to create pleasure and nothing more is a foolish waste similar to that of burning all the money in your wallet in order to light a candle.

Sex always is a creative act. Sexuality is what gives forth all forms of creativity. It is already well known that sex creates children, families, and relationships. However what is ignored is that *sex creates a state of mind*. Rejecting sex creates a repressed psychology. Using sex for its sensual pleasures creates a psychology locked within desire and degeneration.

The esoteric philosophy does not use any of the previously mentioned options. The fourth option is often called *transmutation*. This is when sexual energy is refined for a superior use (a superior creation). Transmutation is the process of harnessing one's own sexual-creative potential in order to create a new spiritual nature within. This is the true meaning of being "born again." The root of every religion contains the message of sexual transmutation. True human sexuality is transmutation, yet society today enacts animal sexuality.

Transmutation is a word that has its history in Alchemy. The prefix "trans" means to go across, and "mutation" is the process of changing. Hence, transmutation means to change from one substance into another; from one energy-matter, into another energy-matter. Sexual transmutation, therefore, means to change the basic, crude, or unrefined sexual energy, into a refined, subtle, volatile, spiritual energy that manifests itself in such ways as spiritual devotion, divinely influenced masterworks of art and music, and a supreme clarity of the mind.

> Throughout history, a universal idea has prevailed that sexual energy for non-procreative purposes can either be 'used up' in sexual activity or 'contained' for upholding the development of the body and the mind. This sex energy was seen as the fuel for opening these channels of experience, not only in the East but in the alchemy of the Europeans during the sixteenth and seventeenth centuries.
>
> – Gabrielle Brown, Ph.D., *The New Celibacy*
>
> Those who practice transmutation awaken many latent talents from within. It becomes second nature to create and express, being in tune with the essence of creative energy. […]
>
> All the energy of the body becomes directed in the channel of sex when the consciousness is coupled or coordinated with the will to release or dissipate this energy. The mental processes then become slow and sluggish, as does the body, if carried to excess. A remedy to this is the reverse. The mind will then become awakened, and the body will begin to glow.
>
> – Satguru Sivaya Subramuniyaswami, *Raga Yoga*

A careful study of various schools of religion finds that sexuality is considered sacred at their inception. Jesus asked his disciples to follow him in his ways. They all practiced sexual transmutation. They did not reject sex, but they did not fornicate either. Peter was married according the Gospel (Matthew 8:14). Peter was the first Pope. Peter founded the Church, and he was married.

As time passes sexuality becomes rejected, and crude asceticism replaces transmutation in its middle life. The Dark Ages mutilated and castrated the doctrine of our Lord Christ. The monks and nuns no longer knew that one was useless without the other, that a priest is invalid without a priestess, etc. The result of abjectly rejecting sex led to abominations, secret affairs, fanaticism, burnings at the stake... Pedophilia develops as a result to this type of abuse to sex.

As a reaction to the absurd forms of asceticism, sexual hedonism arrives in a final period, when religion begins to decline and dissolve. Throughout history, any particular religious sect could be in any one of these three states. Right now the religions of the world are in decline and sexuality is being abused everywhere. When we begin to take a look it is evident that we do not understand what sexual desire means and what religion is attempting to tell us. The way religion is taught today is completely off base on many issues and it needs to be viewed from a new angle. We have foolishly thrown out and ignored what religion has to say about sexuality, and this is leading to a lot of pain in our lives.

If you take the time to read the works of the yogis mentioned earlier in this work, you will see they agree that the proper use of the sexual energy is essential for vitality. The heart of every religion agrees upon the sexual problem. Jung, the famous psychologist, also discovered the value of sexual energy; his work is the product of sexual transmutation, or sublimation. Freud's doctrine is based entirely on the sexual energy.

Someone who is making proper use of the sexual energy becomes very creative. He will become two or three times as productive at work, his sleep will become more restful, he will actually enjoy getting up in the morning and living life. However, the physical and social repercussions are insignificant to the positive mental states that become easier and easier to achieve and maintain. Virtue and happiness are fructified by the sexual energy. Therefore, not only will someone become a healthy, productive member of a family, business, and society, but they will become increasingly happier in life. What more does one want? These are not profound statements, or some wild theory, anyone can experience this for themselves. The effects of the transmutation of sexual energy are experimental, verifiable and reproducible within the interior laboratory of the mind.

The sexual problem presented in this book is the problem of becoming a true human. Sex always creates something, and it either creates in a way to sustain harmony, or in a way to destroy it. Our current psychology was made the way it is today through the abuse of sex. As a society we are unable to have lasting and loving relationships, and we are increasingly grasping at sexual hedonism as a replacement for love, but this ultimately only leads to a life of bitterness. All of this is due to the underestimation of the sexual problem, which itself is due to ignorance.

Through the correct use of the creative energy, one can change the state of their mind. The sex and the brain are linked through the pineal gland and the pituitary gland. Transmuting the sexual energy transmutes one's state of mind.

The common person believes to be a real human, but from the viewpoint of esotericism this is not the case. The outcome of various and distinct modifications of the sexual energy make a person what he or she is. Therefore, a person who makes use of animal sexuality is not a human, but an animal. Lust, insatiable passions, brute desires are things of an animal quality; it is a very low and crude expression of sex. Likewise science correctly states that we are nothing more than animals with intellect. The esoteric philosophy is more specific, stating that although intellectual animals, we can change what we are and be "born again" as a real human.

How does one become a true man or a true woman? Obviously, being that the sexual nature of a person is the fundamental axis upon which one's self is constructed, modifying one's sexual behavior results in the becoming of something new. Likewise, exchanging animal sexuality for human sexuality is the method to become a true human being.

THE MIND & THE EGO

> Mind is the great Slayer of the Real. Let the Disciple slay the Slayer.
>
> — The Voice of the Silence

> More than all that you guard, guard your mind, for it is the source of life.
>
> — Proverbs 4:23

> Develop the mind of equilibrium. You will always be getting praise and blame, but do not let either affect the poise of the mind: follow the calmness, the absence of pride.
>
> — Buddha Shakyamuni, *Sutta Nipata*

Common logic erroneously concludes that the chatter endlessly reverberating within the amphitheater of the mind constitutes the Being, the "I Am." This is not true: the endless chatter inside of us is the *ego*. Therefore, let us now begin to discuss what exactly the ego is. The first thing we must understand is that this term is used by nearly every psychological and spiritual school in existence. Some schools use *ego* to describe their spiritual "I," while others use it strictly according to Freudian psychology. In this work we will be using it differently.

The ego is inside our mind, or, it is better to say the ego is mind, a mental substance. The ego is a type of mental matter. What do we mean by mental matter? We are affirming that all energy is matter, and all matter is energy. They are both forms of something greater. This "something," for the lack of a better word, is that which is behind both matter and energy. It is similar to the way that water has different forms: it can be liquid, a solid, or a vapor. Likewise, this "something" is the principle behind both matter and energy. According to Kant, we would say that matter and energy are the *phenomena* that come from the same *noumenon*. Matter and energy are forms of something, but the *thing in itself* is something beyond form and motion, something the mind cannot directly observe or know about.

Most of us have gazed upon that famous equation of Einstein's: $e = mc^2$. This equation states that all matter is energy, and this something very important to understand because it means that our mind is directly related with matter. The mind is not apparent in the first three dimensions. It has, as the occultists say, its existence within the Fifth Dimension. When we are speaking of the mind we are not speaking of the brain. The brain is the lowest physical manifestation of the mind. The use of the word *mind* should be understood as "that matter of our soul which originates thought." When we say "the mind is matter," what we are attempting to elucidate is that the mind has a real existence, just as a physical table or chair. Radio waves exist, and we believe they exist, though we cannot see them. We know of radio waves in an indirect manner, through the results of those waves which produce the music flowing from our radios. So, in a similar way we must regard the mind. We cannot see it here in the physical world, but we know its results: such as thoughts and chemical reactions in the brain.

Understanding that the mind is a piece of matter, obviously it is an object that can be modified. Throughout many lives we have been modifying our minds in an increasingly degenerate slope. This has left our minds are in an extremely deep state of hypnosis. Hypnosis is hypo-gnosis, meaning "under the state of gnosis; without knowledge." The mind today is being held captive by a certain type of crystallized energy which prevents true knowledge (gnosis) from being acquired, leaving us in ignorance (without gnosis). This hypnotic energy is the ego. Having a concrete existence, the ego is real as well; it is not to be considered a flimsy theoretical idea or concept. The ego does not appear because we believe in it, and likewise it does not go away when we reject it. We can create and destroy ego, just as we can modify any other type of matter or energy. In our current daily and "normal" activity that we have been conditioned throughout our lives to perform we crystallize ego and strengthen ego. When we strengthen the ego, we enslave the mind to the ego with larger chains.

There is another term one must understand: *consciousness*. Consciousness denotes not just existence, but the awareness of existence, the knowledge of existence. The relationship between the consciousness and mind is dependent upon how the words are used. For example, Buddhist texts that have been translated into English often speak of awakening the mind, however in this discourse we will usually speak of awakening the consciousness. In reality the inner content of both these messages are identical, yet here we may at times make use of the words in a particular way. To differentiate, the mind is the creator of thought while consciousness is the state of Being. In reality the ego actually entraps the consciousness, like a genie trapped in a bottle. Yet, it is the consciousness that animates the processes of the mind, therefore, a mind being used by a sleeping consciousness is a sleeping mind.

The word ego means *self*, or *I*. The ego expresses itself as *me*, *myself*, *I*, *mine*, etc. If one where to destroy the ego, individuality would remain, but it would be a true individuality. The ego is a false individuality. True self coalesces with the whole universe as one thing, yet the diverse aspects of the ego cannot even agree among themselves. We always contradict ourselves, and we always have conflict and problems because the ego itself is disorder, disharmony, confusion and chaos. Life reflects our state of mind.

Once again, when speaking of creating ego, it means to actually create something, as if building a machine. It is not merely a concept, eventually one must understand through direct experience how the ego forms. Ego is a particular type of *crystallization*, or, *condensation* of energy. Just as a water vapor condenses out of air into water upon a plane of glass, so can the vibrations of life condense improperly – somewhat like a parasite – upon the surface of the mind. These vibrations condense improperly when we make use of the creative energy incorrectly. This leaves the mind infused, infested, with a malignity we refer to as the ego. Ego bottles consciousness up within it and leaves the consciousness hypnotized.

The ego is the cause of dreams. The ego is incarnated fantasy, in other words, the ego is the opposite of reality. The ego projects its desires into the world of dreams, and this is what we see when our body is sleeping. During the day our ego remains active, projecting in the same exact way in what is called daydreaming. Some daydreaming is more conscious than others. Our current normal state of mind is a continual state of dreaming. The beginner may deny these things, but in reality, when we begin to investigate these matters, we come to realize that our entire life is spent as a sleepwalker. It does not take long to experience that reality first hand. We can do this by recalling all those moments when we are on "autopilot," those times when we were there, but we were not aware. The more we investigate, the more we realize that we are continuously on what some call "autopilot."

There are different levels of dreaming. Areas of the day exist where we cannot remember anything at all, while other memories are more or less hazy to varying degrees. Therefore, the state of sleep is very fluid. The state of the mind is always in movement.

Let us understand that behind the mindless chatter composing our internal status is an instrument called the mind, which is currently asleep. The mind is being held captive by the ego, the sum of our desires. A desire is an aversion or craving of experience. When we begin to free the mind of desire, awesome transformations occur. So it is first urgent to understand why it is necessary to remove our ego.

Desire is the *will* that incarnates in one to recapitulate a certain scenario. Desire is the will to live out a certain thing we like, again and again. The inverse of desire is aversion, which is a craving to remove ourselves from a particular event of life. They are both ultimately the same thing. Did you know that it is unbalanced to desire the things that "make you feel" good, and to avert from the things that "make you feel" bad? For many people, it seems strange to say that something one desires can actually cause pain and suffering in the end. People familiar with Buddhism will understand this better. Buddhism teaches that desire and aversion are parents of suffering.

It is a difficult concept for many, yet it is necessary for us to grasp it. We have to become a little more sophisticated in our understanding of that person called "me." The "me," the "I," the "ego," has causes and conditions for its life, birth and death. It is the "I" that we live as, and it is the "I" that we die as, yet, we know very little about this "I." When one learns the causes and conditions, then one can modify these causes and conditions in order to bring about that which one yearns for, namely, happiness.

When we crave something, when we want a certain physical or emotional sensation to arrive, unconscious elements within our psychological space distort, misinterpret, and ignore reality. The "I" is like a translator who does not know how to translate the words of the external world into the words of the internal (psychological) world. The ego is like a secretary that receives lots of files and archives them into different folders incorrectly. If we observe our mind, our ego, we can see that as soon as some event or impression of life appears in front of us, we judge it, we label it as *this* or *that*. At that moment we have lost the ability to see that moment as it really is. We just sort of see something, compare it to our past, to our ideas and desires, and choose to see that moment only from that viewpoint: we file it away incorrectly. Doing this makes it impossible to see what that moment really is.

For example, if you have a conversation with someone you do not like, that aversion you have with that person will filter all of his or her words so that they will somehow fit what you expect. It does not matter what that person says, if you continue to have enmity for that person, then you have already filed that moment of life away even though you did not actually listen to a word. You, as the ego, already believe to know everything about that moment of life, so you never actually observe it for what it is. The ego, the secretary, does not do us any good because we base our action upon what is in all our folders, that is to say, our memories. But if the memories are false, if the folders where stuffed according to misconceptions, then any action, word, or thought based upon them is also mistaken. That leads to suffering.

We end up, *without consciously attempting to do so*, interpreting life in the wrong way, and this leads to mistakes, to suffering. We hear want we want to hear. We see what we have already concluded that we want to see. The unconsciousness associates the current moment of time with all its historical data and makes the "now" fit the data of the past. This is why older people have a harder time accepting what is new, because instead of seeing the new, they see what they saw in the past, and they cannot comprehend it. The current moment should be experienced without the rancid norms of yesterday – it should be lived in a pure and incomparable fashion.

The mind is a comparison tool. Yet the unconsciousness abuses this tool by always mechanically associating the sensorial data of the current moment with what it has stored in memory. If a person were to become more attentive, then this willpower can be liberated from the unconsciousness and one can begin to see the moment of now with a little more objectivity. It is imperative that we become conscious of our mental actions in order to dominate the unwieldy animal mind.

Few people have control over their own mind: few can tell the mind to stop thinking, to stop worrying, to stop feeling hurt. The mind of the today's civilized and modern man endlessly tortures itself. People today cannot sleep because they cannot control their thoughts at night, their minds runs on and on without the slightest bit of control. Therefore, in these times it is more imperative than ever to learn how to work with the mind.

When the world is seen subjectively, we in turn act incorrectly. When we act incorrectly, pain and suffering of all types are the outcome. This is not just physical pain, but more importantly, emotional and mental pain. Desire is born from the incorrect application of the mind. Desire is an action of the mind and the heart, and likewise it provides suffering of the mind and the heart. Aversion is the same as desire, yet inverted. Craving and aversion are delusions of the mind, because in reality no thing has inherit existence, and therefore, no thing has inherit value in order to like or dislike.

The values we place on events, ideas and things are false values. The true nature of these false values become known when reality crashes in and all those good intentions and mental deliberations bring nothing but more confusion, and the angst that, in the end, nothing seems to ever turn out to be what one thought it was.

The content of this work is to help the reader understand the teachings that, when enacted, liberates the mind from the ego. Obviously the ego will despise teachings that provide its death, and for this reason many people are unable to read something like this, as they are not interested in a doctrine that wishes to assassinate their ego. This is because they are not able to differentiate between unconsciousness and consciousness – thus they feel that to destroy the ego is to destroy their very self. This is of course true to an extent, but we must remember that what must die is the animal self, the unconscious self, the mechanical self, the self of vices and defects. It is this very "false" self that is based entirely on desire. We need to comprehend our own desire.

Until we come to understand why we think what we think, why we feel emotions we feel, and why we desire what we desire, then it is absolutely *absurd* to accept "good" *or* "bad" sensations of life as true, correct, or real. Nevertheless, ostensibly we continue to ignore why we feel what we feel, why we think what we think, and instead just go with the flow of emotion, thought, and movement. We believe that if we are thinking or feeling something, then it must be true and correct. We often point out to ourselves how stupid other people act, yet we always believe we are acting correctly in the moment of now. In reality we ignore our own sophisms, and ignoring *the why* makes us ignorant. Ignorance to reality produces pain. Thus, we have to begin to struggle to understand the real value of the things we hold dear about ourselves.

To intellectually understand how the products of the ego cause suffering is not enough. Millions of people study Buddhism, or religion in general, yet those who liberate themselves from suffering are almost nonexistent. Therefore, to *conceptually* agree with how suffering is produced by ignorance is of little or no value. It is simply a prerequisite to understand how it occurs in our lives. If we do not gain direct self-knowledge, then we have nothing of value. If we wish to change our lives we need direct experience, gnosis.

Life and all of creation is a balance of the transformation of energies. Physics states that when energy is applied to a system, the system is put into movement and that energy of the system is diffused through various means until equilibrium is found. So, if we were in front of a huge swinging pendulum and pushed it far away from ourselves, what is going to happen? Obviously that pendulum is going to return using the same force we applied to it.

When something comes our way mentally, we need to be careful not to take that thing and throw it back into the world, because that causes imbalance, and that imbalance will be known through suffering. For example, let us say that this pendulum is at rest and on this pendulum there is a picture representing a desire or an aversion. This picture represents our likes and dislikes, certain concepts in our head that take pleasure in the experience of liking something, or disliking something.

It represents something we identify with. Do you see where you fit in this? The picture represents something we like or hate. It could be a person we gossip about, our job that we are too proud to work at happily, our family that we are embarrassed about, the fear we have in finding ultimate security, anything that we spend time thinking about, anything that expends enormous mental energy, anything that sends us into emotional disequilibrium just from the mere thought of it. So, in synthesis, the pendulum is *fascination*, any type whether it be how much we a like something or how much we hate something. Accordingly, this pendulum represents an impression of life, something we crave or something we avert from. It is important to realize this concept.

The pendulum is an impression of life. But what do we mean by *impression*? Life is nothing more than our impression of it. Our impressions are not reality even though we are fooled into believing otherwise. Evidence of this fact is that everyone views events of life in different ways. Each of us places unique values upon the impressions of life. A certain event in life could be sad for one person, yet not for another, even though they are physically in identical circumstances. It is therefore the psychological circumstances that make up the difference. It is our psyche that places the values upon the impressions of life.

Reality is one thing, the impression is something else. The ego feeds off the incorrectly valued impressions of life. It is the impression that we are fascinated with, it is the impressions (perceptions) that can be altered, so it is good to work with transforming the impressions of life. When we transform the impressions of life we transform life itself because life is nothing more than an impression of it.

So what happens when an impression of life makes us angry? Obviously we push the pendulum-impression away from us to avoid getting angrier, but what we ignore is that this pendulum is going to eventually swing back at us, giving some other impression we cannot handle.

Let us say we had an argument where a lot of insults were traded. We all know that returning an insult will only make the matters worse. But we do it anyway because we cannot control ourselves. We do it because we are fascinated with the argument and we are fascinated with our own pride. Does that last sentence make sense to you? Do you now realize, although you may never have thought of it previously, if you were truly a humble and kind person that you would never say a hateful thing to anyone, ever? Do you also realize that if there is no hate inside of you, then it is actually impossible to hate anyone in the external world? Do you know that it is possible to not even have hate, resentment, anger, frustration, etc.?

True humility and kindness takes no effort to enact within the moment. Once a virtue is manifested within, it acts without effort. In the same fashion that we are provoked to act in harmful ways it is possible to change one's very self to return only compassion and humility towards the insulter. In this way, true happiness is found within you. When we express hatred, that emotion is coming from within, from a manifestation of hate that has been formed within our psychological country. The expression of hate or any other infrahuman vice results in the strengthening of that vice.

Recall an argument in which you believe to have said something correct, but said it with a lot of emotion. Take a moment to really observe, in yourself, why and where that emotion came from. Ask yourself if that was the best way to handle that situation. Remember that pride lives within every argument. Reevaluate. Are you still sure that what was said was correct and had absolutely no ulterior motive? Enumerate every emotion that occurred and find every single motive. Be honest to yourself if you are interested in changing yourself. One motive may have been to tell the truth, but behind that are many others that wish to cause anger and grief. In other words, there are a lot of pendulums swinging about and causing all sorts of havoc, and when we take a look at any argument we readily see our ulterior motives. Every argument has more than one motive. It is quite easy to see this, just think of all the different, conflicting negative emotions we have. However, it is one thing to see it, and another to comprehend it.

The motive to produce pain in someone else comes from the pain we have in our soul. Anyone who, at any moment, attempts to cause anything but happiness towards another person is suffering under their own psychological misery. The will to produce pain, guilt, unhappiness, envy, etc., within another person, are not human motives. Those are wills of an infrahuman nature and have no place living in our psychological country. The fact that we are not true human beings is nothing more than that. Some may be insulted with the idea that they are not human, others may feel that the idea of the esoteric philosophy is to feel guilt or shame for not being what they should be. This not the case, what one must be interested in is the truth, nothing more or less. To state that we are not human is the truth, and that is all. To state that we are good and honest people is a lie. To state that others are the reason happiness eludes our life is simply not true. The state of our lives is due to our own action, our own karma. To feel regret for making our lives a mess is something logical, but it is not the goal of the esoteric philosophy. If one truly respects themselves, they will respect others, and will repent against wrong action. What offends many people is the fact that they do not believe they have made any mistakes.

Negative emotions are the mental expressions that disrupt *harmony*. Positive emotions are the mental expressions that set harmony back in order. Do you know that a single kind response could reduce the most horrendous argument into sweetness? It is the truth. It is absolutely necessary to deeply love our enemies with all of our heart. It is necessary to love the person who hates you. Practice this, and if you fail at transforming your negative energy into positive energy, then observe why. Why is it difficult to love our enemies? We must come to know these things.

The reason it is so difficult to love our enemies is because our consciousness is sleeping due to the conditioning of the ego. The ego causes the personification of disharmony. We have a tremendous amount of ego and to leave it un-personified is impossible, this is why we are here to discuss what is called *psychological death*, or *mystical death*. The only way to achieve the virtue of loving one's enemies is to destroy those egos living inside of our psychological space that act in ways unbecoming a human.

A human being is the Word made flesh, but what we are is Satan made flesh. Satan is the ego and the ego is created through the creative energy, the sexual energy. The ego is the outcome of the fornication of the creative-sexual energy that occurs when we are fascinated with the impressions of life. When we are fascinated with an argument, we make use of the creative energy to create hateful words and perform hateful actions. For example, the ego of hate becomes identified with the argument and provokes us to act in accordance, to misuse the creative energy to create in its likeness, more hate, and to express that hate to do deeds of hate. To say that we are the sons of Satan may a bit difficult to believe, yet this is the teaching of Christ.

> I know that ye are Abraham's seed; but ye seek to kill me (*your intimate Christ*), because my WORD hath no place in you (*because your "Inn" or psychological interior is full of animal vices*).
>
> I speak that which I have seen with my Father: and ye do that which ye have seen with your father (*Satan*).
>
> They answered and said unto him, Abraham is our father. Jesus saith unto them, If ye were Abraham's children, ye would do the works of Abraham.
>
> But now ye seek to kill me, a man that hath told you the truth, which I have heard of God: this did not Abraham.
>
> Ye do the deeds of your father (*Satan, the ego*). Then said they to him, We be not born of **fornication**; we have one Father, even God.
>
> Jesus said unto them, If God were your Father, ye would love me: for I proceeded forth and came from God; neither came I of myself, but he sent me.
>
> Why do ye not understand my speech? even because ye cannot hear (*understand*) my WORD.
>
> Ye are of your father the devil, and the lusts of your father ye will do. He was a murderer (*of the truth*) from the beginning, and abode not in the truth, because there is no truth in him (*only ignorance or lack of gnosis*). When he speaketh a lie, he speaketh of his own: for he is a liar, and the father of it.
>
> And because I tell you (*the ego*) the truth, ye believe me (*the intimate Christ*) not.
>
> – John 8:37-45

We believe that our state of being is the product of God, that we are just and that we are not born of fornication. We believe that because we were born with a particular psychological defect, it implies that defect was the design of God. This is a lie; defects are the design of Satan, and Satan is the result of fornication.

Fornication is the misuse of the sexual energy in any of the three spheres of thought, feeling and action.

It may be well for the reader to disregard everything he or she understands Satan to be. The reason for Satan's existence is not to fear people into being good. Satan always has been and always will be an interior psychological element. Religion in its true form has always been psychological, and this affirmation should be a clue as to how ignorant we are concerning many forms of religion. The Word of God has no place within our soul because it is a den of liars and thieves. We have to make space for God to live within our temple. The Word of Satan creates monsters. It will create hate, violence, enmity and arguments. It will even kill love, and that is truly lamentable. Every time we insult our loved ones, we are in fact killing that love, until the day exists that there is no love at all. Then, only cold emotions, understood protocol and bank accounts exist between the couple. Let us now understand John, where it is written:

> In the beginning was the Word, and the Word was with God, and the Word was God.
>
> – John 1:1

It is the Word that is God, and it is the Word that creates. When God said, "Let there be Light," he was creating, because He uttered the Word, the LOGOS. The Logos is the vibration of creation. We create with the Word too, but on a microcosmic level. God is the macrocosmos, the Human is the microcosmos. Man said, "Let there be light..." Woman said, "...and there was light." This is love.

The word comes from the *larynx*. The larynx is sexual, and we know this because every boy and girl who grows up has a shift in his or her voice signifying sexual maturity. It is a sign that they are sexually fertile and have the ability to create. In accordance with the Hermetic axiom, *"As above, so below,"* or *"As Earth as it is in Heaven,"* the larynx of God is the instrument of Cosmocreation. The larynx is sexual and this is something irrefutable. God can create the Universe with the DIVINE FECUND LARYNX. The Divine Larynx is a uterus where the Word is gestated.

The profane larynx can only create and destroy within the emotional and mental worlds. We actually *create* anger. We actually use energy to create negative emotions, not just arguments, but the secret, invisible slander and gossip that is only known within the deep corridors of our own mind. Every time you even think ill of someone, then you have created hate in your mind, and that hate will be there until you remove it.

We make choices in life without the slightest of effort when we act unconsciously. So, it is necessary to make a conscious choice in order to supersede our mechanical and unconscious impulses that choose for us. We are not really conscious of our negative emotions, we just sort of do it, we just feel an impulse and we react to that impulse. So we end up just reacting to events like a programmed machine. The conscious decision we must make is to stop ignoring our unconscious actions: to awaken. We need to be conscious of love.

We need to come to love everyone, especially those who wish to be our enemies, because that takes tremendous conscious effort, sacrifice. This is how we sow the seeds of happiness. We need to understand love. People form ideas and rationalize their hate of others. We end up thinking it is "ok" to hate someone because of what they have done to us. All of this type of action causes suffering.

It is very courageous and difficult to truly love, because only love can exist where there is no ego, no "I want." Everyone believes they know love, that they know how to love, but if this was the truth, our world would be very different. From love comes happiness, because happiness is transmuted love.

The majority of people are not interested in climbing towards the summit of love. They are too afraid to reduce the "I" to ashes, they are too afraid to leave behind their conditioned cravings and aversions. Regrettably, they will never surrender the identity of the "I" because they do not understand what lies beyond it. These people only know pleasure and pain. We mistake pleasure for love, and strangely we become attached to the very things that cause our suffering. Unfortunately it is rare for someone to actually consider his or her own identity as something bad. However, the Divine Rabbi said:

> And he said to them all, If any man will come after me, **let him deny himself**, and take up his cross daily, and follow me.
>
> – Luke 9:22

The true identity is the Being. The Being has nothing to do with our concept of "I" or our idea of individuality. The Being is a state of non-being according to our understanding of existence, nevertheless it is the true existence. The "I" is many "I's" because each "I" is a desire. It is, *"I like this," "I am not that," "I want," "I hate."* One "I" is not the same as another, they contradict each other. There is even *"I love,"* which is very sad because the "I" cannot love, it thinks it can, it believes it has a conception of love, but the *"I love"* often disappears because it was just another fleeting desire. Then the relationship fails, the woman cries and the man turns his back for a new "love." Therefore, let us begin to understand what lies beyond desire. Let us trade pleasure and pain for true happiness.

Psychological Gymnastics

> Full attention, natural and spontaneous, in whatever we are interested in without artificialities, is truly perfect concentration.
>
> Any error is multi-faceted and inevitably operates in the forty-nine dens of the subconsciousness.
>
> A psychological gymnasium is indispensable; fortunately we have it in life itself.
>
> The path of family life with its infinite, sometimes painful details, is the best chamber of the gymnasium.
>
> – Samael Aun Weor

Life itself is a school, and there are many lessons to learn. If we do not make an effort to learn a lesson, we must repeat the class until we are able to pass its test.

Life is a series of lessons. Lessons that we do not learn will always repeat themselves, and each time the lesson becomes harsher. Let us observe anyone's life that is continuously plagued by the same problems, someone who has become torpid, someone who is stuck in their situation of life. A person like this is not learning the lessons in the schoolhouse of life.

Can we find psychological emancipation of life's problems if we are not paying attention to life's lessons? No, obviously not. So the first thing to do is to begin to observe life.

The lessons of life are the problems themselves. It is good to look into yourself and find what lessons in life you are not learning. What mistakes do you always make? What problems do you have today that you have had yesterday, last year, last decade? Have you changed your position, your job, your home, your spouse and yet the same problems continue to follow you? Let us be quick to learn that the problems of life are psychological and can not be solved at their root by changing external circumstances.

Everyday life is like a psychological gymnasium. Going to work, dealing with family, paying bills, and all the associated problems that are presented to us provide very difficult trials and tribulations. It is astonishing to contemplate that what is very difficult for one person is quite easy for another. This is because everyone's state of mind is different. Everyone has different lessons and levels of being to attain. The higher our level of being, the greater degree of freedom we possess, because when this occurs life no longer dominates our sentiments and reasoning. Instead, for the one who overcomes, he is no longer a servant, but a master of life.

In order to pull ourselves up from our current fallen state a certain mental discipline is required. After all, it is our state of mind that defines us, and to change our mind we need discipline and willpower. However, by discipline we are not speaking about harnessing "mental power," or ignoring our feelings. The discipline that is required is a vigilant consciousness, a consciousness that is aware of its own state of being. Some think that in order to overcome grief, one must simply grind their teeth together, put their head down and just withstand the pain until those emotions are pushed down forcefully, until they "go away." In reality they are merely pressed into the subconsciousness and this is the wrong way to deal with grief. Those who attempt to repress their feelings multiply their suffering. Doctrines that advocate that type of practice only increase the bars of our prison. Rather than strengthening the mind, let us bring fruition to the mind. We need to make the mind a fertile ground that is capable of giving birth to new concepts. We need a flexible mind, not a rigid one. A rigid mind only knows what it knows and rejects what it does not already know.

When properly taken advantage of, the psychological gymnasium of life transforms the mind into something more flexible. The flexible mind can take in the events of life without immediately reacting to them. The mechanical and stiff mind is like a pool of water that is in constant turbulence due to all the rocks of life that are thrown into it. Turbulent water is impossible to work with. The mind needs to become calm in front of life's tempests. A tranquil mind reflects life with clarity. Being agitated, franticly emotional, stressed or depressed are outcomes of a diseased mind.

The problems of life are like rocks that are thrown into a pond. If the water reacts to the rocks, there is no way to see the reflected firmament and the rock below with any clarity. If the water were able to take in the rock without a mechanical reaction, then both the sky and the submerged rock become clear. Likewise, inner tranquility against life's terrible ordeals allows one to understand life instead of being a victim of it. To see the rock, a problem of life, with perfect vision can give us the wisdom to solve that problem. For a wise man, *to see is to know*. Vision and wisdom come from the same root ("weid"). For us, to see the causes of life's problems is the first step. We cannot alter what cannot be seen.

The ego is the "self," but this self is based upon something fundamentally harmful and violent to the rhythm and harmony of the universe as a whole. This is why the ego suffers, and, because the consciousness is trapped in the ego, we feel that suffering. The ego is an aberration, an error of the mind that perpetuates itself. It is like a cancer of the mind because it destroys its host. The liberated consciousness, with no ego, receives and transmits energy, thoughts, ideas, sentiments, will, etc., but the ego takes that perfect harmony and disrupts it: it elaborates itself at the expense of the world around it. So, in this way we have to understand that the ego is what blocks the correct flow of energy. Psychological gymnastics is the method to restore the correct flux of energy.

The physical body is just a machine that receives, transforms, and transmits energy. Beyond the dense physical vehicle (body), there are other vehicles, such as the vehicle of vitality which gives life to the physical body, the emotional vehicle which elaborates sentiment, and the vehicle of the mind which is the foundation of thought. All of these vehicles transform energy, and when that process is performed perfectly, then one becomes a perfect vehicle of that energy, and through that one becomes indistinct from the movement of that energy itself, like how a wave is indistinct from the ocean itself. That perfect harmony is the bliss of Heaven or Nirvana.

Everything has a source, and ultimately, that energy emanates from what is called the Absolute, also known as *Barbelo* in Gnosticism. The Absolute is something beyond God. When Man becomes a perfect transformer of the intelligence of God, then he has become an incarnation of that intelligence called God. That intelligence or energy that can be called God has no form itself, but it can incarnate within anyone who knows how to do it. However the ego prevents the correct transformation and transmission of energy because the ego only uses that energy to edify itself. It is like a single wave thinking it is more than the ocean itself. Thus, the ego prevents the reception of God.

Psychological gymnastics is a term that is saying, *"Ordinary life itself is the best thing that can give us the tools to achieve happiness."* A practical life, the family life, the work life, with all of the stressful situations, all the accidents, the arguments, the things we usually wish to run away, hide and ignore, all the events that we blame our unhappiness for, all the temptations, trials and tribulations, are in actuality the very key to happiness. Instead of ignoring daily life, we have to work to observe it, comprehend it and transform it.

Over six hundred years ago, a monk who knew this, who knew the psychological work of Christianity, wrote the following:

> So long as we live in this world we cannot escape suffering and temptation. Whence it is written in Job: "The life of man upon earth is a warfare." Everyone, therefore, must guard against temptation… No one is so perfect or so holy but he is sometimes tempted; man cannot be altogether free from temptation.
>
> Yet temptations, though troublesome and severe, are often useful to a man, for in them he is humbled, purified, and instructed. The saints all passed through many temptations and trials to profit by them, while those who could not resist became reprobate and fell away. There is no state so holy, no place so secret that temptations and trials will not come. […]
>
> Many people try to escape temptations, only to fall more deeply. We cannot conquer simply by fleeing, but by patience and true

> humility we become stronger than all our enemies. The man who only shuns temptations outwardly and does not uproot them will make little progress; indeed they will quickly return, more violent than before.
>
> Little by little, in patience and long-suffering you will overcome them, by the help of God rather than by severity and your own rash ways. Often take counsel when tempted; and do not be harsh with others who are tempted, but console them as you yourself would wish to be consoled.
>
> The beginning of all temptation lies in a wavering mind and little trust in God, for as a rudderless ship is driven hither and yon by waves, so a careless and irresolute man is tempted in many ways. Fire tempers iron and temptation steels the just. Often we do not know what we can stand, but temptation shows us what we are.
>
> Above all, we must be especially alert against the beginnings of temptation, for the enemy is more easily conquered if he is refused admittance to the mind and is met beyond the threshold when he knocks. [...]
>
> In temptations and trials the progress of a man is measured; in them opportunity for merit and virtue is made more manifest.
>
> When a man is not troubled it is not hard for him to be fervent and devout, but if he bears up patiently in time of adversity, there is hope for great progress.
>
> Some, guarded against great temptations, are frequently overcome by small ones in order that, humbled by their weakness in small trials, they may not presume on their own strength in great ones.
>
> – Thomas à Kempis, *The Imitation of Christ*, ch. 13

We can be certain that the message of this chapter is wholly within Christendom. Sadly, all the supposedly good Christians know nothing about the practical psychological work that Christianity demands. They, today, personify the same values that the Pharisees illustrated in the scriptures they so ignorantly adore. They love to study the Bible, but they ignore what the teachings say, which is: individually we must all become something we are currently not. This implies the psychological effort that Thomas a Kempis outlined in his work; a work so profound that the only book to have sold more copies throughout history is the Bible itself.

Let us become practical: If your boss is a tyrant and personifies everything you do not like in a person, you can take advantage of that. The situations of life are the situations we need in order to understand ourselves. In our example here, we have someone who can expose our psychological defects. There is a saying: *"If the water does not boil at 100 degrees, then the impurities will always remain..."* With this cryptic sentence we can see that without the *heat*, the *pressure*, or the *resistance*, nothing is transformed. The most difficult situations of life provide the most psychological pressure for us to take advantage of, because these situations make all our vices and defects boil up to the surface. We can take advantage of that if we know to observe our mind and its inner workings. If we do not know how to take advantage of that, then our vices remain and even increase.

In this sense, the more you hate someone, the better the teacher they are for you to gain self-knowledge. If a family member's action always brings out resentment from within you, then you have a marvelous opportunity to gain self-knowledge, and nothing is more valuable than self-knowledge. This is how you can begin to observe the ego, how it wishes to act, to discover its *modus operandi*. Only from there can one work to change it. If you were to truly remove that resentment, then that would liberate the consciousness trapped in that resentment. When you free the consciousness the ability to be joyful in any situation arrives without any effort at all.

If you are interested in self-knowledge, cease daydreaming. Stop playing that movie in your head that you love to play and begin to take advantage of life.

Observe. Observe when something makes you very emotional. Do not judge, just observe. If you feel justified in your anger, for now that is okay, but observe that anger, and observe that logic that is justifying your anger. If you feel that your pride is ok, then, do not try to reinforce it, but do not try to repress it either. Observe it. Whatever you do, do not do it mechanically. Do it with conscious attention of what you are doing. Observation will make us realize how mechanical, irrational and reactionary we are, and this gives us a bookmark to come back to later. We often see people acting foolish, yet we very rarely catch ourselves acting foolish. If we were to see ourselves, within the moment of now, as we see others, then we could arrive at self-knowledge. Later, in meditation a superlative retrospective analysis is performed to deeply comprehend the situation.

> If you want to succeed in life you should dissolve the "I." If you want to dissolve the "I," you should disintegrate all your defects. If you want to disintegrate your defects, do not condemn or justify them, **comprehend** them.
>
> When we condemn a defect, we hide it in the profound recesses of the mind and when we justify a defect, we strengthen it horribly but when we comprehend a certain defect, then we disintegrate it completely.
>
> – Samael Aun Weor, *Introduction to Gnosis*

Life gives us the experiments we need in order to understand ourselves. When someone we hate approaches us, and we feel sick from their very presence, instead of giving that person a sneer or a sarcastic remark, observe the emotions this person stirred up inside you. Observe how they have complete control over you. Observe how you are a slave to your emotions. Observe your psychological slavery.

It is very easy to simply *know* of our ego as an intellectual concept, yet this is something insignificant, therefore we must begin to self-*observe* the ego. The way we can unveil the hidden mysteries of ourselves is by pointing our light of conscious attention into our personal darkness. We need to know ourselves before we can change ourselves.

Observation is often misunderstood. Observing is not the same as knowing. It is easy to know of our defects, to superficially list them, but this is not the same as observing them and truly comprehending them. Observation is a continuous and active process that is far beyond an intellectual understanding. We have to go deeper than the intellect. We have to breach the doors of the unconsciousness and this is something that is done only with a mental discipline of self-observation and meditation.

One will find that paying conscious attention is difficult, and indeed it is impossible for any average person to pay conscious attention for even five minutes. We will find the mind is always worrying, always thinking, always stressing, and always dreaming. This is because our consciousness is *asleep* due to its captor, the ego. In truth, if one really begins to apply the methods of the esoteric philosophy, this one will find that the natural and ordinary state of the mind is *silence*.

In order to awaken we must work for it, because we have performed a lot of work in placing our minds in sleep. Life itself will provide the situations that bring out our psychological defects, our negative emotions, our false preconceptions, our sophisms and specious viewpoints into the foreground so we can *observe* our ego. This is a guarantee because the ego has profound karmic ties, and the deeply karmic situations the ego creates are same situations that it is fascinated with, and the same situations one can use to overcome the ego.

Judo is the technique of using the energy of an opponents attack against the attacker. Psychological judo, therefore, is the technique of transforming the values of the impressions to work against the negative impulses the ego wishes to perform. This is only possible through self-observation, because one must be aware of and observe the impressions of life and the fascinations the ego undergoes.

We get angry, resentful or sarcastic when someone gives us a repugnant impression of life. It is often thought that when someone gives us an impression like this, that negative energy is reflected back in our response of anger. It is thought that we are *given* anger. This is not true, because as we have already discussed, the impressions of life are valueless. It is the ego that puts value on the words of another. Someone who has no ego does not respond to hate with more hate, because they have no hate to give. Someone with no ego has comprehended all the reasons for his hate, as they have been all removed, so this one only returns love. Someone with no ego is a true human being, and he would have no ability to act as an animal.

When we are very emotional, fanatic or angry, it is an ego jumping out of the background and into the foreground. That ego is always there, but it is very difficult to see that ego, until a particular impression of life occurs, like gossip, or hateful words, or beautiful imagery, in which the ego feeds upon and consequently makes itself known. When a particular psychological aggregate (ego) is fascinated with an impression of life, it takes control of our psyche and acts in accordance with its own type. It joins in the gossip, it inflames the argument, etc. It is within these very moments that we must observe our ego. It is also these very moments that are most difficult to observe, due to the very fact that we are *identified* at that moment with the ego.

When an ego of jealously appears and we are acting in a sleepy manner, we instantaneously become identified with that ego and begin to project jealousy into the world. However if we are being attentive, with an alert perception, when a particular ego makes itself known in the foreground of the mind, a degree of separation can occur. This separation is essential. Separation is to observe the impulse of jealously in our hearts without becoming totally identified with it, without enacting it.

Someone who is successful at this will see all the negative emotion that wishes to express itself, but at the same time the person will understand that this negative emotion is nothing more than an ego, nothing more than a delusion of false values. Thus, the portion of *awakened consciousness* observes the ego, which the *sleeping consciousness*. When this occurs we are in observation. The first step to transformation is to know what we are transforming. We must observe. Therefore, do not run away from life. Instead of ignoring problems and doing our best to simply withstand them, observe them and conqueror them. We can only remove a defect that we have previously understood. How can we work with something if we do not even understand it? Therefore, let us begin with observation.

When we begin to observe we find that we are constantly throughout the day experiencing some form of mental agitation and emotional frustration, however we rarely look into the root of these mental and emotional states. The truth is we are ignoring the worst of ourselves and identifying with illusions. These are all forms of suffering. We ignore our worst attributes and what we do not ignore we justify. Suffering is ignored through many vices: gambling, debauchery, drugs, alcohol, arguments, work, television, hobbies, etc.

Sometimes the best way to solve a problem is to talk a walk, to rest, to read or relax. This is because the when the mind stops thinking about the problem the solution becomes evident. However, we have to observe what activities are conductive for solving our problems, and what activities are not.

Many of our activities do not in anyway whatsoever solve our problems, and what is worse, we form vices related with these activities, perpetuating our suffering. Nevertheless, because we are trapped in our delusions, we believe that these very activities are what provide the "enjoyment" of life. The enjoyment of life should be found within each moment of it, because the enjoyment of life is intrinsic to the fabric of reality. Yet, the psychological aggregates remove the ability to always experience that enjoyment. The psychological aggregates only "enjoy" certain things, and this enjoyment is what we are seeking through our bad habits. What is horrible is that we fail to see the duality of that ego's existence. If one thing gives the ego pleasure, it is inevitable that something else will give it pain. The ego may enjoy certain impressions, yet it suffers when impressions of life do not satiate it.

Return and Recurrence of the Ego

> Time in itself, as the fourth dimension, intrinsically contains two fundamental properties; the temporal one and the spatial one.
>
> Undoubtedly, the chronometric side of life is in reality just the unstable surface of the spatial question. Before the wise Einstein had surprised the world with his famous theory of Relativity, any cultured man conceived time as a straight line. Today, intellectuals accept the fact that the above factor is curved.
>
> Yet, in this 20th century, there are still people who think with a medieval mind.
>
> – Samael Aun Weor, *The Perfect Matrimony*

Certainly, we can add and subtract the values of time to quantify the sequence of events that constantly occur. We can say with confidence that a television program is thirty or sixty minutes. We can put a value on that event: it is so and so minutes long. But where are the minutes? Where exactly does time go? Are those minutes assigned to a program now in the past? Where does time come from? Do we really have any idea at all of what time is? We must realize that however we wish to quantify time it ultimately has no value. Time is meaningless. As Einstein said, "Time is relative." Time is not fully defined because a partial definition is a non-definition. It is better to say that time is undefined, and its phenomena are therefore ultimately flawed and subjective. Time does not exist.

If there is no absolute nature of time then we cannot rely on anything that has to do with it. Nevertheless, we know that through time we are born and we eventually die. We understand that our fatality is tied with time. We realize that our entire existence is time based. Within our life are many years. Within many years are many months, and within a month are a number of weeks. The composition of a week is seven days, and one day is composed of twenty-four hours. Here we see that the hour is definitely a quantity of time, yet paradoxically, we also know that time has no calibration. Exactly what our existence is composed of does not seem to make sense in terms of time.

Observing this, we notice that all of the quanta of time break down into cyclic events: every day repeats itself, every year the seasons occur. Creation is a series of cyclic events and the laws of creation ensure this fact. Gravity pulls us around the great luminary, just as every object gravitates towards another. Our sun, in turn is attracted to a central luminary, etc., etc.

The great clue that time gives us is its cyclic nature. All events in time are recapitulations. Every event is the blueprint for another and every event is the result of a previous blueprint. The profound significance of the Uroboros is unveiled with this clue. The serpent consuming its own tale is the circle of life and death. It is the 10th Arcanum of Tarot intimately related to The Ten Commandments. It is the Buddhist's Wheel of Samsara, it is the Wheel of Fortune.

The esoteric philosophy states that humans live chained to the Wheel of Samsara. Time itself is a closed curve that Buddha called Interdependent Arising. Each event is the effect of some other event, and that effect transforms itself into a cause of something else. In total, each cause-effect is a self-feeding chain of events.

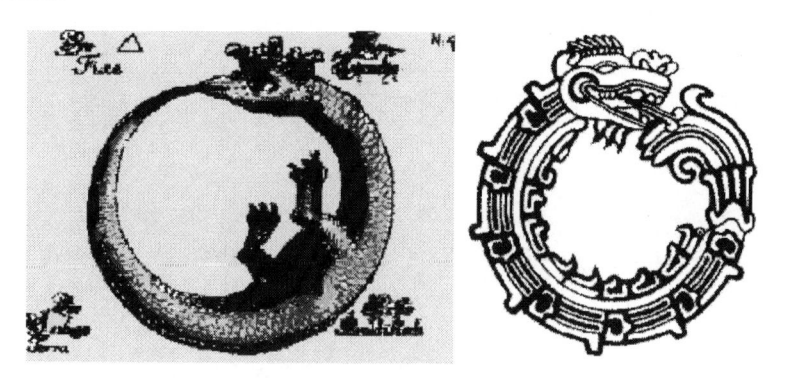

The Alchemical (left) and Aztec (right) Uroboros.

The concept of what we improperly labeled reincarnation, that is, multiple successive lives, comes as a very foreign concept to the occidental personality. Firstly understand that reincarnation is for those who have firstly incarnated, that is to say, incarnated God. The normal and ordinary person simply *returns* as legion of psychological aggregates.

In reality, western persons should not be surprised that life is a recapitulation just as any other process of time is. In fact it is unique that western culture finds the concept of multiple lives to be odd. Pythagoras taught the doctrine of metempsychosis, Hinduism teaches of the transmigration of souls, Buddhism speaks of rebirth, and in fact, return can be found in both Judaism and Christianity if one looks in the right places.

Each life we live is in general the reenactment of our previous lives. This is called the Law of Recurrence. Although possessing the same general set of characters, events and scenery, each life has its modifications. These modifications are either for the better or for the worse. In other words we have a general path, but upon this path we can choose to improve ourselves, or we can let ourselves degenerate. Each choice leads us down a path of modified causes and conditions. On the grand scale though, it is very difficult to change the path of life in a radical manner. This is the superior transformation we have spoken of, it is a type of transformation is few achieve.

"How is it possible," one may ask, "that within each successive life, of all the infinite possibilities one may have, out of free will, we will choose to make the same general choices?" This is a very worthy question and it is has to do with the part of us that belongs to the cyclic events of time. The short answer is that we *do not* have free will, or otherwise stated – conscious will. Our will is exclusively defined by our desires: we are a conditioned machine that reacts to the impressions of life.

What we have is unconscious will, animal will, group will, but not conscious and individual will. Before we can answer our question fully we must understand there is a part of us that belongs to time and a part that belongs to what the occultists call eternity. The part of us that belongs to time is the ego. The ego is the sum of the untransformed impressions that occur through all of time. Our true self however is timeless: it is outside the laws of time. The ego is not our true self, our true self is not a product of time. The True Self, the Being, is ineffable and eternal.

If we manage to correctly transform impressions by always staying vigilant, and comprehend our subconsciousness through meditation, the amount of interior space occupied by ego will begin to lessen. The correct transformation of impressions leads us to make better choices in our lives, and the lack of this transformation leads to worse choices. These are the modifications made in each life: it is tied with the quantity of ego. Time is a circle and sometimes we spiral up, other times we spiral down.

The ego is a product of time, and therefore it can only exist within the nature of time. In other words the ego has its birth, life and death within time, it cannot process itself anywhere except where it has been created. There is a mistaken concept that when the physical body dies, the psychology that was personified through that body dies as well. This is a mistake because *psychology is soul*. To think that the soul dies along with the flesh seems silly, but we will readily believe that the *causes* of our pain in life will magically go away when we die. We must begin to comprehend that it is our very soul (psychology) that is causing our pain and misfortune here and now, and where we take our soul is where we take our suffering.

When the physical body sleeps, obviously we are still alive and our psychological processes remain uninterrupted. When sleeping, without the external physical distractions, we are able to fully emerge ourselves in our internal dreams. What we must realize, is that when we are driving a car, eating, working, etc., we are always dreaming because we are always psychologically sleeping. We dream all day and our dreams at night are just a continuation of this process.

Some people say they do not dream. They say, "I just close my eyes and seven hours later I awake as if only a moment had past." These people are more profoundly asleep than others, when one does not recall their dreams it is because they were too profoundly asleep to even perceive their dreams. They need to awaken enough to even perceive their dreams. Many people who are unable to see their dreams feel indifference or repugnance towards this doctrine because, due to their own pride, they feel themselves to beyond this "idea" of people being psychologically asleep, both day and night.

Fascination is the cause of all dreams. One must pay attention to their mental wanderings in order to understand fascination. Incredibly, one will find that we are fascinated with nearly everything. Many people are fascinated with their workplace, with how much money they are making versus how much they could be making. We are fascinated with some valueless goal of the minute, only to be replaced by something else once it is accomplished, and if we fail at accomplishing a particular goal, we become cranky as a child with a stomach ache. Often, we are even fascinated with our own problems, and we enjoy spilling our woes upon others. All this dreaming requires enormous energy and it is very important to remove all dreaming if one is interested in awakening consciousness. As it turns out it is very difficult to realize this fact within the moment of a dream. The trance is very elaborate and requires the application of an intricate didacticism in order to awaken from it. This is what religion, yoga, the occult sciences, etc., are attempting to produce: an instructional teaching to awaken consciousness.

When we stop dreaming totally, we begin living totally conscious. This is something very rare, and therefore in the beginning the aspirant, using all of his will, may manage only one or two minutes of contiguous observation during daily life before falling asleep again. However, with practice, the time and quality of self-observation increases. Quality is important. If we are not obtaining information about the self, then we are not gaining the knowledge required for comprehension, which leads to true, fundamental, psychological change. One can practice self-observation for thirty years, but if the quality is not good, then little change will be made. This work is a lifetime effort, even when proper effort is applied. Proper effort simply means to observe without thought or expectation, and to see everything as if it had never been seen before.

Through the correct application of self-observation we will come to know through direct experience that our interior processes (thoughts and feelings) and the state of our physical body (awake or asleep) are discrete. In other words, the physical body and the psychology it personifies are *independent* of each other. Therefore the death of the physical does not correspond to the death of our psychology. What we are stating is that the ego in fact lives beyond the death of the physical body.

Everyone is nothing more than a point in infinite space which holds certain values. Death is the *action* of subtracting of these values, however, *the values themselves remain*. Thus, to die is to merely shift from one dimension to another. The ego is a sum of values - it does not die with the body. When the body is dead those values continue to process themselves. If the physical body is dead, the ego facilitates our return to time. If subtraction of those values produces death, then later those values will process themselves as addition to give birth again. If the values do not change the outcome of those values are predetermined. If 2 + 2 = 4, it will always forever be such, and every time we are born, we are the same equation because we hold the same values. The values are the psychological aggregates, and the equation is our lives.

Egos are the chains that retain us to the wheel of our own circumstance, *samsara*. The ego does not die with the body. The processes of the ego continue after death. In other words the circumstances that remove us from Eternity remain even when the flesh is dead. When we die we enter into Eternity, into perhaps what we could say is Heaven. However our desires caused so much karma through incorrect action that our ego, which in turn is entrapping the consciousness, must return to time and to the physical dimensions. Then we begin to live out the same desires we had in our previous life. The ego is the cause of karma; it is the reason for our recapitulations. The ego itself *is* karma. Unfortunately our karma is very large because the ego is never satisfied and we continue to ignore that to feed desire is to strengthen desire.

The ego is a temporal movement of energy that impels the physical return to time in order for its expression. Is the drunkard ever satisfied when he is at the bar? Is the gambler ever satisfied with his earnings? The "Duan Juan" with his women? The intellectual with his theories? The emotional with her movies and novels? The ego is never satisfied and this is why it always returns. Examining life and time, we can conclude that the fulfillment of desire is a contradiction because desire is a product of time and all products of time repeat. Hence the only thing left for our ego, in a logical sense, is death.

Our desires must die in the same fashion they were born. This process concerns the untransformed impressions that we receive in life. Impressions that are currently incorrectly stored within our interior constitute the ego, and it is this energy that must be comprehended through meditation. Through this the ego is decreased, because the *flawed internal processes* it was using to misuse energy no longer exist. The knot (ego) that was blocking the correct flux of energy, the correct transformation of energy, will be corrected. This is the agenda of meditation: to comprehend ourselves by internally dieing.

Let us to ask the question again: *Why are our successive lives always the same?* This is because although we may have a new body, the processes that brought us here (karmic egos) are constant, and while they remain as such, the same processes (egos) will dominate our life. Therefore, the same mistakes, the same errors, the same people appear in our lives. It is only logical to repeat: *The desires we create and carry within this life will carry on to the next and this is why our circumstances will always recapitulate.* For this reason the scriptures emphasize the necessity of the internal death. If we remove the values, it is obvious they can no longer process. When all the values are removed, destroyed, then what remains is 0=0, or if we compress the equation: ∞. When the false values are removed what remains are the infinite possibilities of the human being.#

> It is necessary for every Son of Man *(the Solar Hero of all ages and sects: Krishna, Jesus, Hermes, Quetzalcoatl, etc.)* to suffer many things, and to be rejected by the Elders *(those who are respected by society, or the instinctual type)*, and by the chief Priests *(organized religion, those with power, etc., or the emotional type)*, and by the Scribes *(those who are considered wise, or the intellectual type)*, and to be slain, and to ascend on the third day... I tell you the truth, some who are standing here will not taste death before they see the kingdom of God.
>
> Whoever wants to come after me, let him deny himself *(destroy the "I")*, and take up his cross daily *(understand and live the Christic Mysteries, the Cross of Man and Wife)*, and follow me *(on the narrow path of conscious suffering and sacrifice for humanity)*.
>
> For whoever wishes to save his life *(those full of ego)* shall lose it, and whoever loses his life for his love unto me *(those wish to die, to make the sacrifice, within)* shall save it.
>
> What good is it for a man to gain the whole world, and yet lose or forfeit his very self?
>
> – Luke 9:22-25

Happiness is unconditionally impossible if the ego is present. Nirvana, Heaven, Paradise, the wonderful afterlife we like to dream about is impossible if the ego is not destroyed and we become perfect people in the *here and now*. The perfection of man is what in Christianity is called an Angel, in Buddhism it is a Buddha, to the Greeks it is Hercules and to the Mayans it is the Feathered Serpent.

Unfortunately people make the excuse that time will perfect us. People want to better themselves throughout time. Many schools have made a mistake in believing that all souls will by the mechanics of nature perfect themselves. It is true that in Nature, our souls evolve as elemental creatures in the mineral, plant and animal kingdoms. This gives us our animal will we spoke of at the beginning of the chapter. However, individual will is different – it does not arrive through the mechanics of time. When time gives us something, it is owned by time. Consciousness is self-knowledge, and it cannot be given by time. Therefore we must search a direct and radical path outside the mechanical forces of nature. When this is achieved one no longer exists within these mechanical forces and therefore true freedom reigns.

The Wheel of Samsara, depicting the animals, humans, demi-gods and gods in the cycles of time.

The SACRED SOLAR ABSOLUTE is far beyond the Mechanistic Nature of Time and exists only as Absolute Abstract Movement and Repose. Bearing this in mind, we must deeply comprehend that no process of time, a vehicle exclusively of a mechanical nature, has any consequence upon this aforementioned singularity. God is freedom in movement and repose, a single Will, a single Law. Mechanism is many laws, many wills, it is contradiction, *relativity*, subjectivism, no absolute truth, etc. Time is subjective and mechanical. It has nothing to do with the Great Reality, the Truth.

"Life is processed in surges that rotate." Evolution is merely a process within the agenda of Nature. Every plant and animal on earth mechanically transforms energies for the Earth to live. This "biological skin" of the earth is something like a stomach, for it processes the energies of the world for its sustainment. Some organisms are evolving, but one day they will begin to devolve, because that is the law. Energy is entropic unless something is applying pressure for its sustainment, but Nature does not give us the pressure required to awaken consciousness, because that is not the agenda of nature. To find this pressure, we must *incarnate* it. This is pressure is willpower. The true Human being is the incarnation of individual willpower.

To ride life in a mechanical manner, to float down the river of life without willpower is something "lunar." That type of life is related with the lunar cycle, it is something that is always moving, but always in circles and never going anywhere in an Absolute sense. When an intellectual animal wishes to become something more than a cog or gear in the great machine of nature, then that animal has what is called, "A spiritual yearning for the Truth." Then the intellectual animal steps off the mechanics of evolution and entropy and steps upon The Path of the Razor's Edge. This is the Narrow and Straight Gate, the Middle Way, the Fourth Way, The Great Rebellion, etc. This path has many dangers within and without.

The Alchemists say, "We must turn the moon into the sun." Man perfects himself by living the Christic Drama, and, in victory becomes a Solar Hero: a true Hercules. This has not to do with evolution, but an Internal Revolution. The Internal Revolution is the Death, the Death of the "I," the ego. The Christ of all times and ages is always a revolutionary.

Eternity is that which is beyond Time. Eternity is not Time stretched to the infinite. This is because time does not exist in eternity. It is the eternal now, it is something fundamentally different than time.

The Gods have their center of gravity within eternity. There are many aspects of eternity. There are many levels of Heaven, there are many aspects of Nirvana.

Beyond eternity is the Absolute. Both man and God tremble at the Absolute. The Absolute is beyond God.

When we study these matters we realize that even within the realms of Gods, cyclic events continue to occur. This is stated in Buddhism and Hinduism. We call these things the Great Day and the Great Night, or *Mahamanvantara* and *Mahapralaya*.

On the dawn of the Great Day, the Gods are born, and at the conclusion of this day, all of creation is swallowed up into the Absolute during the Mahapralaya. Even the Gods die. When a God dies willingly then he enters the Absolute willingly. When a God willingly gives up His power, His omnipotence, His ubiquity, His Being, then He "gets lost" in the bosom of the Great Common Cosmic Eternal Father, the Adhi-Buddha, Ain, Sat, Tao, The Absolute. Then He becomes NON-BEING, which is the Real Being in the most absolute sense. Likewise, when the intellectual animal willingly gives up his animal nature, then he can become a true Human Being.

God is Deity, Elohim of the Semitics. Beyond God is the Absolute, the Aelohim, the Unknowable, the Ain in Kabbalah, Sat in Sanskrit, Brahma of the Hindus, the Tao: THAT WHICH HAS NO NAME. That is our true point of departure and that is where we are going to return.

I died from the mineral kingdom and became a plant;
I died to vegetable nature and became an animal;

I died to animality and became a human being.

Next time I will die to human nature and lift up my head among the angels.

Once again I will leave angelic nature and become that which you cannot imagine.

– Rumi

THE TREE OF GNOSIS

> And out of the ground the LORD God made every tree grow that is pleasant to the sight and good for food. The Tree of Life was also in the midst of the garden, and the Tree of the Knowledge of Good and Evil.
>
> – Genesis 2:9

The Tree of Gnosis is the same Tree of the Knowledge of Good and Evil mentioned in the Bible. The true meaning behind this symbolic tree is a mystery to the Roman Church. The Tree of Gnosis is where one studies true Gnosticism.

Remember, dear reader, it is stated that "Adam *knew* Eve" when they had children. The cornerstone of Gnosticism is the mysteries related with that "knowing" of a sexual nature. In Jewish esotericism, the most secret doctrine is the doctrine of *Daath*. Daath is Hebrew for *knowledge*, or gnosis, and daath is the word used in Genesis to describe sexual relations.

True Gnosticism is the knowledge of good and evil, which is tied at its root to sexuality. All of those who say otherwise are lacking or ignoring the essential Gnostic foundation. Indeed, the cornerstone of all secret doctrines is sex. Sex is a topic of offense, it is a weakness, a stone of stumbling, a stone that causes one to fall into fanaticism and ignorance. This is the stone of sex Adam and Eve stumbled upon when they fell from paradise. Adam and Eve fell not simply by disobedience, but by sexual disobedience.

Adam and Eve represent an entire wave of evolving souls that had reached the pinnacle of mechanical evolution many millions of years ago. They were beginning to become aware of their own natures and as souls were primed to take the next step and become human beings. So, in a way, their "eyes" were closed because they still possessed the innocence of ignorance: they knew not what was good or evil. They, like any animal, were imparted with the instinctual inheritance to reproduce in the animalistic way. Animals do not have reasoning when it comes to reproduction. They simply act. This instinctual inheritance was and is guided by "Jehovah Elohim," or as we can say, those superior vehicles of intelligence (souls) that had already reached the Angelic state, and were responsible for the management of the evolving and devolving life forces on Earth.

Once these evolving souls were ready for human bodies, they were born within them, yet because they were still innocent, they were still guided by Jehovah Elohim. As such, they were taught how to reproduce in a superior way, the way of a human. They were taught to unite, and how to transmute within the sexual act, and how to reproduce within the sexual act. In those times, the male body had the ability to release a single sperm in order for it to unite with a single ovum. There was no need to ejaculate 100 million spermatozoa in order to reproduce. Because of this, neither the males nor the females ever reached orgasm or ejaculation. Instead of spilling or wasting their sexual energy, their creative-sexual potential was transmuted into a paradise of the body and soul. The Earth was a living paradise.

There was something sinister at work however. Something was slithering, like a serpent, in the blood of this newborn humanity. Temptation, the great gift of Mephistopheles, was too great and sexual disobedience was the outcome. This innocent humanity began to copulate like animals, which was a backwards step. They began to reach orgasm again. Now, because these souls were imparted with reasoning of a human, their eyes opened to lust when they experienced the sexual spasm, and from that all the sin of the world was generated. The gates of Eden were closed, and humanity fell into perversion.

The serpent is that force in the blood that gives a man his erection and the woman her voluptuousness. The serpent is at the epicenter of gnosis, which is why it coils around the Tree of Knowledge. The serpent is both the strength and wrath of God.

This temptation is obviously related with Jehovah, as it was Him, the Demiurge Architect-Creator of the World, who placed a tempting serpent in the midst of paradise. Many people have read about the Gnostic Demiurge, the lion-faced ruler of the chaos whose name is also Yaldabaoth, and His antithesis (and mother), Sophia (wisdom). Nevertheless, even after much study, few people correctly understand these things.

Yaldabaoth is the karma of the universe. Without Yaldabaoth, the universe would not exist, and Sophia could not cry Her Thirteen Repentances to rid herself of the attacks of the Self-willed. Yet, without the Thirteen Repentances, Sophia would not be wise. Existence is due to an unbalance of energy, or karma. Sophia will always create Yaldabaoth as long as there is cosmic debt (karma) or cosmic capital (dharma).

Existence comes into being in order to equilibrate the energy of every cosmic unit. Every cosmic unit, or monad (spirit), has a Sophia. The sum of all "Sophias" is also called Sophia. Likewise, Yaldabaoth must be understood in similar way. Only when Sophia has completed her journey from the top, all the way to the very bottom, and back to the top again, she will no longer mistakenly create Yaldabaoth. Only when the Sophia of a monad achieves the Thirteen Repentances will she no longer create her son, Yaldabaoth.

Each of us has our own individual Yaldabaoth and Sophia. Each person has the Self-willed, the ego, that crucifies Sophia, who is our inner spirit. The Thirteen Repentances are the psychological works that rid us of the shackles of the lion-faced rulers (karmic debts).

From a cosmic standpoint, Yaldabaoth is a divine emanation. Yaldabaoth is both the good and evil of the universe. Why then do Gnostic texts refer to Yaldabaoth negatively? This is because the Gnostic must fight against Yaldabaoth, due to the fact that the Gnostic must go beyond good and evil, which is precisely the realm of Yaldabaoth.

So, on the cosmic level, the Gnostic must go beyond the realm of Yaldabaoth, beyond existence, which is the Thirteenth Aeon. On an individual level, the Gnostic must die to the "Self-willed" (the ego), and in doing so overcomes the lion-faced rulers (karma) that attack Sophia. On an individual level, Yaldabaoth is the self-willed, or in other words, the separateness or false-individuality that manifests itself as the ego in our psyches. Likewise, the forty-nine demons of Yaldabaoth are the forty-nine levels of the unconscious mind.

Karma is The Law (as it is described in the Bible) that holds the universe in place, without it the universe could not exist. Yet it is also The Law which prevents us from escaping the limitations of existence. Realize, that for the Gnostic, *existence itself* is a form of bondage, because true Being is *Non-Being*. The Gnostic wishes to go beyond all forms of existence.

The Gnostic works on the "Straight Path" to the Absolute. The Gnostic is not complacent with even the rank of an Angel, God or Archon ("ruler"). The Gnostic wants to go all the way to the Absolute, and because of this, the other Archons (who are complacent with their existential omnipotence) behave and work, in a way, against the Gnostic struggling towards the Absolute. This is the essential principle behind the struggle of Yaldabaoth and Sophia.

These are very strange concepts to us, yet, this is the way it is. A great deal of meditation is required to understand Gnosticism. It cannot be haphazardly interpreted based upon our subjective whims of the day. We have to understand that even Christ is a stranger among the Gods, because the Gods' center of gravity is within existence, yet the center of gravity of Christ is Barbelo, the Absolute, the Nothingness, the place where true freedom reigns.

The being named Aberamentho, known to us as Jesus, came not just to save this miserable humanity, *but also Gods*. We understand that his doctrine is the highest doctrine taught on this Earth, which makes it very difficult to comprehend. Many aspects of his doctrine only reach their deepest significance after we have already accomplished the complete removal of the ego and have gained entrance into the superior realms of existence.

An aspirant of Gnosticism is a Gnostic only to the percentage upon which he has died to his ego. A complete Gnostic has no ego. A complete Gnostic is already an enlightened being. So, obviously, the Gnostic doctrine is very advanced and not easily understood by us, mere aspirants. There are many Gnostic groups today that have no relationship with what we are explaining on these pages. They depict the Demiurge and the Archons in the same way as fundamentalist Christians depict Satan. They are lacking comprehension and as a result they do not understand the supremely elevated nature of these teachings. People are confused because the ancient Gnostic texts have a way of describing things that is very foreign to our intellect. The Demiurge is described as "evil" for example; yet, the actual meaning of evil in this context is not so crude as a cliché villain depicted in storybooks.

It is very interesting to contemplate the outcome of Sophia's folly. She creates what is described as a lion faced serpent. The serpent, we know from studying the Bible, is a symbol of wisdom, of gnosis. This is why Jesus recommends we become as wise as a serpent. But what is the lion? The lion represents The Law, or karma. This is the lion that Samson and Hercules must defeat.

The serpent in Eden is related with all of this. When we make the wrong use of the serpent, then we are trapping Sophia in the realm of Yaldabaoth. Only when we overcome the temptations of the serpent can its power elevate us beyond the realm of Yaldabaoth, because the serpent is the essential creative power of everything. The serpent is the power that Yaldabaoth used to create, yet it has its ultimate source beyond creation. This is why it is stated that Yaldabaoth stole a portion of Sophia's power in order to create. Sophia's rightful place is in the Absolute, the Nothingness, the Thirteenth Aeon, yet due to karma, Sophia is dragged to the lowest spheres of creation. All of this is written and explained in the *Pistis Sophia Unveiled* by Samael Aun Weor.

When the serpent is used in combination with chastity, then the creative and destructive power of God is realized in man. However, when the serpent is too tempting, fornication is the result. The definition of fornication is the orgasm. Because of fornication, the male body has now totally lost the ability to release a single seed in order to reproduce. The woman still retains that ability, albeit at a mechanical level (ovulation). The body can be educated to reproduce without the need for orgasm. It is possible to reproduce without the sexual spasm. This is the true primeval sexual system, the system of Eden. This is the system that one must use to return to paradise.

By disobeying the commandments of God, we have come to know good and evil very well. We all know the joys and bitterness of life, yet now it is time to leave this cage is return to bosom of the Pleorma, knowing good and evil. In order to return to our departure point, we must obey, by resisting the temptation to "eat" the fruit of the Tree of Good and Evil. When we reach orgasm, the most wonderful and beautiful power of man is depleted and wasted all for the name of desire. The orgasm is the expression of animal sexuality. Sexual transmutation is the expression of human sexuality.

There are four rivers in Eden. Eden, as with every symbol in the Book of Genesis, is multifaceted. One of these facets is the symbol of the paradisiacal man. Two of the Edenic rivers are related with fluids of the brain and spinal cord, and of the mind. The other two rivers are related with the fluids of the sex, and of creativity. Adam is the brain of man and woman. Eve is the sex of man and woman. Eve is the one who eats the fruit, because the fruit is eaten during sexual intercourse. Eve passes the defiled fruit to Adam, the brain and mind, and as a result corrupts it with the ego. Thus it is stated in the Bible.

> So when the woman saw that the tree (*of knowledge, gnosis, daath, or creative potential*) was good for food, that it was pleasant to the eyes (*and all sensations*), and a tree desirable to make one wise (*to know good and evil*), she (*the sex*) took of its fruit and ate. She also gave to her husband (*the mind*) with her, and he ate. Then the eyes of both of them were opened (*to sensation*), and they knew that they were naked (*no longer innocent*); and they sewed fig leaves together and made themselves coverings (*for their sexual organs had now been defiled, and their mind had been defiled, and they could no longer look upon the world with their new sight without the corruption of lust. Thus, they covered their sex in the "shadows" because their creative potential now lives in Hell*).
>
> – Genesis 3:6, 7

Eve eats the fruit of the Tree of Knowledge of Good and Evil every time the sexual spasm takes place. The mind and the sex are two poles of the same thing. There cannot be a serious discussion about mental clarity or enlightenment without tackling the serious problem of sexual desire. It is only when Eve stops eating the fruit will Adam stop receiving its negative consequences. In other words, it is only when fornication ceases that true illumination can arrive.

> Now the angel who talked with me came back and wakened me, as a man who is wakened out of his sleep. And he said to me, "What do you see?"
>
> So I said, "I am looking, and there is a lampstand of solid gold with a bowl on top of it, and on the stand seven lamps with seven pipes to the seven lamps. Two olive trees are by it, one at the right of the bowl and the other at its left."
>
> – Zechariah 4:1-3
>
> Then I answered and said to him, "What are these two olive trees—at the right of the lampstand and at its left?"
>
> And I further answered and said to him, "What are these two olive branches that drip into the receptacles of the two gold pipes from which the golden oil drains?"
>
> Then he answered me and said, "Do you not know what these are?" And I said, "No, my lord."
>
> So he said, "These are the two anointed ones, who stand beside the Lord of the whole earth."
>
> – Zechariah 4:11-14

The two lamp stands that carry the golden oil are the two principles of man and woman, called Adam and Eve in Genesis. These lamp stands are worthless if they do not carry the golden oil, the transmuted sexual waters, to the bowl that rests atop the lamp stands. The bowl, the chalice, is the mind. The Gnostic must fill his chalice with the sacred wine of light.

> To whom coming, as unto a **living stone**, disallowed indeed of men, but chosen of God, and precious, Ye also, as lively stones, are built up a spiritual house, an holy priesthood, to offer up spiritual sacrifices, acceptable to God by Jesus Christ.

Wherefore also it is contained in the scripture, Behold, I lay in Sion a chief corner stone, elect, precious: and he that believeth on him shall not be confounded.

Unto you therefore which believe he is precious: but unto them which be disobedient, the **stone which the builders disallowed**, the same is made the head of the corner, And a **stone of stumbling, and a rock of offence**, even to them which stumble at the word, being disobedient: whereunto also they were appointed.

— 1 Peter 2:4

The living stone, the sexual nature, is the where the Spirit of God (the creative potential of God) can be used to create the Spiritual House. This is how one is born of the spirit. One is "born again" by making use of the sexual nature, not in fornication, but through transmutation. This is what Jesus was symbolizing in his first miracle. He transformed the waters into the wine at the Wedding.

Jesus is not stating that it is acceptable to have many glasses of wine at a wedding; it is absurd to believe that Jesus would make use of a miracle to promote drinking. What Jesus is teaching is that the individual Inner Christ that lives within each person must take the "waters" of the Wedding and transform them into Wine. The wine is the transmuted water, and within the Waters lays the Spirit of God. The sacrament of the wedding is the sexual act performed without orgasm. This is how the water is transmuted into wine. The "Wine" is the Blood of Christ, it gives a type of spiritual intoxication, a mystical *agape*, a rapture of a nature that is far beyond the fleeting illusions of pleasure and pain.

As Jesus tells Nicodemus, flesh gives birth to flesh, but it is the spirit that gives birth to the spirit. The sexual act with the orgasm is a fleshly and defiled act of sexuality. The sexual act without the orgasm, with sexual transmutation, is a purely spiritual experience.

Transmutation can occur if one is single, yet the most superior form of transmutation is only for couples. Transmutation is the expression of true human sexuality.

Transmutation is the path to be "born again," and it is the only path to be "born again." Instead of sexual transmutation as the path to God, celibacy has been taught. Celibacy is the rejection of sex. Celibacy is different than transmutation or chastity. Celibacy was born from not knowing the mysteries of transmutation. Transmutation as a single person has been forgotten and replaced with celibacy. The original monks and nuns knew transmutation, yet, this was forgotten and replaced with celibacy. Celibacy can be a form of fornication because it is an abuse (waste) of the sexual energy. Those who are celibate totally reject the sexual energy, they do nothing with it, they do not understand that the Spirit of God dwells within the sexual energy, and thus by totally rejecting it, they are, in fact, performing fornication.

This does not mean that everyone who practices continence is a mistaken path. All the true Saints, all the Avatars ("messengers" of God), the Angels ("messengers"), and the Buddhas were all already born again, therefore they no longer needed to perform the sacred act. Sexuality is the most secret portion of religion. The external doctrines never mention the spiritual power of sex because such power is too easily abused. Eventually these external doctrines become like empty shells because they had forgotten the inner doctrine. As a result, many teachers today affirm that this Master, this Prophet, or this Buddha was totally celibate since the beginning of time. Such affirmations are incorrect. Without sexual transmutation with a partner (in one lifetime or another) the level of spiritual enlightenment possible is limited. Complete spiritual mastery is impossible without the power of sex.

The problem is that people already believe they are a true human, people believe that they already posses a soul, when in fact only those who are born again possess a soul. That is why Luke 21:12 states *"in your patience you will possess your souls."* Currently we do not have a true human soul, we have an animal soul. An animal soul is developed through animalistic sexuality and a human soul is developed through sexual transmutation.

The true, superior, esoteric meaning of a virgin has not to do with sexual abstention. A virgin has nothing to do with the presence or lack of a woman's hymen. A virgin is one who is absolutely chaste on all the levels of the heart and the mind. A virgin is one who enacts immaculate sexuality. Immaculate means: spotless, perfect, flawless. Those who contain a even one small dint of lust, of desire, on any conscious, subconscious, unconscious, or infraconscious layer of the mind is not a virgin. It does not matter if a man or woman has refrained from sex in their present lifetime, if they have lust, then they are not a virgin. The reason they have lust is due to fornication in previous lives. This humanity lost its virginity in Eden. To meet a true "virgin" today is to meet a Prophet or an Angel.

Understand that one who has desire cannot be a virgin. A virgin is chaste, and chastity has much more to do than with the sexual act itself. Chastity is a state of the mind, a state of the heart, and a state of the body. The mind must be chaste, the heart must be chaste, and the body must be chaste. The Immaculate Conception is not a physical conception. The Immaculate Conception occurs when one is born again of the Holy Spirit through chaste sexual union.

Mary was an initiate of the Gnostic mysteries and practiced sexual transmutation, with her husband. Mary had a husband, and she was born again in the Spirit through the creative power of God, which exist within the Spirit of God, which exists within the sexual "waters" of man and woman. She purified herself of all sin, of all imperfection and reached the state of virgin. Thus, she was capable in giving birth to the Savior of the World.

No one can become a born again virgin without practicing sexual transmutation; no one can be born without sex, and no one can be born of the spirit without the spirit being active during sex. The sexual act of the spirit is the holiest of holies. It is the Arc of the Covenant.

When a man and woman unite physically and renounce the animal instinct (orgasm), that energy that usually manifests itself in a pleasure of the senses is refined and sublimated through one's soul. This act of sacrifice fills one's heart with true love and compassion. The same energy that produces a child, and pleasure, can produce the Spiritual Man. The nature born man is the Natural Man, the animal-man, the nature of the animal man is to fornicate. Yet, the Spiritual Man, the Heavenly Man is the true Human, the one who is a Twice-Born, because they have been born of the flesh and of the spirit.

All of the sacraments of the Gnostic Church (the original Christian Church) are related with Daath, or sexual-tantric knowledge. The circumcision is a pact of chastity, in order to prevent fornication (orgasm) during the later sacrament of marriage (intercourse). What does Paul, the great Gnostic, say about this? Paul states that the physical circumcision is meaningless, what is important is the spiritual circumcision (Phil 3:3).

Paul also states that when we become married, we must act as though we are not married (1 Cor 7:29). What can be concluded with such a strange statement? The principle and foundation of marriage is sex. Therefore, how can one practice marriage as someone who is single? Unless you know the key, it does not make any sense. The spiritual circumcision, and the way to be married and yet be as if single, is to perform the sexual act without the sexual spasm. That is the key.

Paul advocates chaste sexual relations for those who still have lust. Yet, for someone like Paul, if you are already a Gnostic, if you are already born again in the spirit, then you do not need the sacrament of marriage, for you have already completed its goal. Paul was a virgin, therefore, he no longer needed the sexual act. When Paul mentions that virgins do better if they do not marry, he is speaking to the initiates who understand his words, and they know that a virgin is someone who has re-conquered their original virginity that was lost in Eden. With this in mind, who can honestly say they have no lust? Once we understand the meaning of virginity and spiritual circumcision, then Paul's inner teachings on love and marriage are unveiled.

Now, contemplating all of the topics discussed in this chapter, let us read from The Gospel of Philip:

> When Eve (*sexuality*) was still (*in harmony*) with Adam (*the brain*), death did not exist. When she was separated from him (*because the Eve-Sexual aspect in humanity ate the Fruit of the Tree of Good and Evil,*) death came into being. If he (*the Gnostic*) enters again (*into Eden, where Daath-Sexuality is located*) and attains his former self, death will be no more (*because Adam-Eve, reunited, will be allowed to eat the Fruit of the Tree of Life, which gives immortality*).
>
> A bridal chamber (*where the sacrament of sex is performed*) is not for the animals (*because animals fornicate*), nor is it for the slaves (*of sensorial phenomena, of lust*), nor for defiled women (*those who profane the temple of the body with the violent sexual spasm*); but it is for (*those*) free (*of sexual lust,*) men and virgins.
>
> Through the Holy Spirit we are indeed begotten again, but we are begotten through Christ in the two (*the Cross of Man and Woman*). We are anointed through the Spirit. When we were begotten (*by our Father-Mother, Jah-Hava or Jehovah in Heaven*), we were united (*with our Adam-Intellect-Solar and Eve-Sexual-Lunar aspects together in harmony*). None can see himself either in water (*sexual potency*) or in a mirror (*of a reflective mind*) without (*the*) light (*of comprehension brought about through meditation*). Nor again can you see in light without mirror or water (*of the Holy Spirit, the Ens Seminus, where the image of truth, or face of God, is reflected*). For this reason, it is fitting to baptize in the two, in the light (*of an illuminated mind*) and the water (*of a purified libido*). Now the light is the chrism.
>
> If the woman (*the Eve aspect of The Holy Spirit in every man and woman that represents the life giving force, the sexuality,*) had not separated from the man (*the Adam aspect of The Holy Spirit, correct understanding or intelligence,*) she should not die with the man. His separation became the beginning of death. Because of this, Christ came to repair the separation, which was from the beginning, and again unite the two (*in a positive aspect as conscious sexuality, Eve, with conscious intelligence, Adam*), and to give life (*again*) to those who died (*to their Spirit*) as a result of the separation (*negative polarization of the mind and sex*), and unite them (*in Eden, under the Tree of Good and Evil, the place of departure*). But the woman (*the Divine Sexuality in man and woman*) is united to her husband (*Divine Intelligence in man and woman*) in the bridal chamber (*of chaste sexuality because the Gnostic Wedding is the result of the transformation of impressions and the transmutation of the libido*). Indeed, those who have united in the bridal chamber (*without fornication*) will no longer be separated (*because the Gnostic sexual act*

transforms the Man and Woman into the Divine Androgyny). Thus Eve (*sexuality, who became a whore*) separated from Adam (*intelligence, to become subjective egocentric intellect*) because it was not in the bridal chamber (*of sexual transmutation, but instead through the orgasm*) that she (*degenerate sexuality*) united (*in fornication to become negatively polarized*) with him (*as subjective egocentric intelligence*).

– The Gospel of Philip

Meditation Fundamentals

> Not to seek any form of psychological security, any form of gratification, requires investigation, constant watchfulness to see how the mind operates, and surely that is meditation, is it not? Meditation is not the practice of a formula or the repetition of certain words, which is all silly, immature. Without knowing the whole process of the mind, conscious as well as unconscious, any form of meditation is really a hindrance, an escape, a childish activity; it is a form of self-hypnosis. But to be aware of the process of thinking, to go into it carefully step by step with full consciousness and discover for oneself the ways of the self – that is meditation. It is only through self-knowledge that the mind can be free to discover what is truth, what is God, what is death, what is this thing that we call living.
>
> – Krishnamurti

It is only proper to be dressed and clean before we start our daily activities. So, every day, we look into a mirror, we comb our hair, apply makeup, straighten our tie, pull our socks up, tie our shoes, etc. Often times, extraordinary lengths are taken in order to enhance our physical appearance. However, what efforts do we undertake to better our psychological state? It should not surprise the reader that our psychological state is more important than our physical state. Nevertheless, we forget to take care of our mind and consciousness.

That which we consider "self" is not simply one thing. It is a culmination of many parts, and each part is a different. There are many different parts, many "I's." Each psychological aggregate, or ego, is an "I." What we mean by this is that every time we say, "I want to look beautiful," a portion of our psyche that is vain is personified.

Every type of desire we have carries with it a small amount of independence: it is an authentic "I," a little "I," which in the aggregate is the ego. Therefore, not all parts of our psyche are vain, another part says, "I don't want to appear self-centered," and that "I," that ego, worries about the actions of the "I" of vanity. So we see very easily that our mind is diffused through each of its desires. This diffusion of will makes a real individuality impossible.

On the other hand, the ego causes all of our contradiction, friction, anxiety, confusion, depression, and all the personification of negativity that exists within our interior. This is because one "I" lives in conflict with another "I," and both live within that which we call *myself*.

Our individuality is diffused into a million different, quarrelling, contradictory "I" centers, each with its own desires and a pseudo-self-identity. In reality none of the "I" centers has a real self-identity, but each "I" takes our true essence, our true existence, and traps a part of it. Each "I" is just a little piece of mental matter that is sleeping to its own desire. The "I" puts the consciousness it entraps into a trance, and it leaves the consciousness without the ability to perceive the world in an objective fashion.

Desire can manifest itself as a daydream or a dream at night. This dream is like a film that is incessantly running in our head. The ego just wants to feel, to touch, to experience the thing it dreams about over and over again. It does not understand that having desire creates an unbalance and that unbalance will cause pain. The ego makes use of the consciousness in a negative fashion, by taking the impressions of the moment through the comparison of previous moments.

What occurs is that the moment of now is not actually is "seen" by the ego. Instead, the impressions of life are mechanically modified in accordance with associations accumulated throughout the memories of the past. The ego always sees a translation of life instead of life itself. The ego always sees the current moment in comparison to other moments. What is better is to perceive each moment spontaneously, to see it without comparison, without dualism, and without labeling or rationalizing. In other words, we need to apply our willpower in order to authentically be in the moment, to experience the moment without thinking. When the ego is active, we act in ways and on levels of consciousness that we have no perception of (i.e. unconsciousness), and this leads to misfortune. When we activate the consciousness we can begin the technique of self-observation. This technique is also referred to as awareness or mindfulness.

Living in a state of sleep (because the "I" causes the consciousness to sleep) causes mistakes of life to be made, and what is worse is that we ignore that we make mistakes. It is necessary to understand the reasons behind our actions. If we truly wanted to know ourselves, we would realize how flawed of a person we are. However deep inside we do not want to know that, it is something that does not concern us, and this is why we ignore it. Always thinking the best of ourselves, we unconsciously ignore our errors.

This ignorance later returns as pain, and hence we ask, "Why me? Why does this terrible thing have to happen to me, and today of all days?" We ask these questions yet we do not really want to know the answer, we just want to act in some manner that we are fascinated with, such as being cranky, irritable, moody, having a short temper, angry, hateful, despiteful, arrogant, envious, depressed, etc. We are not actually looking for the answers because it is obvious that they are to be found within our interior. Reality may be harsh, but it is also the gateway to happiness.

Most people live their entire life attempting to satisfy the same desires, but they will never be satisfied because every experience of that desire strengthens the chains to that desire: the outcome is more desire, not less. Often when middle age hits, these poor souls just wish to be happy, but they cannot find it, not in a real, objective, or truthful sense. As a society we are failing to find our right to happiness. Happiness is the natural phenomenon of an awakened consciousness. A consciousness free of desire is happiness in itself.

In order to awaken consciousness we need to make efforts to be observant though our entire day. We need to observe all of our actions and reactions in a continuous manner. We need profound observation, which takes no thought and is spontaneous.

The modern mind of today's culture is in a degenerate state: it struggles to be aware of itself, to be at peace, to be tranquil, to take in the world without judgment, etc. The mind should be a receptive organ, but it is normal today for the common woman and man to have a projective mind. The projective mind transforms our internal contradiction into external contradiction: arguments, deceit, hate towards others, jealousy, pride, etc. These types of things are not normal, they are the products of a diseased, degenerate psyche.

One may agree or disagree with this description of our internal status. However, only someone who continues to ignore their contradiction can deny that it exists. In reality, opinions mean nothing, and in order to truly comprehend our psychology we must stop ignoring it and begin observing it. This is in itself is the first step of meditation.

Meditation is a science of the consciousness. Meditation actives the powers of the consciousness. Meditation is the way to acquire information that no other method can obtain. Without meditation, there is no gnosis. A Gnostic who does not meditate is like a lamp without electricity.

The fundamentals of meditation are relaxation and observation. Some say that meditation is nothing more than observation, but we will say that when meditation is true, then there is nothing outside of one's existence to observe, because everything has been united into an integral whole. How can you, for example, observe the tree, if you are already that tree? How can you see something else if you are already being that something else? These are very interesting ideas, yet, for those who experience it, it is reality.

Observation is essential. Observation is the process of perceiving the state of being without rational processes of the mind, without thought. In depth observation is the prelude to meditation. We do not need to think in order to observe. For many people that is a novel concept, but it is true. Thinking or reasoning, processes of the mind, have nothing to do with observing or perceiving, which are qualities of the consciousness. Unfortunately, the consciousness is entrapped in the ego, which leads to our sleeping consciousness. This is why it is so difficult to consciously observe even for five minutes.

Meditation is not "spacing out" or daydreaming. That is the opposite of meditation. Meditation is not any type of hypnosis. Meditation is the way to experience reality. Meditation is the process to gain self-knowledge, gnosis. Meditation allows us to directly experience reality. With meditation we access the superior aspects of our self in order to understand, to comprehend, to make light in the psychological darkness of our consciousness. This is where we truly come to know ourselves.

Meditation is a devoutly spiritual act that has a direct relationship with sexual energy. The brain and the sex, as well as the mind and creativity, are two sides of the same thing, and how we use one affects the other. Every diabolic and spiritual act is fueled through the modification of the sexual energy. Sexual energy is the raw material of psychological energy, and likewise it can be modified in either a regenerative or degenerative fashion. The methods of this book are teaching how to modify the sexual energy in a regenerative fashion.

Those attempting to meditate without concern towards their sexual disposition are missing a vital factor in the development of their awakening of consciousness. They may achieve particular experiences however the true doors of wisdom will remain closed. Attempting to gain self-knowledge without transmuting the sexual energy is as absurd as attempting to run a combustion engine on crude oil, or attempting to run an engine without any fuel at all.

Obviously, if we waste the sexual energy, we cannot transform it, however even if we do not waste it, it still must be transformed. Likewise, oil must be cleaned of impurities and transformed in order to become volatile so that, as gasoline, it will power your car. We must teach our body and our mind to sublimate sexual energy in order to advance our spiritual work. Creative energy is the great mediator between the Creator and its Creation. When we transform the creative energy we transform our whole being.

Being aware in the moment, during any moment – and preferably every moment of the day – is how we begin to train the mind and strengthen the consciousness for meditation. Through this practice, our mind becomes less identified with life's daily problems and enters into a more receptive and reflective state. It is this state of mind which must be our foundation for meditation, because it is impossible to penetrate the depths of the mind if it is not within a calm and receptive state.

Meditation is like a calm body of water. In this state it is easy to see through the water. If it is full waves, then everything is distorted. When we throw a rock into a lake, the lake responds by creating ripples. Everyday, many rocks (impressions of life) are tossed into our lake (the mind), and we respond by creating ripples of all sizes. There are so many ripples in our lake that we do not even realize that it is a lake at all because we cannot see the bottom anymore. The receptive mind takes these rocks but does not react to them automatically and mechanically. That is to say, the lake remains completely clear and calm and simply accepts the rocks.

Then, we can observe the rock, laying at the bottom, in complete clarity. Instead of re-acting, we can make conscious, willful actions. This is something only possible through vigilant awareness. It is necessary in order to understand what the impressions of life are. We come to realize that the impressions of life are just that, and nothing more. To react like an ignoramus or a tyrant, to become depressed or angry does not change what that impression is. Acting in such ways actually produces more suffering, not less. To transform the impressions of life into something superior, on the other hand, is something much more intelligent. It is therefore in our best interest to understand why we continue to act without intelligence.

To meditate is fundamental. There is no reason why it should not be practiced by all on a daily basis. In the Yoga schools there are many preliminary stages of meditation. Feel free to read about them, but here we are going to only list two important factors, as this is only an introduction. First, in order to have any success at the science of meditation, one must make the effort to be observant at all times of the day. Meditation is not something to be done in isolation from everyday life. If we are very mechanical and psychologically asleep during the day, the mind becomes increasingly agitated. An agitated mind will not sit still and silence will not arrive out of an overly agitated mind. This is why we must extend our self-observation into every moment of life. Then we become less mechanical, less sleepy.

The meditator will benefit in proportion to how well he or she has transformed the impressions of that day. If we have had many moments of stress, anger, frustration, pride, envy, greed, lust, etc., then when we sit for our meditation at night, it is obvious that our mind will be a mess. Many people quit meditation because of this, but in reality this should not cause discouragement. Meditation should be attempted regardless of the state of our mind because even if we get nothing but a slightly more relaxed mind, then we still will have improved our internal status, which is a wonderful thing.

What we need here is *correct effort*. We cannot act stupidly and mechanical throughout the day and expect the mind to be in a good state for superlative meditation. But we must also realize that if we were able to correctly live life then we would already be masters of meditation. In synthesis, we must work and we must not be discouraged by our setbacks.

The second aspect is comfort, as meditation is a child of comfort. We need to be absolutely comfortable to meditate. First, finding a suitable chair or bed is essential. Many schools make a big deal about particular positions. Ultimately, our body position is not overly significant, except that our spine should be straight. Find a position that does not cause discomfort. Once we have found comfort, we must first relax the body, and then the mind.

If one is having trouble, then deeply inhale and exhale in a slow, natural but profound manner a small number of times. Inhale slowly through the nose, hold it for a second, and then exhale out through the mouth. The breath with naturally flow quickly out of the mouth because the lungs will be full of air. This type of breathing should be relaxing. If done correctly, it will sublimate creative energy and clarify the mind a bit.

Then make a careful analysis of every aspect of the physical body. Every muscle should be relaxed. Systematically work from the tips of the toes to the eyebrows. Take a long time to become relaxed, you will be wasting you time if you attempt to rush it. Do not make a superficial check, beginners must go through each muscle and question, "Are my feet relaxed, or am I tapping my foot right now? Do I have my fist clenched tight, or is it really relaxed? Am I breathing correctly, or is it a shallow, hurried breath?" It may surprise the reader that we do not even know how to properly relax, so we need to be very diligent or we will not find absolute comfort. In my experience, many people forget to relax the facial muscles, so take extra care around the eyes, the jaw, and the areas around the ears. Some people can go to sleep while grinding their teeth, so it is quite easy to keep these muscles tense and still be "relaxed," let us be sure they have no tension whatsoever.

Simply relax, forget about time. You must become so relaxed that you can feel every part of your body simultaneously. So you can even feel your heart beating. It is a level of relaxation that is virtually unknown to western society. If one is successful at doing this, they will find themselves more relaxed then they could probably ever remember. This alone, the deep relaxation of the body, helps tremendously in reducing stress and the normal problems of life.

We must become drowsy but with a level of awareness. An experienced practitioner of mediation can easily fall asleep while still remaining psychologically awake. Once physical serenity is accomplished we must move on to the mind. We have to find a fine balance between attentiveness and sleepiness. This is something difficult. We have to find a degree of separation, as we spoke of in a previous chapter, in order to use the mind to observe the mind.

The goal of meditation is to acquire information. Those who meditate for relaxation are only using the preliminary exercises, because true meditation occurs when relaxation is already achieved. Those who meditate just to achieve samadhi are mistaken. Samadhi is the outcome of proper meditation, but it should not be our reason to practice. To desire samadhi is a contradiction, because samadhi is the absence of desire.

Samadhi is a broad term; in general it means "union." Samadhi is a union with God, or the Great Reality. Samadhi occurs when the rational processes and the sufferings of the "I" are transcended, and the consciousness becomes totally integrated and activated. Nevertheless, there are many different types and levels of samadhi. The consciousness, due to its temporal emancipation, irradiates pure joy when samadhi is experienced, and this is also the state to gain true wisdom.

Finding temporal emancipation and reaching absolute emancipation are very different. Temporal emancipation is found in meditation, but true emancipation only arrives when the ego has been destroyed.

Samadhi comes from the correct use of *imagination* and *willpower*. We need imagination to see something in the mind and we need willpower to observe this mental image without becoming emotional and identified with it. We need willpower to sustain a passive *separation*. We fail in separation when we become identified with our mind and fall asleep. It will be more common, however, for the beginner to fail before even achieving separation. We must have a will for separation, but this is not enough.

The *power* is required for willpower. The power is the creative potency circulating in the blood of the practitioner. This is called *ojas* in Sanskrit. Together, a correct will, and a source of power, form our will-power.

A calm, flexible, fructified mind is required to find separation. A rigid, degenerate mind will crack and partition itself. A rigid mind will not be able to separate itself from its problems. A rigid mind gets frustrated and when it fails at meditation, it becomes identified with its failure too. The problems of the mind are what need observation. To observe something, we must not be that something and this is why we need passive separation. An overly active separation results in dissociation, which is the denial of emotion, and this is as incorrect as identification. To find separation, a level of physical sleepiness is required. To observe our separation, a level of mental awareness is required. If we can master this fine balance, then we will have achieved the fundamentals of meditation.

There are many things we can use our imagination to meditate upon. We are going to discuss retrospective analysis. This is simply the observation of our memories. Any memory will do. Whatever is on the mind will be fine, because obviously whatever is bothering the mind is the current source of the most discomfort. Memories of the mind are stored like a movie in a database. When we are watching our own movie (memories), let us be an observer. Instead of becoming an actor in the movie, just observe as an audience. If we identify with the movie, we have become the movie: our emotions begin to run all over the place and then we have fallen psychologically asleep. In other words, we lose separation.

When we begin meditating, many psychic aggregates will *immediately* appear and these are the rocks we have spoken of. Most of us will immediately begin to daydream, worry, stress due to this or that particular aggregate. Huge mental waves appear, we lose our mental equilibrium, and the exercise concludes in failure. If we are lucky enough to remember our original purpose, we can make efforts to begin our practice again. Otherwise we may fall asleep in a physical sense (because we have already begun the psychological sleep), or we may become frustrated. However if we remember our purpose and ourselves, if we do not identify with the psychic aggregates, some success will be found eventually.

Psychic aggregates are the millions of mental (psychic) pieces that in sum (aggregates) constitute a portion of the ego. In the average person today, the ego constitutes about 97% of the mind. This means that about 97% of everything we do is rooted in subconscious, unconscious, or infraconscious will. Anything that is not conscious will is desire, and all desire is subjective, created in ignorance, and produces suffering.

To identify with the psychic aggregates means that when an aggregate appears on the projector of the mind, we begin to feel that emotion again. It is as if we were reliving that specific moment of time that left an *emotional impression* upon our mind. When this occurs, suddenly we feel sad or happy, or frustrated, or hurt, or angry again. This constitutes a sleeping consciousness, or in other words, levels of unconscious will. Each of us can know for ourselves that these emotions spring from unconscious will because, from a conscious standpoint, we do not wish to relive many of our terrible memories, yet, we end up suffering their emotional impressions again and again because portions of our willpower is trapped within psychological aggregates (that is to say, *egos,* or *desires,* or *unconsciousness*) related with these emotions.

When observation is truly profound we stop becoming emotionally attached to our problems in life and begin to see them as they are. Consequently we begin to see how to solve those problems always reappearing in life. We come to understand that many of our external problems stem from a *single psychological problem.* Then we can work on changing an internal flaw, and thereby correcting many external problems. This is a wonderful but difficult process. It is difficult because when we think about our worst problems, it is inevitable that our most emotional feelings come about. Then we begin to identify with our emotion, we begin to dream, we begin to waste our energies foolishly, and worst of all we lose our awareness.

If we become that which we wish to examine, then we are attempting to do something impossible. Instead of becoming identified immediately with our memories and their phenomena (the emotions that stir up because of them), we must reflect upon why we felt in such a way, at such a time. We must understand the root of the cause, the reason why we were put into a situation that led to this emotion in question.

If we remain in a receptive state, not identifying with the ego, we can then discover the ego's processes, logic, and eventually its cause. If we have the joy of comprehending in the most fluid sense a psychic aggregate, we have then accomplished a reduction to its corresponding personification, that is to say, its ego. But this is not something trivial. To *know thyself* is terribly difficult, but it is for good reason that all the all the sages give us this advice.

The comprehension of a desire is the foundation of its death. When comprehension occurs, that ego is no longer hidden within the depths of our psyche because we are now conscious of it. This aids us. It gives us power to *consciously act*, a power only the BEING has, instead of *being acted through*, the only type of movement the ego is capable of. The desire no longer mechanically controls us and we regain a portion of authentic will. Mechanical reaction is the phenomena of a sleeping consciousness. This is the darkness in the Bible. Willful action is the result of vigilant consciousness. Vigilant consciousness is the key to happiness, and its birth is only found within the Halls of Death.

> The light shines in the darkness, but the darkness understood it not.
>
> – John 1:5

To observe, let the mind flow like the Great Breath of Life. Do not silence the mind by force. A blank mind is not a silent mind – that is a mind thinking of blankness. If the mind refuses to quiet, we need to control it. Rather than feed the mind with "blank" thought, let it run out of fuel and coast to a stop. When we are "stopped" then we can begin to enter ecstasy.

Our mind is like a train, it seems like an unstoppable force, however once we stop feeding it fuel, eventually it will coast to a stop. We need to be patient and very vigilant in order to find success here. Meditation takes time and effort, but we improve though practice. Most people will find it terribly difficult. This is because all day we are feeding the train fuel, so when we attempt to meditate, it is going at a thousand miles per hour and we are just along for the ride.

Understandably, one who has never even thought about meditation is going to find it difficult to make time for it. If nothing else however, it is a good practice to simply take time to completely unwind the body. Throughout the day, make an effort to completely relax and, for at least a single moment, *stop thinking*. We need to begin taking a minute out of the day, while in our office chairs, or in the kitchen, at a desk, wherever, to just relax the body completely and become aware of it. Take yourself out of the day and its problems, and observe, for just a moment, from an outsider's perspective. The problems of life solve themselves when we become separated from them and see that the solution lies within *understanding the problem itself*. This practice will improve the day's impressions, and although it is very easy to begin observation it is terribly difficult to remember to do it. Observation also happens to be the foundation of meditation, so if one finds it impossible to meditate, just relax the body while doing this practice. This foundation will grow stronger and it will help you.

Freeing the mind from ego is not easy. We strive to keep the mind awake and free and it is easy to slip back into a sleeping consciousness. To know thyself is a process that takes a lifetime, because only with practice will meditation become profound. The layers of the mind are many, and they reach down far into the very root of darkness. Nevertheless we must begin now, not in the future. The future never comes. We must begin here and now. Ultimately, those who believe they do not have time for self-observation and mediation are lying to themselves.

The more observant we become during the normal daily routine, the more profound our meditations will become, because meditation is an amplification of our normal observations. It takes a lot of diligent work in order to awaken any serious percentage of consciousness. This does not mean it must take years to see the positive effects of meditation – that can be known immediately through correct effort. Nevertheless, we need to be patient and we need to be profound and unyielding in our battle against our own self. This is why Jesus says *"deny yourself,"* it is so we can break the bondage of the ego to express the real self, the Being.

Take a moment to free your mind of stress, of mindless chatter, of tension, of worry and anger, and just relax and observe.

Pratyahara

Upon beginning meditation all we see is darkness. But as it was said earlier, we use our imagination to view our memories. Then pictures appear upon the screen of the mind and when this occurs something additional also occurs. This will be an *emotional attachment*. Obviously, as we have already stated, do not become that emotion, but, do not avoid that emotional attachment either. We are going to repeat it again: What is needed is separation. Because we are being vigilant, we are making use of our tiny bit of free consciousness. The tiny seed of awakened consciousness is called the *Essence*. We can separate the essence from the ego, thus the essence observes the ego.

When emotion successfully attaches itself to the ego, then we have become identified with ego and have lost separation. Emotion makes the image become more "real" in our mind by giving it emotional depth. It is at this moment when fantasy is likely to occur. We need to recognize emotion, but do not become emotional. To deny or accept emotion like an automated machine is a lack of vigilance. The trick is to remain a level of separation between the consciousness and the ego. What we gain from this is the ability to observe why that emotion is appearing in connection with our memories. When the Essence provides that "something additional," it is not the type of emotion we are familiar with. This is called superior emotion, intuition, samadhi. The Essence, which is beyond the rational processes of the mind, when activated though willpower, can give us divine knowledge about the self. The ego, when empowered through identification, provides negative emotion.

If we watch an entire "movie," it will eventually end. When this happens that memory will vanish from the screen of the consciousness and something else may appear. *The second memory will be related with the first.* Now once again we must remain in separation, but, we must also spontaneously recognize how the latter memory is related with the former. The connection will be unknown at first because it is something unconscious. However, one will find that intuition springs forth spontaneously when the mind is silent. Thus a common link will be given to the mind (from the consciousness) when it is in a receptive state. This is how we will understand that something common produced both memories. This is a form of comprehension.

As this process repeats itself, more memories play out and the comprehension becomes more profound, until the mind has no more memories to play that are related with its current agitation. When the mind has nothing left to give us then samadhi occurs. Samadhi is what occurs when we escape the rational mind. What has been outlined here is only an example of how samadhi may occur.

We have emphasized separation. This is separation of attention. However, this act correctly applied, provides as an ultimate consequence a profound integration of all the dispersed aspects of the consciousness (dispersed because they are asleep to the multiple ego). Thus, when this integration is achieved, one is absorbed in immeasurable happiness.

There are many things we need to do throughout the day to place the mind within a superior state for meditation. Really, we are looking for a silent mind all day long, but if we could already do this, we would not have any ego and already have an awakened consciousness. Accordingly, to prepare the mind for meditation, one must be aware of "being" throughout the day. One must stop the internal chatter in our minds. One must not react to the impressions of life in an inferior way because this feeds the egos to act, which agitates one's state of mind. If one makes these efforts correctly, they will begin to change.

> The stillness and silence of the mind has a single objective: to liberate the Essence from the mind, so that when fused with the Monad or Inner Self, it (the Essence) can experience that which we call the Truth.
>
> During ecstasy and in the absence of the "I," the Essence can live freely experiencing the Truth within the World of the Mist of the Fire.
>
> When the mind is in a passive and receptive state, absolutely still and in silence, the Essence or Buddhata is liberated from the mind, and ecstasy arrives.
>
> The Essence is always bottled up in the battle of opposites, but when the battling ends and silence is absolute, then the bottle is broken into pieces and the Essence remains free.
>
> When we practice meditation, our mind is assaulted by many memories, desires, passions, preoccupations, etc.
>
> We must avoid the conflict between attention and distraction. A conflict exists between attention and distraction when we combat those assailants of the mind. The "I" is the projector of such mental assailants. Where there is conflict, stillness and silence cannot exist.
>
> We must nullify the projector through self-observation and comprehension. Examine each image, each memory, and each thought that comes to the mind. Remember that every thought has two poles: positive and negative.
>
> Two aspects of the same thing are entering and leaving. The dining room and the washroom, tall and short, pleasant and unpleasant, etc. are always two poles of the same thing.
>
> Examine the two poles of each mental form that comes to the mind. Remember that only through the study of these polarities can one arrive at a synthesis.
>
> Every mental form can be eliminated through its synthesis. For example, the memory of a fiancée assaults us. Is she beautiful? Let us think that beauty is the opposite of ugliness and that if in her youth she was beautiful, in her old age she will be ugly. The synthesis: it is not worthwhile to think about her; she is an illusion, a flower that will inevitably wither.
>
> In India, this Self-observation and study of our Psyche is properly called Pratyahara.

Bird-like thoughts should pass through the space of our own mind in a successive parade, but without leaving any trace behind.

The infinite procession of thoughts projected by the "I" is exhausted in the end, and then the mind remains still and in silence.

A great Self-realized Master said, "*Only when the projector, in other words, the "I," is completely absent, will the silence* (which is not a product of the mind) *then befall. This silence is inexhaustible; it is not of time, and it is immeasurable. It is only then, when THAT which is, arrives.*"

This whole technique is summarized in two principles:

1. Profound reflection.
2. Tremendous serenity.

This technique of meditation with its non-thinking puts to work the most central part of the mind, the one that produces ecstasy.

Remember that the central part of the mind is that which is called Buddhata, the Essence, the Consciousness.

When the Buddhata awakens we remain illuminated. We need to awaken the Buddhata, the Consciousness.

The Gnostic student can practice meditation seated in the Western or Oriental style.

It is advisable to practice with the eyes close to avoid the distractions of the exterior world.

It is also convenient to relax the body carefully, thus avoiding any tension in the muscles.

The Buddhata, the Essence, is the psychic material, the inner Buddhist principle, the spiritual material or raw matter which will eventually give shape to the Soul.

The Buddhata is the best that we have within and awakens with profound inner meditation.

Indeed, the Buddhata is the only element that the wretched intellectual animal possesses in order to arrive at the experience of that which we call the Truth.

The only thing that the intellectual animal can do (being unable to incarnate the Being due to the fact that he still does not possess the superior existential bodies) is to practice meditation, to self-awaken the Buddhata and to know the Truth.

– Samael Aun Weor, *The Revolution of the Dialectic*

The Fourth Way & the Human Machine

> Self-observation brings man to the realization of the necessity of self-change. And in observing himself a man notices that self-observation itself brings about certain changes in his inner processes. He begins to understand that self-observation is an instrument of self-change, a means of awakening.
>
> – G. I. Gurdjieff

> Man is a machine. All his actions, words, thoughts, feelings, opinions, and habits are the results of external influences, external impressions... It is possible to stop being a machine, but for that it is necessary first of all to know the machine.
>
> – G. I. Gurdjieff

> Among themselves, certain stronger "I's" dominate other weak "I's," however, their strength comes from the energy of the Cylinders of the Human Machine. All of the "I's" are the outcome of the external and internal influences. True individuality does not exist within the Intellectual Animal. Present humans are merely Machines.
>
> – Samael Aun Weor, lecture entitled *The Human Machine*

G. I. Gurdjieff refers to the man as a machine because the physical body is merely a *vehicle* that can be controlled by elements of lower or higher nature. The biological organism is the most advanced piece of technology that we know of. In everyday life it may not feel like what we called "technology" because our body is much more sophisticated than anything this current society has produced. Our technology, often portrayed in terms of "modern miracles" and the savior of the overly troubled human condition, is in reality very flimsy, inept and incipient. Our current technology does not solve anything foundational to our current human problems. It is because the true driving factor of our technology is to make money, not solve our problems.

Modern science knows very little of how the physical body actually works. Today's material science is now diving into the study of our DNA and RNA, mapping the human genome, but they still know very little about how these chemical compounds actually function. Molecular biologists use the moniker "junk DNA" to describe the vast majority (97%) of our genetic sequence because they can find no function for it; but new findings now tell them that the functionalisms of DNA and RNA are much more intricate that previously imagined, and "junk DNA" is anything but.

The fundamental knowledge of the matrix of biological systems as they process themselves interdependently to sustain all the necessities of a living body is largely unknown. Science does not have anything close to a complete or accurate working model of the body. For example, when a new type of pharmaceutical drug is developed, the consequences of the drug are unknown and only through empirical observation can we find the effects of what are essentially unknown causes. If an accurate model of the body were known, then the effects of modern drugs would be known with exactness before a single person is submitted to them.

Much of this ignorance is because modern science does not yet accept the existence of a vital depth to the body, which is the fourth dimensional aspect. This is related with the ch'i (life energy) of Eastern medicine. Without knowledge of the vital depth, a complete understanding of biology is impossible. Within the vital depth is the root of metabolism, the root of the five senses, the basis of hormonal-chemical energy and the whole science of endocrinology.

THE THREE BRAINS

All creations are formulated through the *Law of Three* and organized through the *Law of Seven*. This is why the numbers three and seven are especially significant in religion. For example, in the Hebraic book of Genesis, the triple aspect of God created man over the course of Seven Days. The human machine, being capable of creating in its own sphere of influence, handles the creative Law of Three through its three primary centers:

- Intellectual Center (Cerebrospinal Nervous System)
- Emotional Center (Grand Sympathetic Nervous System)
- Motor-instinctive-sexual Center (Vagus, or Parasympathetic System)

Although it is often thought that the Sympathetic and Parasympathetic systems are involuntary, it has been shown that through yoga and meditation these centers come under control of the student. The difference then, between a student of meditation and the common man is understood once we realize that the everyday man rarely controls the emotional center or even his intellect. The emotion and intellect must be under control before the motor-instinctive-sexual center can be controlled, yet there are many who have achieved this. What is required is a yogic discipline.

The intellectual center is the source of rational thought. The intellectual center is what differentiates the human machine from the rest of the animals. No other animal has the rational abilities than that of the intellectual animal called "man." Through the intellectual center we can deliberate, deduce, label, contemplate, and in general form logic. The physical location of this center is the brain. The emotional center is located in the "heart" (the solar plexus). When we are accused of something, we point to our heart and say, "Who, me?" So now we can see that this is this area where emotions are developed and felt. The motor-instinctive-sexual center is actually composed of three different "cylinders," but in synthesis we can state as one entity it located at stomach, sexual organs, and along the entire spinal column. It is the basis of all movement and provider of all the raw energy of the human machine.

Each center of the human machine operates at a particular frequency. The intellectual center is the slowest at accomplishing its tasks. To illustrate this point, observe someone who can type quickly on a keyboard. This person is not thinking or intellectualizing the movement of each finger as he types, and thus a skilled typist has no trouble is typing fifty or sixty words per minute. However, if this person were to think about what keys needed to be pressed, his typing would slow down to a crawl. This is because the typist normally uses his motor brain, *not* the much slower the intellectual brain, in order to type. Therefore, when he attempts to move his actions into the intellect, the process slows considerably.

The emotional center is faster than the intellectual center as well. This is evidenced by the fact that we always experience an emotion regarding an impression of life before we have time to form logic about it. We just feel things - we do not have to think about what we feel. We just feel without thought, although thought comes soon after. It is good to begin to observe this fact in everyday life.

Still, the motor-instinctive-sexual center is the quickest. The sexual impulse happens so quickly that we do not even know it occurs. The ordinary man walking in a busy shopping mall is consistently looking at everyone around him. The ego of lust localizes itself in the sexual center and looks at the women it lusts after. This occurs so quickly that the poor man in our example would deny it ever happening when confronted. The sexual impulse is extremely fast and the only way to interrupt the sexual impulse from acting in a mechanical way is to be observant. A man will even say that it is impossible to resist a glance upon the entrance of a beautiful woman, and he would deny that it is lust, but this man simply is ignorant of self-observation.

Society has placed a lot of emphasis on the intellectual center. As a result we have a lot of educational intuitions, degrees and certifications. The intellectual ability of a person is thought to be the pinnacle of education. In truth, this is only one third of education. The ability to think logically and "scientifically" is something good, and we all can possess these abilities, but to totally neglect or underestimate the emotional and motor-instinctive-sexual brains is a tragedy of modern culture. What we are interested here is to gain an *equilibrated* psychology, which means all three centers are neither abused nor atrophied. Real intellectual education is the teaching of not what to think, but how to think. The ability to solve problems and to learn new abilities is a creative facility. Obviously then, a mind potent with creative energy has the ability to solve problems and the ability to find new ways to solve problems. Older people many times cannot learn new ways of doing things because their mind has throughout the years become infertile.

> Normally we live on different levels of our interior temple. There are people who always live in the lower levels; those are the ones that are concentrated exclusively in instinct and fornication, the fourth and fifth levels (instinctive and sexual centers, respectively), levels that have been used in a negative way.
>
> Others live on the third level (motor center) and never leave it; they always move following the patterns of predetermined customs, along the line of certain habits. They never change; they are like a train that always runs over the same tracks. These third-level types of people are so accustomed to their train of habits that they are not ready to surrender them.
>
> Others live on the first level (the intellectual center); others, on the second level (negative emotions). Those who live in the intellectual center want to turn everything into rationalism, analysis, concepts or arguments, and they never leave that place. Others live in the emotional center dedicated to the vices of movies, racetracks, bullfights, etc., in reality, a very limited and narrow world.
>
> They live enclosed and enslaved by negative emotions, never thinking of escaping from such places. It is necessary to insist upon giving opportunity to our consciousness.
>
> – Samael Aun Weor, lecture entitled *The Science of Meditation*

The three primary psychological classes of the intellectual animal can be correlated with the three types of people often cited in the Bible: Elders, Priests, and Scribes. Each has its mechanical lifestyle as quoted previously, as well as corresponding spiritual pursuits. Gurdjieff named them Fakirs, Monks and Yogis, corresponding to action, emotion and intellect. There is wisdom found in all these paths, but there is a Fourth Way. The Fourth Way is the path of the balanced human being. The Fourth Way is the path of psychological transformation and sexual-alchemical transmutation.

Each "I" plays an internal "king of the hill" within the emotional, motor-instinctive-sexual and intellectual centers of our interior. At any point a certain "I" pushes the current one out and then a new Ego Will is personified. An "I" can be in any one of the three centers. Impressions of life hit all three centers, and they are dealt with in different ways, depending on our vigilance or lack of vigilance in a particular center. This causes great contradiction. When an "I" implanted in the sexual area wants pleasure, but the "I" in the emotional center knows it is wrong, the pressure of opposing centers can be enormous.

The often cited example occurs when a man is greeted kindly by a woman. This woman just happens to have good manners but the man takes the impression of her kindness incorrectly. That impression goes into the man's sexual center because the ego of lust has grabbed it, and now this man believes he is the object of her desire. The man may violate her, or he may just spread promiscuous gossip (lies) to his acquaintances. Thus the outcome of this type of situation is some kind of emotional pain, an argument, hurt feelings, anger, etc., and I think we understand this. Observe what happened here: that impression was mechanically accepted in a negative way by one of the "I's" that controls the human machine. Instead of lust, that impression of kindness should have been *transformed* correctly through humility, and placed in the emotional center.

To take in the impression of those around us in a superior way, throughout the whole day, throughout one's whole life, is terribly difficult. This is because we do not have an organ that mechanically transforms the impressions of life correctly. Our stomach mechanically digests the food we eat, our lungs mechanically aspirate the air, but the mind does not have an organ that will mechanically transform impressions. This means we have to make a conscious effort to transform and discriminate the impressions of life. For example, if we had a choice to drink gasoline or to drink water, we of course choose water, we discriminate between gasoline and water because one is clearly poisonous for the body, and it is the exact same way with impressions. Negative impressions produce psychological degeneration, but we are so conditioned into "drinking gasoline" (mechanically taking in the negative impressions of life) that we actually believe it is normal and even healthy.

So, in reality, there are three types of food: comestibles, air, and impressions. Common food is transformed, air is transformed, but are the impressions transformed? Impressions are only transformed when we are making the effort to do so.

The expression of negative emotions affects the mind in a way that is often mistaken for happiness. The expression of negative emotion, the "venting" of negative energy, produces a temporary psychological deadness and relief. For one instant our desire is satisfied. After we get very emotional, very upset, what occurs afterwards is a feeling that we have removed that stress from within. Through this, the impulse was expressed and it produces a feeling, both psychological and physical, that is normally taken comfort in.

Regrettably, this feeling of satisfaction is produced at the expense of those we have negatively expressed ourselves towards. A fundamental law of the universe is that every movement of energy is a sacrifice, or, transformation. Nothing comes for free, energy is neither created nor destroyed. Energy can be only transformed. So, in daily life, we must choose to sacrifice our own action or to submit others to be sacrificed by our action: to be the victim of our anger or any other negative emotion. If that was the only outcome of acting mechanically, it would be bad enough, however, what is worse is that acting unconsciously only strengthens the psyche to repeat wrong action in the future.

So, we can conclude, both through theoretical and experiential avenues, that any ego's negative impulse that has been expressed in the past inevitability resurfaces in the future. More specifically, any particular ego-aggregate that is fascinated with an impression of life will always resurface, again and again, each time to "blow off" steam. This "blowing off" is the ego transforming psychological energy in such a way that satisfies itself, but at the cost of producing discord in the world around us. Each time this is done, the habit is fortified and the ego becomes a larger beast to handle. Therefore, expressing ourselves this way does not solve anything.

On the other hand this way of acting is how, through many years and many lives, we crystallize our psychological defects. The expression of negative emotions increases the suffering of both the person performing the negative emotion, and everyone involved with him. This is undeniable. Yet, because it feels so good *to the ego* to act in this way, we continue to do it, even though *the consciousness* is ultimately in misery. Therefore, instead of wasting our energy through the venting of our emotions in a negative fashion, it is better to transform the energy into something positive. In order to accomplish this we must learn to discriminate between what is good for the consciousness and what is bad for the consciousness. This is a technique called the transformation of impressions.

How do we transform impressions? Firstly, we have to be self-aware. The transformation of impressions does not occur mechanically because as we have already stated, there is no organ to automatically transform the impressions of life. We have to digest our impressions, to process them, not simply accept or reject them.

Impressions arrive through one or more sensations. There are five types of sensation: visual, auditory, smell, taste, and touch. Any particular impression that arrives through the sensations has to be rigorously intellectually analyzed and later deeply comprehended. Understand that by *comprehend*, we are referring to meditation, which is a tool or technique that is vastly superior to the intellect.

When we look at, for example, a car traveling down the road, we do not see the vehicle itself, we only receive an impression of that vehicle. The impression is not the *thing-in-itself*, it is only a perception or representation. There are many characteristics of the car that we do not perceive. For example, there is no impression that arrives through our sensations related to the exact temperature of the car's engine, especially from a distance. Nevertheless, that information can be attained from a distance with high precision using infra-red technology.

Therefore, although many people refuse to admit that the impressions are not the thing-in-itself, the truth is that the impressions are only subjective representations. Any representation of an object is only that, just a representation. The thing-in-itself can only be known with totality by becoming one with the thing-in-itself. This is achieved when in meditation the consciousness leaves its cage of the mind and expands to the infinite, leaving any sense of "I" behind.

If impressions are not objective, but subjective, then it is obvious the values of the impressions of life are within the subject, in other words, within the mind. When the consciousness is asleep, the ego translates all the impressions incorrectly. Sensation that is left untransformed crystallizes into desire.

In the common man, visual sensations of pornographic imagery are mechanically processed in the mind and translated according to animal desire that is looking for nourishment. Vulgar music processes itself similarly. A cup of liquor, with its delightful odor, enters our nose, is passed to the olfactory system of our brain and then to our mind which by manner of its fascination, sleeps profoundly. In such a state of fascination, the ego mechanically translates those sensations into desire, and later we end up consuming those "spirits" until our inebriation.

In today's society, if one sees the image of a swastika, the ego immediately translates that image into an expression of hatred, suffering, bigotry, and evil. But such was not always the case. In fact the swastika is a universal symbol of spiritual prosperity and it has only been in the last century that it has come to be viewed as evil. If you saw a map of Asia with many swastikas on it, what would think? How would you translate that? We have to see the world without translating it, without assuming anything. Those swastikas on a map of Asia are icons that denote Buddhist temples. But, according to our translations, the swastika is evil. The translation is wrong! To see the world in such superficial representations and presumptions leads to ignorance. In daily life we translate everything, every single impression, when we lack self-vigilance. The ego translates everything according to its particular likes, dislikes, cravings, aversions, fears, and dreams. It is all unnecessary and leaves us without gnosis, without the ability to know reality.

Some people, when hearing anything that sounds religious, automatically translate those impressions in relation with subconscious psychological trauma formed from many unfortunate prior experiences. Others translate the appearance of their own religion as faultless, yet upon the appearance of another spiritual doctrine, find themselves repulsed simply due to its different manner of appearance. In reality their essential content may be identical, yet, by mechanically labeling or translating all our impressions of life we fail to process the impression itself. Such translations are by no means rational, let alone intelligent, they are simply mechanical translations done according to the mode of the translators: the psychological aggregates. Practice self-observation by being serenely receptive to the impressions of life as they are, not how you want them to be.

The Three Traitors

The first three types of people mentioned previously represent the Tower of Babel. Esoterically, this is called the Kingdom of the Confusion of Tongues and the in the Kabbalah it is *Malkuth*. In this kingdom no one understands each other and everyone believes themselves to be just and superior to others. The Fourth Way is the path that leads out of the labyrinth of theory and into The Alchemical Citadel. It is here that path of initiation begins. Few people enter this path.

When the three centers, or three brains as they are also called, are used in an inferior and mechanical fashion, they are referred to as the *Tree Traitors*. The Three Traitors are those psychological elements carried inside that betray our internal God.

> In the profound Inner Work, within the sphere of the strictest psychological self-observation, we are to experience directly all of the cosmic drama.
>
> The Intimate Christ has to eliminate all the undesirable elements which we carry within.
>
> The multiple psychic aggregates within our psychological depths scream for the crucifixion of the Innermost Lord.
>
> Without question, each of us carries Three Traitors within our psyches: Judas, the demon of desire; Pilate, the demon of the mind; and Caiaphas, the demon of evil will.
>
> These Three Traitors crucify the Lord of Perfections in the very depths of our Soul.
>
> This has to do with the three specific types of fundamental inhuman elements in the cosmic drama.
>
> Without a doubt, the drama has always been endured secretly in the depth of the supreme Consciousness of the Being.
>
> The cosmic drama is not the exclusive property of the Great Kabir Jesus, as is always supposed by learned ignoramuses.
>
> Initiates throughout the ages, Masters of all times had to undergo the cosmic drama within themselves, in the here and now.
>
> However, Jesus the Great Kabir had the courage to perform such an intimate drama publicly, in the street, and in broad daylight. He did this in order to bring out into the open the significance of Initiation for all human beings, without distinction of race, sex, caste or color.
>
> It is wonderful that we have someone who publicly taught the innermost drama for all the peoples of the Earth.
>
> Not being lustful, the Intimate Christ has to eliminate from within the psychological elements of lust.
>
> Being in himself peace and love, the Intimate Christ must eliminate from within the undesirable elements of anger.
>
> Not being covetous, the Intimate Christ must eliminate from within the undesirable elements of greed.
>
> Not being envious, the Intimate Christ must eliminate from within the psychic aggregates of envy.

Orestes and the Three Furies.

Having perfect, infinite modesty, being absolute simplicity, the Intimate Christ must eliminate from within the sickening elements of pride, vanity and conceit.

The Intimate Christ, the Word, the Logos Creator, living always in constant activity must eliminate from within us, in Himself and by Himself, the undesirable elements of inertia, laziness and stagnation.

The Lord of Perfection, accustomed as he is to fasting, to moderation, never a friend of drunkenness and voraciousness, has to eliminate the abominable elements of gluttony.

A strange symbiosis is that of Christ-Jesus, the Human-Christ, that rare mixture of the divine and the human, of the perfect and the imperfect, an ever constant challenge for the Logos.

Most interesting of all is that the Hidden Christ is always triumphant. He is someone who constantly vanquishes darkness, is someone who eliminates the darkness from within, in the here and now.

The Hidden Christ is Lord of the Great Rebellion: the one who has been rejected by the priests, by the elders and by the scribes of the temple.

Priests hate him, that is, they do not comprehend him. They wish that the Lord of Perfection would live exclusively in time, according to their unbreakable dogmas.

The elders, that is, the Earth dwellers, good heads of households, sensible, judicious people, abhor the Logos, the Red Christ, the Christ of the Great Rebellion, because he is beyond their world of habits and antiquated, reactionary, petrified customs from so many yesterdays.

The scribes of the temple, the scoundrels of the intellect abhor the Intimate Christ because he is the antithesis of the Antichrist. He is the declared enemy of all the decaying university theories which abound so widely in the markets of bodies and souls.

The Three Traitors mortally hate the Hidden Christ and lead him to death within us and within our psychological space.

Judas, the demon of desire always exchanges the Lord for thirty pieces of silver, or better said, for liquor, money, fame, vanity, fornication, adultery, etc.

Pilate, the demon of the mind, always washes his hands, always pleads not guilty, is never at fault, constantly justifies his actions to himself and to others, seeks excuses and loopholes in order to evade his own responsibilities, etc.

> Caiaphas, the demon of evil will, unceasingly betrays the Lord within ourselves. The Intimate Adored One gives him the shepherd's staff to lead his sheep pasture, but the cynical traitor converts the altar into a bed of pleasures, fornicates incessantly, commits adultery, sells the sacraments, etc.
>
> These Three Traitors compel the adored Intimate Lord to suffer in secret without any compassion whatsoever.
>
> Pilate forces him to put the crown of thorns upon his temples; evil "I's" scourge him, insult him, curse him in the innermost psychological space with no mercy of any kind.
>
> – Samael Aun Weor, *The Great Rebellion*

When the emotional brain is mechanically used by the ego, it is Judas. The demonic ego-intellect is Pilate. The demon of will (related with sex) is Caiaphas. This is Jubela, Jubelo, and Jubelum in Masonic tradition. It is Apopi, Hai, and Nebt in Egyptian mythology that murder Osiris. It is the Three Furies of Greek mythology, the three enemies of Moses, the three daughters of illusion that tempt Buddha. The Three Traitors resound themselves everywhere and they live in the here and now.

There are two types of animals: irrational animals and the intellectual animal. The intellectual animal is mistakenly called "human" today. The physical presence between an intellectual animal and a human is indistinguishable, yet a human has a soul of a human, while an intellectual animal has a soul of an animal. The human *proper* is therefore not an animal. This world is populated by intellectual animals or we can say humanoids, but not humans. There are a few humans, but very few. The word *humanity* is used nevertheless out of respect.

The irrational animals constitute all the other animals that are not the intellectual animal. The Three Traitors are born as the three aspects of the soul in an animal: desire, mind, and will. Irrational animals perform the will of God collectively, they contain three vestments of the soul at the level of an animal in order to be able to receive the intelligence of God in accordance with the Holy Triamazicamno (the Law of Three, the Trinity). Within an irrational animal these vestments of collective intelligence are of an evolutionary type.

For example, all the oak trees contain a collective soul. They grow and experience life as the oak. All the lions contain a group will: they always act in the way of a lion. A lion cannot be anything but a lion. A frog can only be a frog. Thus, animals live and experience the good and evil of life in as a collective soul of their group. They have three vestments which constitutes their soul: collective desire, collective mind, and collective will.

The intellectual animal, although always boastful about its magnificent presence, is just another group thought, group willed animal that moves, acts, and feels in herds. Yet, they contain something more, they contain the intellect. The intellect is a tool to discriminate phenomena, and it is the tool required to overcome instinctual, group-will, and crystallize a true individuality. So, there is a little bit of difference between different humanoids, but not much. It would be a lie to say that the intellectual animal has true individual will or individual mind. Intellectual animals think in groups, believe in groups, etc.

The three traitors betray the purpose of the intellectual animal, which is to become a human. The three traitors constitute the three vestments ("bodies") of the intellectual animal soul, inherited from the collective intelligence of "Mother Nature." These bodies are the same mentioned previously: the Lunar Body of Desire (Emotion), the Lunar Mental Body and the Lunar Body of Will. With the gift of intellect one is supposed to individualize through freewill. The problem occurs when intellectual animals choose to disobey the commandments of God, principally: *Thou shalt not eat from the Tree of Good and Evil*. The Tree of Good and Evil is the sexual organs. The fruit of the Tree of Good and Evil is the Sexual Energy; this is the 'fruit' or 'hydrogen SI-12' that Peter D. Ouspensky elucidates upon. When one reaches orgasm (eats the fruit), these three vestments are strengthened with animal qualities not suited for the higher purposes of the intellectual animal, which is to become a human being.

There is no law in the kingdom of irrational animals against adultery and fornication because these animals, through the creative-sexual energy, understand the intelligence of God in a collective fashion fit for the level of being of an animal. However, the intellectual animal has been told that in order to become a human, he must stop his ways as an animal and develop a new nature within, the nature of a human being, one who has individual will.

Because this humanity has failed to do this, we have complicated our psyche with many infrahuman elements, which in sum constitute the ego. The three animal vestments of an evolutionary type have become in the intellectual animal devolutionary elements. This is the genesis of the Three Traitors.

It is necessary to remove the three traitors through psychological death, but this is not all. It is also necessary to be born again. When the sexual energy is transmuted by restraining from the animal impulse in the mind, heart, and sex, new vestments are crystallized out of individual will, vestments that can receive a much higher voltage of God. In this way, the human is exalted by God and he becomes divine.

Transforming the Being-Exioehary

Let us now read from the chapter entitled *The Holy Planet "Purgatory"* from Gurdjieff's *Beelzebub's Tales to His Grandson*. Gurdjieff wrote this book in a way to stimulate in the reader the reception of ancient wisdom in a pure form. He did this, in part, through the usage of strange and new vocabulary, so that the reader could not mechanically associate these strange words with the many spiritual concepts the reader has previously misunderstood. Thus, instead of using the phrase "sexual energy," the term "being-exioehary" is used, and the phrase "being-Partkdolg-duty" is used to describe the actions of self-sacrifice. Transforming the being-exioehary is a phrase for the same process of sexual transmutation.

Exioehary is an esoteric name for sexual energy (in any form), and the more specific *being-exioehary* is the sexual energy in the biological organism as it is formed mechanically through the digestion of comestibles combined with the processes of the inhalation of air. Without the "mechanical shock" of the processes of the inhalation of air, the evolution of the energies that become the being-exioehary is impossible. The shock occurs when the vital energy (prana) of the solid food is crossed with the vital energy of the air. The crossing of these two types produces the shock, because power of any form is invariably the outcome of the *crossing* of elements. Luckily, life is impossible without breathing, so there is no need to worry about the completion of the crystallization of the being-exioehary, that is to say sperm, semen, hormones, etc., in today's average individual. Gurdjieff writes:

> In order to transform [comestibles] completely into new higher substances and in order to acquire vibrations corresponding to the vibrations of the next [octave of energy] [...] it requires just that foreign help which is actualized [...] in the 'being-Partkdolg-duty,' [...] which factors until now serve as the sole possible means for the assimilation of the cosmic substances required for the coating and perfecting of the higher being-bodies... (p. 792)

Therefore, this process of creating the being-exioehary (semen or sexual energy) is performed automatically in the body, but transforming it into subtler substances cannot take place via mechanical shock (such as breathing). What is required to further transform this energy into something superior is that which is called being-Partkdolg-duty, a term that means, according to Gurdjieff, "conscious labors" and "intentional suffering." These two phrases can be summarized as the whole work of psychological annihilation: the conscious actions one must perform in order to destroy, or, sacrifice, the "I." In other words, it is the work performed on the path of the self-realization of the Being.

Two distinct outcomes arrive from the application of being-Partkdolg-duty: The First Conscious Shock and the Second Conscious Shock.

The First Conscious Shock occurs through the practice of the transformation of impressions. As it was already stated, the transformation of impressions only occurs when one is inner self-remembering, when one is consciously receiving and digesting the impressions of life. When an impression provokes a negative response from the ego, to deny that response and to consciously act in accordance with being-Partkdolg-duty, this "pressure" of the denial of the animal self as a consequence transforms the energies in the human machine into something more subtle. This newly distilled or purified energy, in turn, provides the nourishment of higher or more rarified states of consciousness, which we can call *happiness*.

The Second Conscious Shock is the transformation of the being-exioehary by performing being-Partkdlog-duty in the sexual act itself. This is done by connecting sexually, but refraining from orgasm and ejaculation. The consequence of this act is the shocking of the being-exioehary into subtler forms of exioehary (sexual energy) that engenders the human soul, as apposed to physical bodies. The crossing of man and woman provides the power of the soul, because the power is always in the cross of life. Gurdjieff refers to the soul, which is triple in aspect, as the "higher being bodies" and Samael Aun Weor refers to them as the Solar Bodies. This is the *To Soma Heliakon*, The Golden Body of the Solar Man, it is the sacred Mercabah, the Chariot of Atman.

Gurdjieff never explicitly taught the method of the Second Conscious Shock, which is in other words white tantrism or sexual magic. But he did stress the importance of the sexual energy, stating that being-exioehary is the human machine's most sacred possession. He also cautions that it is necessary to perform the First Conscious Shock if one practices continence because a failure to do so will leave the being-exioehary stagnant, leading it to devolve and thus devolving one's psychology with it. However, it is stated that the habitual removal of the being-exioehary from the organism has become humanity's chief vice:

> The beings of the present time [...] do not use these same substances of being-exioehary at all consciously, neither for self-perfecting nor for conscious reproduction outside of themselves of new being similar to themselves.
>
> And these sacred cosmic substances [...] serve [...] for the involuntary conception of a new beings similar to themselves, who

is without their cognized wish a distressing result for them from the [exchange of sexual fluids] during the satisfaction by them of that function of theirs which has become, thanks to the inheritance from the ancient Romans,[1] the chief vice of contemporary three-brained beings. [...]

I must sadly remark that the mentioned depraved inherency already completely fixed in their common presences is for them [...] already an 'automatically acting' means of destroying to their very root even those impulses which sometimes arise in them from manifestations worthy of three-brained beings and which evoke in them the what is called 'thirst-for-Being.'

[Contemporary society has] ceased to use these sacred substances inevitably formed in them, consciously for the coating and perfection of their 'higher-parts' as well as for the fulfillment of their being-duty foreseen by Nature herself, which consists in the continuation of their species, yet even when this latter does accidentally proceed, they already accept it and regard it as a very great misfortune for themselves, chiefly because the consequences which must proceed from it must for a certain time hinder the free gratification of the multitudinous and multiform vices fixed in their essence. [...]

Whereas, this same 'being-act' which [...] has been turned into their chief vice, constitutes and is considered everywhere in our Great Universe for being of all kinds of natures, as the most sacred of all sacred Divine sacraments. (p. 793-795)

At the present time, very many of these 'monasteries' exist [on Earth], and these innumerable 'monks' who enter them do indeed strictly abstain from the ejection from themselves in the customary way of the being-Exioehary or sperm formed in them; but of course, no sensible result at all is ever obtained from this abstinence of theirs, and it is not obtained, because the thought has ceased even to enter the heads of these unfortunate 'contemporary' monks that although it is indeed possible, by means of these substances of Exioehary formed in them, to perfect themselves, yet this can proceed exclusively only if the second and third being-foods[2] are intentionally absorbed and consciously digested in one's presence, and this is possible exclusively only if all the parts of one's presence have been accustomed beforehand consciously to fulfill both sacred being-

---

[1] Sexual indulgence, orgies, etc.
[2] Air and the impressions of life.

Partkdolg-duties, that is to fulfill 'conscious labors' and 'intentional sufferings.' (p. 807-808)

In light of such evidence, it is clear that Gurdjieff knew the science of sexual transmutation. However, he – like all other eroticists before him – did not explicitly teach what to do with the sexual energy, only that it was something important. This is because they were forbidden to speak about the Great Arcanum, the Great Secret.

Blavatsky and Olcott

The Great Arcanum is known as sexual magic in western occultism. A practice by this name has been popularized in its negative, fatal antithesis by some highly intellectual, yet, mistaken personages who will remain unnamed here. Due to many factors, western occultism has become very degenerated and distorted. Therefore we must be very clear about what sexual magic is in its unadulterated form.

Sexual magic is a very simple practice: One must make love without becoming identified with sensuality, passion, physical sensation, and, especially without orgasm or ejaculation. This is because the orgasm and ejaculation do not return the values of the seminal energy back to its ultimate source in order to create the soul in the supradimensions. Instead, through the orgasm, the creative energy goes into the infradimenons and creates the ego.

The creative energy comes into our physical presence through the sexual organs and when it is activated through the cross (sex) and sublimated, that energy returns to its source (the spirit) full of the values of the experience of the soul. Within the sexual energy is the condensation of the universal spirit of life, which is the *intelligence* of the Creator. When this energy is received and consciously handled it is subsequently impregnated with the values of the experience of the consciousness and returned to the spirit. Through this process of the Holy Eight the soul realizes the spirit and the spirit realizes the soul. The Holy Eight is the sign of the infinite: one loop represents the spirit, the other is the soul. The Holy Eight is impotent without the crossing in its center. No movement exists without the cross, and no values return if the values are ejected from the organism.

The impressions of sexuality must be consciously transformed in the three brains to transmute the energy of each brain in accordance with the Law of Octaves. No energy can be wasted, especially the sexual energy. The Kabbalists know that *El-Shaddai is the power of Shaddai El Chai*, or, in other words, the sexual energy is the power of God.

Blavatsky, the yogini disciple of Master Kout Humi, was not authorized to teach how to transmute the sexual energy. Nevertheless, she practiced sexual magic. She had to remarry to Colonel Olcott after being widowed by Count Blavatsky in order to practice sexual magic and crystallize her Being's Solar Bodies. There was no occultist prior to Samael Aun Weor that publicly taught sexual magic in the unadulterated form.

Many followers of the doctrine of Gurdjieff are very mistaken on how to deal with the sexual energy. The key is written here, it is sexual magic.

Sexual transmutation completes the circuit between God and man. God delivers his values through man, and if man returns those values by transmuting them back, a circuit is created, and the higher the quality of transmutation, the higher the degree of gnosis that is received. Of course every circuit has a resistance; the resistance that exists within man provides the creative potential for his internal illumination. The resistance of man is temptation, Lucifer. This is why Lucifer is the creator of light. Light traveling through the nothingness of space is not seen, because there is nothing for it to be seen with. Without resistance light is not "Being." A large ego is very bad, but a large ego that has been overcome provides more light than a small ego that has been overcome.

The most gratifying sensations are sexual sensations. The most pleasing sensations for the "I" are those created in the sexual act. The processing of the sensation of the orgasm transforms psychic energy. Likewise, the sexual act performed without the orgasm also transforms psychic energy, but in the opposite way. The "I" is established and sustained through the sensations of the orgasm, it is the foundation of the creation of loose cathexis. Likewise, nothing is more detrimental to the life of the ego than the renunciation of the orgasm combined with the technique of sexual sublimation. Nothing is more absurd to the "I" or "self" than the renunciation of the orgasm, because this transforms loose cathexis into bound cathexis.[3]

In relation to the three centers of man the following can be said:

1. Sensation-desire is transmuted into sensation-willpower when the animal impulse is refrained.
2. Sexuality engenders superior emotion when lust is transmuted into love while in the sexual act the sexual energy is sublimated from the sex up to the heart.

---

[3] Psychic-sexual energy in Freudian terms is called cathexis. Three fundamental types of cathexis exist: free, loose, and bound. Free cathexis is used by either the loose or the bound cathexis. Loose cathexis is formed principally through the mechanics of the orgasm. Loose cathexis is the ego. The values of the spirit constitute the bound cathexis.

3. Transmutation brings forth powerful mental comprehension, because man and woman united in the sexual act is the living Cross, and the power of God lives within the Cross of Life.

The Tao Path includes three paths, and Tao is itself is the fourth. Much has been said about the four paths. We Gnostics travel along the fourth path in full consciousness. During the sexual act, we transmute the brutal instincts of our physical body into willpower, the passionate emotions of the astral body into love and the mental impulses into comprehension. As Spirit, we perform the Great Work. This is how we travel along the four paths in practice. We do not need to become fakirs for the first path, neither monks for the second, nor scholars for the third. The Path of the Perfect Matrimony permits us to travel the four paths during the sexual act itself.

– Samael Aun Weor, *The Perfect Matrimony*

SEEING THE EMPTINESS

> Forms that we see directly are just mere appearance to mind
> They exist falsely because the way they appear
> Does not correspond to the way they exist,
> Just as a human body is conventionally accepted as clean when in reality it is impure.
> Buddha taught the impermanence of things
> To lead people gradually to a realization of emptiness –
> The lack of inherent existence of things.
> *"Then it is incorrect to say that things exist even conventionally."*
> No, there is no fault, because things exist by conventional valid cognizers.
> From the point of view of worldly people, seeing things is seeing reality;
> But worldly people never actually see reality
> Because the real nature of things is their emptiness.
>
> – Shantideva, *Guide to the Bodhisattva's Way of Life*

The ego is a malleable, moldable element. It exists within our psychological space and grows larger when we do not correctly transform the impressions we are constantly receiving throughout life. When we incorrectly transform love, it becomes lust. When we incorrectly transform criticism, we implant revenge, or hatred within ourselves. If we do not transform the impression of wealth within our interior, greed crystallizes within. Just as the food that enters our bodies must be transformed into its basic elements via digestion, we must digest our impressions to correctly nourish our interior. We must remain in love, not lust; we must correct our errors rather than seek revenge; we must use financial moderation, not hording or excessive spending. This is what the great avatars have told us.

We must transform our impressions to make use of the flux of the energy of life properly. The ego does not take in energy of the cosmos correctly. The ego implants the impressions of reality within our psyche in accordance to its own *flawed subjective logic*, its own subjective reality that has nothing to do with the objective truth. The energy of the world (the impressions, the experiences we have in the world) should never cause us to react in an inferior fashion such as envy, fear, pride, or hatred. If any of these emotions are found within then we have already failed at transforming an impression. Normally, we are not even lucky enough to catch ourselves. It is normal to never even consider conscious transformation. If we remember ourselves within the moment of reacting upon an untransformed impression, by this act we have already begun to reinterpret and to transform it correctly.

To read how to transform impressions is nothing compared to moments in which it must be done. The aspirant will find that he must struggle terribly to remain in the state of now. When we catch ourselves in the act of a negative emotion we have a wonderful opportunity to ask ourselves why we are frustrated, why we are angry, etc. In this way we can find what brought us to that point. That is Psychological Gymnastics - life, when intensively lived, is our Psychological Gym.

Really, one should never be angry at anything. Some point to the account of Jesus throwing the merchants out of the temple, or when he called the Pharisees "a generation of vipers" as evidence to the contrary, but this is not so. Anger is a reaction to frustrated desire. What Jesus did were not things born of frustration, but of perfect cognizance and love. When Jesus stated, *"I did not come to bring peace, but a sword,"* this means, *"I did not come to make peace with your ego, but instead to destroy it by fire."* This is a work of love even if it appears treacherous to our concepts of love and hate.

Those who feel it impossible to never be angry are not being sincere within themselves. They should work harder for their psychological emancipation. For example, the 14th Dalai Lama speaks about a monk that was imprisoned by the Chinese communists for a number of years where he had to suffer many unspeakable things. This monk told the Dalai Lama that there were a few times that he was in danger. Yet, he was not speaking of his own physical life, but in danger of losing loving kindness and compassion for his torturers. Therefore, those who think this doctrine is impossible are simply not ready for it. Negative thought, emotion, and action are the product of the failure to understand the inherent "emptiness" of life.

Shunyata is a Sanskrit word used in Buddhism often translated as *emptiness*. Yet, this emptiness is not related to the way the most western personalities understand this concept. When western people use the word emptiness to describe their life, they are using it to depict a depressed psychological state. For example, "I feel empty inside," "My life is empty of meaning," etc., etc. This is not shunyata. Shunyata is translated as emptiness or voidness, but the experience of realizing shunyata in any particular moment provides what could be paradoxically described as "fullness," "totality," or "completeness." When Buddhism talks about emptiness it is speaking of all things being empty of inherent self-nature.

Take the concrete example of a single room cabin placed in the wilderness. What makes it a cabin? Can a cabin exist without four walls? If you take one of the walls away, is the cabin still there? Does the cabin exist within the wall? No, the wall is made simply of wood; a "piece" of the cabin is not within the wood. Yet, placing the wall back in its place, the cabin is once again complete. The cabin cannot exist without the sum of its parts also existing in the proper way.

Examine each part of the cabin. The walls are made of wood. What makes wood what it is? A configuration of wood cells exists as a log, and each of these cells cannot exist without a configuration of molecules. Likewise, each molecule is composed of atoms. Each atom contains electrons, protons, and neutrons. Each atomic particle is composed of quarks, etc., etc., etc. Everything can be broken down into parts. Even if somehow a "thing" was found that could not be broken down, it would still have parts because if it did not, it could not be used to make more complex things. Anything that has spatial extent requires that it has a front, a back, a shape – different parts.

At the level of atoms, the distance from one atom to another in relationship to the diameter of the nucleus of the atom is "astronomical." There is more emptiness in the atoms composing the wall of a cabin than there is matter! And this goes for all matter. All matter is mostly emptiness. The vast majority of matter is emptiness or voidness. What prevents your hand, for example, from passing through a wall is not that there is some "thing" or "things" (atoms) in the way, but more so because there is an atomic energy field that prevents the atoms from one's hand to pass by the atoms of the wall.

Now, let us go a bit deeper. Let us relate the doctrine of emptiness with relationship to the self. We regularly believe that our existence is an independent, discrete phenomenon that exists in and of its own self. In reality, our existence is the constitution of innumerable parts that exist as they are due to the interaction with other constitutions that are also empty of true independent self. In other words, we have experiences with other people, and with the world itself, and the outcome of those experiences make us who we are. If we were to remove all the little pieces that in sum make up "who we are," there would be nothing left. There would still be existence, but it would be non-existence according to our understanding of the word. This is something one must comprehend in meditation.

Now let us observe any moment of time. What is a moment of time composed of? We can say that each moment arises, sustains, and fades away. Yet, by doing so we have stated that a moment depends upon three aspects: an arising, a sustainment, and a falling. Therefore, a moment cannot simply exist in and of itself. It is empty of self-nature. Furthermore, each part of the moment, the arising, the sustainment, and the falling, are each a moment themselves. Each of these parts would also require their respective parts in order to exist, and so on and so forth. What exists between each moment? Emptiness. What exists in each moment? Emptiness.

Emptiness is not nihilism. Emptiness does not refute existence. Emptiness refutes independent existence. All existing things share interdependence. All interdependent things are empty of self-nature. Everything is always changing because the interdependent quality of existence. Nothing exists without emitting into existence the reflection of the other aspects of existence. For example, if we were to construct a lattice which upon every point of intersection we placed a jewel of varying color, obviously when light shines upon this lattice, every stone reflects the colors the others. The light itself is impersonal, yet each stone shines in a unique way. In order for this lattice to become realized in our own self, we need to make a diamond soul (*Neshamah* of the Kabbalah, the *Vajrasattva* or *Dorjesempa* of Buddhism). What we have now is coal in our hearts. We have to convert the coal into a diamond, and this is done with intense heat and pressure. Heat and pressure are the difficult situations in life that, when triumphed, crystallize virtue in our interior.

> "Why so hard?" the kitchen coal once said to the diamond. "After all, are we not close kin?"
>
> Why so soft? O my brothers, thus I ask you: are you not after all my brothers?
>
> Why so soft, so pliant and yielding? Why is there so much denial, self-denial, in your hearts? So little destiny in your eyes?
>
> And if you do not want to be destinies and inexorable ones, how can you one day triumph with me?
>
> And if your hardness does not wish to flash and cut through, how can you one day create with me?
>
> For all creators are hard. And it must seem blessedness to you to impress your hand on millennia as on wax.
>
> Blessedness to write on the will of millennia as on bronze — harder than bronze, nobler than bronze. Only the noblest is altogether hard.
>
> This new tablet, O my brothers, I place over you: Become hard!
>
> – Nietzsche, *Thus Spoke Zarathustra*

Karma arrives from action. When one acts in a way that imbalances the forces of the universe, then that imbalance will return to the actor. This is understood, to one degree or another in the minds of many aspirants, however, because of our three dimensional psychology, we do not understand that karma is more than just physical action and consequence.

Every movement of energy is karmic. What a person thinks generates karma. What a person feels generates karma. To even think ill of a person will be the cause of future suffering. It is not enough to appear polite to people while internally slandering them. Appearing respectful, honest and humble to people is an act that we play in order to appear as if we truly possess these qualities, yet internally we all know our mind is a tavern where we incessantly gossip and slander our fellows. We ask internally "Why does he always have to act like that? What is wrong with him? He annoys me so much." Nevertheless, we always feel as if our own action in daily life is correct. It is very rare that in ordinary live do we view ourselves in an objective fashion, yet because we are so identified with life, we often act in very immature and animalistic ways.

When you find yourself slandering others for their strange or offensive action, remember to self-observe and take a moment to actually see the world from their point of view, from their psychological program that they have conditioned themselves to run. The program our nervous systems (three brains) run is deterministic, it acts in the way it has been programmed to act. The programs that run in our minds have no choices to but to act in the way they act. The programs can modify themselves but they can never destroy themselves. The mind cannot destroy or create itself. Something beyond the mind is necessary to radically alter the mind. This is why we must meditate; this is why we must work with sexual super-dynamics.

It is good to place our self in the shoes of others. It is good to understand that everyone is a programmed machine, yet this is only possible when we begin to see our own programming. When we work with a personal computer, it at times does not work the way we wish it to, it may lose our data, a program may crash at an ill time, etc. Sometimes we yell and curse at the machine when it misbehaves, yet we later realize that such action is very silly and that as a programmed machine, it is merely doing what is has been programmed to do.

Nevertheless, when those people we interact with make mistakes, we give rarely give them any such tolerance, at times we may even silently keep track of what others owe us, of how many times they have done us wrong, we keep grudges in our hearts and become tyrants without mercy for even the smallest of trivial mistakes that we have become totally identified with. People today are programmed machines, yet living beings, therefore why is it so easy to forgive an inanimate machine when it does us wrong as opposed to one who has the ability to know hatred and kindness?

Criminally, the answer lies within this very question: the reason we hurt others is because we know that we can hurt them, while it is impossible to hurt a machine that has no feelings. We cure this criminal behavior (and it is indeed a crime against one's soul to not forgive mistakes) by comprehending that those people with a sleeping consciousness have no authentic freewill. The only people who possess authentic and total freewill are those who have awakened the consciousness. Therefore, those who have freewill are very few.

We must deeply comprehend that the loving kindness and compassion taught by the Buddha is not to love other people's ego or personality, but to love that Buddha-nature that exists within each person (even if it is only in a sleeping state). The Buddha-nature is the *Buddhata* in Zen Buddism, the *Tathagatagarbha* in Tibetan Buddhism, it is the Essence of Being in each person that has the ability to unfold into the inner Buddha. To see the Being within each and every person is only possible when we remember our own Being while practicing self-observation. Inner self-remembering must be combined with self-observation.

It is absolutely necessary to purify our minds of all desire. This is the only way to walk the path of happiness. Anger is frustrated desire. No desire, no anger. There can never be anger without desire. Anger is painful. Desire is the cause of pain. Yet once again we will stress that this has nothing to do with repression. To never personify anger we already have, well, that is truly impossible. Often, someone reads that anger equates failure and immediately assumes we are speaking of repressing our already manifested desire. This doctrine is not about building psychological walls or disconnecting from the situation to not feel our anger. It is crucial to understand this, because mechanical repression or indulgence is a waste of time. We are speaking of the transformation of energy into a superior aspect.

When an impression that usually causes anger hits us, we have to do something with that impression, because it is energy. We cannot deny that energy because that is impossible. It is impossible to superficially reject our anger or happiness or any emotion. We must take the energy, not as something negative but as something positive, and this means we must consciously transform it. When we see the inherent emptiness of the impression, we have transformed that impression.

For example, an image of a beautiful man or woman assaults our mind, and we become identified with desire. Yet, if we were in that very moment to comprehend that beauty is an illusion that fades away with time – that if in youth one is beautiful, then at an old age they will wither away and die – then we will have seen the inherit emptiness of that impression. To see the beauty of someone is fine, but to desire it is another thing. Why desire something that will go away, if you desire beauty then when that beauty leaves one will experience anguish. Therefore, what is the use of this desire? It is meaningless, has no purpose other than fascination and pain. This is how we transform the impressions: when the truth is realized, the transformation is already complete. Therefore, this has nothing to do with repression.

Conscious transformation can only take place if we are in a moment of self-observation. Transforming an impression means we must often make a *sacrifice*. We must see the impression hit us, produce for example a feeling of hurt towards our pride, however if we are vigilant, we will transform that energy that is causing hurt and resentment into humbleness. We will observe that our pride is a flaw that we have come to know about within our psychological gym of self-observation.

What happens when we do not make that sacrifice is that our psychological equilibrium is lost and we begin to send negative emotions to the world. Then no one wishes to be around us, we are wretched people and in conclusion it is all a chain of misery. In life, someone gives us a miserable impression and we mechanically proliferate that misery. This is the Wheel of Samsara and the Interdependent Arising of Suffering.

Samael Aun Weor often states that self-observation must be combined with inner self-remembering. This is a problem for some because they do not understand exactly what inner self-remembering is. The phrase "inner self" denotes something beyond our mundane "self" or "personality," while the word "remembering" quantifies a state of being. This is not an intellectual remembering, it is not the recollection of a specific memory of the mind, but something much more real. For example, remember the smell of a flower, and by association the state of being that scent places you in. It is not necessary to remember a specific time that one has actually smelled a flower. That is remembering a specific instance, what we are after is the remembering of the smell itself, to remember what that smell is, in and of itself, without relationship to space or time. The flower is a representation of beauty, but the actual beauty itself exists within eternity: what you must remember is the beauty of the eternal flower.

In Buddhism, the "inner self" is the Lotus Flower, and to remember the inner self is to remember the effluence of God flowing within you and within the entire Universe. That effluence is a contiguous stream of high voltage energy, in potential form, that only has the ability to be realized when one remembers it. When one remembers that they are a part of God, it instantaneously elevates the state of the mind and places the psyche actively in connection with the universal impersonal Cosmic Christ (Avalokiteshvara or Chenrezig).

Merely self-observing without inner self-remembering is like trying to make a car move without using any gas to move it. At first, inner self-remembering may feel quite unusual and very little will be noticed from the practice. With time, the student will come to realize exactly what this method is, and notice how the "taste" of the impressions of life change when they are truly in a moment with God (inner self-remembering). In other words, the impressions of life become less fascinating, it is becomes easier to see the inherit emptiness and therefore easier to transform the impressions of life. This is how life itself is radically transformed.

Buddhists chant *Om Mansi Padme Hum* in order to inner self-remember. The literal translation of this mantra is *The Jewel of the Heart of the Lotus*, however its inner meaning is *Oh, My God that is Within Me*. If I were to tell you that a particular monk may chant this mantra for 5 or 6 hours, a common reaction would be that it must be very boring. In reality though, anyone who uses this mantra correctly will be in a true state of happiness. When the latent forces of the divine are activated within one's mundane and ultra physiologies the whole idea of "boredom" washes away into a sea of ecstasy. Boredom is a product of the ego, and we normally live so far away from happiness that we mistake it for boredom. The ego is bored of God because it is interested only in activities that produce fascinating sensation, which it lamentably mistakes for happiness, and in reality produces suffering.

ཨོཾ་མ་ཎི་པདྨེ་ཧཱུྃ།

Om Mansi Padme Hum

Although modern science knows nothing about it, it is commonly known throughout the esoteric world that the thoughts of an individual attract its likeness. This is called the Law of Psychological Affinities. When we are angry, we will attract angry "atoms" of energy and this energy will be synthesized into our blood stream. We are what we eat: Not just the food we eat, but the mental impressions we process too. Mental impressions are the food of the mind. Those who do not transform mental impressions get mental indigestion. So, take this advice: Think positively! Aspire, be well and love others. Then you will attract wellness, and people will notice that (even if it is mostly unconscious), and it will help you in everyday life.

Is it possible for us to transform everything correctly? No, it is truly impossible for us to simply say, "I not am going to be angry anymore." We all know that is a path of failure and misery. The Magnum Opus - the great work of self-realization - is not something theoretical, it is something we must live, here and now. We must become practical. The Cosmic Drama is not an ideology to accept or reject, as if changing one's opinion. We can change our political party by simply saying, "I now follow this political party, I vote for them now." However we cannot just wish to change ourselves by merely thinking about it or believing in it. Someone who lives strictly in the mind and its theory will never see anything real and they will never change in a superior sense. Therefore, this is something critical to understand. Change first requires knowledge, gnosis, of what it is that must change. In order to become something different, you must first stop being who you are.

You have to die. How does one become what they are not? If one thinks they are not, then by that fact alone they still are. We need comprehension in order to change; we need meditation, willpower, patience and sacrifice. We need to go beyond the mind; we have to reach the transcendental.

Realize that it takes a sacrifice because it is difficult to transform negative impressions. Our ego wants to react, it wants to express its pride, it enjoys itself, it wants to take the energies of the world and form negative emotion, but this will unknowingly cause a disharmonious atmosphere, and what happens then? Everyone begins expressing negative emotions, no one is happy, the misery continues, more ego is stirred up into action, and then our home or office is like a wretched inferno. Remember that we transform our emotions not only for ourselves but as well for the love of others, because if we do not wish our neighbor happiness, if we do not love them with our whole Being, we will always be selfish.

The impressions of life hit everyone differently. What makes one person sad makes another angry. So we must understand that *each impression exclusively holds the value we choose to apply to it*. We choose to be angry. We choose to be sad. We choose it because we are choosing to be asleep, we are choosing not to make a sacrifice and transform the impression. We are lazy, we do not want to change and we will go to great lengths to justify our psychological flaws preventing our change.

Many will disagree with this. Many believe that certain things will always make us sad, or angry, and that it is impossible to feel otherwise. These types of people are slaves to their emotions because their unconsciousness controls their every move. These people have no control over themselves. Let us be honest though, because there are very few who are not guilty of being asleep. Sometimes the impressions of life strike us so profoundly that we cannot help but feel an array of inferior emotions. Nevertheless, we must remember that it is not the impression itself that makes us sad, but rather the inferior transformation of the impression that makes us feel sad. What is impossible for one is easy for another because this latter person has fewer egos, a balanced psychology, a strong sense of Being. This is not because this person is special. Rather, it is because they have done the work, in this life or another. A person like that has reaped what he has sowed.

Negative emotions are anger, hate, envy, pride, depression, lust, greed, etc... These emotions are extremely contagious and they are literally a form of psychological sickness. They are destructive and hence they truly are inferior and degenerate. When we express our inferior emotions we spread our destructive energy to everyone around us. Then, our entire world is filled with negativity, a mob mentality develops, and disaster is the only outcome that can occur. Therefore, we must be more than ostensibly pure. To appear is one thing, but we must actually become, otherwise this is a waste of time. When we think ill of someone, we condense energy that through the Law of Psychological Affinities, reaches the subconsciousness of that person. Thoughts travel through time and space to reach its subject. Consequently, when a person has transformed their own subconsciousness into consciousness, then this person has the ability to read other people's minds like an open book.

When we do not digest our impressions correctly they are then fed to our ego. Obviously feeding the ego causes it to grow and reserve more of our interior space. When do we not digest our impressions of the world correctly? We do not digest our impression of the world correctly within the moments when our consciousness is asleep. It takes supreme effort to stay vigilant, to keep an aware, novel experience of life in the constant moment of now, but this is the requirement for change.

The key to breaking the chain of the Interdependent Arising of Suffering is self-observation.

Sexual Transmutation

> How can the oversexed person talk of having a creative mind?
>
> Do they not know that the thoughts which are not penetrated by the Determinative Energy of Nature (sexual energy) become disintegrated?
>
> Do they ignore that the Determinative Energy is the sexual force?
>
> How can an individual whose pineal gland is atrophied, because of fornication, talk of having courage, willpower and triumph?
>
> Is it perhaps that the intimate existent relationship between the pineal gland and the sexual glands is unknown, and also because the pineal gland is the messenger of the center of thought?
>
> How can an individual whose brain is weakened, because of the vice of coitus, talk of mental concentration?
>
> – Samael Aun Weor, *The Revolution of Beelzebub*

The true source of energy in every person is the sexual center. It is obvious that physically this is located within the sexual organs. This energy is diffused throughout the entire endocrine system. Powerful emotions are ultimately fueled by the sexual center. If these emotions are negative, then the outcome is a negative crystallization, if the emotions are positive (love, altruism, kindness, happiness, humility, etc.), the likewise a positive crystallization occurs.

When the especially reserved mental energy has been depleted, the mental center makes use of other reserved areas of energy not suited for the mental center. The esoteric philosophy affirms that each center operates at a specific frequency, and to deplete the normal energy of a center will damage it with foreign energy. Sexual energy is very quick and it is fuel for the sexual center. It needs to be processed to enter the emotional center correctly because that center operates at a slower frequency. However, if the emotional center has been depleted, it will make use of that energy within the sexual center, and this will damage the emotional center. Consequently, it is unhealthy to become emotionally "sick" or intellectually drained because when the raw sexual energy is used in the intellectual and emotional brains the result is similar to placing the wrong type of fuel in a combustion engine. The result of chronic abuse of these energies leads to emotional disorders and mental complexes, syndromes, etc.

When any aspect of sex is abused it creates degeneration. This is obvious once it is understood that sex is something in constant activity. Sex is ether creating or destroying, it is never idle, and this is why we must understand how to correctly make use of our energy.

> There is conscious as well as unconscious action. The Yogis possess a third kind, the superconscious, which in all countries and in all ages has been the source of all religious knowledge. The superconscious state makes no mistakes, but whereas the action of the instinct would be purely mechanical, the former is beyond consciousness.
>
> It has been called inspiration, but the Yogi says, "This faculty is in every human being, and eventually all will enjoy it."
>
> We must give a new direction to the "sun" and "moon" currents and open for them a new passage through the centre of the spinal cord. When we succeed in bringing the currents through this passage called "Sushumnâ", up to the brain, we are for the time being separated entirely from the body.
>
> The nerve centre at the base of the spine near the sacrum is most important. It is the seat of the generative substance of the sexual energy and is symbolized by the Yogi as a triangle containing a tiny serpent coiled up in it. This sleeping serpent is called Kundalini, and to raise this Kundalini is the whole object of Raja-Yoga.
>
> The great sexual force, raised from animal action and sent upward to the great dynamo of the human system, the brain, and there stored up, becomes Ojas or spiritual force. All good thought, all prayer, resolves a part of that animal energy into Ojas and helps to give us spiritual power. This Ojas is the real man and in human beings alone is it possible for this storage of Ojas to be accomplished. One in whom the whole animal sex force has been transformed into Ojas is a god. He speaks with power, and his words regenerate the world.
>
> The Yogi pictures this serpent as being slowly lifted from stage to stage until the highest, the pineal gland, is reached. No man or woman can be really spiritual until the sexual energy, the highest power possessed by man, has been converted into Ojas.

No force can be created; it can only be directed. Therefore we must learn to control the grand powers that are already in our hands and by will power make them spiritual instead of merely animal. Thus it is clearly seen that chastity is the corner-stone of all morality and of all religion. In Raja-Yoga especially, absolute chastity in thought, word, and deed is a sine qua non. The same laws apply to the married and the single. If one wastes the most potent forces of one's being, one cannot become spiritual.

– Swami Vivekananda, *Lessons on Raja Yoga*

Perhaps now we understand the quote introducing this chapter. The esoteric philosophy has always known that the loss of sexual energy degenerates the mind and body. The esoteric philosophy readily states that the quickest way to age, to become old, to calcify the body, and to become mentally arrested is to misuse the creative-sexual energy. This is for both the man and woman, because the woman has her special reserves of sexual potency too. This is known perfectly well throughout many schools of Yoga and in Tibet.

If we wish to obtain mental equilibrium, then we must stop abusing all our energies. The same energy that we use to create a new child also is used in the formation of anger, lust, envy, pride, and all the other infrahuman elements that currently exist inside of us. These elements are a different condensation of that energy, but in synthesis, all of the energy that comes into body goes through the sexual center. Air and food put these energies in our blood, and the blood is transformed into the semen. This is the trinity, the Law of Three: Father, Son and Holy Spirit. Semen is representative of the Holy Spirit, because it is that which impregnates. Blood is analogous to the Christ, the Wine of Christ. Thirdly, the breath of life is the Father, this is the first principle, this is what each newborn inhales as soon as they are born into this world and what every dieing man exhales as their last breath.

The air is needed for the Cerebrospinal Nervous System (intellectual center) to function. The blood is needed for Grand Sympathetic Nervous System (emotional center). The sexual energy, which is stored as semen and the various chemicals of the endocrine system is needed for the Parasympathetic Nervous

System (motor-instinctual-sexual center). It is obvious that the sexual energy is a very refined and expensive substance for the human machine to manufacture. Therefore it is easy to understand not only that it is the most potent and useful energy but also the most detrimental to abuse.

To use this energy correctly one must make use of conscious willpower. Nature and its machine, the rational animal that is mistakenly referred to as the human being, mechanically transforms the energies of life into the sexual-creative energy as we know it. This energy is then deposited in our sexual glands in order to further the economy of that intelligence which created the rational animal. However, if one wishes to become free of nature's laws, and become subject to the superior laws – allowing more freedom and consequently more happiness – then one must use *willpower*. Willpower, in other words, *conscious action*, can transform sexual energy into a superior vibration. This superior vibration is the fuel one needs to awaken consciousness. Change is impossible without willpower. No superior creation can occur without transforming sexual energy into a superior vibration. The *will* is human, and the *power* is the transmuted sexual energy.

Nature exists in order for Beings, the true Being in each one of us, to gain understanding of themselves. Nature's rigid and mechanical laws give the structure, the crutch required for ignorant Beings to begin to know themselves. When a Being becomes conscious of its own self, then it becomes a God, a Deva, a Buddha, etc., etc. When a human soul rebels against Nature, it is stating, "I no longer need these crutches to walk. I am no longer a servant of Nature, Nature now serves me." This is not an act of resentment, because we must realize that Nature is necessary and a part of God's creation. Good and Evil is *necessary* in order for us to understand it. When we understand Good and Evil, then we have understood ourselves, then we become Gods who are beyond Good and Evil.

Nevertheless, Nature is a terrible filter. Few people understand themselves. Instead of rebelling against Nature, people are rebelling against their own Inner Being. People choose the mechanical laws of Nature instead of true freedom and happiness. Today we are born in a society that profanes the sexual force in every form possible. It is even seen as taboo or dogmatic to state that masturbation is a crime against one's own Being – nevertheless, this is the truth of the matter. People feel rebellious when they become "sexually free" from all the taboos of yesterday, but in reality they never understand what those taboos meant, and they continue to live within Nature, providing the energy required for her sustainment. The authentic rebellion is against today's degenerate social norms. The only way to rebel against nature is to develop something that Nature did not give us: this is the authentic Human Soul. For this we must psychologically "die" (as an animal), and be reborn into the Human Kingdom. This is what it means to be reborn in the Kingdom of God. Masturbation is the use of the sexual-creative energy to create ego and therefore to further one's bondage to Nature.

> Unfortunately, although it is pitiful to realize it, nowadays many children of twelve and thirteen years of age are already copulating. Moreover, those who are not yet copulating commit the crime of masturbation. They eliminate their hormones, degenerate their brains and atrophy their pineal gland through masturbation. This is how they become sure candidates for a mental home.
>
> It is well known that after coitus, the phallus continues with certain peristaltic movements conducive to receiving vital energies from the feminine uterus in an attempt to replace its wasted creative principles.
>
> However, when masturbation exists, instead of assimilating vital feminine energies with such peristaltic movements, useful principles for existence, the masturbator absorbs cold air, which passes directly to the brain. The outcome of this is idiocy, mental degeneration or insanity.
>
> The vice of masturbation is, unfortunately, also very popular among the feminine sex. Obviously, with such a vice, many women that could have been genial or good wives have prematurely become degenerated, have aged quickly, have lost their sexual potential, and have become true victims of life.
>
> – Samael Aun Weor

There is nothing at all healthy regarding masturbation. Many sexologists believe otherwise. They state that masturbation is a good way to alleviate stress, a way for youth to deal with their sexual energy. In reality this is terrible advice. It is better to be creative, to paint, sing, to exercise, to place the mind in meditation. The truth is that masturbation removes the ability for the brain and nervous system to function well. If masturbation was something good for the three nervous systems of the biological organism, than youth today would be healthy, without disease or so many problems in life. Instead, what we find are many children embodying mental disorders with names such as ADD or OCD. Instead of renouncing masturbation we give them the latest pharmaceutical pills. Sadly, these pills do not fix anything, they only hide the effects of the child's weakening psychology. Due to the abuse of the sexual energy throughout many lifetimes the brain has become atrophied. Therefore it is essential to regenerate the brain.

To regenerate the brain we must renounce all impulses to waste the sexual energy through negative emotion, negative will, and negative use of the sexual act itself. Sexual energy has the power to awaken consciousness through the restraint of the animal impulse and the expression of virtue. Neither Buddhists nor the Hindustani yogis are ignorant to the power of the vital energies because they understand the value of determinative energy. Our ultra-modern, degenerate society does not know that the determinative energy is the sexual energy.

> The man who has a bad habit of masturbation or who suffers from wet dreams, should give up the evil habit at once. You will be entirely ruined if you continue the practice. Do not be worried. Forget musing over the past mistakes and think positively and with confidence about your ability to get rid of evil habits. Give up negative thinking. Let the past not bother you. Let bygones be bygones. The disease is aggravated by getting worried about it. Let not weakening thoughts enter your mind. Do not be anxious over sexual energy you have already wasted in past. Up to this time you were blind and ignorant. You had no idea of the disastrous effect of this evil practice. Wake up now and girdle up loins to preserve seminal energy in the remaining life.

Remember, the aim is not to suppress the seminal energy but to sublimate it. You do not know how to sublimate it. Learn the techniques of sublimation. But before that you should know what is the meaning of sublimation of seminal energy. [...]

If the sexual energy is transmuted into ojas or spiritual energy by pure thoughts, it is called sex sublimation in western psychology. Sublimation is not a matter of suppression or repression, but a positive, dynamic, conversion process. It is the process of controlling the sex energy, conserving it, then diverting it into higher channels, and finally, converting it into spiritual energy or ojas shakti. The material energy is changed into spiritual energy, just as heat is changed into light and electricity. Just as a chemical substance is sublimated or purified by raising the substance through heat into vapor which again is condensed into solid form, so also, the sexual energy is purified and changed into divine energy by spiritual sadhana.

Ojas is spiritual energy that is stored up in the brain. By entertaining sublime, soul-elevating thoughts of the Self or atman, by meditation, japa, worship and pranayama, the sexual energy can be transmuted into ojas shakti and stored up in the brain. This stored up energy can then be utilized for divine contemplation and spiritual pursuits.

Anger and muscular energy can also be transmuted into ojas. A man who has a great deal of ojas in his brain can turn out immense mental work. He is very intelligent. He has lustrous eyes and a magnetic aura in his face. He can influence people by speaking a few words. A short speech of his produces a tremendous impression on the minds of the hearers. His speech is thrilling. He has an awe-inspiring personality.

– Swami Sivananda

A person's approach to sexuality is a sign of his level of evolution. Unevolved persons practice ordinary sexual intercourse. Placing all emphasis upon the sexual organs, they neglect the body's other organs and systems. Whatever physical energy is accumulated is summarily discharged, and the subtle energies are similarly dissipated and disordered. It is a great backward leap. For those who aspire to the higher realms of living, there is angelic dual cultivation. Because every portion of the body, mind, and spirit yearns for the integration of yin and yang, angelic intercourse is led by the spirit rather than the sexual organs. Where ordinary intercourse is effortful, angelic cultivation is calm, relaxed, quiet, and natural. Where ordinary intercourse unites sex organs with sex organs, angelic cultivation unites spirit with spirit, mind with mind, and every cell of one body with every cell of the other body. Culminating not in dissolution but in integration, it is an opportunity for a man and woman to mutually transform and uplift each other into the realm of bliss and wholeness. The sacred ways of angelic intercourse are taught only by one who has himself achieved total energy integration, and taught only to students who follow the Integral Way with profound devotion, seeking to purify and pacify the entire world along with their own being. However, if your virtue is especially radiant, it can be possible to open a pathway to the subtle realm and receive these celestial teachings directly from the immortals.

– *Hua Hu Jing*, v. 22

In the view of Tantra, the body's vital energies are the vehicles of the mind. When the vital energies are pure and subtle, one's state of mind will be accordingly affected. By transforming these bodily energies we transform the state of consciousness.

– The Fourteenth Dalai Lama

Pranayama

There are specific exercises one can do in order to transmute the sexual energy. The most profound transmutation occurs between man and wife unite when they finish without the sexual spasm. Bachelors can perform a breathing technique called *pranayama*. *Prana* is life force, the breath of life, and *ayama* means restraint. Pranayama is a breathing exercise that moves the sexual-creative energy inwardly and upwards, as opposed to downwardly and outwards. Thus, the sexual energy is transmuted according to the law of octaves.

> Sit down comfortably: the eastern way (cross-legged) or the western way (on a comfortable armchair). Relax your bodies as children do.
>
> Inhale deeply, very slowly, and imagine that the creative energy rises through the spermatic channels up to the brain; mentally pronounce the mantra HAM like this: HAAAAAAAMM. Exhale, short and quick, as you pronounce aloud the mantra SAH: SAAAAHH...
>
> Undoubtedly, you inhale through the nose and exhale through the mouth. While inhaling, you "mantralize" the sacred syllable HAM

(mentally, since you are inhaling through the nose); but you can articulate the syllable SAH with sound while you exhale.

The marvelous symbol that in the East makes the chaotic waters of life fertile is Ham-Sah, the Third Logos.

Usually, the sexual forces flow outwards from the inside in a centrifugal way and that is why there are nocturnal emissions; when you have a dream based on the Sexual Center, there occurs an emission, a loss of Sacred Sperm or Spermatic Liquor...

If one organizes one's vital systems and instead of propitiating the centrifugal system, uses the centripetal system, that is, if one makes the sexual forces flow inwards from the outside through transmutation, then there are no emissions even if there may be erotic dreams.

One needs to organize one's sexual forces if one wants to avoid emissions; such forces are closely linked with one's nourishment, with the prana, with life - that is obvious. Therefore there is a profound relation between one's sexual forces and one's breathing, so that when both are duly combined and harmonized, they bring about fundamental changes in one's physical and psychological anatomy.

To make the sexual energies "re-flow" inwards and upwards in a centripetal way is what matters; only thus is it possible to produce a specific change in the office and functions that the sexual creative force can fulfill. During meditation one needs to imagine the creative energy in action, making the energy rise to the brain in a rhythmic, natural way by means of vocalizing the mantram HAM-SAH, not forgetting to synchronize the inhalations and exhalations of air in perfect concentration, harmony and rhythm.

Let us make it clear that inhalation has to be deeper than exhalation simply because we need to make the creative energy flow inwards from the outside; that is, we need to make exhalation shorter than inhalation.

With this practice there comes a moment when all the energy flows inwards and upwards. Clearly, the creative energy so organized - in a centripetal way - becomes an extraordinary instrument for the Essence, a means to awaken Consciousness.

I am teaching you genuine White Tantrism; this is the practice used by the Tantric Schools in the Himalayas and the Hindustan; this is the practice through which one can achieve Ecstasy or Samadhi, or whatever you want to call it.

They have spoken much about the Illuminating Void and clearly we can experience it ourselves. It is in that Void where we can find the Laws of Nature as they are in themselves and not as they seem to be. In this physical world we only see the mechanism of causes and effects but we do not know the Laws of Nature in themselves, whereas in the Illuminating Void we can recognize them in a simple, natural way, just as they are.

We have been told that a suction pump is needed in order to form a void; we have such a pump in the spinal column and the channels Ida and Pingala through which the creative energy rises to the brain. We have also been told that a dynamo is needed; we have that in our brains and strength of will. Finally in any technique, obviously there must be a generator; fortunately, our generator is the creative organs, sex, the sexual force.

Having the system and all the elements, we can form the Illuminating Void; the pump, the dynamo and the generator are the elements that we need in order to achieve the Illuminating Void in meditation. Only through the absolute Void can we get to know that which is real.

In fact, the Illuminating Void is produced because the creative energies flowing inwards from the outside, impregnating the Consciousness and eventually making it leave the ego and the body. Extracted from the ego as if out from a bottle, in the absence of ego and outside the physical body, the Consciousness undoubtedly goes into the Illuminating Void and receives the Tao.

Therefore, the creative energy combined with meditation serves to awaken the Consciousness. Unquestionably, it draws the Consciousness out from the ego and into absorption in the Illuminating Void.

Meditation combined with Tantrism is tremendous. HAM-SAH is the key...

– Samael Aun Weor

A *mantra* is a vocalization. Vocalization transmutes creative energy because the larynx is, as we have already stated, a sexual organ. To make one's body and soul fertile, the sexual energy must be conserved. Obviously if we conserve the sexual-creative energy without transmuting it, the result is nocturnal pollutions (wet dreams). Therefore it is a two step process. We conserve in order to transmute, thus it is the vibration of the fecund larynx that transmutes energy. One may perform pranayama as much as they wish, whether it is fifteen or forty minutes. The practice is absolutely marvelous. It is good to vocalize before and during meditation.

Vocalization is a normal act of sexuality. However, most of us only understand the negative aspect of the vocalization that pronounces itself during orgasm. It is very difficult to keep the larynx from not acting during intercourse, and the very thought of these negative types of vocalizations can bring lustful thoughts to our minds. Mantras are the diametrical opposite of the uncontrolled animal spastic vocalizations. A positive vocalization during the sacred chemical copula would be a mantra such as *IAO*. This mantra elevates the couple into ecstasy, but only when animal desire is transcended, thus allowing the Holy Spirit to enter into the heart of the couple made one. Animal desire is transcended when sensation-desire is transformed into sensation-willpower, in other words, when the transformation of sexual impressions successfully occurs and the orgasm is not reached. *IIIIII AAAAAA OOOOOO*, pronounced Eee, Ahhh, Ooo, while remembering God is an excellent practice of sexual transmutation. IAO is the name of God among the Gnostics.

TRANSMUTATION IS NOT REPRESSION

> Wanting to confine sex is like wanting to bottle up the sun. A man like this is the most abject slave of sex without any benefit or true pleasure. A man like this is an unhappy sinner. A woman like this is a sterile mule, a vile slave of that which she wants to enslave (sex).
>
> – Samael Aun Weor, *The Perfect Matrimony*

The sexual energy has an evolutionary curve and a devolutionary curve. When the sexual energy is in its evolution, it is a regenerative element, but when it devolves it becomes a degenerative element. If sexual energy is not used when it is evolving, it will begin to devolve, and what was once a regenerating element becomes a degenerating element because it has not been used in a timely fashion. This is like leaving fruit out too long on the table. Fruit becomes rotten if left out too long. In conclusion, the one who is attempting to muzzle the sex will eventually transform into something degenerate because their seeds will have become a rotten, and the result is a rotten brain.

This result is not overnight, it is something that occurs very slowly throughout many years. Likewise, the practice of sexual transmutation is not something that will transform one's self in a week or a month. People want to change without effort; some practice for one or two months and state that while transmutation might work for others, but it did not "work for me." This is arrogance. The effects of sexual transmutation are something that grows slowly within the person in time, like a tree growing from the mud of the earth. These studies are not for people of little or no patience.

When sexual energy is used within mechanical ways it creates mechanically. However transmutation is not something mechanical. Transmutation takes a conscious will. It is dynamic, fluid process that takes continuous effort and refinement.

To profane the sexual energy is to misuse it. Therefore, do not confuse this doctrine with celibacy. Celibacy is the denial of the sexual force. To repress the sexual force is like bottling up the sun. Very advanced masters can renounce the sexual act without abusing its energy because they transmute it perfectly through their soul. They have already become human, therefore they naturally transmute. However, the practice of celibacy without knowledge of transmutation is a crime. Those who do not provide any conduit for the energy of life to flow through damage their own psyche. Evidently, this is a major problem in many religions that have forgotten the science of transmutation. When we bring the sexual force into movement, but sublimate this force rather than expel it, the fuel of transformation is acquired.

Bring the creative energy into delightful movement by listening to or playing music, by writing poetry, creating art, by diligently solving the problems of work and family life, through vocalizations of sacred mantras, pranayama, meditation, through loving your inner being, your spouse, your family, and all the sentient beings of the world. This is sexual transmutation, yet of an inferior type. The superior type of sexual transmutation is the chaste-sexual act, where orgasm is refrained and the love between man and woman sublimates and transmutes the creative energy, giving birth to spiritual consciousness instead of engendering children and strengthening desire.

The elder brother of the 14th Dalai Lama says thus:

> The sexual act performed normally may give a slight notion of the nature of this higher consciousness, but more than that it cannot do, since the energy, instead of being trapped and put to use, is expended... creating a new physical body instead of spiritual consciousness.
>
> – Thubten Jigme Norbu

The history of all times affirms the doctrine of sexual transmutation. We know that it is White Tantra, Sexual Yoga, *Maithuna* of Buddhism, the Christian *Mystical Agape*, the *Chastity* of Medievalism, the *Baking* of Alchemists, etc., etc. Intellectual ignoramuses, those who have only educated the intellect, deny that sexual transmutation is the basis of all religion. When we attempt to search about these matters of sex, all we find is a false interpretation that is taken for reality. All of these matters upon sex have become lost like the Midnight Sun because the self-sufficient, boastful vagabonds of the intellect do not know the Midnight Sun (the Father). Deplorably, this is how the most holy rite of husband, wife and God, THE HOLY MA-TRI-MONY is converted into a facilitator of carnal passion, orgies, prostitution, etc. The ignorance surrounding sex has transformed this society into the Great Harlot. Instead of understanding the mysteries of Eden (sex), we have become prostitutes knowing nothing more than the vain sensual pleasure that can be extracted from the divine act when it is profaned through animal desire.

ONLY SEX CREATES AND DESTROYS

Obviously, the psychological aggregates themselves cannot destroy their own existence. The ego did not self-manifest itself and it also cannot destroy itself. Therefore, how was it created? What can destroy it? Has anything ever been created without sexual energy?

Two facts must be comprehended:

1. Sexual energy is the only energy which creates and destroys. This is why the creator-destroyer in Hindu theology is Shiva-Shakti, the Divine Couple in erotic, but chaste, embracement.
2. A *harmonious* creation and destruction can only take place through the Law of Three. Physically speaking this is man, woman, and the Holy Spirit (Shiva).

The sum of life and death is absolutely sexual in nature. Sexuality is Shiva and his wife Shakti, in Hinduism they are the creator and destroyer, often posed in chaste sexual union. This is because sex is both a creator and a destroyer. Death, itself, is nothing more than the movement of energy into a different form. The sexual energy is the only 'thing' with the ability reduce our psychological aggregates to dust. Therefore, if one is interested in real and integral self-change, they must work with the sexual energy, the creative energy. There is no other way. This is the exact, precise and definitive reason why religions throughout the world all state that one must make use of the sexual energy wisely, and that there are detrimental repercussions for the abuse of sex.

Those who abuse the sexual energy crystallize, *create*, within themselves, certain *infrahuman* (animal) qualities known as psychological aggregates, or simply the ego. These are formations of the outcome of the modification of the sexual energy, because sexual energy does not only create physically, but also emotionally, mentally, and spiritually. When we understand that one's psychology is founded in one's sexuality, then we can better understand that the qualities of energies in our sexual brain are directly related with the qualities of energies in our emotional and intellectual brains. Furthermore, the elaboration of all thought and emotion is directly linked to creative-sexual energy.

This is why creative-sexual energy is the universal determinative energy of life.

The author of this book understands that what is being stated here regarding the sexual energy can been seen as absurd or scandalous to the reader. This is due to a very rudimentary, incipient, or incorrect understanding of religion, psychology, endocrinology, tantrism, etc., etc. Let us struggle to find the truth, because it is only the truth that shall set one free. In no way must one believe in these matters. These matters are not something to accept or reject. Regarding the sexual transmutation, the only way to know is through action: one must experience it.

Sexual Energy Exists On All Levels

There are infinite degrees of sexual energy. There is atomic sexual energy in electricity and magnetism. The atom itself is sustained through the magnetic-sexual attraction of electrons and protons. The destructive aspect of this same principle force can manifest itself through atomic and thermonuclear bombs which not only destroy life, but infect the three dimensional world with the maleficent radiation of the inferior dimensions. There is sexual energy in the plasma of distant nebulas which are birthing new cosmos, and in the darkness of black holes. There are different modifications of the sexual energy in the sex, emotion, and intellect. Rarified and what we can call super-rarified sexual energy enlivens the spirit and all of the superior facilities of the soul.

The mind, as anything, is the outcome of the creative-sexual energy. In order to change the psychology in a truly radical sense one must work with the sexual-creative energy. The mind can label itself and recondition itself, it can observe itself and become more aware of itself. Nevertheless, without God, the Creator, nothing can be created or destroyed, and those who work without regard to divinity will fail totally in these studies. Therefore, it is necessary to cultivate the heart; love; faith. Some people work for self-development without the love for mankind in their heart, and without concern for God. There are psychologists who attempt to change the mind without the power of God, and they only manage to replace one form of conditioning with another. The work of awakening the consciousness is impossible without the creative power of God.

The altar of God is the human body, and its sacrifice is the love of another. When the Man and Woman unite they become like Gods hovering over the Waters of Life. Blavatsky tells us quite frankly in *The Secret Doctrine* that Eden can be translated as *voluptuousness*. The tree in the center of "The Garden of Voluptuousness" is the sexual organs. Sex is something terribly important and the whole basis of Judeo-Christian tradition verifies this. The ritual of circumcision is a pact of chastity. The Bible speaks of vows taken while placing one's hand on the thigh, or below the thigh. This is the sex. Sacred phallism reigns universal, yet never is its profound nature understood. According to the Book of Revelation, on the thigh of the White Rider, whose name is the Word of God, is written the following: THE KING OF KINGS AND LORD OF LORDS.

JEHOVAH IS A CREATOR GOD

The Hindu Lingham[1] is identical with "Jacob's Pillar" – most undeniably. But the difference, as said, seems to consist in that the esoteric significance of the Lingham was too truly sacred and metaphysical to be revealed to the profane and the vulgar; hence its superficial appearance was left to the speculations of the mob. [...]
Both India and Egypt had and have their sacred lotuses, symbolic of the same "Holy of Holies" – the Lotus growing in the water, a double feminine symbol – the bearer of its own seed and root of all. Viraj and Horus are both male symbols, emanating from androgyne Nature, one from Brahma and his female counterpart Vach, the other, from Osiris and Isis – never from the One infinite God. In the Judaeo-Christian systems it is different. Whereas the lotus, containing Brahma, the Universe, is shown growing out of

---

[1] A stylized phallus that represents Shiva, the Holy Spirit.

> Vishnu's navel, the Central point in the Waters of Infinite Space, and whereas Horus springs from the lotus of the Celestial Nile – all these abstract pantheistic ideas are dwarfed and made terrestrially concrete in the Bible: one is almost inclined to say that in the esoteric they are grosser and still more anthropomorphic, than in their exoteric rendering. Take as an example the same symbol, even in its Christian application; the lilies in the hand of the Archangel Gabriel (Luke i. 28). [...]
>
> [H]ow could those who invented the stupendous scheme now known as the Bible [...] feel reverence for such a phallic symbol [...] as Jehovah is shown most undeniably to be in the Kabalistic works? How could anyone worthy of the name of a philosopher, and knowing the real secret meaning of their "pillar of Jacob," their Bethel, oil-anointed phalli, and their "Brazen Serpent," worship such a gross symbol, and minister unto it, seeing in it their "Covenant" – the Lord Himself! Let the reader turn to Gemara Sanhedrin and judge. As various writers have shown, and as brutally stated in Hargrave Jennings' Phallicism (p. 67) "We know from the Jewish records that the Ark contained a table of stone ... that stone was phallic, and yet identical with the sacred name Jehovah ... which written in unpointed Hebrew with four letters, is J-E-V-E or JHVH (the H being merely an aspirate and the same as E). This process leaves us the two letters I and V (in another form U); then if we place the I in the U we have the 'Holy of Holies'; we also have the Lingha and Yoni and Argha of the Hindus, the Isvara and 'supreme Lord'; and here we have the whole secret of its mystic and arc-celestial import, confirmed in itself by being identical with the Linyoni of the Ark of the Covenant."
>
> – H. P. Blavatsky, *The Secret Doctrine*

Bluntly stated, Jehovah is a creator god and in no way could one divorce creation from its sexual nature. The Arc of the Covenant is sex. But not sex in the way it is performed today. In the past, in order to be instructed in the mysteries of sacred sexuality one had to reduce their "I" or "Satan" significantly. This is because the teachings of sex are very powerful and can be manipulated slightly in order to give nefarious results. The public unveiling of the Secret Doctrine, the Esoteric Philosophy, has occurred because the state of society has become so dire that the dangers of publicly teaching this doctrine no longer outweigh the dangers of its adulterations – and such adulterations do exist in abundance on the shelf of any bookstore.

Never profane the sexual energy unless you intend to spit on face of God himself. The Hebraic letters of Jehovah, Iod-Hei-Vau-Hei, can be kabbalisticly synthesized in the following way: Man-Woman-Phallus-Uterus. The greatest power lies within the sexual virility. The sexual energy is the foundation of all change, both physically and psychologically.

The Spirit of God lives within the sexual energy. Transforming, sublimating, transmuting, this energy within one's self is what leads to that which we call happiness, love, and spiritual abundance. When one prays to God with a truly open heart, to the point they are even crying with an overabundance of joy, then this person has already performed an act of sexual transmutation. When a couple honestly loves each other in a spontaneous and natural way, then an act of sexual transmutation has taken place. When the mind is quieted and one is overcome in rapture or Samadhi, sexual transmutation was the root of that experience.

All the creative genius of Leonardo Da Vinci, Dante Alighieri, Beethoven, Homer, Richard Wagner, Nikola Tesla, to name just a few, were all the outcome of the transmutation of creative energy. All of these men were devoutly religious in their own way and their creative genius is the outcome of harnessing the "Spirit of God" within themselves, which in the "normal" person is usually thrown away or rejected as something unimportant.

THE AQUARIAN SYNTHESIS-RELIGION

We can find countless schools in the East, and even some that exist in the West, which teach how to transmute the sexual energy, and one will progress accordingly, but these schools do not reveal, or have forgotten the most powerful methods to work with the consciousness. The essential ethical and moral teachings of religion, the teachings summarized in this work, have been known to the world since the beginning of civilization. What is unique about the doctrine spoken of here is its clear sexual nature.

The true spiritual schools that do not speak openly concerning sexual transmutation are foundational and related to the past. These schools are wonderful and necessary. They perform a service to humanity, yet, because they do not teach sexual magic they are limited in comparison to the doctrine taught on these pages. These schools cannot bring the student to the Final Liberation.

The Gnosis of Kali Yuga, the Aquarian Synthesis-Religion as taught by Samael Aun Weor, is entirely revolutionary to the ways of the past. The Aquarian Synthesis-Religion led by Samael Aun Weor guides the aspirant from the beginning all the way to the Final Liberation.

To make a comparison: The tools of the foundational schools can be likened to a hatchet. The Aquarian Synthesis-Religion in comparison hands the student a rather large doubled headed axe. Both tools use the same principle to get the work done, but obviously one performs the job done more efficiently, with much more power. Likewise, one has to know how to use an axe correctly in order not to cause more harm than good.

Obviously, these matters are very serious. These studies are not recommended for the "curious cat." These studies are recommended for the astute, temperate, and the enduring aspirants who devoutly wish to remove their suffering. This is because those who sincerely enter into the esoteric philosophy sign a Faustian pact.

The Serious Nature of the Faustian Pact

As the story goes, Faust made a deal with Lucifer. If he could defeat Lucifer he would gain the divine knowledge, and if not, Lucifer would have his soul. Lucifer is something within our own inner being. He is a reflection of God, an "Angel" who carries out God's will. Those of you who are scandalized by this affirmation must read the Book of Job, that book contains a lot of wisdom of how Lucifer works.

Lucifer is divine, yet we have transformed him into something perverse, and we have made him suffer endlessly. This is why Lucifer is crying in Dante's poem; Lucifer wishes to rise again, yet because he lives within us, he is suffering. Lucifer is the bearer of light ("luci" is *light*, "fer" is *to carry*, as in "ferry") that lives within the depths of each one of our spirits, he is the Morning Star, which is Venus, which is Love, yet we have made him perverse, and now he suffers.

The will of our inner spirit is to know itself, and it knows itself through its creation. Remember, creation is sexual. The creation of the human being, the true man, is necessary for the spirit to know himself. It knows Itself through an animal, It understands Its creation through animal sexuality, but It must also know Itself, which is creation, in a superior way through human sexuality. The spirit also wants to know Itself through super-human sexuality, which is the Love of the Verb of Christ, the Logos, and even beyond this, things beyond our conception. This is how man is exalted by God.

Lucifer plays his role of tempter, because the only way to achieve human sexuality is through human virtue. Virtues are something created, manifested, crystallized. A virtue is born through the triumph of temptation, and Lucifer is the tempter. Every virtue one has is the outcome of the work of Lucifer. Every virtue is the outcome of the modifications of sexual virility; a virtue is a psychological creation, a way of being. Lucifer has the light, and when you overcome temptation, you then receive that light, which means that you awaken your consciousness: you become enlightened.

The story of Lucifer and Faust are rarely understood correctly. If Faust fails, he fails the temptations of Lucifer and the very tools he needed to succeed become the very cause of his failure. The aspirant ends up living the drama of Faust. Thus, Jesus was tempted in the desert, and he succeeded. Job also succeeded.

Adam and Eve did not succeed. Adam and Eve represent all of humanity.

What is Happiness?

Few today have the urge to know their own self, and therefore they will have no urge to achieve human sexuality, no urge to achieve human virtuosity. What is criminal however, are those people who know in their hearts what they are longing for, yet do not follow with action. Perhaps it is good to reflect and count how many elderly people we know of that are truly and genuinely happy. It then becomes outstandingly clear that nothing really amounts in ordinary life, other than death. It seems the best thing that happens is acceptance of the harsh reality: disappointment, evilness, suffering and pain, intermingled with some periods where these things happen to be absent. In no way does the common lifestyle actually triumph over the problems of life. In no way can one say with any honesty that society is showing the didacticism for authentic happiness. People claim to the four winds they are happy, but the reality is seen when they transform into an angry or hurt person the second you say one or two unkind words to them. Psychological slavery is not happiness.

Regeneration and Degeneration

All that present culture knows is the external because it is degenerate. All that we are taught is the external because society has imprisoned itself within the first three dimensions of space due to the degeneration of the senses. In consequence it is no surprise that we aspire only to the external attributes. How can we blame anyone but ourselves? We are degenerates because we grow in a degenerate society. Depending upon how it is modified, sexual energy, being The Creator, the generator, has exactly two outcomes: degeneration and regeneration. Therefore, because we modify the sexual energy in a negative way, it has produced the degeneration of not only our physical senses, but our supra-senses. Accordingly, only the sexual energy, modified in a positive fashion, can reverse degeneration. Everyone can try all they wish to become a better person, but they will fail if they continue to modify the sexual energy in a fashion that is not conductive for the liberation of the consciousness.

Pure & Empirical Knowledge

> It is one of the commonest of mistakes to consider that the limit of our power of perception is also the limit of all there is to perceive
>
> – C. W. Leadbeater

> Esoteric science is the science of what takes place esoterically, in the sense that it is perceived not outside in nature but where one's soul turns when it directs its inner being toward the spirit. Esoteric science is the opposite and counterpart of natural science.
>
> – Rudolf Steiner

Believing themselves to already know everything, there are skeptics do not accept what is said this book. They believe to already contain the whole of wisdom concerning "God" and "religion." They believe that they have knowledge, or the method to gain the knowledge of the whole of creation, of the infinite. Regardless of their statements, in reality they only have empirical knowledge.

Materialists may chuckle in amusement when we state that the esoteric philosophy is a science. Every science contains empirical knowledge but many do not believe what the esoteric philosophy states because they do not accept pure knowledge - which is precisely the esoteric science's distinguishing characteristic.

The incredulous say that occult powers - what are called *siddhis* in the East - such as traveling in the subtle body, clairvoyance, telepathy, the power over the elements, recollection of previous lives, reading the history of nature, etc., are nothing more than the fantasy or mental illness of religious cranks and charlatans. There is a degree of truth to these because most who claim these powers are either mistaken or is attempting fool others. Nevertheless, it is unfortunate that these former types - the "soothsayers" and "merchants of souls" - are unjustly grouped together with luminaries such as St. Paul or Joan of Arc.

One who gains occult powers, in the true and healthy way, does so by awakening consciousness, through intense efforts of charity, sanctity, and chastity (transmutation). Clairvoyance is nothing more than clear consciousness: awakened consciousness purified of desire. Those who are looking for attention, to be on television and on the cover of many books, looking to gain power over others, are obviously not awakening consciousness. Usually these people who claim to have such powers are full of ego, and if they truly have powers, they have the power of the awakened ego, not the awakened consciousness.

It is extremely sad to state that the vast majority of "psychics" should learn how to be silent until they remove their ego. Until this occurs, their sight is distorted. The lives of many people have been filled with tears due to such people. Those who develop positively always have extreme humility and charity. Charging money for healing or anything similar that is what the Bible calls "selling doves," and it is against The Law.

Amongst the surging popularity of dialectical materialism, H. P. Blavatsky founded the Theosophical Society in 1875. Blavatsky actually demonstrated her powers to many people, and through incredibly erudite works such as *Isis Unveiled* and *The Secret Doctrine* the Theosophical Society was globalized. The genius of Blavatsky is quite outstanding. Albert Einstein's niece stated that a dog-eared and greatly annotated *The Secret Doctrine* was the book beside her uncle's death bed. Nevertheless, many materialistic scientists claim that Blavatsky was a crank. In fact, there exist entire books to "prove" that she was a charlatan. Of course, they ignore statements in *The Secret Doctrine* concerning the dual nature of light which precludes, by several decades, the official acceptance of the same fundamental idea in the sphere of exoteric science.

Lamentably, Blavatsky is still very much surrounded by the rumors and slander of her critics. There are modern Buddhists scholars who totally dismiss Blavatsky's works of Buddhism. They must ignore that she was the first person to give access to the west portions of the sacred and profound Kalachakra tantric literature.

It is obvious that Blavatsky had access to the occult doctrine. Blavatsky was a scientist in the fullest sense of the word and her books are the outcome of something far superior to what we understand as empirical observation. Perhaps critics do not know that the 14th Dali Lama himself states about her work *The Voice of the Silence*: "I believe that this book has strongly influenced many sincere seekers and aspirants to the wisdom and compassion of the Bodhisattva Path."

C. W. Leadbeater and Annie Besant were other clairvoyant Theosophists surrounded by controversy. Leadbeater's critics constantly slander him, stating was an abuser of children and taught them masturbation. In reality he taught them a technique of sexual transmutation called the *vajroli mudra*, which is the absolute opposite of masturbation. Leadbeater's action provoked so much controversy that he was forced to leave the Theosophical Movement.

Certainly, he paid dearly for teaching something what could not be taught publicly at that time. Few people even today can understand the true meaning of transmutation, in the previous centuries the public was simply not ready for it in the former, Piscean Era. Luckily Besant reinstated Leadbeater to the Theosophical Society some years later.

Pure knowledge comes from that space which exists beyond the mind's thoughts and reasoning. It is beyond what we commonly call mind itself. Nevertheless, that which is experienced can be brought into the mind. The esoteric philosophy states that pure knowledge is attained through methods of synthesis yoga. Unfortunately, official science has mostly rejected this notion.

Today, the university student is forced to sip from the pungent cup of theories. These theories make their creators unbearable and self-sufficient: they feel as if they really have knowledge, when they really have nothing of value at all. They boast of sapience inside their Temple of Theories, calling it a University, but in no way does the contemporary university contain the wisdom of the universe. Theosophy, especially today, is also filled with people who know nothing but theories. Most Theosophists do not practice synthesis yoga because they believe their mystical theories will evolve their consciousness in a mechanical fashion.

Many Theosophists, like the students in many other highly regarded spiritual schools, hate sex. They find sex to be crude, animalistic and disgusting. The topics of tantrism and sexual transmutation frighten them. This is the unfortunate outcome of the Piscean Era. In this previous Era of the Fish the topic of sex was intensely hidden. The methods of the Piscean Schools are to stay single, meditate on the ego, and devote one's self to a spiritual life. The sexual teachings were hidden to all but the most adept. The Aquarian Era is upon us now, and the Aquarian Era is entirely sexual. So today, in the Aquarian Era, we can speak of sexual transmutation publicly, and we can work with transforming our sexual nature by using the sexual act itself. The unfortunate outcome of our current Era however is the profound sexual degeneration found today.

The reason so much controversy surrounds Theosophy is unfortunately because these clairvoyants, although possessing superior facilitates, where not perfect. There are many mistakes made by Leadbeater and Besant, but perhaps nothing was more profound than the Krishnamurti case.

Leadbeater noticed a boy, Jiddu Krishnamurti, with an outstanding aura on a beach in India. Because of his beautiful and pure aura, believed that Krishnamurti was the reincarnation of the Lord Savior and the Society publicly heralded him as such. Lamentably, Leadbeater and Besant did not understand what Krishnamurti was: although he was a man of a high degree of awakened consciousness, he was not the Lord Savior Christ of the Word. The Theosophical Society had already partitioned itself, but this incident in particular caused Rudolf Steiner to start a new movement called Anthroposophy.

Although Krishnamurti was not the Savior of the World, a profound wisdom flows from his writings that in no way could be feigned. Thus Leadbeater indeed found a spiritual teacher, but he did not correctly interpret his sight and made a terrible mistake (however it was Besant that was mainly responsible for the pompous announcement). According to Samael Aun Weor, if Krishnamurti had not been traumatized as a boy (by being heralded as the Second Coming), he would have given an even more profound doctrine for us to study. Krishnamurti made mention of occult powers but never made the mistake of H. B. P. in displaying them to others.

Let us conclude this story with two transcendental axioms:

1. The superior facilities of man are divine, and the improper use of such powers cause great suffering.
2. Great exaltation is preceded by terrible humiliation.

Rudolf Steiner did not agree with Leadbeater and this was a principle reason for his departure from the Theosophical Movement. Steiner is another certifiable genus and clairvoyant. Rudolf Steiner's works have a Christian esotericism, while traditional Theosophy contains a Buddhist and Hindustani esotericism.

Samael Aun Weor was physically incarnated from 1917 to 1977. He was born with an awakened consciousness of a high degree of objective reasoning, and therefore understood that it was necessary for him to develop a strong intellectual culture in order to deliver a doctrine of synthesis in order to help humanity. Thus, he states in his work *The Three Mountains* that in his youth he studied entire libraries of occultism, religion, philosophy, ancient wisdom, etc. This, in complement with his study of his previous lives and the entire history of nature he provided unfathomable resources of wisdom. He began his public life in 1950 with the initial printing of *The Perfect Matrimony*, which is the first ever truly public teaching of sexual magic and sexual transmutation.

The reaction polarized those who read it into either great veneration or contempt for the author, with the latter population arising from a variety of factors. Firstly, the Catholic Church denounced the book entirely, and at one point even incarcerated Samael Aun Weor for "healing the sick without permission." Secondly, those occultists who jealously guarded the Arcanum A.Z.F. (sexual magic) did not want the public to have the knowledge due to their Piscean traditions. Third, the many infra-sexuals who existed that hated the idea of sexual magic, because they either cannot accept anything but fornication, or because they reject sex altogether as something animalistic and disgusting.

Samael Aun Weor delivered the most potent and practical doctrine to acquire direct knowledge: gnosis. In fact, there are so many different practices and techniques the student is given that he can easily become overwhelmed. Samael Aun Weor writes about many different fantastic things, yet, he asserts that the real function of the doctrine is only manifested when the student directly experiences them. He clearly stated that he was not looking for believers or followers, just people to awaken their consciousness and experience the transcendental realities normally unknown to mundane existence. Entire droves of students would flock to his presence, and just as many would leave his movement because they did not like to hear what he was actually saying. This is because Samael's doctrine is very radical, very direct, and very potent.

Unfortunately, some students of Samael Aun Weor felt it was necessary to proclaim that they were the successors of his doctrine. Many "Masters" have appeared, claiming to teach his doctrine, but in reality they distort it and fool their students. Therefore, the reader must be very careful, for merchants of souls exist that will take advantage of those who are naïve. No "successor" of Samael Aun Weor is needed, because Samael Aun Weor is still very active in the internal worlds, guiding his students and helping anyone who asks for it. Any student who learns how to consciously project themselves in the astral body can speak to Samael Aun Weor face to face. Anyone who wishes to be aided in their spiritual pursuits can ask for help, and they will receive it if the supplication is sincere.

We can divide the public exposure of esotericism into three categories. First, the introduction to the general public regarding fundamental concepts such as: karma, reincarnation, Kabbalah, alchemy, the superior worlds, and the fundamental principles that unite all religions. One must understand that prior to Theosophy, karma and reincarnation were topics virtually unknown to the western world. Theosophy was the introduction of these topics, and therefore its application is mostly intellectual.

Later, schools such as Anthroposophy and The Fourth Way appeared that taught the basic methods of how to apply this wisdom. They are good and necessary schools; however, ultimately, they are incomplete because while they speak much about the mind and the heart, they say very little about the sex, and what they do say is quite ambiguous. Therefore, the doctrine Samael Aun Weor delivered (approximately 75 books and thousands of lectures in the span of 27 years), is just the culmination of what began in the 1800's.

It is interesting to contemplate that even though all the material produced by these schools fills many walls of bookshelves, all of it is merely "esoteric kindergarten," it just the crumbs of the true bread of wisdom. Real esotericism is found in the internal worlds. This is where pure knowledge, objective knowledge reigns, and all the contradictory theories wash away into a unified, living reality.

It is not science that the esoteric philosophy opposes for as we have already mentioned the esoteric philosophy is science. Rather, the problem stems from materialism. There are philosophical materialists and practical materialists. The former are more difficult to find today, yet the latter are found everywhere. They claim to be religious, to be spiritual, yet in their practical lives they live according to materialism. To believe in spirituality is meaningless if one lives materialistically. To live materialistically is not qualified simply by owning many things, it is whether or not one is attached to these things. Someone poor with few material items can still be materialistic.

Materialists have formed a very scintillating logic that hypnotizes many people into believing that all phenomena begin with physical matter. Materialists have a very firm belief that the mind is within the physical brain. Materialistic science teaches that consciousness arrives from the functions of the brain. Unfortunately, this is because materialistic theories, especially those ultra-modern, degenerate views of sexuality discussed throughout this book, certifiably destroy the brain and all the nervous systems.

A degenerate brain has a limited empirical scope, a *skeptikos*: thus they become a "skeptic." A degenerate brain cannot observe the superior worlds. Someone who cannot observe the subtle dimensions can only believe in them. When a belief contradicts what has been observed the outcome is a rejection of that belief, especially when the observer does not know his own ignorance.

Today's skeptic is usually one who has done a lot of reading, someone who is "smart," someone who has the "scientific" explanation to everything. They are pleased when they bedazzle one with their use of scientific jargon. They believe that by identifying and labeling something that they have understood it.

Obviously, there have been in history many intelligent people who did not abuse the intellect. The problem begins when confusion between intelligence and intellectualism exists. Let us be perfectly clear when stating that the intellect in itself has no intrinsic value. Intellectualism is just a product of the personality, a product of conditioning, of memories and of time, a way of speaking, a way of acting, a way of opining, repeating, mannerisms, etc. Authentic intelligence is not any form of conditioning or learning, it is absolutely conscious, unique and divine.

Skeptics become increasingly refined at their trade with the more theories they know. Then, they can speak and write a lot about theories, spend time debating, comparing, etc., etc. Skeptics never accept anything when one presents it as the truth, because the skeptic knows that he can never approach truth. The skeptic indeed has never understood truth because skeptics only know their antithetical opinions. Skeptics lack discrimination, they have no idea of objective realities, only what is logical, what can be argued, what can be justified. Skeptics even enjoy being called a skeptic, as if it is a virtue!

Skepticism, the battle of antithetical ideas, breeds nothing but confusion and ultimately insanity. A brain stuffed full of undigested ideas breaks down and degenerates: by theorizing upon everything, the skeptic becomes a know-it-all nihilist. An undigested idea is confusion: a Thesis and its conflicting Antithesis with no resolving Synthesis. Comprehension is the synthesis or the reconciliation of opposites.

A concept cannot solve a problem. A theory cannot resolve other theories. How can we manage a way out of our labyrinth of theories with more theory? Theory leads to more theory, confusion, complication, mechanization, suffering, that is all. The antidote to suffering is knowledge, but not intellectual knowledge, not knowledge from the mind, but direct or pure knowledge. Intellectual knowledge is the knowledge of the subject, and it therefore subjective and fallible but objective, pure knowledge is the knowledge of the object and it is perfect.

Being trapped within the subject (the mind), the skeptic only has the idea, the theory, the concept of objective knowledge in which by virtue of their own ignorance he ultimately rejects.

Believing that the intellect is the Self, the skeptic takes intellect far out of its proper place. In reality, the intellect is not the Self, and even if it sounds impossible, the "I", the ego, or what we commonly view as our identity is also not the Self.

In order to gain a glimpse at what exists beyond the mind, there is a specific science one must follow in order to gain direct knowledge. The first step is to completely give up the notion of being perfect, ineffable, or a "good" or "normal" person.

Glancing at all the books he has read, the skeptic believes himself to be wise and accomplished; remembering all the time spent in school and the degrees and titles earned, he stupidly believes himself to be important and worthy of praise. Humility is impossible for the skeptic.

Skeptics believe that through time they will become wise, intelligent, but in reality they only become wretched intellectuals, who nurture themselves from the bitter cup of theory and doubt, who are unable to see anything without comparing and contrasting it with other theories stuffed in their heads. It is better to drink the manna of God, to achieve divine inebriation by sipping from the cup of meditation. This is only possible with a total transformation, a complete revolution of the consciousness.

> Accepting or rejecting any doctrine or concept reveals a lack of mental maturity.
>
> When we reject or accept something, it is because we have not understood it.
>
> Whenever understanding exists, accepting or rejecting is unnecessary.
>
> The mind that believes, the mind that does not believe and the mind that doubts is an ignorant mind.
>
> The path of wisdom does not lie in believing, not believing or doubting.
>
> The path of wisdom consists in inquiring, analyzing, meditating, experimenting.
>
> Truth is the unknown from moment to moment. Truth has nothing to do with what one believes or stops believing, neither does it have anything to do with skepticism.
>
> Truth is not a matter of accepting or rejecting, it is something to experience, live and understand.
>
> – Samael Aun Weor, *Fundamentals of Gnostic Education*

Materialism is founded on self-supporting principles, a circular logic. Someone who believes in materialism obviously has never experienced the Emptiness. This leaves one to form a materialistic ideology which, by consequence, leads to activities ensuring they will never experience that which they already do not believe in. What is even worse is they ignore and label those who testify their pure knowledge. Materialistic philosophy is a circular judgment based on limited empirical observation. Nevertheless, when we speak about occult phenomena, they say, "Those things are all in your brain, they are not real." These foolish unfortunates know nothing of their own consciousness and yet they believe they understand other's minds with clarity. What can we do in front of such invincible ignorance? Those who wish to reject, will reject it, and those who wish to accept, can accept it, and those who wish to know for themselves will work for it.

> I know that there are still many men in the world who are so far behind the times as to deny the existence of such powers, just as there are still villagers who never seen a railway train. I have neither time nor space to argue with such invincible ignorance; I can only refer enquirers to my book on Clairvoyance, or to scores of book by other authors on the same subject. The whole case has been proved hundreds of times and no one who is capable of weighing the value of evidence can any longer be in doubt.
>
> – C. W. Leadbeater

The yogic techniques of the East expand the scope of empirical investigation and open the door of objective knowledge, leaving all theories behind. Materialistic people however completely reject the exercises found in this book precisely because they *believe* it to be false. This is why such clairvoyants are not considered in official science or theology. It is not because they were methodically unscientific, but rather because society has a degenerate brain and it believes that empirical observation reveals a totalitarian objective reality which lies exclusively within the first three dimensions.

Regrettably, people are not concerned in anything but what they already believe in. Science believes it already knows what knowledge is when in reality it only knows the most rudimentary techniques of empirical observation. Quantum mechanics is proving that our ideas of matter are not as they seem. Nevertheless many scientists will readily reject the very idea of transmutation of sexual energy, occult powers, etc., because it does not fit within their empirical observations. They reject pure knowledge without ever attempting to access it.

To blame someone for not believing in something they have never observed would be unjust. Therefore it is good to note that the esoteric science does not work with blind belief. What is necessary is reserved belief, a working belief, an "open mind" as stated in the beginning of this book. Let there be no fear in rejecting official science when ample evidence is against it, because what is considered impossible today is "scientific fact" tomorrow. This is the way science creeps along. This is also not to say that modern official science does not have merit. Materialism and expert cynicism are the problems. There is much technological advancement that helps us, but there are far more technological things in this world that are destroying us psychologically. Yet, because it is not destroying our physical bodies, we believe them to be of no harm at all.

The ego will make a lot of convincing logic to prevent someone from following out the instruction of the esoteric science. This is because the ego does not wish to die. We must experience these greater realities things first hand because logic is an inferior tool to direct experience. How can we directly experience these things? The answer is exclusively through awakening consciousness.

The Liberation of Good & Evil

It is through not understanding, not realizing four things, that I, Disciples, as well as you, had to wander so long through this round of rebirths. And what are these four things? They are the Noble Truth of Suffering, the Noble Truth of the Origin of Suffering, the Noble Truth of the Extinction of Suffering, the Noble Truth of the Path that leads to the Extinction of Suffering.

– Buddha Gautama Shakyamuni

My friends, everything in this world in which we live is temporary; ideas are temporary, persons pass away, things pass away. The only thing that is stable and permanent is the Being and the only reason for the Being to be is to be the Being itself.

– Samael Aun Weor

Good and evil are descriptors, that is, they describe the state of an object. Good and evil are not inherent as many erroneously believe, but rather opposing states of existence. Good, in the most practical sense, is something that is in order, in place, in harmony. Evil on the other hand is just the opposite; it is something out of place, out of order, out of harmony. For example, water in and of itself is neither good nor evil. Water that nourishes a biological organism is obviously a good thing. However, when the water of the Mississippi River floods it is certainly not good, for it is producing damage and a lot of suffering. Likewise, fire in your kitchen is good, yet that same fire burning down your kitchen is bad, or in other words, evil. Therefore the fire itself is not good or evil, but forms of fire are.

Any ego we possess in our interior psychological country is either good or evil. Obviously any ego of hatred, arrogance, pride or vanity is bad, but what can be said of good egos? Many people believe that if they destroy the ego that accomplishes work at the office, then one would no longer perform the duties required to obtain money, or a mother may think that if she removes the ego that travels to the grocery store then no one would exist to do the shopping. While these good egos may provide a service for ourselves and others, when they (the "good" egos) are removed it is obvious that the liberated consciousness takes their place. The liberated consciousness, through its own essential nature, always acts in a superior way than the consciousness trapped in the ego. Therefore the consciousness will always be a better worker than the ego of the office will ever be, it will always provide for the family in a genuine, pure and authentically loving manner, far beyond the mechanical, reactionary action of the ego.

There may be an ego of charity within us, and in this way we may give alms to someone on the street, however, if this unfortunate homeless person is an alcoholic and makes use of his money to support his vice, then what good has been done? That ego believes to have done well, yet in reality it has not. The ego does not know the truth, it only deals with appearances and it has no method of knowing the truth of the moment. Therefore the good ego is not "good" at all.

When the ego performs a deed of service, it believes to have sacrificed and has aided humanity, yet in reality the ego does not know sacrifice. Upon observation, it is evident that the ego always wants recognition for its "good" deeds, therefore when the ego performs its "deeds" it is looking for a payment, not of money, but as a pat on the back, a plaque or a medal, some type of recognition. It says, "Look at me, look at what I am doing, look how good I am, look how I have sacrificed." True sacrifice is action that is performed without any expectation whatsoever, which is something the ego can never do because its very existence is one of craving for that which it is fascinated with. In this example the "good" ego is fascinated with recognition. Service is one thing and the ego can do many good services, but only the awakened consciousness can perform sacrifice.

THE FOUR NOBLE TRUTHS

It is necessary to liberate ourselves from the confines of good and evil, from craving and aversion. The Buddha Gautama Shakyamuni taught a method to liberate the consciousness from good and evil. The Buddha said that life itself is dukkha, or suffering. He called this the First Noble Truth. Interestingly, many people disagree with the message of Buddha because they do not believe it. In reality though there is nothing to believe or reject because suffering is self-evident.

All forms of delusion are forms of suffering, and we are under the spell of many delusions. For example, one must come to realize that we are all under the delusion that we exist independent of the outside world. We think that we are a person and that our actions, thoughts and feelings are enclosed within our little world and that within our little world we are a king or queen to think and feel as we please, without any consequence to others whatsoever. We believe that the only action that causes repercussions is physical action, but reality is different because to think or to feel causes karma too.

People believe they can get away thinking of others in hateful manners, but all of that action results in karma, suffering. Therefore, what is in your head and in your heart is just as important as what you physically do in life. No action goes without its consequences, both good and evil, both physically and super-physically. Those who are interested in achieving liberation must sanctify their every thought, word and deed, which is only possible by liberating the consciousness trapped in good and evil.

All forms of delusion and ignorance are suffering and therefore anyone who states that they do not suffer only ignores their suffering, which in reality can only lead to more suffering.

Not knowing the exact reason for your existence in the universe is suffering.

Not having a clear idea of what is right and wrong in a particular moment is suffering, and choosing the wrong way is also suffering.

Inflicting pain in others lives because of ignorance is suffering, and not knowing the pain you cause in other's lives is also suffering.

Not knowing the moment when you will die is a form of suffering.

Being a slave to the impressions of life is suffering.

All desire is suffering.

It is clear that suffering exists within everyone, yet to comprehend this within the intimate depths of our own heart is something beyond a mere intellectual understanding of suffering.

To comprehend the state of suffering is a profound step to liberate one's self from suffering. To begin to see this state requires that one removes a bit of pride and a bit of shame, because we are proud of who we want to be and we are ashamed (secretly) of who we really are. The truth cannot arrive if pride or guilt is present for they are artifacts that distort the image of truth. Pride does not want to admit that it suffers, and the shame is the same pride but inverted.

Some may state that they neither contain pride nor guilt. Nevertheless, these same people are always those who have never self-observed their self and they have never meditated upon their self. Therefore, such statements are nothing more than flimsy rhetoric, and they do not resist an integral analysis.

When one accepts they have a psychology, one has begun to look for change. This opens the door to change, nevertheless, actual change requires much more. Meditation is the only way to see the psychological ego with any depth and integrity, thus those who wish to change must develop a routine of meditation.

The intellect is the first level of the mind, yet, the mind contains forty nine levels, therefore it obvious that in order to submerge into the depths of the subconsciousness it is necessary to meditate. It is necessary to search deep within the mind in order to comprehend the mind. It is necessary to comprehend the mind in order to have any chance to change the mind.

Change occurs through death of the old and birth of the new, therefore to change the mind is to achieve psychological death and alchemical rebirth. These two factors require the transmutation of energies.

Just as only a mechanic can change a machine, only the creative-sexual energy can change the mind. The machine cannot change its own self, what is required is the creator, the mechanic, and it is obvious that the essence of the Creator exists latently within the creative-sexual energy.

The Second Noble Truth we must understand is that nothing is permanent. Everything ends, everything changes, nothing continues forever, yet, because our mind is conditioned to certain cravings and aversions, we suffer when these changes occur. We dream because the mind is fascinated with certain impressions that it wishes to relive. The mind is bored with its own condition, and it dreams about conditions it believes is the antidote to its boredom, yet because all phenomena are impermanent the mind will never be finished with its boredom (suffering). It is ostensible that we are always looking for the *next* thing because we believe that the next thing will always be that one thing that gives us contentment. In reality, that next thing never brings happiness. The action of doing that next thing simply distracts us from our current psychological state. It allows us to ignore, to be ignorant of, our suffering.

The temporal aspect of man is that type of mental matter that clings to the craving and aversions of time. The mind is a form of energy that the consciousness, another form of energy, uses as a tool to order and label the universe around it. When the mind begins to crave and avert a certain label of a sensation, however mundane or complicated, then the element of time is produced within the mind. The element of time is personified as the ego. Hence the temporal phenomenon begins: we crave those sensations that give us pleasure and avert from those sensations that produce pain. Thus mind entrapped by the ego modifies the impressions of life in a negative fashion, which plant the seeds of suffering in our lives.

When the mind entrapped by the ego says, "I like this..." and "I do not want that...", then the mind is no longer able to do its job of making order of the experiences of the consciousness. Instead of *observing* and transforming the situations of Good and

Evil we just turn off the observing factor and *indulge* in aversion or craving. In other words, we ignore our experiences because we are too identified with what fascinates us. When we are craving or averting from things, when we are *identified* (identity, ego) with something, we are not *observing*, we are not *remembering*.

What is that we must remember? Remember that life is not how it appears to our hypnotized mind. Remember that everything, both pleasant and unpleasant, passes away. Remember your inner Being. Remember that every action has a result, and only by knowing the right actions in life can we find true happiness in life. Remember that only the awakened consciousness truly knows.

Third, we must comprehend that if everything ends, then even suffering must end. Therefore, fourth, there is a way to liberate one's self from suffering. Many messages have been delivered to humanity in order to achieve liberation. This liberation occurs when our delusions are destroyed and our karmic actions are exhausted. In order to destroy our delusions we meditate. In order to exhaust our karmic actions, we perform charity to humanity and enact the will of our interior Being. In order to liberate one's self from good and evil one must work with the Tree of Good and Evil that exists in the center of the Garden of Eden.

> Said the students again to Rabbi Simeon, since sexual desires and impulses were the cause of sin and transgression, wherefore do they exist?
>
> Said Rabbi Simeon: If the Holy One had not created a spirit of good that emanates from the active light, and spirit of evil that emanates from the passive light or darkness, man would have been a neutral ignorant kind of being unable to distinguish and contrast things essential to mental growth and spiritual development and progress; therefore was he created dual in nature, endowed with sexual feelings and rational functions, from the right and orderly discharge of which, or otherwise, he enjoys or suffers, as it is written: "See I have set before thee this day, life and good, death and evil" (limiter. xxx. 15).
>
> –Zohar, Genesis Ch. IV

Innocent ignorance is one thing and rational ignorance is another. We all possessed innocent ignorance until we ate the Fruit of Good and Evil, because we then became aware of Good and Evil, giving us the will to handle them as we see fit. What we now *choose* to do is ignore our experiences and to ignore the will of God and this leaves us in ignorance that is painful. This is a *rational ignorance* because we make the *decision* to ignore. The elementals of nature are innocent, they do not know good and evil thus they respond to good and evil in the same way, in a way that is collective and directed by greater intelligences. These greater intelligences either follow the will of God, such as Angels, or those who follow their ego-will, such as Demons. Thus, in this way can a magician, such as Moses, part the waters by commanding the elementals of the water accordingly. Yet, these same Undines (water elementals) will also follow the will of someone who has awakened their consciousness negatively (Demons) because the Undines are innocent of good and evil.

The intellectual animal has gained the knowledge of good and evil – the knowledge of the Gods – yet unlike God the intellectual animal avoids and seeks certain things and this is the cause of suffering. It is painful because we ignore and attempt to avoid the bad things in our psychology instead of understanding them. For example, we expect God to forgive us even though we ignore that we have not forgiven our enemies. We expect God to love us even though we hate our enemies. We expect justice when we falsely judge others. We expect kindness when we fill the lives of others with hateful thoughts, jealously, sarcasm, criticism, etc.

Beyond the intellectual animal is the realm of authentic human beings. A human being is one who knows the knowledge of good and evil yet does not crave or avert from either phenomena. The Bodhisattva is beyond good and evil because he makes use of his own incarnated intelligence to properly handle good and evil. When God is slandered, he is happy, and when one praises God, he is still the same, he is happy. Yet, when someone slanders us, we become ashamed of the truth, or atoms of anger animate us, and when one praises us, we fill with abominable pride and arrogance. Thus, we remain enslaved to our sufferings.

Kabbalistic Good and Evil

It is written, 'And God saw that the wickedness of men upon the earth was great and all the imaginations and thoughts of their hearts were only evil continually.' (Gen. vi., 5.)

Said Rabbi Jehuda: "'Thou art not a God that hath pleasure in wickedness, neither shall evil dwell with thee' (Ps. v., 5). Observe that he who gives way to the temper and suffers himself to be led and guided by it, defiles not only himself but also those with whom he comes into personal contact. As already stated, though the wickedness of the antediluvians was great and their evil deeds were many, yet was the Holy One unwilling to destroy them, but long-suffering towards them, notwithstanding, and their shameful propensities and heinous practices, of which it is written 'that they were only evil continually.' Their evil actions are denoted by the word (Ra) (pollution). Of Er, the eldest son of Judah, who was guilty of this sin; it is written that 'he was wicked in the sight of the Lord and the Lord slew him.'" (Gen. xxxviii., 7.)

Said Rabbi Jose: "Is not this sin synonymous with what is termed rashang (wickedness or wrongdoing)?"

"No," replied Rabbi Jehuda, "for rashang is applied to intentional evil ere it becomes an actuality, but Ra refers to him who defiles himself by the dissipation of his vital powers and thus gives himself up to the unclean spirit called Ra. He who thus renders himself impure will never attain unto the Divine Life nor behold the face of the Shekina, whose disappearance from the world previous to the deluge was owing to the vice termed Ra. Woe unto him who indulges in it, for he will never experience the joy of living in the presence of the Holy One, but will drag on through life as a degraded captive and miserable slave of Ra, the unclean spirit; so true are the words, 'The fear of the Lord leadeth to life, it bringeth peaceful nights free from visits of the impure spirit Ra' (Prov. xix., 23). And therefore it is written, 'Evil (Ra) shall not dwell with thee' (Ps. v., 4). Only the pure in life and thought and deed can say, 'Yea though I walk through the valley of the shadow of death, I will not be afraid of Ra, for thou art with me and causest me to dwell in the house of the Lord forever.'" (Ps. xxiii., 4-6.)

— The Zohar

"Ra refers to him who defiles himself by the dissipation of his vital powers..." Therefore, we can see that defilement is when one has given himself up to the unclean spirit called Ra, or evil. Evilness, properly understood, equivalent to the ritual or religious "uncleanliness," which in turn is equal to the expulsion of sexual energy from the human organism. Thus, all of the Judeo-Christian tradition must be reevaluated with this understanding. When this done, it becomes obvious that the original sin is the orgasm.

דעת טוב ורע

"DAATH TOB vey RA," Knowledge of Good and Evil. Spelled, right to left: Dalet-Ayin-Tav Teth-Vav-Beth Vav-Resh-Ayin. The last Vav, although appended directly to Resh-Ayin, means "and."

Of course, nobody is teaching the lay – certainly not the clergy or the scientists – how to transform sexual energy, because they do not know it themselves, and if they do, they keep it secret. The modern scribes (theological experts) and Pharisees (religious leaders) do not know the truth behind the baptism and the circumcision: these rituals are symbolic of a sexual pact to "cut" away sexual desire, and to wash away our filthiness, our sin, in the chrism of the transmuted waters.

Thus, although many are circumcised and baptized in accordance with tradition, no one is following in practice what these rituals symbolize, and therefore everyone is giving themselves up to the unclean spirit called "Ra." Ra means pollution or defilement in Hebrew, but is usually translated simply as *evil*.

The Tree of the Knowledge of Good and Evil must be understood as The Knowledge of Purity (Good) and Defilement (Evil). Society today still does not have knowledge of Good and Evil, because society still does not have dominance over its sexual energy or mental habits.

Man and woman are dominated by their sexual desires, and cannot control their urges, and therefore they are submitted to a torment much like Prometheus. What does mean? It means the fire of life is sex! Yet, it burns and torments the mind in the one who cannot wield its power intelligently.

The axis of Good and Evil in our body is the sexual organ, and it is through the use of sex that we increase our goodness or evilness in the kabbalistic sense. Graciously, if the intellectual animal does not wisely make use of its own axis of good and evil properly, the axis of good and evil that exists at the center of Earth will deal with those energies for him. This is how Earth eventually returns these souls to an original state of innocence. Unfortunately this process is very painful, much more painful than to deal with good and evil through one's own individual axis of good and evil (the sexual organs).

Thankfully, there is a limit to evil, and it is called Hell in Christianity, but also known as Tartarus, Avichi, Druj-Demana, Xibalba, Uffern, and many other names which are too abundant to list. Hell is the only way failed souls will stop being evil, the only way they will be liberated from their suffering. Yet, the path through Hell is very painful. Suffering increases, step by step, before the threshold is crossed. Each step painfully destroys the outer shells of the soul, which is the ego, yet at the termination of this process, the Essence of the soul emerges as an innocent, purified Elemental.

When the Earth transforms the energies for us in Hell there is no knowledge gained from it, however when we self-transform the energies we gain wisdom. Therefore, there are two paths: The Lunar Path and the Solar Path. The Lunar Path is to be "recycled" by Earth, to eventually be free of ego and return to THAT which we came from, but without wisdom. The Solar Path is to deal with the forces of good and evil within one's own self, to become a manager of the forces of the universe, in other words, to become a God. The Solar Path is the path of Gods.

The Battle of Opposites

> Joy and sadness, pleasure and pain, good and bad, triumph and failure; these constitute the battle of the opposites upon which the "I" is founded.
>
> – Samael Aun Weor

Good and Evil are the archetypical opposites that one must overcome. To identify with good is to become what is called in the Bible a Pharisee. To identify with evil is to become what is called in the Bible a Sadducee. These groups existed in history, yet the message about them contained in the Bible is allegorical. Jesus states that we should not accept the leavened bread of the Pharisees and the Sadducees. The bread itself is the Wisdom, the Doctrine, the Dharma, yet the leaven is the corruption that the Pharisees and the Sadducees add to the wisdom.

Remember the three minds: the sensual mind, the intermediate (mystical) mind, and the inner mind. The first mind elaborates the data of the external sensory perceptions and therefore cannot know the truth. The second mind is the receptacle of metaphysical and religious beliefs, which are also not the truth. The third mind only functions within the awakened consciousness, thus, it can know the truth. The third mind, the inner mind, is the way to know God.

The modern "Sadducees" are the practical and philosophical secular materialists who are totally incredulous to anything beyond their sensual perceptions. They operate in the sensual mind and oppose those who operate in the intermediate mind or the interior mind because they do not understand these minds. Many scientists, academics and intellectuals fall into this category.

The "Pharisees" operate in the intermediate mind, they believe in their religious doctrine, they study with intensity, yet they do not know the reality of what they study, and when it (the Truth) arrives in their life they reject it entirely, feeling as if they are super-sapient. Everyone who does not fall into the previous category and does not make use of the inner mind inevitably falls into this category.

The Pharisee and the Sadducee exist everywhere, both within us, and outside of us. They corrupt the real doctrine, they live identified with good and evil. It is necessary to live beyond good and evil, and this only occurs when we operate within the inner mind. The conflict between religion and science is an illusion created and sustained by the sleeping masses within these two previously mentioned spheres. What is necessary is to live beyond this illusion.

To live beyond good and evil is to correctly handle the "good" and "evil" energies in all their manifestations. In reality, good and evil do not exist, they are just descriptors; the limit of good is evil, and the limit of evil is good.

> Good and Evil do not exist. Something is good when it is convenient and evil when it is not convenient. Good and Evil is a matter of egotistical conveniences and whims of the mind. [...]
>
> Every moral bases itself on these two small words, good and evil; that is why every moral reformer is, as a matter of fact, a reactionary.
>
> The terms good and evil always serve to justify or condemn our own errors.
>
> Whoever justifies or condemns does not understand. It is intelligent to understand the development of evolutive forces but it is not intelligent to justify them with the term good. It is intelligent to understand the processes of the involutive forces but it is stupid to condemn them with the term of evil.
>
> Every centrifugal force can become a centripetal force. Every involutive force can become evolutive. Inside the infinite processes of energy in its evolutive state, infinite processes of energy in its involutive state exist.
>
> Inside each human being there exists various types of energy that evolve, involute and transform themselves incessantly.
>
> To justify a specific type of energy and condemn another is not understanding. The vital thing is to understand.
>
> The experience of Truth has been very rare among humanity due to the concrete fact of mental imprisonment. People are imprisoned between the opposites, good and evil.

The Revolutionary Psychology of the Gnostic movement is based on the study of the different types of energy that operate within the human organism and within nature.

The Gnostic Movement has Revolutionary Ethics that have nothing to do neither with the morality of reactionaries nor with the conservative and retarded terms of good and evil.

Within the psycho-physiological laboratory of the human organism there exist evolutive, involutive and neutral forces that should be studied and profoundly understood.

The term good stops understanding of the evolutive energies due to justification.

The term evil stops understanding of the involutive forces due to condemnation.

To justify or condemn does not mean to understand. Whoever wants to finish with his defects should not justify nor condemn them. It is urgent to understand our errors.

To understand ANGER in all the levels of the mind is fundamental so that serenity and sweetness are born within us.

To understand the infinite shades of COVETOUSNESS is indispensable so that philanthropy and altruism are born within us.

To understand LUST in all levels of the mind is vital in order that true chastity is born within us.

To understand ENVY in all the areas of the mind is enough so that the sense of cooperation and the joy for other's wellbeing and progress is born within us.

To understand PRIDE in all its shades and degrees is the basis for the exotic flower of humility to be born within us in a natural and simple way.

To understand what the element of inertia called LAZINESS is, not in its grotesque forms but also in its more subtle forms, is indispensable so that the sense of activity is born within us.

To understand the diverse forms of GLUTTONY and GREEDINESS is equal to destroying the vices of the instinctive centre such as banquets, drinking sprees, hunting, carnivorousness, fear of death, desires of perpetuating the ego, fear of annihilation, etc.

Teachers of schools, colleges and universities advise their students to improve themselves as if the ego could become better, they advise them to acquire specific virtues as if the ego could obtain virtues, etc.

It is urgent to understand that the ego never improves itself, that it is never more perfect and he who covets virtues strengthens the ego.

Total perfection is only born within us with the dissolution of the ego. Virtues are born within us in a natural and simple way when we understand our psychological defects not only at the intellectual level but also in all the subconscious and unconscious areas of the mind.

To want to improve oneself is stupid, to desire sanctity is envy, to covet virtues means strengthening the ego with the poison of covetousness.

We need the total death of the ego not only at the intellectual level but also in all the nooks, regions, areas and corridors of the mind. When we have absolutely died, only that which is perfect is left in us, that which is saturated with virtues, that which is the Essence of our intimate Being, that which does not belong to time.

Only by understanding in-depth all the infinite processes of the evolutive forces that develop inside us in here and now, only by understanding in an integral form the various aspects of the involutive forces that process themselves within us from moment to moment can we dissolve the ego.

The terms good and evil serve to justify and condemn but never to understand.

Each defect has many shades, secret depths, and profundities. To understand a defect at an intellectual level does not mean to have understood it in the distinct subconscious, unconscious and infraconscious areas of the mind.

Any defect can disappear from the intellectual level and continue in the other areas of the mind.

Anger disguises itself with the toga of the judge. Many covet not being covetous. There are those who do not covet money but covet psychic powers, virtues, love, happiness here or after death, etc.

Many men and women are moved and fascinated in front of people of the opposite sex, "supposedly" because they love beauty: their own subconscious betrays them, lust disguises itself as the aesthetic sense.

Many envious people envy saints and do penance and beat themselves also desiring to succeed in being saints.

Many envious people envy those who sacrifice themselves for humanity and then wanting to also be great they scoff at those they envy and hurl against them all their defamatory drivel.

There are those who feel proud because of their position, their money, their fame and their prestige and there are those who feel proud of their humble condition.

Diogenes felt proud of the tunnel in which he slept and when he arrived in the home of Socrates he greeted him, saying, "Trampling your pride, Socrates, trampling your pride." "Yes, Diogenes, with your pride you trample my pride," was Socrate's reply.

Vain women curl their locks, they dress and adorn themselves with everything they can to awaken envy in other women, but vanity also disguises itself with the robe of humility.

Tradition speaks of Aristippus, the Greek philosopher, who wanting to demonstrate to the whole world his wisdom and humility, dressed in a very old robe full of holes, he grasped in his right hand the rod of Philosophy and went through the streets of Athens. When Socrates saw him coming, he exclaimed, "Your vanity shows through the holes of your clothes, oh Aristippus."

Many are those who are in misery due the element of laziness but there exist people who work very hard to earn a living but who feel laziness in studying and knowing themselves in order to dissolve the ego.

There are many who abandon greed and gluttony but unfortunately they get drunk and go hunting.

Each defect is multifaceted and develops and processes itself in a step-wise way from the lowest step of the psychological ladder to the most elevated step.

Within the delicious cadence of a verse, crime is also hidden. Crime also dresses itself as a saint, as a martyr, as a chaste person, as an apostle, etc.

Good and Evil does not exist. Such terms only serve to look for evasion and to elude the profound and detailed study of our own defects.

– Samael Aun Weor, *Fundamentals of Gnostic Education*

LEGION, HUMAN, CHRIST

> In the name of Truth, I solemnly declare that the Being is the only real existence, and before the ineffable and terribly divine transparency of the Being that which we call I, Ego, Myself is just outer darkness, wailing and gnashing of teeth.
>
> – Samael Aun Weor

We have arrived at the fundamental question: To Be or Not To Be. To Be is to be the Being. The Being is the Being and the purpose of the Being is to be the Being.

To Be is something that is only known to the Being because that is what the Being is. Really it is impossible to further elaborate upon the Being. The abstraction of being into a theory or concept is something false. Concept itself is antithetical to being.

A consciousness that is mechanical and sleeps is not being. A sleeping consciousness lives within its own darkness and ignores its own lack of autonomy. The sleeping consciousness does not act itself but rather it is acted upon by that aspect in which it dreams of.

Being fascinated with an argument, the sleeping consciousness reacts to stimuli with resentment and hateful words, exactly as it has been programmed to. The sleeping consciousness has been programmed to ignore those aspects that refute its logical imperative. A sleeping consciousness has no choice but to become hurt by hateful words and return hate with more hate. The sleeping consciousness is conditioned not only to do such, but to furthermore ignore all degenerative consequences possible and systematically justify those consequences which cannot be ignored.

Creation itself is the sum movement of energy. Every movement of energy is either regenerative or degenerative. In other words, all movement of energy has a direction and this direction either sustains creation by destroying itself or destroys creation by sustaining itself. To have a physical world we need physical laws in order to sustain it. The study of physical laws (physics) has shown that in order for a system to exist it cannot create or destroy energy and that all energy is in constant transformation from one form into another.

Music is on some absolute level either harmonic or disharmonic. Good music is more than the total of the notes that compose it because it is harmonic. Obviously if the notes of Beethoven's 9th Symphony were reordered we would not have the same thing because we would not have the same impression of what those notes give. There is something beyond mere notes of music that provide it something transcendental within the hands of a great musician who knows the Music of the Spheres.

> The aim and final end of all music should be none other than the glory of God and the refreshment of the soul.
>
> – Johann Sebastian Bach

> Music is the one incorporeal entrance into the higher world of knowledge which comprehends mankind but which mankind cannot comprehend.
>
> – Ludwig van Beethoven

Every great song is an expression of Being and when this occurs each note is a reverberation of that Being. However if those notes, under the trace of their own beautiful sound, where to sustain themselves out of time and order then that superlative expression called harmony is lost. When notes are played out of harmony, the value of those notes in the aggregate is exactly the same as the sum of the notes. In other words, unlike harmony, nothing extra or transcendental occurs from disharmony.

Harmony is that phenomenon which occurs when a set of notes in the aggregate constitute something beyond the sum of each note itself. In good music every note has its proper moment of rise and fall, its harmonic life and death within the composition. Music is a Creation because the notes that compose it are in constant movement. Any attempt to sustain or kill a note out of time will degenerate the harmonic nature of the music it composes.

Each note dies in order for harmony to live. Each note lives and dies within the eternal moment of now. As "now" occurs, each note is played. No note is played in the future or in the past. Every note exists in the moment of now. Every note dies and is transformed within the moment of now into another note. Each note contains a specific quality. Each note is important and in the aggregate all are equal, but none of them are equal in and of themselves because every note is unique.

> As death, when we come to consider it closely, is the true goal of our existence, I have formed during the last few years such close relationships with this best and truest friend of mankind that death's image is not only no longer terrifying to me, but is indeed very soothing and consoling, and I thank my God for graciously granting me the opportunity...of learning that death is the key which unlocks the door to our true happiness. I never lie down at night without reflecting that — young as I am — I may not live to see another day. Yet no one of all my acquaintances could say that in company I am morose or disgruntled.
>
> – Wolfgang Amadeus Mozart

If a note does not die then it degenerates harmony while sustaining itself. Emergence of the transcendental occurs when each note has proper evolution and devolution (rise and fall). Through its harmonic death, each note paradoxically lives within its superior harmonic aspect. Proper death facilitates the regeneration of harmony. Without regeneration, harmony dies because it is entropic.

Harmony returns to the absolute without a proper host to facilitate its becoming. Harmony needs a proper host in order for its sustainment. Harmony can never stay the same because it is either being regenerated or degenerated.

Creation is the harmony of the Being. To Be is to become, to live and die within the moment of now. Creation is the Great Fire, I.N.R.I.: Fire Renews Nature Incessantly. This is the Theosophical Fohat, the Pythagorean Monad, or simply the Being. This is the esoteric significance of the "INRI" upon the cross of that Divine Rabbi from Galilee we call Jesus.

> I believe in God, Mozart and Beethoven, and likewise their disciples and apostles; - I believe in the Holy Spirit and the truth of the one, indivisible Art; - I believe that this Art proceeds from God, and lives within the hearts of all illumined men; - I believe that he who once has bathed in the sublime delights of this high Art, is consecrate to Her forever, and never can deny Her; - I believe that through Art all men are saved.
>
> – Richard Wagner

The ego is the disharmony that wishes to sustain itself but unknowingly at the cost of destroying something far greater. The ego vibrates a malignancy into the world. The ego is the cause of all pain and suffering, war and famine, political, economical and religious pride and all the fortified borders in existence. To remove the ego is to harmonize with creation. The ego is the lack of Becoming. The ego wishes to do good, but that is something ultimately impossible because the foundation of the ego is something degenerative, not regenerative.

The ego is a knot that impedes the correct flux of energy that would otherwise regenerate The Becoming of Now. Christ is the Holy Negation, the eternal regeneration of The Becoming of Now, a great burning fire of light and infinite splendors.

The authentic self is expressed when the ego is removed. Until that time the pseudo-Man has not even individuality. The true Man is an individual. Until Man has conquered Himself he is nothing more than Legion. Until Man has conquered Himself he will never be able to conquer the world, this solar system, this galaxy or universe. The true Human Being is the microcosmos.

Let us read the Hermetic Wisdom:

> In truth certainly and without doubt, whatever is below is like that which is above, and whatever is above is like that which is below, to accomplish the miracles of one thing.

This is what has been written on the Emerald Tablet of the Thrice God Hermes. This is what is meant by "on Earth, as it is in Heaven." Creation is cosmically recursive. The Earth is a Creation. The Solar System is a Creation. The Galaxy is a Creation. The Human Being is a Creation. When the intellectual animal incarnates its Being then he has becomes a living Zodiac, the

Hebraic Adam Kadmon, a Cosmic Human, the Microcosmos, or simply an authentic Human Being. When the intellectual animal becomes the King of his own self, then by the hermetic axiom ("as above, so below") he has become King of the Earth. These people become true Gods with powers over creation.

The intellectual animal is attempting now to conquer the solar system even though he has yet to conquer Earth or even his own self. The intellectual animal is a slave to its own passions and the cause of all the misery on this world. A *true* human being is a lyre upon which the music of the spheres resounds. The perfect christified human being is an angel who is a harmonic note of the Army of the Voice. The Angel, the Diva, the God, the Buddha, these are in total the Ruach Elohim, the Host of the Christ, the Army of the Word, those who utter of the Verb of Gold through the Divine Fecund Larynx.

The intellectual bipedal mammal is just a machine used by nature to transform energies. The earth itself is a living organism and the skin of the earth is the biological membrane composed of all the animals and plants living on its surface. The true human being is something different. Earth is not interested in creating human beings. Earth has created the ecosystem to sustain itself. However, the Solar Logos, whose physical macrocosmic manifestation is the Sun, has deposited the seed of the human being within the intellectual animal. This seed is within the sex. When the seed is expelled in the physical word, it creates in the physical world, however, when it is properly transmuted, it creates the microcosmos. In Buddhism the seed is called the Buddhata.

The Solar Logos is interested in its incarnation, but it can only *Be* in the one who has properly prepares himself. Jesus received the Cosmic Christ when he was baptized by John. The Holy Spirit is that dove that Moses named the Ruach Elohim, the one who utters the Logos.

In order to use the sexual energy in a superior fashion (transmutation) we must awaken consciousness, because the sleeping consciousness only knows how to fornicate. The consciousness is sleeping *because* it fornicates, therefore the mechanical-sleeping consciousness cannot transmute the sexual energy. Sexual energy is the basis of all the energy of our body, and this known through endocrinology, but the ego only knows how to use this energy to please itself: to dream, to get angry, to get sad, to get drunk, to be lazy, to be proud, to have arguments, to gossip, etc. All of this is the misuse of the sexual energy. At the end of the day we use so much energy improperly that it leaves us tired and physically sleepy. Psychologically we sleep profoundly.

When we are able to successfully experience the state of now in a continuous fashion life becomes an incredible sequence of synchronistic events. The vast majority of our problems in life are due to the fact that we are *never paying attention.* This leads us to do extra work to make up for our "lost" time.

What do you think of a person who is reading a book while driving a car? It is obvious that they should have their eyes fixed entirely on the road in order to pay attention to that which is important now. We have many accidents in our everyday lives because we are not paying attention to the eternal moment of now.

Our internal preoccupations lead us to forget about the now. We are never paying attention to the now. We are always in the past, reliving our mistakes and adventures, reminiscing of a better time, or worrying about the future. Meanwhile our "car" is heading straight for a tree and we are totally unaware. Staying in the moment of now requires an act of will most people are unaware of. We must be extremely vigilant like a watchman at war.

The only true war is the war on oneself. The only authentic use of *Jihad* is the war on oneself. Martian expression is the war on oneself. Mars is the God of war, but it is the Internal Warrior, the Innermost. Our Atman is Martian because It has to fight the ego for its self-realization.

The authentic Human Being is something exceedingly rare. A Human is a Hu-Manas, a Spirit-Mind. Only when the ego is removed from the human machine can the mind reverberate the spirit. Today, the human machine (the three dimensional terrestrial biped) is plagued with the malignant vibrations of the ego. Instead of authentic human beings, society is populated with intellectual animals.

The human being is divine. The human being is a reflection of the spirit. The intellectual animal is merely the outcome of mechanical evolution. The human being is not the physical body. The true human being is the Hindustani Atman, the sephiroth Chesed. The physical body is the inferior aspect of true human being. The true human is in the superior worlds, a King of Creation.

> When we say, "I am hungry, I am thirsty," etc., we are affirming something absurd, because the innermost is not hungry, neither thirsty. The one that is hungry and thirsty is the physical body. Therefore the most correct way to say this is, "My body is hungry, my body is thirsty."
>
> The same happens with the mind when we say "I have a powerful mental force, I have a problem, I have such a conflict, I have such a suffering, some thoughts are arising in me," etc. We then are affirming very grave errors, because these things are from the mind and not from the Innermost.
>
> **The true Human Being is the Innermost, He does not have problems. The problems are from the mind.**
>
> The Innermost must whip the mind with the terrible whip of **willpower**.
>
> The human being that identifies with the mind falls into the Abyss.
>
> **The mind is the donkey that we must ride in order to enter into the heavenly Jerusalem.**
>
> – Samael Aun Weor

We should not identify with the processes and problems of life. Everyone experiences pain. Everyone has their loved ones die. Everyone fails. The problems complicate themselves when we feel that life itself has personally forsaken us. Problems are just mental shapes of the mind. When the mind cannot find the synthesis between conflicting ideas then the mind has a problem. To solve the problem one needs comprehension. Comprehension and intuition are facilities of the Being. The Being is able to express itself only through a mind that is calm and receptive.

It is clear that this book is not for everyone because not many people are interested in becoming what they are not. People are content with their animal existence and being subservient to the laws of the earth. We think that we are strong and powerful, but really the intellectual animal is very weak. The intellectual animal is victim of every earthquake and flood. The intellectual animal is nothing more than an expendable resource for the mechanics of the earth. The common "man" is nothing more than an intellectual animal and I do not know of any scientist that will disagree with this. Nevertheless, we take a lot of pride in calling ourselves a human being even though we have no true being at all. Instead, we have a mechanical reactionary product of the evolution of time: the ego.

Most people like being animals. The lustful or "passionate" ego enjoys its hedonism. An ascetic ego rejects sex and feels superior and righteous, and it enjoys its false righteousness. The drunken ego dreams of its drunkenness and rejects all aspects of seriousness. The fanatical religious member is fascinated with pride and secretly or outwardly hates all other sects. The hard worker is fascinated with the hard work. A father enjoys releasing anger towards his family because it is easy. A mother justifies her yelling back. An executive loves his money and his new car. In synthesis: people enjoy their degeneration.

People rather die than to kill their suffering. People enjoy suffering. The esoteric philosophy states that the intellectual animal is the product and pinnacle of natural evolution. The only thing left for the intellectual animal is devolution, degeneration and death. It is better to enjoy the harmony of the Being through psychological death than to renounce the Being by remaining bounded by animal desire. This is the message of Christ: "What good is it for man to gain the whole world, and yet lose or forfeit his very self?" Animal desire is going to die regardless, because it creates karma in the rational animal, but only conscious sacrifice sustains and reverberates the joy of the Being.

Instead of the Being, within each of us lies a legion of demons. In fact, it is best to say that our existence is nothing more than the compilation of a legion of demons. The ego is demonic or as the Christians say, satanic. Literally, neither in any dogmatic sense nor in agenda to cause fear, the ego is Satan. That is the true meaning of Satan in the Bible. The ego is, as well, the Anti-Christ, the Beast whose number is 666.

The Sixth Arcanum of the Book of Tarot is Indecision, the choice between the Harlot and Virgin, and we have chosen the Harlot, and we are the Great Harlot. We are thrice six because we are "six" in our intellectual center, "six" in our emotional center, and "six" in our sexual center. Our three brains are 6, 6, and 6. We are the ego, we are the Anti-Christ. This is a definitive fact that we must submit ourselves to, the truth is the truth, and the truth is that everything the ego is, is everything the Christ is not. Whosoever carries the ego is one with the Anti-Christ.

The Anti-Christ has the power of ubiquity, it is everywhere, it is within everyone. The Anti-Christ, with his false materialistic values, creates "wonders" in science that only "fools" would reject, such as the Hydrogen Bomb, contraceptives, the grafting of fruits and vegetables. The Anti-Christ does not even suspect his own ignorance, he is like a child playing with nitroglycerin and pretending to have total sapience.

In all reality the ego does not have a center. Rather, it is diffused through all its desires and needs. *The ego has no permanent will.* Its will is always changing. We must ask ourselves, "Why do I contradict myself? Why do I often change my mind?" Everyone is a hypocrite because no one has a permanent center of consciousness. Our consciousness is always centered on different needs and desires and this is the cause of our contradictions and hypocrisy. This is why no man or woman who has ego is trustworthy.

Our ego is a multiple entity. There are multiple "I's" within the ego. Each "I" contradicts the other "I's." The "I" that swears fidelity towards their spouse ends up fornicating with others. The

"I" that wishes to be charitable is overcome by the "I" that is greedy. Today we see many people ashamed of their own actions. Sometimes we are ashamed of actions as we carry them out. This is because one "I" feels ashamed for the actions of another "I" that arose in a fit of passion, jealously, greed, envy, lust, etc. Truly, this is neither happiness nor freedom. We have become slaves to our desires. We have no authentic will of Self. The Bible speaks of this multiple entity as a legion of demons that has overcome a man of destitution.

> When he saw Jesus from a distance, he ran and fell on his knees in front of him. He shouted at the top of his voice, "What do you want with me, Jesus, Son of the Most High God? Swear to God that you won't torture me!" For Jesus had said to him, "Come out of this man, you evil spirit!"
>
> Then Jesus asked him, "What is your name?" "My name is Legion," he replied, "for we are many."
>
> – Mark 5:6-10

All of us have a true name that is *Legion*. The "I" is Legion. Only the Intimate Christ has the ability to remove the ego.

The systematic identification and removal of all our "I" centers is necessary to awaken consciousness. Otherwise we will never possess the continuity of Will, the will of the Father here, as it is in Heaven. Only the True Self has the power to act. The False Self, the ego, has all action occur *through* it, it is a medium. Our true nature is omnipotent and only It knows when to speak and when to keep silent. The ego is merely a contradiction of values and it never knows the correct way. We are all lost in the labyrinth of the mind and its theories, logic and presumptions. The mind does not have the ability to understand that which is real.

Each "I" we carry believes to be the authentic self. It is completely unaware to the other "I's" inside. We have a difficult time realizing this because although we are constantly being controlled by different egos, our bodies remain the same. *It is the internal states that change*, but society does not teach us about the internal so we never are aware of this very apparent fact. We come to understand that each "I" is ignorant when we begin to see and understand its desires. Then we come to see, through our consciousness, that we are not this "I" and in fact it is some type of crystallized impression left on our interior that incessantly wishes to *relive* that impression. Only then we will truly know what desire is. If we do not begin to awaken consciousness than the ability to see is more than impossible. Our egos can be identified through constant vigilance and study. This is a process Benjamin Franklin did to improve his interior self.

Interior perfection can be achieved through the radical disillusionment of the "I."

The "I" is multiple contradictions. The Human Being is a true individual without contradiction. The Christ is a multiple singular consciousness. The Christ is supra-individuality that manifests itself everywhere and incarnates within any Human who is properly prepared. We must first remove the ego and crystallize the Solar Bodies of Emotion, Mind and Will. Then, if one so chooses, the Solar Initiate can incarnate the Christ. This is a path rarely taken because it is a path more bitter than bile; the masses spit on the face of Christ, because he represents everything that the Anti-Christ is against.

The Brain, Mind, and Sleep

> True illuminates have no dreams. Dreams are for those who are asleep. True illuminates live in the higher worlds, out of the physical body, in a state of intensified wakefulness without ever dreaming.
>
> – Samael Aun Weor, lecture entitled *Mental Representations*

The science of neurology theorizes that the consciousness of man exists within the neocortex. The neocortex is a section of the cerebral cortex, which is the frontal area of the brain. When Buddhist monks where analyzed during deep meditation, they noticed that the cerebral cortex was much more electrically active. Many other studies, such as one carried out by Massachusetts General Hospital noted that regular mediators contained a significantly thicker cerebral cortex and an overall less atrophied brain.

There is a definitive link between the brain and the consciousness. Yet, the idea that the consciousness is stored in electrical activity of the brain is totally rejected by the esoteric philosophy. There exist documented cases in which people have hydrocephalus (water in the brain) to such an extent that no significant cerebral cortex exists, let alone a neocortex. These individuals who have no substantial neocortex, the supposed center of consciousness, live perfectly normal lives. One student (who had achieved an honors degree in mathematics) discovered that his brain was virtually nonexistent when it was examined by British neurologist John Lorber. This man lives today with a thin layer of brain cells in his skull which surrounds a large body of cerebrospinal fluid.

The esoteric philosophy states that the brain is the lower counterpart of the mind, and the brain's mechanical, electrical and chemical processes are the *results* of the subtle mind influencing it. The (intellectual) brain is a mailbox for the intellect. It is a machine that receives thoughts from the mind.

The mind is the messenger of thought, just as the postman is the messenger of the mail.

Strictly speaking, the mind is not the same as the consciousness, yet sometimes these words are used interchangeably, particularly in some Buddhist texts translated haphazardly into English. It is better to state that the consciousness is the root of perception, and that the mind is a *tool* of the consciousness that allows one to label or organize experience in an individual, subjective fashion. In turn, the consciousness is a vehicle of the Being.

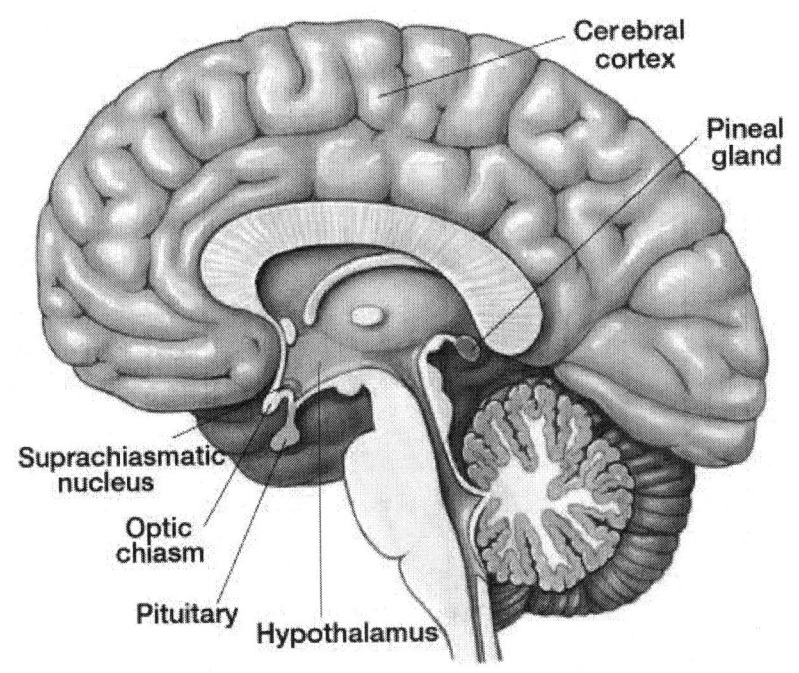

The mind has a center of gravity in the fifth dimension, the consciousness has its center of gravity in the sixth dimension, and it is through the consciousness that one experiences objective reality, because no "I" could ever exist in the 6th dimension.[1]

---

[1] We will speak of the seven fundamental dimensions in later chapters.

The reality is that all the marvelous systems of the body are tools for the mind to drive its vehicle, the human machine. The intellectual brain is just one of those machines. The consciousness is not exclusively interfaced through the intellectual brain because every cell contains consciousness. Every atom in space contains consciousness.

There is much discussion today about how some people, due to their chemical imbalances, are only able to live, perceive and react to life in certain ways. Depression, for example, is thought to be caused by the imbalance of neurotransmitters such as serotonin and noradrenaline. The solution is thought to be found in developing drugs to supply these chemicals in an overabundance. But, truly, this is nothing more than treating the effects while ignoring the causes. What is the cause of causes of an imbalanced machine?

A brain that is chemically imbalanced is the result of abusing the human machine. This is done principally through the abuse of the sexual center. The reason for this assertion is understood when we comprehend the relationship between the brain and the sex. The pineal gland, located in the center of the brain, is the director of the sex. When the sex is abused, the pineal gland becomes atrophied. Modern medicine states that after puberty the pineal gland inevitably calcifies, yet, the sages of India know well that this gland only degenerates when the vital values are extracted from the organism through the indulgence of lust. Fornication destroys the brain.

There are many secondary causes of chemical imbalances, such as the abuse of psychedelic drugs. The rumors surrounding the dangers of psychedelia, while often exaggerated, are based in the truth. One may not go "insane" by taking a single dose of some psychotropic chemical (organic or not), nevertheless the abusers of these drugs may find themselves distraught years later. When the time comes when they want to put aside such foolishness (often disillusioned), they may find themselves suffering from depression or the inability to concentrate, to harmoniously handle the events of life, etc. Other causes of chemical imbalances are due to the abuse of the emotional center. A person who can never control explosions of anger obviously cannot go unaffected by this, often through heart disease, yet the results of such emotional abuse may only manifest themselves in their next life. Some people have lost their mental equilibrium through the abuse of the intellect. Schizophrenia can result.

The famous DSM (Diagnostic and Statistical Manual of Mental Disorder) has grown significantly since its inception in the 1950s. In 1962 the DSM-II was 134 pages long, describing 182 "disorders." In 1994, the fourth revision of the same manual contained 886 pages to describe 297 disorders. In other words, according to the American Psychiatric Association, about one hundred new mental disorders, or supposed types of chemical imbalances, either came into existence or was simply discovered over the course of just three decades.

Even if, over the next thirty years, ten thousand new types of mental disorders were discovered, and even if the halls of their intuitions are filled with sincere doctors, without a revolutionary paradigm shift, modern psychiatry (and psychology for that matter) will continue to totally and completely fail to cure mental illness.

Let us remember that one thing is to treat symptoms, and it is another thing to actually cure them. Modern psychiatry has totally failed to resolve the cause of the so-called chemical imbalances in the brain. Through pharmaceutical drugs, apparently the brain chemistry can be modified, yet these drugs, in no way whatsoever actually solve the cause of the imbalance in the first place. The reason is our mind is shaped by the actions we made not just in our previous weeks or years, but in our previous lives. Because such a topic lies outside the scope of psychiatric science, it is obvious that it will never be able to radically cure mental illness.

The best thing one can do to resolve the cause of chemical imbalance is to practice sexual transmutation, and to meditate. Sexual transmutation invigorates the brain and reactivates the pineal and pituitary glands. When the glands of the brain are secreting the correct levels of hormones, our entire body becomes balanced.

The pineal gland is named after the pine cone, and this is because (according to modern biology) the shape of this gland resembles its namesake. While this is certainly true, the real reason is much more profound. Any advanced ancient culture (prior to their degeneration) knew the importance of this gland, which sits the center of the brain and is called by many Asian masters as the "third eye." Luminaries of all times have their pineal gland fully active and glowing: it gloriously shines in the superior dimensions and forms the halo of saints.

Examine the staff of many Pagan deities, such as Dionysus, and you will find it adorned with a pine cone. The staff itself, unbeknownst to modern academia, represents the spinal column, and the pine cone is the symbol of the pineal gland. Likewise, the artistic rendition of the sahasrara chakra, which is located at the crown of the head, resembles the budding pine cone.

The soul of the pine tree, the elemental of the pine, has all the knowledge of the "reed" (spinal column). The gland that sits atop the spinal column is absolutely pineal, and this is why the ancients called it such. This is why many temples are built with pine, and are built in the presence of pine trees. The Christmas tree, crowned with the Star of Bethlehem, is related with the pine. We can say the following: The inner Star of Bethlehem is the pineal gland. When the connection between the pineal gland and the sexual organs is made complete, then the Son of Man has been raised upon the staff (spinal column) as Moses raised the Serpent (Kundalini).

To invigorate the pineal gland, pronounce the vowel "I" for one hour daily:

Iiiiiiiiiiiiiiiiiiiiiiiiiiiiiiiiiiiii...[2]

---

[2] This is to be pronounced as a Latin "i," like the "e" in "tree."

While vocalizing, concentrate on the center of your brain. Visualize your pineal gland glowing and vibrating. The vibrations of the vowel "I" pulse the pineal gland and invigorate it. Likewise, the pineal gland will produce more hormones and these will vitalize the blood stream. When the pineal gland is regenerated, it allows the student to see the Ultra of nature. Like a microscope views the infinitesimally small, so does the pineal gland view superior dimensional phenomena.

This type of healing does not occur overnight. Those who are looking for healing of serious mental disorders should, in addition to these practices, supplicate (pray) to the hierarchies of the Archangel Raphael. Serious psychosis is serious karma and must be handled very carefully: any abrupt termination of medication would rarely be advisable if, without the stupefying effects of antipsychotics, such a person quickly becomes harmful to himself and society.

DREAMS

The first state of consciousness is called Eikasia.

The second state of consciousness is Pistis.

The third state of consciousness is Dianoia.

The fourth state of consciousness is Nous.

Eikasia is Ignorance, human cruelty, barbarism, exceedingly profound sleep, a brutal and instinctive world, an infra-human state.

Pistis is the world of opinions and beliefs. Pistis is belief, prejudices, sectarianism, fanaticism, theories in which there does not exist any type of direct perception of the Truth. Pistis is that consciousness of the common level of humanity.

Dianoia is the intellectual revision of beliefs, analysis, conceptual synthesis, cultural-intellectual consciousness, scientific thought etc. Dianoetic thought studies phenomena and establishes laws. Dianoetic thought studies the inductive and deductive systems with the purpose of using them in a profound and clear way.

Nous is perfect awakened consciousness. Nous is the state of Turiya, profound perfect interior illumination. Nous is legitimate objective Clairvoyance. Nous is intuition. Nous is the world of the

> divine archetypes. Noetic thought is synthetic, clear, objective, illuminated.
>
> Whosoever reaches the heights of Noetic thought totally awakens consciousness and becomes a Turiya.
>
> The lowest part of man is irrational and subjective and is related with the five ordinary senses.
>
> The highest part of man is the world of intuition and objective spiritual consciousness. In the world of intuition, the archetypes of all things in nature develop.
>
> – Samael Aun Weor, *The Perfect Matrimony*

Eikasia is obviously our unconscious, subconscious, and infraconscious levels of mind. We visit our **infraconscious inferno** through our worst nightmares. Subconsciousness is a level that more accessible, it just below our vigilance. Our subconscious speaks to us through our dreams on a regular basis. The terms subconsciousness and unconsciousness are merely describing grades of psychological *darkness*.

Dreams with monsters and beasts attacking us occur when we begin to work with our darkness. When we stir up our darkest diabolic elements they begin to show themselves in the light and only then do we begin to understand what the ego truly is. Tempting dreams will occur to someone who is attempting to begin to understand their unconsciousness. It may seem strange to say it, but when we fight against our own desires, they react and begin to express themselves as tempting dreams. Each ego has its own autonomy within the depths of the consciousness, each one is a real, literal "I".

If we understand the useless waste of energy that anger results in, then we begin to yearn for the removal of our interior processes that cause anger. If we are truly diligent, aware and if we truly deny our anger in a fundamental and causal sense - in other words if we comprehend our anger - the ego no longer has the pleasure of expressing itself physically. However it is important to note that this does not mean the ego has been totally dissolved.

Each "I", each desire, each ego is a real creation, a real entity, a real crystallization of matter that formed by failing to transform impressions of life. So it should be very clear that the ego will, in a sense, attack someone attempting to remove it. This occurs because each psychological aggregate feeds upon impressions, it desires the impressions that create it and sustain it. In a desperate attempt to express its desire the ego will attack within a dream. That is to say, within a dream a scenario will appear in which we would usually get angry, or lustful, or envious or proud, etc. We will have nightmares.

A student had a dream in which he was attending an illustrious event. It was quite like a storybook: There were beautiful rolling hills that surrounded an enormous castle in which this event was taking place. Around on the greens various tents were arranged, each of them had activities for the guests, and the subject of this dream was attending to them. He was having a wonderful time, even if in this dream he was acting completely mechanical (like a robot). It was as if the dream was happing *to him*, instead of him dreaming *it*. Well, as it goes, the more he looked around, the more he realized how large a party this was. Indeed, it seemed as if everyone of importance was there. How surprised he was suddenly discovering this party was for him! He became quite jubilant in this dream, which was fuelled with feelings of pride and vanity. He was like a little child at his birthday: one who becomes completely attached to all the attention received. Thus, in this dream, he was doing just that: *dreaming*. His consciousness was very fantasized by its own projection and was totally unaware of his own existence due to the deep state of fascination he was within.

Later in this dream our subject began to speak with one of his good friends. They were having a pleasant conversation about personal matters, when seemingly out of nowhere this friend began to criticize the dreamer. He called him a liar, that he was not one to be respected and that in general was not a very good person at all. Our dreamer was shocked! Those words deeply hurt him, and he could do nothing else but *react* by returning some hateful words.

Our student was very surprised upon awakening from that dream. He erroneously believed that he would have never reacted so foully upon the words of another. Nevertheless, it became obvious that the ego of revenge was very much alive within. He mistakenly thought that he did not carry such negativity within his interior. This is because another ego, *pride*, believed that he was doing very well in self-observation.

These types of experiences give us the necessary data to become aware of certain aspects of our condition that we otherwise ignore. We may believe that we feel we had worked on in this or that psychological area in earnest. If we are not careful, we will miss these very important opportunities of harsh reality. These types of experiences are the best tool to help us.

It is foolish to believe or opine concerning self progress and internal achievement. On the path of self-realization, appearances are routinely nothing more than that, an illusion, a mirage that keeps us from the truth. Instead of worrying about how well we are doing, let us simply be very humble. Let humility grow, live in the moment, transform the impressions of now.

During that dream the consciousness of the student was completely asleep: the impressions given to him, instead of being transformed into to humility, were crystallized as anger. Full of this impression, which was *indigested*, he returned hateful words. He desired to hurt his friend as revenge. He wanted to hurt him because he *identified* with those words; they were words that contradicted his self-esteem. However those critical words against the dreamer were nothing but the truth. We have all lied, we have all committed many wrongs in our life, therefore how can one deny what was said? It was through pride that he *lied* to himself and *justified* the hateful words he responded with. This is how the ego lies, justifies and reacts. And all that emotion, all that energy used to produce hate, for what purpose? Pride.

Within the dream he succumbed to anger, the ego of anger found that improperly digested impression delicious. The ego of anger and pride fed off that energy. Really, everyone who has ego is a liar. Only the one who has removed the ego, the one that reflects the ineffable splendors of the luminous Being can be considered, in truth, a person to consider unconditionally trustworthy.

A corollary of the story is that if we cannot overcome psychological faults within our dreams, then all change, progress or supposed advancement has been ultimately superficial. If our dreams continue to exert the qualities in which we are attempting to rid of ourselves then we must say we have not yet accomplished anything of importance. Dreams are the movie playing in our subconscious. We convert the subconsciousness, the animal instinct, into consciousness, and even supra-consciousness: intuition.

We must start here and now in the physical if we ever wish to be awake in the moments of subconscious temptation. One starts in the physical, which is coarse and rigid. Slowly we work out towards what is more subtle and darker. When we are dreaming, our emotions and feelings are intensified. The world of dreams is what the occultist refers to as the Astral World. This world is less mechanical than the physical. The physical world is more mechanical, time exists in a rigid fashion, whereas the superior dimensions contain less and less mechanical aspects. Within the Astral and Mental Worlds, the Fifth Dimension, we experience happiness with more ease because that word is more subtle. In those worlds, to merely think of something is to be that something. For example, if you mentally lusted over the sight of someone of the opposite sex, that lust is being played out in the Fifth Dimension. When you dream, you are perceiving the Fifth Dimension, and instead of merely thinking about this act, you find yourself actually performing it. This is why in dreams anger shows its face much easier, just as fear, pleasure or pain does. In such a state we are experiencing ourselves in a much more *intense* or direct way. For anger to appear in the physical, it must first be within our mental counterpart.

It is easy to repress anger within the physical body, and many people become experts in this. They simply try to deny their mental feelings and thoughts to express themselves in a physical manner. Nevertheless, no matter how much we exercise this capacity it is impossible to leave any thought or feeling totally unpersonified. In reality we personify everything, it is just to what extent within our most subtle motions that we personify a defect that we attempt to repress. The ego always betrays even our most valiant efforts at removing ourselves from it. It is always there. It may be the way you move your eyes, the tone, inflection or tempo of voice, etc.

Only psychological death removes the ego and death only comes through comprehension. We have to understand our status in life. The very act of understanding who we are will modify our action in life. Thus our lives will change for the better, in a natural way. You do not need a book that gives you a ten pointed list of what you must do in order to change your life. That is a ruse, a lie, it will not work. But books like that are popular because that is what we want to hear, we have been so indoctrinated into society that we actually *want* to be told what to think. We enjoy our prison of insanity. We do not even want real freedom, we do not even care about how to think.

In this chapter we have stated that removing our internal flaws within a physical sense is only superficial, it is only one effect of a deeper cause, therefore we must remove the very psychological processes that produce the cause and effect relationship of these thoughts.

Dreams constitute the mental movie that we direct and star as lead role. A dream is our creation, yet, we are unable to control this creation. The subconsciousness provides the scenes of life it desires to live out, and as a result our dreams occur according to the most dominant ego-desire of the time. During a tempting dream, if we have reached some comprehension regarding that ego, we will easily succeed in triumphing over temptation. If we did not comprehend that portion of our ego, then we will be failures and the ego will continue to propagate itself on that level of consciousness. In order to become aware of your dreams, in order to have "lucid" dreams, all you have to do is become aware of the moment of now. If you are aware in your wakeful state, you will become aware in your dreaming state. Thus, you will remember your dreams and this is a great boon for self-change.

To resist temptation in the physical is easy in comparison to the temptations of the subtler dimensions. The majority of people do not even remember their dreams. That is how asleep we are. Even when we do remember our dreams we realize that we did not have any say whatsoever regarding our choices and decisions of that dream. Everything seems to happen *to us*, instead of us having any will of our own. When we begin self-observation, our dreams become more vivid and eventually, little by little, they become clearer, more concrete and in control, but these matters do not take leaps. It takes time and patience. A dream journal will allow one to notice reoccurring dreams. Reoccurring dreams are the easiest way to know something about our unconsciousness.

Here is a good question: If dreams are mental projections, then how do we resist our own mind? This is possible because the consciousness is not mind. The consciousness *precedes* mind and when it is awakened, only when it is awakened, can we understand and perceive directly, *before* the ego-mind distorts reality. When this occurs, the awakened consciousness is something that is no longer sleeping inside the inferior crystallization of the mind, known as the ego, and instead uses the mind as an instrument of *observation*. Conversely, the sleeping consciousness uses the mind as an instrument of *identification* ("I"). The mind is that instrument that organizes sensation. Consciousness is not sensation, but rather a state of being.

When we learn about ourselves in successively increasing fidelity we slowly become *enlightened* because we have turned the darkness into light. The awakened individual does not dream at all because this one, instead of living in the Fifth Dimension in a dream state, lives as an Awakened Being.

When we achieve true liberation from a mental defect on a level of consciousness it opens up new consciousness to us. Then we begin the process of investigation again within a more refined and subtle way. Each time a layer of the ego is removed, the next layer is darker and denser, each time it is more subtle and difficult.

There are forty-nine levels of the mind. Each defect, each psychological aggregate, exist on one or more of these levels. Some defects exist only on the top or superficial layers of the mind. Other defects reach down the forty-ninth chamber of the mind. A sincere devotee of wisdom may be humble and kind in the first thirty levels of the mind, but at the thirty-first level he is an arrogant and cruel person. This is partly why in similar situations we act differently. One scenario of life may stimulate within us a reaction from only the fifth layer of the mind. Yet, in another situation, life's circumstances may agitate the twentieth level of the mind, and on this level, different aggregates live. Some people say, "I used to have a very short fuse and get angry all the time, but now I have a much longer fuse... but you still don't want to be around me when I go off..." This is because the levels upon which their raging egos exist are now at a deeper level of the mind. These people need to continue to work on their ego, to eradicate even the most subtle forms of their anger, because it is still alive and it is trapping their consciousness. When the anger is comprehended, that consciousness previously trapped is liberated, and the virtues of patience and kindness are the fragrant result.

> Only those who have penetrated into the world of objective intuition, only those who have reached the solemn heights of Noetic thought are truly awakened and illuminated.
>
> – Samael Aun Weor, *The Perfect Matrimony*

DREAM YOGA

Do you want to awaken within your dreams? Do you want to "project" your "astral" body in the superior dimensions? If so, practice dream yoga.

We need to clarify that the astral body is just a fanciful term for the body of emotions. The intellectual animal only has the *kamarupa*, or body of desire. Note that the legitimate astral body is a Christic body forged in Vulcan's furnace (sexual magic). Everyone leaves the physical and experiences the astral world every time their body falls asleep, but not consciously. Therefore, what we are attempting to achieve is the *conscious* departure from the physical world into the astral world with no dreaming of any kind.

First, practice self-observation throughout your day. Divide your attention by using the "Key of SOL:" Subject, Object, Location.

Subject: Remember the subject from moment to moment. The subject is one's self. Always remember yourself. What is "you" is divided into millions of parts, which generic names such as: pride, envy, lust, hatred, jealously, anger, etc., etc. In each moment, observe yourself: Who is the one feeling? Who is the one listening? Who is the one talking, acting, and eating? Who is the one that is jealous? Who is the one that is angry? Who is the one that is stressed? The answer is not "me," it must be more than that, because what is "me" is very complicated, it is a book of too many volumes.

Realize that you are nothing more than a child of God in each moment. In this way, you will find yourself less fascinated with the impressions of life. When fascination ends, the awakening of the consciousness is inevitable. When fascination ends in the astral world, a lucid dream is the result. From there, we can have objective experiences.

Object: What are your surroundings? From moment to moment, observe the world around you, objects in your presence. In dreams, our surroundings often make no sense whatsoever. If you practice during the day to observe your surroundings, then this habit will be carried over while in the astral world. How many people are in the room? How many lights are there? See the surroundings as something new, like a child. You may find yourself in your house, except the carpet is a different color. Why is it a different color? If you notice this, then you immediately you will discover that you are dreaming. But, if you always enter into every place and do not take the time to observe it carefully, you will do the same in your dreams, and you will not be able to use this to awaken your consciousness.

Location: Perhaps you notice that you are on top of a mountain. Ask yourself, "How did I get on a mountain? I have never been here before. Am I dreaming?" Perhaps you find yourself at work. So, recall how you arrived at work. Was it a logical sequence of events? Or did it occur strangely, as if you just appeared "here" (as it occurs in dreams)? You may find yourself at school, yet, you no longer attend school, so why would you be there? You may find yourself talking to your diseased loved ones. Don't you want to awaken so you can talk to them consciously? To do so you must awaken here and now, from *moment to moment*. Perform these questions silently in each moment, each time you find yourself in a new locale. Thus, the awakening of the consciousness is the outcome.

There are tests you can perform as well. If you apply these methods of observation, you will eventually notice times when something feels different. You will think, "Am I dreaming?" Yet, how do you know if you are in the astral world? You exist there every night and never suspect that you are anywhere but the physical world. When you are clearly awakened in the astral world, the clarity of this world is *exactly* that of the physical world. You can even say that the clarity and "realness" of the subtler dimensions is *greater* than this physical world. The only thing that makes dreams incoherent is the sleeping consciousness. Therefore, never assume you are in the physical world if you wish to have success in dream yoga. The beginner cannot tell the difference between vigilance in the physical world, and vigilance in the astral world. Therefore, one must always question appearances by performing tests.

One test is to see if you can fly. In the astral world one can fly without much effort at all. To do this, perform a little jump into the air with the firm intention of flying. Do not doubt that you will not fly. If you doubt, if you are skeptical, then you will sabotage your experiment. If you need to, excuse yourself to the bathroom and attempt the little jump there.

Another test one can perform is to see if the matter around you is physical matter or astral matter. Astral matter is elastic and porous. You can, for example, pull your finger, or your nose, to see if stretches. If you are in the astral world, they will stretch. Also, you can try to put your hand through a wall. This can be done without effort in the astral world. Yet, you have to awaken first, and doubt nothing. Just observe without expectations. If you attempt to place your hand through, for example, a wall but expect yourself to fail, then it is obvious that you will arrive at your preconceptions.

The astral world, the world of dreams, is a great mediator. The astral world is both subjective and objective, depending upon the state of mind. An objective experience can easily transform into a dreaming, subjective experience. Likewise, the opposite can occur when one awakens from a dream state and becomes fully conscious in the astral world. The subjective nature of the astral world means that there are innumerable testimonies concerning this world. The best thing to do is throw away all those theories and stories and instead become conscious in the astral world.

Every student must become adept at astral projection. This allows for work to be done during the night as well as the day. Angels and Masters can be invoked in the astral world, temples can be visited, etc. Samael Aun Weor delivers hundreds of keys and clues to astrally project. The reader is advised to consult his works for a wealth of information upon this topic.

SOTERIOLOGY: SALVATION HAS REQUIREMENTS

> Jesus said, "If those who lead you say, 'See, the Kingdom is in the sky,' then the birds of the sky will precede you. If they say to you, 'It is in the sea,' then the fish will precede you. Rather, the Kingdom is inside of you, and it is outside of you. When you come to **know yourselves**, then you will become known, and you will realize that it is you who are the sons of the living Father. But if you will not know yourselves, you dwell in poverty and it is you who are that poverty."
>
> – Saying 3, The Gospel of Thomas

> Neither shall they say, Lo here! or, lo there! for, behold, the kingdom of God is within you.
>
> – Luke 17:21

Everyone holds a particular opinion of the afterlife. Many feel comfortable in believing in a place of rest or supreme joy. Others are indifferent, some are afraid, etc. But in the end, what do we really know? Everyone has beliefs because this is all they can afford. Modern religions are not providing the tools for their adherents to acquire self-knowledge of that which is beyond the physical world.

The esoteric sciences do not deny the paradisiacal realities, however everything is paid with a price. Salvation, or liberation, is quite expensive. Although it may seem cruel, heaven is not something given to anyone for free. Heaven is won, and it is only for the courageous. The scriptures clearly state that Heaven is for the few.

An incredible degree of sincerity and courage are required to seriously contemplate these matters of life and death. For many, death is too morbid or frightening and any mundane excuse to think about anything but death is almost constant. It can be horrifying to look into the mirror and come to terms with the fact that our flesh and bones will one day rot away into dust. It brings sadness into our hearts to remember our dear friends and family no longer living physically. Nevertheless, every life is crowned with death. Therefore, we need to be sincere; it is important to meditate upon death. Those who avoid these topics do not realize it, but by doing so they will suffer more when the inevitable occurs.

If we want to know the truth we must first be truthful to ourselves. We enjoy simply *believing* in being happy after death. We like that viewpoint, so we believe it. Someone says, "It would be cruel if not everyone went to Heaven, and God is compassionate." Yes, God is compassionate, but not in the way many people think. God's compassion is beyond the comprehension of the everyday man, just as a parent's compassion is beyond the comprehension of a child.

How often do children do what is best for their development? How often do children not understand that the very actions they despise of their parents are, in fact, what is best for them? A child needs to go through many experiences, some painful, in order to reach responsible adulthood. The compassion of God is similar, but much more profound and "mysterious" (difficult to comprehend), because the development of a soul does not happen in one year or even one hundred years, but an entire eon, or more.

In the 16th century the Roman Catholic Church degenerated into the selling of sacraments and ecclesiastical positions. In a word, if you were wealthy, you were assured salvation. This idea, of course, is lunacy and has nothing to do with actual Christian Doctrine. As a response to this systemic degeneration, it was necessary for those involved in the Great Reformation to usurp the tyrannical power of the Church and hand it back to the people. This was done by focusing not upon the participation of sacraments or association with the Church, but by relying upon the content of the scriptures which, indeed, do not make much mention of the necessities of brick and mortar intuitions. As a result, Protestantism focuses upon individual qualities of a person and not mere membership to a Church. This is very good;

yet, the fallacy of Protestantism is their focus with belief and the mere acceptance of their doctrine as the pathway to salvation.

Martin Luther and all those who followed established necessary corrections which helped restore certain aspects of the Christian doctrine. Nevertheless, the idea that simple blind faith is the door to Heaven is a bit foolish. Luther would not agree with modern Protestantism, because it has swung too far in the opposite direction of what it originally opposed. Today, anyone can be saved according to Protestantism just by accepting Jesus as their personal savior. This line of reasoning is today supported by an incipient understanding of a few verses of the Bible.

No event in the universe happens out of a belief. No event occurs "just because." Every event is the exclusive outcome of a cause and effect relationship. We do not realize that when our consciousness leaves our body, we dream. Therefore, when our body is no longer alive, this will be the state of our consciousness. Thus we need to awaken consciousness, so when it is out of the body – either because the body is dead or the body is sleeping – we can experience the superior worlds. The cause of our sleeping lies within our own action and the effects are pain and suffering, not only physically but beyond these conditions as well. Nothing, and no one, can awaken consciousness without conscious work. No one but you can awaken your consciousness.

Christianity is often quoted as saying, *"Heaven is by the grace of god,"* and yes, by His grace we can enter Heavenly Jerusalem. However there is a lot of misconception about this. An integral study of the Bible clearly states that although *soteria* (salvation) is only possible through the grace of God, it does not mean that everyone reaches salvation, or that, as it is mistakenly believed by some, there is nothing one can do to alter the salvation of one's soul other than to believe in Christ. Although John 3:16 states that all those who "believe" in Christ shall have everlasting life, we have to understand the context of "believing" in Christ.

First we have to point out the difference between the Christ, and the man, Jesus. Jesus incarnated the Christ. Christ is a universal force that is everywhere. It is a terrible mistake to render a cult of personality around Jesus or Christ. Christ is not a person; Christ is beyond all sense of individuality. The Christic principle exists in all religious forms. Christianity is a highly synthesized mixture of Pagan, Egyptian, Hindu, and Jewish religions. The Christ principle is exists in all these religions, under many different names: Jupiter, Osiris-Ra, Vishnu, Odin, Chokmah, etc. The Fathers of the Church knew the realities of their religion's origins. The Fathers of the Church were perfectly aware of these things and made use of the facts in order to convert pagans. For example, Justin Martyr wrote in his *Apology* (circa 150 AD):

> And when we say also that the Word, who is the first-birth of God, was produced without sexual union, and that He, Jesus Christ, Our Teacher, was crucified and died, and rose again, and ascended into heaven, we propound nothing different from what you believe regarding those whom you esteem sons of Jupiter. And if we assert that the Word of God was born of God in a peculiar manner, different from ordinary generation, let this, as said above, be no extraordinary thing to you, who say that Mercury is the angelic word of God. But if any one objects that He was crucified, in this also He is on a par with those reputed sons of Jupiter of yours, who suffered as we have now enumerated.
>
> – Justin Martyr

Therefore, anyone with diligence can discover for themselves that Christianity is just another of the countless religious forms that expresses the same Universal Cosmic Common Religion according to its own time and place.

The only differencing factor between Christianity and all other religious forms that have appeared on this planet is that its founder, Aberamentho (Jesus), is the legitimate Savior of the World. To call Aberamentho merely an avatar or prophet would, in the strictest terms be a misclassification, because he is beyond that, he is the Savior. Aberamentho's mission is beyond that of an avatar's mission, it is related with the handling the extreme karma this world has engendered, and, because he has and is modifying the karma if this world for its betterment. This is what it is meant when it was written in the *Pistis Sophia* that Jesus changed "the Fate and the sphere over which they rule," and due to this, he really is the Savior of the World.

However, and this important factor is too easily overlooked, just because Jesus is the savior of the world, does not mean he is automatically the savior of your interior, psychological world. The exterior Jesus (the man), and the inner Jesus (the Inner Savior or Inner Christic Principle) are two distinct things. Jesus, the man, taught the doctrine of the inner Savior, the Intimate Christ that lives within.

Christ is not interested in the formation of a personality cult, however Christ *is* interested in incarnating within you, yet this task requires tremendous efforts. So, how is Christ going to incarnate within each person? How is our inner spark going to become one with the great Fire? Simply believing is not going to do that. Christ is no more or less powerful, no more or less motivated, to perform His great works based upon how many people believe in him.

In light of this information, the reader may ask why John 3:16 and many other Bible passages use the greek word *pisteuvw* or *pistis*, meaning faith, as a legitimate pathway to salvation? The answer to this question becomes clearer when we take a look at the words *belief* and *faith*:

> Faith is the direct perception of what is real, it is fundamental wisdom; it is the experience of that which is beyond the body, the affections and the mind.
>
> We must distinguish between faith and belief. Beliefs are found stored in the Intermediate Mind. Faith is a characteristic of the Inner Mind.
>
> Unfortunately, there is always a general tendency to confuse belief with faith. Although it seems paradoxical, we emphasize the following: "Those who have true faith do not need to believe."
>
> This is because genuine faith is living knowledge, exact cognition, and direct experience.
>
> For many centuries people have confused faith and belief. Now it is very difficult to make them understand that faith is true knowledge and never futile beliefs. [...]

> In order to enter the kingdom, the treasure of faith is essential. As long as the psychological split has not been produced within each of us, faith is more than impossible.
>
> Faith is pure knowledge, direct experiential wisdom.
>
> Faith has always been confused with vain beliefs; Gnostics must never make such a serious mistake.
>
> Faith is direct experience of the real, the magnificent vivification of the Inner Human Being, authentic divine cognition
>
> – Samael Aun Weor, *The Great Rebellion*

The Gnostic text we already mentioned, entitled *Pistis Sophia*, gives us a further clue. Pistis, which is *faith*, becomes one with Sophia, which is *wisdom*, through the Gnostic Mystery of her Thirteen Repentances. This is the *pistis* we need, we need faith-wisdom, or experiential wisdom, or simply gnosis. The type of belief being purported today as faith is wrong, because our beliefs, even if they are supposedly holy, do not bring wisdom. Now let us read John 3:16 in the context of Gnosticism:

> For (*the Innermost*) God so loved the (*inner psychological*) world, that he gave his only begotten Son (*the Intimate Christ, which is born the stable of the dirty mind, is washed in the sexual waters, and is crucified among the masses of psychological aggregates*), that whosoever have faith (*not belief, but faith: meaning direct experience or gnosis*) in him should not perish, but have everlasting life.
>
> – John 3:16

This is the true Gnostic doctrine, the same primeval Christianity that is taught by the Ante-Nicene Fathers. The founders of Christianity have more in common in what is called Gnosticism today than what is called Christianity today. It is self evident, that even Irenaeus, the supposed great prototypical "Anti-Gnostic" spoke truths that if were spoken by any other person would be considered "Gnostic" or heretical. If any modern Christian today integrally read *Against Heresies*, they would know that amongst many other "Gnostic" allusions, Irenaeus states that Jesus lived for much longer than the dogmatized 33 years imposed by the Church. In fact, he devotes an entire chapter to discuss his argument against it.

They, however, that they may establish their false opinion regarding that which is written, "to proclaim the acceptable year of the Lord," maintain that He preached for one year only, and then suffered in the twelfth month. [In speaking thus], they are forgetful to their own disadvantage, destroying His whole work, and robbing Him of that age which is both more necessary and more honourable than any other; that more advanced age, I mean, during which also as a teacher He excelled all others. For how could He have had disciples, if He did not teach? And how could He have taught, unless He had reached the age of a Master? For when He came to be baptized, He had not yet completed His thirtieth year, but was beginning to be about thirty years of age (for thus Luke, who has mentioned His years, has expressed it: "Now Jesus was, as it were, beginning to be thirty years old," when He came to receive baptism); and, [according to these men,] He preached only one year reckoning from His baptism. On completing His thirtieth year He suffered, being in fact still a young man, and who had by no means attained to advanced age. Now, that the first stage of early life embraces thirty years, and that this extends onwards to the fortieth year, every one will admit; but from the fortieth and fiftieth year a man begins to decline towards old age, which our Lord possessed while He still fulfilled the office of a Teacher, even as the Gospel and all the elders testify; those who were conversant in Asia with John, the disciple of the Lord, [affirming] that John conveyed to them that information. And he remained among them up to the times of Trajan. Some of them, moreover, saw not only John, but the other apostles also, and heard the very same account from them, and bear testimony as to the [validity of] the statement.

– Irenaeus, *Against Heresies*, Book II, Ch. XX, v. V

The only way to reconcile Irenaeus' Gnostic statements with his Anti-Gnostic statements is by assuming that he (or whoever else may have forged his writings) did not have access to the complete esoteric Christian doctrine. It is known by any Gnostic that the number 33 as the years of the life of Jesus is not only symbolic, but imposed by those knew the significance of the number, which is related with the number of vertebrae in the spinal column. The primeval Christianity is what is considered today as *Gnostic Christianity*, and although Irenaeus spoke against many different Gnostic sects, if his doctrine were analyzed today, it would be considered another form of Gnosticism. Today, everyone believes that Jesus lived 33 years, which is a *Gnostic* symbol, which is the very reason why Irenaeus fights so hard to state it as such. How is it that a founding Father of the Church directly opposes the modern, official Christian doctrine taught today? It is all due to ignorance. The literal number of years has no importance upon the actual teachings, which is why the number 33 has been used. Those who knew, the Gnostics, taught of the 33 years to the public but revealed its esoteric significance only to an elite few. However, in modern times, the significance of the symbols of the Gospels have been forgotten and ignored. In its place is an absurd form of literalism which does nothing to aid the process of salvation.

> The narratives of the Doctrine are its cloak. The simple look only at the garment - that is, upon the narrative of the Doctrine; more they know not. The instructed, however, see not merely the cloak, but what the cloak covers.
>
> – The Zohar, iii.
>
> The Mysteries of the Faith (are) not to be divulged to all [...] It is requisite to hide in a mystery the wisdom spoken.
>
> – St. Clement of Alexandra, *Stromateis*

Every sincere Christian should reevaluate his or her knowledge of the Gospels, and relate them not to a historical past, or an interpretation dealing with the external events of the world, but instead always with the *inner relationship with one's self.* Now, in order to remove any doubt concerning the uselessness of simply accepting a Christian doctrine, or merely believing that Jesus was the Christ as the method of salvation, let us quote Matthew that states very clearly that many who speak well about the Lord will not necessarily be saved by the Lord:

> Not everyone that saith (*or believe*) unto me, Lord, Lord, shall enter into the kingdom of heaven; but he that doeth the will of my Father which is in heaven.
>
> Many will say to me in that day, Lord, Lord, have we not prophesied in thy name? and in thy name have cast out devils? and in thy name done many wonderful works? (*Did not we say, "I believe in you? I accept you as my god and savior?"*)

And then will I profess unto them, I never knew you (*because you did not know me, you do not have real faith in me because you do not live the doctrine*): depart from me, ye that work iniquity.

Therefore whosoever heareth these sayings of mine, and doeth them, I will liken him unto a wise man, which built his house upon a rock:

And the rain descended, and the floods came, and the winds blew, and beat upon that house; and it fell not: for it was founded upon a rock.

And every one that heareth these sayings of mine, and doeth them not (*but only recites the doctrine, only says that he believes and that he accepts the doctrine*), shall be likened unto a foolish man, which built his house upon the sand:

And the rain descended, and the floods came, and the winds blew, and beat upon that house; and it fell: and great was the fall of it.

– Matthew 7:21-27

Before we continue further, let us be absolutely clear: we are speaking of the very same Celestial Realms of Buddhism, Nirvana, the lands of bliss where the rivers run of milk and honey, as found in every scripture of every religion. Please do not confuse the use of "Heaven" as an exclusionary method. Many people like to tell us what Heaven is even though they have not seen the Kingdom of Heaven. They only understand these things intellectually. They judge and condemn others, always feeling super transcendent. They lock up the kingdom of heaven within their beliefs before they enter themselves. Few people in the ranks of organized religion have any superlative connection with God. Mostly, they simply read the passages of their doctrine without any comprehension whatsoever.

Jesus said, "I am The Way, and the Truth, and the life; no one comes to the Father, but by Me."

– John 14:6

Enter by the narrow gate; for the gate is wide and the way is easy, that leads to destruction, and those who enter by it are many. For the gate is narrow and the way is hard, that leads to life, and those who find it are few.

– Matthew 7:13-14

The very pompous person reads these passages and says, "Yes, I have found the way, Christianity is the true and only religion. Here it is, the proof, written in the Bible." Just like that they feel by the grace of God that they will enter into Heaven. There is a lot of arrogance and ignorance in that type of thought. To think that Christianity itself is the narrow gate is illogical. How can Christianity be the narrow gate? How is Christianity the difficult path? Without an atom of doubt I will say that Jesus, along with the authors of the Bible, do not speak about the Christian Religion as the one path to God. In all truth, as we know, many are those in Christianity, wide is the door and easy is the acceptance of Christianity. So in what way is Christianity the difficult path of the few?

Read carefully: I am not saying a word against any religion. Rather I am stating that Christianity is the most popular religion in the world, and here in the western world, the most accepted religion. I am bringing into the spotlight of investigation a major contradiction of many preachers and orators. In happens to be that many are full of religious pride.

No claim to any religion will deliver anyone "by the grace of God" into paradise just as no theory will grant anything without its actualization. Religion as theory means nothing without its practice, its actualization – to live the thing in itself. The person who practices religion as a theory – as something that can never actually to be proven – is mistaken. Therefore, do not waste time reading this book as theoretical doctrine, as something to store in memory and pass on at the table of intellectual dialogue, because that is nothing more than a waste of time.

> Among thousands of men, perhaps one will strive for perfection; among those strivers, one possibly achieves perfection, and among the perfect, perhaps one knows me perfectly.
>
> —The Bhagavad Gita 7.3
>
> Jesus said: I shall choose you, one out of a thousand and two out of ten thousand, and they shall stand as a single one.
>
> – Gospel of Thomas, verse 23

The difficult nature of interior illumination is made quite clear in these passages, and all those who find the Narrow Gate, those who truly travel the Difficult and Narrow Path, are the same, regardless of who they are, what their background or religion is. "They shall stand as a single one." Two misconceptions of exoteric Christianity are being made clear. First, Christianity is not an exclusive religion, regardless of what those who preach it say, and second, the exclusivity of salvation is not based on religion but rather on internal *merit*. That is to say, ==Heaven is for those who have conquered Hell==.

> The kingdom of heaven suffers violence, and the violent take it by force.
>
> – Matthew 11:12

What do we mean by conquered? We mean that Lucifer grants us his light when we defeat him. Esoteric Christianity tells us that Satan is our internal physic aberrations, the ego. In ancient Egypt, before the Latin term *ego* was created, these entities were known as the Red Demons of Seth. These demons attacked Osiris relentlessly. In Buddhist terms, the ego is termed as aggregates. This is the Doctrine of the Many. It states that our psyche is made up of not one center, but many centers, many "I's." Of course we know this already. This is why we say, "Oh, I changed my mind, I don't want that anymore!" There it is: we have changed our mind, our ego. We do this constantly. The mind free of ego does not change, it is consistent, it is permanent, continuous. Removing the ego results in a Continuity of Purpose, a Permanent Center of Consciousness.

What do we mean by defeating Lucifer? We mean that we must resist the luciferic temptations as Jesus did in the desert. Fanatics are scandalized by the very idea of Lucifer. These people are unfortunately ignorant. They do not understand the need to polish the dark brass in order to make it shine. Every Light casts its Shadow and those fanatics who scream blasphemies against Lucifer know nothing of these matters, they ignore them entirely. The fall of Lucifer has been misunderstood.

We need to whitewash the devil with maximum expedited urgency. This is only possible through fighting against our own selves, by dissolving all those conjunctions of psychological aggregates that constitute the "I," the "myself," the "itself." Only by dying in ourselves can we whitewash the brass and **contemplate the Sun of the Middle Night** (the Father). This signifies that we must defeat all temptations and eliminate all of the inhuman elements that we carry within (anger, greed, lust, envy, pride, laziness, gluttony, etc., etc., etc.). A trainer in the psychological gymnasium of human existence is always required. The divine Daimon, quoted many times by Socrates, is the very shadow of our own individual Spirit. He is the most extraordinary psychological trainer that each one of us carries within. He delivers us into temptation with the purpose of training us, teaching us. Only in this way is it possible for the precious gems of virtue to sprout from our psyche.

– Samael Aun Weor, *The Initiatic Path in the Arcana of Tarot & Kabbalah*

There is no sense in believing that after death we will all ascend to Heaven in order to live in peace and bliss for eternity. That is delusional. It must be made clear that the reason that this earth is full of so much pain is because we are here. If we were all to go to Heaven, then what would become of it? Have you ever put a drop of ink in a glass of pure water? You understand then, one single drop pollutes the entire glass. All of the water is affected. With this, you will understand that only the Heavenly are in Heaven. Would you attend a public event without taking a shower? It would be absurd to appear in filth, and if you did, you would not be asked to return. In the same sense, only those who are attempting to clean themselves (psychologically) will be helped by those above, and only those who actually perform the work will gain entrance into Heaven.

There is an absurd belief that, in some way or another, Heaven will automatically change what we are inside. If that were true, then God would be a tyrant, because we would have no freewill in these matters. God is not going to save us until we chose to save ourselves. God respects freewill, and if our will is degeneration, then he will respect that, even though it means more karma and pain for us. It is only a matter of the facts that today, there are actually very few heavenly people to be found, and by this notion, we fully understand who the few that Jesus speaks of.

We are the ink, full of darkness. If we were to purify this darkness, then we could be pure ourselves, and by that, our purity would be Heaven. Those who believe it is impossible for man to reach the state of divinity are mistaken. Radical changes simply require profound inner work.

Heaven is found within. Heaven is the peace, solitude, and love that is found when our darkness is converted into the divine Lucifer, Angel of Light. Heaven is internal, it is found in the internal worlds. It is found through the most difficult struggle and profound emotional crisis. The inner worlds, the heavenly worlds, exist "within" the three dimensional world. Heaven is a supra-subtle reality. Only a blissful mind could sustain itself within Heaven. The ego cannot sustain itself in Heaven.

While the path to Heaven is difficult, the gate to perdition is wide and easy. It is very easy to ignore our wrongdoings, and we must make an effort to stop ignoring the outcome of our actions. We must also comprehend what provoked such action in the first place. For example: A hidden self agenda (to appease our desires) may, unbeknownst to our self, trample upon the legitimate needs of another. Later, we wonder why others are upset. The usual and easy solution to this is to believe it is not our problem. Yet, the reality is that we are simply ignoring our own self. We need to comprehend our actions. Every action that leads to conflict is multifaceted and complicated. This is because the psyche of each individual is a total disorganized mess.

Exterior conflict is the always outcome of interior conflict. Know this profound fact first intellectually, then, through conscious efforts, know this from your consciousness. Unlike the mind or memory, when values are assimilated by the consciousness there is no ability to forget them. Thus, when we awaken our consciousness we cannot "forget" the truth of our life, we simply *know* it at all times, within ever increasing fidelities and profundities. When you know the truth, when you are one with the truth, there is no suffering, there is only heavenly bliss.

Have a little compassion for your fellows. If they are angry at you, remember that you are also not an innocent lamb. Besides, when the day comes that you truly comprehend that the angry one is the suffering one, you will no longer accept their hateful words. Knowing this, how can you react in resentment to someone presenting you with undesirable impressions? If you remember the reality of the situation, it is him or her, not you, who is suffering in that the moment.

Anger is terrible. No one wants that anger, and when it manifests within someone, that person is a slave to that anger. But if you do not remember yourself, if you identify with those words, then you become a slave too. When one comprehends the reality of their situation, instead of feeling insulted, one feels spontaneous compassion for their situation (for their inability to sustain mental equilibrium).

When someone insulted the Buddha, he replied, "If someone offers you a gift and you refuse it, to whom does it belong?" The insulter replied, "It belongs to the giver." So, the Buddha said, "Sir, I cannot accept your gift." Samael Aun Weor says that the negative impressions we receive from our fellow men should be like a check that not has insufficient funds to back it. If you do not cash the check then what is it worth? It is nothing. So, do not accept the negative impressions of others. Use the methods of self-observation to comprehend why it is so difficult to perform this task. Meditate on your actions and work to cultivate a true loving kindness for your fellow men.

Do you see another speak about his or her works with pride? If that brings about resentment or jealously from within, then both of you are suffering, however, if you see the pride in another person in a selfless way, you will immediately notice their pride is a form of suffering. Even if they are very "happy" with a smile and a hearty laugh, pride is always a manifestation of suffering. Perhaps you have yet to comprehend this, but in time you will.

Before you can comprehend the manifestations of suffering in another person, you must comprehend your own manifestations of suffering.

In this way, working upon the self is a selfless act. Yet, if you notice the suffering in others and become prideful in that, or do not care about that, then you are working upon yourself in a selfish way. Many people are proud of their spiritual lifestyle. Many people do not covet material items, but instead covet virtues or spiritual powers. The mind is a true labyrinth that few find their way out of. Just when you think you have found the way out, you find yourself fooled again. Do not fall into these traps, because the spiritual aspirant has the power to commit crimes far worse than the common criminal.

So, by living our days with compassion towards our fellow man is how we orientate our lives towards the path to Heaven. Realize however, that in order to be compassionate, we must remember ourselves. If we view the world from our normal center of gravity, which is the ego, then we are obviously viewing and accepting the world from a selfish or egotistical view. However, if through conscious efforts we elevate the frequency of our consciousness, if we activate the free consciousness, this offers a superior vantage point to view the events of life from.

The Inferno or Hell

> The steep path of self-development is… as mournful and gloomy as the path to Hell.
>
> – Carl Jung

Unfortunately, there are many who do not think Hell is a reality because they believe it is something cruel and that would make God cruel. Atheists and pseudo "New Age" movements reject Hell because they do not understand it. They only see it as a concept, and how such a concept can be abused to strike fear into others. They see it this way precisely because they have too much fear. Obviously Hell is used as a tactic to strike fear into others, but these people are mistaken to an even greater degree. Although

Hell is painful, there is nothing cruel about this place, for we pay not a penny more than we owe in our karmic debts. Hell is part of the grace of God, the pity of Christ. Hell is not only a reality, but an absolute necessity.

In the beginning, the soul is nothing more than a spark of light, and somewhat like a baby it cannot even perceive or control its own "movements" is the infinite. Therefore, although there is happiness in this soul, there is not consciousness of this happiness, and conscious happiness is the only true and legitimate happiness. As a result, the purpose of existence is to acquire self-consciousness. In this path to absolute consciousness, there are many levels and phases. The first phase we can denote as the evolution of the soul.

Evolution and its twin counterpart, devolution, are mechanical processes that happen *to* the units undergoing the evolution or devolution. Therefore, these units (souls in this case), do not manage their own evolution; from their point of view the evolution occurs without any special effort at all. This is because higher intelligences, what we can call Angels or Devas, are the ones who are consciously managing the waves of evolution and devolution.

This type of development, evolution, is required for the soul because it provides the necessary experience that a soul needs. An embryonic soul could never manage its own development precisely because of the very fact that it is nothing more than an embryo. For the embryonic soul, the processes of evolution are like a womb in which certain qualities, although mechanical in nature, provide the development required to one day perform conscious acts and thereby develop consciousness itself.

Do not confuse the evolution of the soul with the evolution of the diverse types of animal organisms that exist on our planetary crust. The evolution of species is a different yet related process. The units (that we mentioned above) in this case are physical organisms as opposed to souls. All animal organisms are either in a state of evolution or devolution. Some species are devolving, while others are evolving. The souls within these animals, however, exist on their own evolutionary track.

In the evolution of the soul one progresses through the mineral, plant and animal kingdoms. Through these kingdoms we gain a physical existence, and then the developmental capacities to handle a motor brain, an emotional brain, and an intellectual brain. We pass through the four kingdoms of mineral, vegetable, animal and humanoid (intellectual animal) and we are given these machines we call the three brains. The three brains are the cylinders, so to speak, of the human machine, and we are given them for free, without self-effort. However, in the devolution of the soul, these very things are taken away from us, because in reality they were never really ours to begin with, they were Nature's. This mechanical process of devolution is Hell.

Light shines, and from that, darkness is created. From this we understand that hell is as real as any other aspect of creation. We visit our internal hell with our nightmares. In hell we experience many horrible things – that is no doubt. But we have to eliminate our fear. Everyone will experience Hell in one of two ways:

1. By Conscious Will.
2. By Mechanical Laws of Nature.

The second way is much more painful than the first.

At some point in time our Essence (currently the only part of ourselves which is Holy) was inserted into the great machine of Nature in order to evolve and experience. When the time came, we were born with a very complex machine at our hands. I am speaking of the human body, the human machine: a body-machine capable of *intellectual* concepts.

In the evolution of the soul, the three brains are developed. Instincts are founded in the Plant Kingdom, emotion is developed in the Animal Kingdom, and intellect is developed in the Intellectual Animal Kingdom (Humanoid Kingdom). This is the "ripening" of the soul. However if the fruits are not used to develop a superior creation, the true Human Being, the Kabbalistic Microcosmos, it is obvious that the fruit begins to rot.

The three brains, which were are something positive and regenerative during our evolution, become negative and degenerative during devolution. In others words, as the downward slope of devolution occurs the three brains convert themselves into the Three Traitors. This is what is already happening today. The three brains were tools of Nature in our evolution, but to become a Human Being we must transcend Mechanical Nature.

The human machine is just that, a machine. It is a machine that can transcend its mechanical nature. Nature uses the human machine to process energies for her own economy. Nature, however, is like a jealous mother does not want her son to leave the home. Because, when one wishes to become conscious, one is wishing to transcend the sphere of Nature. Nature of course wants nothing to do with that, and in no way could it, for it would undermine the purpose of Nature.

The human machine is the only vehicle that can reach the Angelic or Buddhic state. This is an extremely significant fact. It took many days to reach the pinnacle of natural evolution, and we as a race have already begun our devolution. The time is now to act because in the day of our intellectual existence is now in its twilight.

When the embryonic, animal soul becomes a human soul (through conscious efforts) this soul has been born again. As a rule, the intellectual animal body is only afforded to the embryonic soul for 108 lives. This is number related with the certain very sacred truths that we can summarize as "nine rotations of the twelve." This is related with the 108 ritualistic movements around the sacred cow of Hinduism, and the 108 beaded necklace of Buddha. This number is significant in many religions and everyone is free to investigate this fact.

The embryonic soul receives the Twelve Aspects of Creation, the Zodiac, and one complete gestation is always related with the Ninth Arcanum. The number nine is the number of gestation. Everyone knows that a baby is due in nine months. The complete gestation of the Creation is nine times twelve. This is why the esoteric philosophy states that we have 108 lives of existence within a human machine before the Second Death. After one complete gestation of the Creation a transformation must occur, which culminates in exactly one of two things:

1. The Second Birth: *Very truly, I tell you, no one can see the kingdom of God without being born again.*
2. The Second Death: *The lake of fire is the second death.*

The "First Death" is the death of the physical body as we have already discussed. We know that the "I" lives beyond the physical existence, and in fact the "I" is the reason for our return to physical existence. But, because the "I" had its birth in time, it will eventually die in time too. This is the Second Death. The Second Death is the death of the "I," the Myself, the Ego.

Every one of us is currently living out our 108 lives as a human. This number is mathematically related with twelve times nine. We know that Heaven is won by the warrior who fights for his self-realization. For example, the *Mahabharata* is the story of the warrior Arjuna who under the direction of Krishna (Christ) must fight against those of his own blood (ego). Therefore it is obvious to those who comprehend these things that if we do not work for Paradise then we will not achieve it.

If we do not work, then Nature will do the work for us through the mechanics of devolution. Nature will devolve everything it evolved. It does this in a very slow and very painful process. Nature will eventually destroy the "I" and this is what Hell is when we enter it as a failure to awaken positively. However, if we choose to be the warrior, then we will destroy the "I" through conscious efforts here and now, and we will awaken consciousness positively.

We must understand that we can only enter Heaven when the ego is dead; the "I" cannot be in Heaven, the sinning Adam and Eve cannot gain reentrance to Eden. So, the processes of Hell kill the "I," and afterwards one exists in the Superior Worlds.

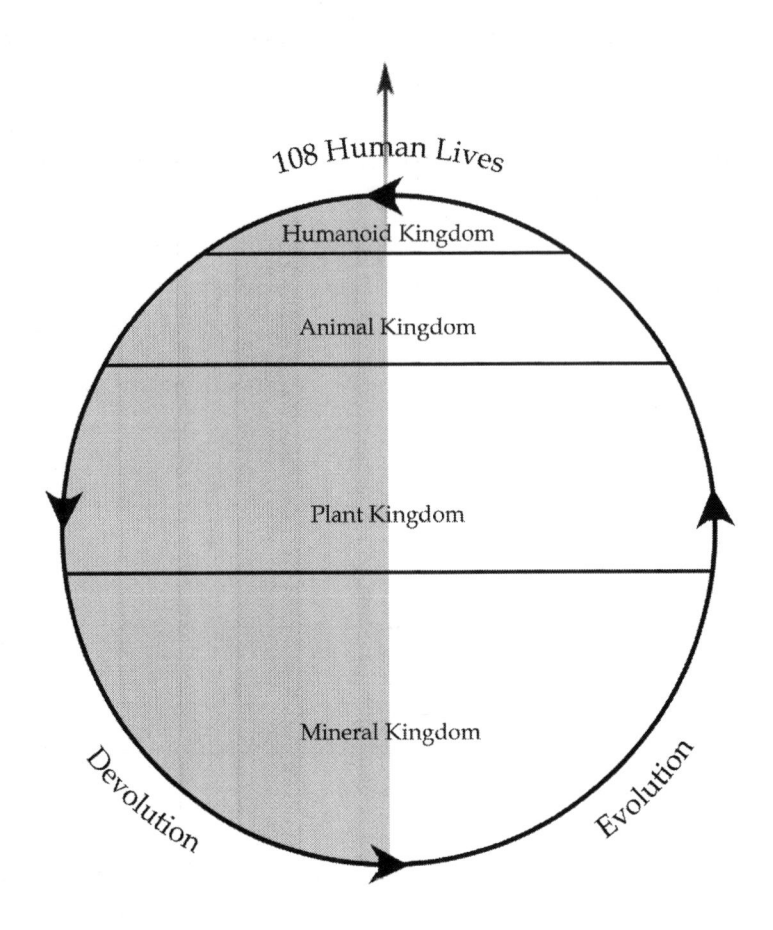

The Wheel of Samsara upon the Mechanical Axis of Time. The Vertical Arrow represents the Direct Path to the Absolute. This Path is only attainable within the Humanoid Kingdom.

If we refuse to take up the duty of our own self-realization, then Nature will send us to hell when our "fruits" begin to putrefy. We have 108 lives fecundate the soul, but after that point the ego-mind has already become terribly rotten. Thus, the embryonic soul, the Essence trapped within ego, becomes totally submerged in Hell in order for our demonic ego to be destroyed. If this did not occur, then nothing would stop the ever growing malignance of the ego. It would continue to grow infinitely. Therefore Hell is the destruction of the ego and our return to a pure state.

Our ego is a product of time and eventually it will die. This is irrefutable. If we enter Hell through the mechanics of nature, then we will return to Heaven upon the same octave we left. Our real objective is to return to Heaven in a superior octave. This only occurs when we kill the "I" ourselves through willful action. When we destroy the "I" we are *rebelling* against the Mechanical Laws of Nature, and by doing so free ourselves from them.

> He who has an ear, let him hear what the Spirit says to the churches. He who **overcomes** will not be hurt at all by the second death.
>
> – Revelation 2:11

If we can overcome ourselves, by ourselves, we will receive a Psychological Death, the Death of the I. The death of the "I" through Thelema (Will) gives us a chance to ascend into Eden. This is why Jesus died before he rose again. This is why Hercules, Orpheus and Osiris descended into the Inferno. In contrast to the Solar Hero, if the "I" dies in the Burning Pit of Fire, that is to say through the Mechanics of Nature, we will return to exactly where we came from. That is the Second Death of the Apocalypse of Saint John.

It is better to work for our Superior Liberation, because the Path of the Failure is more painful. In order to avoid this path, we must work with Psychological Death, with Alchemical Birth, and with Conscious Sacrifice. We die to the ego. We are born through chaste sexuality. We live intensely by sacrificing for the love of humanity. In other words, we must become Alchemists. We must follow the instructions of the great Alchemist known as Jesus Christ. He informs Nicodemus of the Fire and the Water.

> Now there was a man of the Pharisees named Nicodemus, a member of the Jewish ruling council. He came to Jesus at night and said, "Rabbi, we know you are a teacher who has come from God. For no one could perform the miraculous signs you are doing if God were not with him."
>
> In reply Jesus declared, "I tell you the truth, no one can see the kingdom of God unless he is born again."

"How can a man be born when he is old?" Nicodemus asked. "Surely he cannot enter a second time into his mother's womb to be born!"

Jesus answered, "I tell you the truth, no one can enter the kingdom of God unless he is born of water and the Spirit. Flesh gives birth to flesh, but the Spirit gives birth to spirit. You should not be surprised at my saying, 'You must be born again.' The wind blows wherever it pleases. You hear its sound, but you cannot tell where it comes from or where it is going. So it is with everyone born of the Spirit."

"How can this be?" Nicodemus asked.

"You are Israel's teacher," said Jesus, "and do you not understand these things? I tell you the truth, we speak of what we know, and we testify to what we have seen, but still you people do not accept our testimony. **I have spoken to you of earthly things and you do not believe; how then will you believe if I speak of heavenly things? No one has ever gone into heaven except the one who came from heaven – the Son of Man. Just as Moses lifted up the snake in the desert, so the Son of Man must be lifted up, that everyone who believes in him may have eternal life.**

"For God so loved the world that he gave his one and only Son, that whoever believes in him shall not perish but have eternal life. For God did not send his Son into the world to condemn the world, but to save the world through him. Whoever believes in him is not condemned, but whoever does not believe stands condemned already because he has not believed in the name of God's one and only Son. This is the verdict: Light has come into the world, but men loved darkness instead of light because their deeds were evil. Everyone who does evil hates the light, and will not come into the light for fear that his deeds will be exposed. But whoever lives by the truth comes into the light, so that it may be seen plainly that what he has done has been done through God."

– John 3:1-21

Jesus was telling Nicodemus about the Fire and Water, about the Death and Rebirth. All of this helps us understand how the The Bible is an alchemical treatise: it begins with the Genesaic Waters of Life and ends with the Apocalyptic Renewing Fire, INRI. The Waters are related with The Baptism. Dante tells us in *The Inferno* that those who populate Limbo have not been baptized.

> That they did not sin; neither did their virtue bestow
> On them any advantage, for they did not receive
> Baptism, the gateway to the faith you follow.

These lines are rarely understood correctly: Dante is not making an exclusionary statement towards Christianity. Dante is speaking in an allegorical context, that is to say, not the physical baptism but the baptism of the Waters of Life. The element of water is always sexual, it is that which gives life. When we dress ourselves in the Wedding Garments of the Soul, we have been baptized in the Waters of Life. The only thing that belongs in heaven is that which came from heaven. It is made very clear in the Bible that we must be suited correctly to enter Heaven.

> Jesus spoke to them again in parables, saying: "The kingdom of heaven is like a king who prepared a wedding banquet for his son. He sent his servants to those who had been invited to the banquet to tell them to come, but they refused to come.
>
> "Then he sent some more servants and said, 'Tell those who have been invited that I have prepared my dinner: My oxen and fattened cattle have been butchered, and everything is ready. Come to the wedding banquet.'
>
> "But they paid no attention and went off – one to his field, another to his business. The rest seized his servants, mistreated them and killed them. The king was enraged. He sent his army and destroyed those murderers and burned their city.
>
> "Then he said to his servants, 'The wedding banquet is ready, but those I invited did not deserve to come. Go to the street corners and invite to the banquet anyone you find.' So the servants went out into the streets and gathered all the people they could find, both good and bad, and the wedding hall was filled with guests.
>
> "But when the king came in to see the guests, he noticed a man there who was not wearing wedding clothes. 'Friend,' he asked, 'how did you get in here without wedding clothes?' The man was speechless.
>
> "Then the king told the attendants, 'Tie him hand and foot, and throw him outside, into the darkness, where there will be weeping and gnashing of teeth.'
>
> "For many are invited, but few are chosen."
>
> – Matthew 22:1-14

The Waters of Life are the same waters spoken of in regards to the Voice of Many Waters. The Waters give life, and sustain eternal life. The Waters are related to the Holy Spirit. The Angels have lips made fertile by the Holy Spirit. They speak the WORD and create with the WORD. This is all sexual, the larynx is a sexual organ that creates the Verb. The Holy Spirit is the impregnator of life.

> And I heard, as it were, the voice of a great multitude, as the sound of many waters and as the sound of mighty thunderings, saying, "Alleluia! For the Lord God Omnipotent reigns!"
>
> – Revelation 19:6
>
> Now the earth was formless and empty, darkness was over the surface of the deep, and the Spirit of God was hovering over the waters.
>
> – Genesis 1:2

We all contain a personal inferno – the ego. In order to understand and eliminate the ego we have to *consciously* descend into it. This is what Dante was doing in his poem we have already mentioned. Hell is the only place we awaken from our ego. When we *choose* to descend into the depths of our Psychological Inferno the result is an awakening consciousness in its perfection. In stark contrast, the lazy ones who never spent any time improving themselves become completely detached from their Being and are left alone. The result is an awakening of consciousness of *error*.

This concept is fundamental and it is only proper to further speak about this matter. Awakening consciousness in perfection means we know ourselves by knowing our errors and removing them. Our Father is always by our side and will even carry our cross as Simon helped Jesus. The crucifixion and resurrection are horribly painful because all events in Hell are painful. However when we *descend* into the Inferno by Will, we are helped and when we triumph, we experience Nirvana (joy). To *fall* is another thing. To fall is fatality, *radical fatality*: the death of the soul.

The soul is an *interface* to the Spirit. What is the difference between the soul and the Spirit? The Spirit Is, while the soul is something acquired. Therefore, the Spirit never dies because was never born, but to know the Spirit we must incarnate the soul and perfect it. The soul can die and be born; the Second Death and the Second Birth are things of the soul.

So, when we are lazy, when we push our Great Work until the "end of the day," then we become failures of existence. After the mathematical 108 lives are lived, we enter Hell not by our will, but through the mechanics of nature. Our soul becomes divorced from our Spirit, and the egos attached to the soul are destroyed through pain, in a completely mechanical way through Nature. Then the *Essence*, the raw material that never unfolded into the Solar (Soul) Bodies returns to the Spirit.

In this mechanical process referred to as the Second Death, we become aware of ego, we awaken negatively, because it is being destroyed. Our ego is brought into violent movements because nature is destroying it. This is of course painful. When we *fall* into hell, we are falling into inferior laws; consequently our consciousness becomes controlled by more complication (Hell). When we *descend* we do so to become enlightened, to remove our karma related with those inferior laws which keep us bound to hell. The failures fall. The heroes descend.

It is necessary that the ego dies. The ego will one day die. The fate of the ego is deterministic because its death is only a matter of time. There are two ways that the ego can die: Through Nature, or through Will (Thelema). In the Second Death, after the Ninth Sphere of hell our Essence is freed from the dirty clothes it did not wash (the mind with ego). Then it is happy again, but in *ignorance*.

Our Being is perfect but it does not know its own perfection. In order to understand its own perfection the Being sends the Essence into evolution in order to experience and become conscious. When this occurs the Essence unfolds into the authentic Human Soul and reunites with the Spirit. Religion is "regulare" and Yoga is "yug." Both words mean "to reunite." The purpose of religion is to reunite the soul with the Spirit in a conscious manner.

The common western notion of yoga is very incipient. Yoga is simply a word that means, "to yoke," to bring to together, to reunite, just as religion means "religare," which again means to bind or unite. Many in the west think that the totality of yoga is stretching exercises and gymnastics, yet this is only Hatha Yoga. Hatha Yoga is the most dense and unimportant aspect of yoga. Let it be understood that using Hatha Yoga as an ends to the means of uniting with divinity is absurd and a waste of time.

The Being wants To Be Conscious of What It Already Is. The Being is perfect, but to understand its perfection it must know it is perfect. Thus, the Being sends the Essence to evolve and become aware of the Being's perfection, and later reunite with it.

A lot of people ask, "How can something be perfect if it is not conscious of its perfection?" The intellect does not understand these things, therefore, let us meditate on the following: "In order to know, one must first not know."

For a failure, after the Second Death the Essence becomes free of ego. At some point it is reentered into nature within the Mineral Kingdom. Through millions of years, the Essence will next find itself in the Vegetable Kingdom and later, the Animal Kingdom. At the paramount of the evolution of soul lies the Humanoid Kingdom. It is here where one can once again attempt to leave the Wheel of Samara, become Radically Free and live in Authentic Happiness.

Hell is necessary. Without hell nothing would stop the perversions that the soul undergoes. Hell is for the souls who have failed to self-realize. Hell is the mercy of Christ because it allows the spirit to try again. The Spirit works to realize the soul and soul works to realize the Spirit.

Tantrism

> In Tibetan Buddhism, especially if you look at the iconography of the deities with their consorts, you can see a lot of very explicit sexual symbolism which often gives the wrong impression. Actually, in this case the sexual organ is utilized, but the energy movement which is taking place is, in the end, fully controlled. The energy should never be let out. This energy must be controlled and eventually returned to other parts of the body. What is required for a Tantric practitioner is to develop the capacity to utilize one's faculties of bliss and the blissful experiences which are specifically generated due to the flow of regenerative fluids within one's own energy channels. It is crucial to have the ability to protect oneself from the fault of emission. It is not just a purely ordinary sexual act. And here we can see there is a kind of special connection with celibacy. Especially in the practice of the Kalachakra Tantra, this precept of protecting oneself from the emission of energy is considered to be very important. The Kalachakra literature mentions three types of blissful experience: one is the blissful experience induced by the flow of energy; one is the immutable blissful experience; and one is the mutable blissful experience. To me, when Buddha took the celibacy vow, at that level he did not explain all the reasons behind that rule or that discipline. The complete explanation comes when we know the Tantrayana system.
>
> – The Fourteenth Dalai Lama, *The Heart of the Buddha's Path*

> Sexual magic is practiced in esoteric Christianity. Sexual magic is practiced in Zen Buddhism. Sexual magic is practiced amongst the Initiated Yogis. Sexual magic is practiced amongst the Mohammedan Sufis. Sexual magic was practiced in the Initiatic Colleges of Troy, Egypt, Rome, Carthage, Eleusis. Sexual magic was practiced by the mysterious Maya, Aztec, Inca, Druids, etc.
>
> – Samael Aun Weor, *The Perfect Matrimony*

Tantra is a widely used and widely misunderstood word. Tantra, in itself, is a word that describes the continuous movement of energy. Therefore, when something is properly described as *tantric*, it deals with how to control the energy of creation, how to transform it, to transmute it, to be in control of it. This entire book is a discourse in tantra, because it teaches the transformation of impressions and the transmutation of the creative libido from instinct to intuition.

In Buddhism, the word *tantra* can denote a book or a manual of practice, and many have seemingly nothing to do with sexuality. What we have to understand is that sexual energy is the basis of all creative energy, and meditation (the basis of Buddhism) is an exercise in the transmutation of creative energies. Truly, all spiritual exercises when performed correctly are tantric.

Although countless tantras contain sexual imagery, many Buddhists proclaim that this imagery is just a method to show our universal interdependence with all. It is commonly stated these manuscripts rarely have to do with *Maithuna*, Sexual Yoga. Regardless of the fact many so-claimed educated and experienced people affirm otherwise, the esoteric philosophy states that the highest form of tantric practice is the movement of energy between opposite sexes, and for this reason it is not a crime to refer to Tantra as Sexual Yoga itself.

In Buddhism, tantrism is the highest vehicle of the Dharma. The founder of the tantric vehicle (Vajrayana) was Padmasambhava, a name which literally means "lotus born." The whole biography of Padmasambhava is a symbolic tale containing the essential story of the Son of Man. Padmasambhava, the great tantric master, helps aspirants on all levels of the path because he incarnated Chenrezig, the Christ. His wisdom is far beyond the many saintly arhats, the very good shravakas, and even the pratyeka buddhas, because Padmasambhava is a bodhisattva with a compassionate heart. In Tibet, Padmasambhava is revered only second to the Buddha Shakyamuni.

The highest objective of tantrism is a radical psychosomatic transformation within all of its aspirants. Padmasambhava could not have achieved his radical transformation without a consort, that is, without White Tantrism (sexual magic). Yet, his highest teachings are only given to the most elevated monks of Tantric Buddhism. Outsiders do not have complete access to the pragmatic workings of how to practice with a consort-wife, and it would take a lifetime (or more) of diligence to be given access to the practices in Highest Tantra Yoga (anuttarayoga tantra) that are performed with a consort.

Likewise, in the west, the secret doctrine of our Lord Jesus was taught to his seventy disciples. The closest western term for tantrism is *alchemy*. The true essence of this Royal Art, which at its height in the medieval ages contained extremely bizarre sounding formulae, has remained hidden for twenty centuries. Alchemy is a paradigm of chemical nomenclature that is nothing more than a blind concealing its true purpose: how to handle the transformative energies of one's sexual potential.

To acquire the secrets of alchemy or tantrism was always a difficult ordeal. However this wisdom is now being given away for free. The bodhisattvas with compassionate hearts are very active in these days. They are very ready, willing, and capable of helping those who are asking for it. Their only will is to serve you if you are looking for liberation. The doors of esotericism are being opened in all the schools which still possess it, even if it is only slightly, and as a result the Dharma is freely spreading to the west.

Many of the schools and religions of yesterday are good vehicles of the eternal wisdom, yet, they do not teach sexual magic openly because that was never their purpose. Their purpose was to prepare the students by eliminating their ego and desire. Thus, chastity is taught. However, the summit of chastity is sexual magic, and there exists no school of a continuous lineage from antiquity that currently teaches sexual magic openly and freely to the public. Many adulterated schools teach forms of tantrism openly, yet their methods lead to abysmal results.

If one investigates, he or she will discover that the only schools teaching the full doctrine of sexual transmutation and clearly and openly are those based on the doctrine delivered by Samael Aun Weor. This doctrine, the resuscitated Gnostic Wisdom, is not his, nor does it belong to anyone, its origins can be traced back to the root of all religion and all existence.

Everything is composed of energy. Therefore, if you want to achieve transformation that Padmasambhava achieved, obviously it is the energy that composes your very being that must be transformed. But transformed in what manner? This is an important question, because in reality the energy composing one's own self is, by its very nature, already under a constant transformation. However, under normal conditions this transformation occurs within the intellectual animal in accordance to influences unknown to him.

Padmasambhava and Yeshe Tsogyal

"Glorious Guru Padmasambhava, please protect and guide me until I attain complete enlightenment."

The goal of the aspirant is to make the correct efforts that transform the energy in that way which perfectly reconciles the antagonism between opposing spheres of order. Nature is only concerned about achieving the level of equilibration required to sustain itself, to reconcile her spheres of order. There are however, other influences – superior influences to that of "Mother Nature" – that one can attune to, in order to achieve the total psychosomatic transformation that religion and yoga exist in order to accomplish.

These superior influences latently exist within the depths of our consciousness, and physically within the seed of man himself. Consequently, the sexual act is very important, for no other act is both a reconciliation of opposing spheres of thought, feeling, and action, but furthermore between the active (positive – male) and passive (negative – female) principles.

In nature, animal sexuality concludes with the release of energy in the expectation that this energy will be transformed into offspring, wisely conserving the sexual energy until it is time to procreate. Intellectual animals, however, carelessly expel the sexual energy at every moment possible.

To dispose of the creative energy in an unintelligent and materialistic manner is a terrible waste. To abuse the creative energy simply to gratify the senses is truly something morbid, because this can only be done at the expense of achieving higher states of consciousness. People confuse this pleasure with happiness and love. By using this energy to achieve orgasm the body can secrete masses of chemicals into the bloodstream, yet, the outcome of all this does not signify happiness. The orgasm or ejaculation in any form whatsoever is a waste of energy, because it is never necessary. Only lust requires the orgasm, and to use one's creative energy to get a sensation is a massive squandering in terms of its potential.

This form of disposal is a very crude and, in time, a degenerating expression of creativity. Tantrism, on the other hand, is interested in the regenerative expression of creativity. In *anuttarayoga tantra*, to even consider the orgasmic sensations to be spiritually beneficial is a considered a "root downfall."

The regenerative expression of creativity takes place when, although vast quantities of energy are placed in movement, none of it is wasted. As with any organ of the biological machine, there are two fundamental ways the creative organs can be used: for the development of the animal psychology, or the development of the human psychology.

Using the creative organs to expel the psychical, psychic, or spiritual energy is the way to develop or strengthen the animal psychology. Such action (orgasm, ejaculation, adultery, lust, etc.) is the level of sexual expression of an animal. The intellectual animal, in his present state is so because he has already achieved all that is possible through mechanical sexual impulse. The problem is that with emergence of individual will the mechanical sexual impulse has been mishandled and submerged within innumerable psychological aggregates. Our true individual will has become trapped in desire to become ego-will which is anything but individual. The ego is legion in its wills.

Using the creative organs to transform sexual energy, not just the physical manifestation but all of its subtle and superior counterparts is the level of sexual expression of a true human being. This is how a true human being expresses himself sexually. That being said, it is necessary to understand that this world is not populated by authentic human beings, but by intellectual animals.

> Two trees are growing in *(the)* Paradise *(of the biological organism)*. One bears animals, the other bears humans.
>
> Adam ate from the tree that bore animals *(because he fornicated like as animal, and as a consequence bore the psychological image of an animal)* and became an animal and brought forth *(psychological aggregates that act like)* animals.
>
> The tree whose fruit Adam ate is the Tree of Knowledge *(through the orgasm)* so his sins increase. If he had eaten fruit from the Tree of Life *(through sexual transmutation)*, the one bearing humans, the Gods would worship *(or revere)* man and woman, for in the

beginning God created man and woman *(and through transmutation they can bare the image of God)*.

Now *(in modern life)* they create *(using sexual energy in the negative way, a false)* God *(within their psyche)*. In the world humans make *(false)* gods and worship their creation *(which are really animal desires)*. It would be better if the Gods worshipped them!

– The Gospel of Philip

We are here in order to become a true human. Yet, in order to achieve that, one needs to transmute the sexual energy instead of wasting it for sensation. As it turns out, this is a terrible sacrifice to the fornicator. However remarkable it may be though, those who learn how to transmute their creative energy enjoy it. It is not a crime to enjoy sexual transmutation.

Those who realize the benefits of sexual transmutation no longer even consider the orgasm. Why? Because they know that the sensations of sex are just a product, they are *empty*. Sensations come and go but they never leave contentment. Remember what emptiness is. Love itself has nothing to do with sensations felt during sex. The sensations are fine, and to enjoy sensual love is a good thing, but do not make the mistake of ejaculating the semen. That crystalline substance, that wine, needs to be refined and refined again, until there is not a single imperfection. Thus, by not reaching orgasm, the creative potential is fully realized and the image of God shines within Man. Man is only the image of God when he reflects Him, and God is perfect.

Although it may seem absurd, the truth is, if someone is wasting the sexual energy via orgasm or ejaculation, then the level of "love" they know is really incipient, illusory, crude, and fatally mixed with desire. This is a sad fact to contemplate. People are searching for the answers as to why their life is a total mess. It all revolves around the power of sex.

Clearly, the orgasm is the transformation of the creative-sexual energies into physical sensation. It is interesting that we fully understand that the very same energy that creates children is seen as something that can be wasted without any negative consequences. Healthy sexuality is fundamental for our physiological and psychological development. The basis of vitality is sexuality.

A happy marriage is founded in a healthy sexual life. The honeymoon can be sustained for the entire life of a marriage if the man and woman know how to intelligently enjoy voluptuousness. When voluptuousness is vibrating during the sexual act, enjoy, renounce, pray. Use this creative, volatile emotional state to "melt" the hardened mental aggregates.

> Voluptuousness: to all hair-shirted despisers of the body, a sting and stake; and, cursed as "the world," by all the afterworldly: for it mocks and befools all erring, misinferring teachers.
>
> Voluptuousness: to the rabble, the slow fire at which it is burnt; to all wormy wood, to all stinking rags, the prepared heat and stew furnace.
>
> Voluptuousness: to free hearts, a thing innocent and free, the garden-happiness of the earth, all the future's thanks-overflow to the present.
>
> Voluptuousness: only to the withered a sweet poison; to the lion-willed, however, the great cordial, and the reverently saved wine of wines.
>
> Voluptuousness: the great symbolic happiness of a higher happiness and highest hope. For to many is marriage promised, and more than marriage –
>
> To many that are more unknown to each other than man and woman: - and who has fully understood how unknown to each other are man and woman!
>
> – Frederick Nietzsche, *Thus Spoke Zarathrustra*

During the sexual act, if orgasm and ejaculation is refrained, after a period of time a heightened state of consciousness is achieved. This is a form of bliss and happiness, it is a terribly divine and cosmic force called love. In these delightful and paradisiacal moments, focus the light of your consciousness, like a magnifying glass under the Sun, upon a particular psychological aggregate in order to destroy it. While visualizing the aggregate being consumed in flames, petition your Divine Mother Kundalini to destroy this aggregate. The ego cannot resist the power of willfully directed chaste sexual energy against it, and as a consequence it will be destroyed. Using the destructive power of sex, one can destroy their own ego. This is how to intelligently use the power of sex. This is Sexual Magic. This is the magic of sex.

For the destruction to be effective one must know the aggregate being focused upon. It must have already been comprehended in depth. Psychological defects are found in daily self-observation, yet they are comprehended in meditation. Without meditation, the annihilation of the "I" is impossible, because the elimination of the ego is the forgiveness of sins, and forgiveness will only be granted when one no longer possesses the ignorance that produced the ego in the first place.

Psychological aggregates are eliminated in cooperation with man, woman, and the Third Logos (Holy Spirit). It is during the sexual act that one must ask the Divine Mother Kundalini to eliminate a defect. One should never enter into the sexual act without being mindful of the divine, and, properly, without a sacrifice for the altar. The sacrifice must be of the "I."

Deep within the profundities of the "I" sleeps the substance of Christ. Through the immolation of the Lamb, the Son of Man is born. Only when one is ready to give every last drop of blood, every last particle of "I," can one reach the summits Heavenly Jerusalem and receive their spiritual inheritance. The spiritual inheritance is the Treasury of the Light, the Golden Fleece, the hidden Manna mentioned in second chapter of the Book of Revelation.

In the Gnostic allegory, the Demiurge is a limited creator God. This is the "I." When the "I" is dead, then the Demiurge, the creator of Good and Evil, is defeated, and then Sophia, the liberated consciousness, shines with glory and happiness. Sophia weeps when she repents. She weeps thirteen repentances. The intimate Christ saves Sophia. Sophia returns to *Barbelo*, the place where she left. The ego whips Sophia on every step of her path. The tyrant of the Law has no mercy, and too much pain is inflected upon Her. Without Christ, without His Grace, Sophia would be lost forever.

> Two trees exist: the Tree of the Science of Good and Evil and the Tree of Life.
>
> The Tree of the Science of Good and Evil is the sexual force.
>
> The Tree of Life is the Inner Christ of each human being.
>
> The Tree of the Science of Good and Evil must be transformed into the Immolated Lamb of the Heavenly Jerusalem.
>
> This is only possible when we inebriate ourselves with the aroma of that forbidden fruit that is pleasant to the sight and of a delectable aspect, of which God said: Thou shalt not eat of it: for in the day that thou eatest thereof thou shalt surely die.
>
> We must always withdraw from our spouse before the orgasm; thus, we avoid the seminal ejaculation. This is how the Chakra Muladhara awakens. This is how Devi-Kundalini awakens.
>
> This is how we transform the Tree of Science of Good and Evil into the Immolated Lamb.
>
> This is how we transform into living Christs, and we eat of the Tree of Life that is in the midst of the Paradise of our God.
>
> – Samael Aun Weor, *Kundalini Yoga*

This sexual act, the Gnostic sexual act, is both sensual yet ascetic. Ancient Gnostic texts clearly state that the normal marriage is one of defilement, yet this is not because the sexual act itself is filthy. Historians and modern "experts" of Gnosticism are ignorant of the Gnostic Mysteries and they consequently misinterpret the Gnostic Doctrine. These ignoramuses (even if they are truly sincere) believe that the historical ascetic Gnostic sects were totally celibate, and rejected all manner of sex. In reality they were only chaste, not celibate (meaning they performed the sacrament of marriage but did not reach orgasm).

> Indeed, marriage in the world is a mystery for those who have taken a wife. If there is a hidden quality to the marriage of defilement, how much more is the undefiled marriage a true mystery! It is not fleshly but pure. It belongs not to desire but to the will.
>
> – The Gospel of Philip

What defiles man and woman is not sex, but the orgasm. This is the key to understanding Gnostic sexuality. Those who assume to be married, but practice the sacrament of marriage as animal (using the orgasm) are defiling their marriage, and they know not the true quality of marriage. The power of sex, free of all desire, is the only pathway of Gnosticism. The historians have taken the most holy of doctrines and destroyed it in their interpretations. They interpret the Gnostic texts in the same infantile and empiric manners that they interpret Bible with. Thus they are lost in a sea of confusion without even knowing this fact.

> Jesus answered her, "If you knew the gift of God and who it is that asks you for a drink, you would have asked him and he would have given you living water."
>
> "Sir," the woman said, "you have nothing to draw with and the well is deep. Where can you get this living water? Are you greater than our father Jacob, who gave us the well and drank from it himself, as did also his sons and his flocks and herds?"
>
> Jesus answered, "Everyone who drinks this water will be thirsty again, but whoever drinks the water I give him will never thirst. Indeed, the water I give him will become in him a spring of water welling up to eternal life."
>
> The woman said to him, "Sir, give me this water so that I won't get thirsty and have to keep coming here to draw water."
>
> He told her, "Go, call your husband and come back."
>
> – John 4 10:16

The Fountain of Youth is accessed in the sexual act. The Living Water is the water that lives within the organism, it is the *Ens Seminus*. To drink is to transmute the waters. Yet, how does one obtain these waters if the well is deep? Jesus tells the woman, "Go, call your husband..." because the Waters of Life are accessed through the sexual act. The Christ saves through the Cross of Sex. The Christ takes on the psychological aggregates, he dies within them to behead them, and he resurrects within the aspirant. The Christ is born by the cross, dies on the cross, resurrects through the cross, and ascends with the cross.

Every monad, every spark of light, is the creation of the Law of Three. The third aspect of the Law of Three, the Holy Spirit, manifests itself in a duality: Father and Mother. Within the Holy Spirit Father, Shiva, is the masculine polarization of the Trinity. Within the Holy Spirit Mother, Shakti, is the feminine polarization of the Trinity. Through the tantric mystery of Daath, a word that means *knowledge* or *gnosis*, the Innermost is formed. The soul is an exponent or unfolding of the Innermost.

It is the Holy Spirit Mother that is the Divine Mother Kundalini. The Divine Mother has a name in every religion: Mary, Athena Nike, Tonantzin, Diana, Cybele, etc. She is the individualization of the feminine cosmic intelligence that palpitates within the heart of your existence.

The Divine Mother is beyond sensation, beyond the sentiments, beyond reasoning, and beyond the mind. Only She can radically eliminate the psychological aggregates. The mind cannot do it. Only the Divine Mother can do it. The force of the Divine Mother acts within the chaste bachelor in the removal of defects, but only the act of union between man and woman can the destructive force of the Divine Mother reach its maximum potential. Consequently, in order to eliminate the most subtle psychological aggregates, it is necessary to perform sexual magic. This is why the Tantric Buddhists practice with a consort wife.

Likewise, the tantric Hindustani yogis practice sexual yoga in profound secrecy. They know that the magnetic induction produced by crossing the active and passive creative organs, the phallus and uterus, causes certain subtle currents of energy to manifest within the body, and that these currents are powerful enough to awaken latent powers or *siddhis*. The circuit formed is double: the male completes his circuit through his connection to the woman; the woman completes her circuit through the connection to the man.

The primary currents are labeled lunar, solar, and akashic. The lunar and solar passageways are called *ida* and *pingala* respectively. They entwine around the center conduit, the *sushumna*, which travels within the spinal cord itself. These subtle cords begin at the point between the anus and the genitals (the muladhara chakra), and end at the root of the nose. It is through these cords that the transmuted sexual energy, which is no longer physical matter, rises to the brain through these subtle conduits of energy. This current provides an active link between the magnetic center at the root of the nose, which is the pineal gland (related with the ajna chakra), and solar and lunar principles located within the seminal system at the muladhara chakra. This current is the Kundalini.

> The sexual transmutation of the "Ens Seminis" into creative energy is made possible when we carefully avoid the abominable spasm, the filthy orgasm of the fornicators.
>
> The bi-polarization of this type of cosmic energy in the human organism was analyzed since ancient times in the Initiatic Colleges of Egypt, Mexico, Peru, Greece, Chaldea, Rome, Phoenicia, etc., etc., etc.
>
> The ascension of the seminal energy to the brain is performed thanks to a certain pair of nervous cords that in the form of an eight splendidly unfold to the right and to the left of the dorsal spine.
>
> We now have arrived at the Caduceus of Mercury with its wings of the Spirit that are always opened.
>
> This mentioned pair of nervous cords can never be found with the bistoury, because they are rather of a semi-ethereal, semi-physical nature.
>
> These two nervous cords are the two witnesses of the Apocalypse, the two olive trees and the two candlesticks standing before the God of the earth, and if any man will hurt them, fire proceeded out of their mouth, and devoured their enemies.
>
> In the sacred land of the Vedas, these two nervous cords are known with the Sanskrit names of Ida and Pingala. The first one is related with the left nasal cavity and the second one with the right.
>
> It is obvious that the first one of these two nadis or canals is of a lunar type. It is ostensible that the second one is of a solar type.
>
> Many Gnostic students may be a little surprised to find that although Ida is of a cold and Lunar nature, Ida has its roots in the right testicle.
>
> Many disciples of our Gnostic movement might receive the news as unexpected and unusual that although Pingala is of a strictly Solar nature, Pingala really emerges from the left testicle.
>
> Nevertheless, we should not be surprised, because everything in nature is based on the law of polarities.
>
> The right testicle finds its exact anti-pole in the left nasal cavity, as has already been demonstrated.

Ida and pingala entwine around sushumna. These nadis provide the pathway to awaken the seven fundamental chakras.

The left testicle finds its perfect antipode in the right nasal cavity and obviously this is the way it must be.

Esoteric physiology teaches us that in the feminine sex the two witnesses emerge from the ovaries.

It is unquestionable that within women the order of these two olive trees of the temple is harmoniously reversed.

Old traditions which surge forth from within the profound night of all ages, state that when the Solar and Lunar atoms of the seminal system make contact in the Triveni, close to the coccyx, then as a simple electric induction, a third force awakens; I mean, the marvelous fire of love awakens.

– Samael Aun Weor, *The Three Mountains*

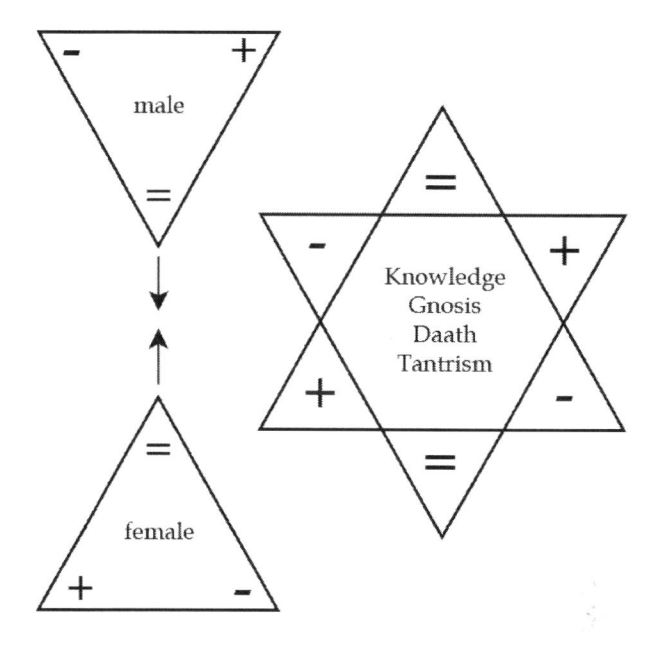

The tantrism of the Star of David. This is also the symbol of Daath and also known as the Seal of Solomon.

THE POWER IS IN THE CROSS

Remember this: *Tantrism is the science of harnessing the energy of the crossing of elements.* When we take advantage of the crossing of elements, we are (in accordance with Mahayana) practicing the highest form of "skillful means" to attain liberation. You cross your life with many people every day, and tantrism exists when you take advantage of your interactions with life. Meditation is harnessing the outcome of crossing willpower with conscious imagination. A family exists through the cross of husband and wife. Ideas are formulated with the crossing of thoughts and experiences. It is through the Creative Cross that all things emerge.

This is why the cross symbol exists everywhere. Recognize the Christian cross, Odin's cross, the Egyptian ankh, the crosses found in the Mayan temples, etc. The swastika or bent cross is a symbol found in nearly every religion: Buddhism, Hinduism, Jainism, Native American traditions, the Grecco-Roman mysteries, etc. The swastika is a spinning cross that moves due to the induction of the crossing of elements.

The tantric Vajrayogini mandala displaying intersected triangles and swirling swastikas.

The symbol of two triangles crossing is the rudimentary symbol of crossing of elements. A triangle is the geometric expression of the creative numeral. The Law of Three is the Law of Creation, which is the passive, active, and neutral forces acting in harmony. Two triangles crossing, one the inverse of the other, is a symbol found in all the world which symbolizes the mystery of tantrism. In Hebraic kabbalah, tantrism is *Daath*, which means knowledge. This is the same as the Greek word gnosis.

> For the Gnostics, the Cross is not, by any measure, a conventional symbol, but the representation of an invariable Law, which covers (without any single exception) the entire gamut, the entire range of the actions of Nature.
>
> Whoever studies the fundamentals of chemistry knows that the reaction of the elements happens only when they are crossed with others; for instance, H_2O, the chemical formula of water, is simply the crossing of two molecules of hydrogen and one of oxygen. So

water, this precious fluid indispensable to organic life, is the outcome of the Cross. The power to produce water is in the crossing of hydrogen with oxygen.

The harmonious march of a system of worlds depends on the cross - the magnetic point where the two forces (centrifugal and centripetal) are found equilibrated. Therefore, the power which supports the worlds is in that magnetic Cross of space.

A masculine cell (named zoosperm) is crossed with a feminine cell (named ovum) in order for the human entity, the outcome of this cross, to emerge. Consequently, the human being is the outcome of the crossing of a masculine zoosperm with the feminine ovum.

"Nothing can come into existence without the power of the Cross."

Nothing can come into existence without the power of the Cross.

The sincere and ideal shaking of hands crosses and harmonizes the mutual affection of two people. Therefore the Cross of the handshake originates the living affection between two souls.

Walking on the street, a handsome youngster finds an attractive damsel; they glance at each other, and from that prodigious, subtle and impalpable Cross (yet palpable in its magical power) affection, love, is born, which later organizes a home. Their Cross will produce astonishing effects, such as the multiplication of their species, the grandiosity of a country, and perhaps the birth of a new genius who will increase the progress of science or philosophy for the sake of the world. The magnetic crossing of two views shows and demonstrates that power is in the Cross.

A seed is introduced within the earth and it crosses its power with the chemical elements which constitute the structure of the planet; thus, trees, flowers, fruits and new seeds are produced, which will eventually increase their species and multiply them ad infinitum. Therefore, the power is in their Cross.

Nothing new can exist, nor can the old be transformed without the Cross. For such causes, we, Gnostics, wise to such excellence, know precisely the power of the Cross and this is why we offer reverence to the Cross. This reverence to the Cross is not based on a belief, but on an absolute and immediate knowledge. We, Gnostics, are mystics of the Truth and are always willing to know all things, leaving aside (as a worthless thing) any type of belief, since belief makes a person foolish, stupefied, and unconscious. Audacious people always take advantage of stupidity and unconsciousness, in order to govern and command the naive crowds, who as sheep follow their chiefs, who are as stupid and unconscious as the crowds.

The cause of all the events of nature is in the Cross, and exceptions do not exist in this.

When someone reveals some philosophical, social or scientific idea, it is crossed with the ideas of those who listen, and this is how new reactions are produced, either for finding the truth of what the speaker presents, or rather (if his knowledge lacks a good foundation) to reject his pretensions of being a sage. Therefore, intelligence is tested and truths are discovered through eliminating what is incorrect, by means of the crossing of ideas.

When our sight is crossed with a being or object, an experience about beings and things is acquired.

The protean substances of the food that we ingest, when they are crossed with our physiological, cellular life, produce crossed reactions that renew the life of the worn cells and create others new. If the substance is not good for our organism, then the biochemical crossing of the substance with the secretions of our specific internal organs produce reactions in order for that substance to be properly eliminated from our organism.

The Cross encloses the mystery of all imaginable powers, whether these are physical, intellectual or moral.

A person who can find some philosophical, scientific, or rational fact, which does not depend on the power of the cross, does not exist. Thus, once again we can emphatically affirm that the power is in the Cross and that the natural and scientific Cross of the Gnostics has nothing to do with beliefs nor with any such instruments of torture.

The Cross of the Gnostics is the power of the Universe constructing atoms, molecules, cells, organs, organism, worlds and any system of worlds.

The intellectual aspect of Gnosis is the outcome of the crossing of luminous ideas, which produce new states of consciousness. In the moral or emotive aspect, the power is in the Cross that produces all the marvelous sensations that ennoble and dignify the soul. Likewise, when musical melodies cross with the psychosomatic hearing capacities of the one who listens, a beautiful manifestation is produced within the sensibility of the soul, producing a harmonious, internal sensation as the outcome of this precious Cross of sounds.

The symbol of the cross is found in every religion.

When a person crosses his sight with the natural beauty of a flower, or a man crosses his sight with the natural beauty of a woman, feelings of divine inspiration appear within the soul; these feelings reveal unto the consciousness the utmost sources of perfection which are found in the harmony of shapes.

When thought is crossed with feeling, then the human being is not only in perfect harmony with himself, but moreover, he has more capacity to confront with success the labor which he is willingly doing.

It is necessary to think as a philosopher and to feel as an artist, because the magical, enchanting amalgam of the soul of the true superman emerges from the precious cross that unites the elevated thought of the philosopher with the divine sensibility of the artist.

This Cross of thought and feeling, in a perfect harmony and concordance, is what allows the development of the mystical and spiritual sides of existence.

Blessed and Divine Cross, in thy precious structure is found hidden all the mysteries of Nature and Life.

– Samael Aun Weor

Troubling Realities

For many pages we have outlined the imperative necessity of taking advantage of sexual magic. Indeed, this provides an excellent opportunity for many, yet, for others it is a troubling and immense problem.

Concerning those who are already married, some will find that their spouse has no concern for practicing tantrism. In this case it is important to emphasize that it is not required for one's spouse to perform transmutation during the act. Of course is it preferable if both the man and wife are in agreement but there are many cases in which one half of the couple refuses the doctrine of sexual transmutation.

What is important in self-realization is the action of the aspirant, not the will or action of their spouse. In the case of tantrism, of course, the situation is difficult if one's spouse rejects scientific chastity. Nevertheless, it is not impossible; the act can be performed with positive benefits for the practitioner even if one's spouse does not care for tantrism. As long as the aspirant does not reach spasm, and he or she is battling their lust to the death, progress can always be made.

What is required for the tantric practitioner is the transmutation of sexual energy, which firstly requires the cessation of the sexual spasm. This, obviously, requires a difficult and emotionally distressing revolution of the "old" habits of sex that one normally develops throughout life. But let it be known it is not impossible. A supreme effort to remember God while in the sexual must be made. It can be accomplished by ceasing any action that is performed solely to gratify senses, and to serenely attune the consciousness to the spontaneous love that inevitably vibrates in any true relationship.

Love – true love, not attachment – is a piercing armor that, when perfectly attuned to, is impenetrable to the afflictions of the sensual mind. When you find yourself identified with lust, it is because one has forgotten where love is. So long as we know how to love, the fragrance of the forbidden fruit elicits no temptation.

Another distressing fact many aspirants face is their age. Some who discover this doctrine are already past the prime age of sexual activity and they find themselves, or their spouses, unable to perform the sexual act. In the case of tubal ligation, vasectomy, or other irreversible sterilization, the sexual act can still be possible, yet unfortunately hindered in terms of transmutation of creative energies. In any of these circumstances one should perform the aspects of the work they can. It is totally worthless to lament one's current state of affairs. Accept who you are, accept what you are, accept where you are in life. Only from there can one change for the better. Work from where you are right now, for you are there for a reason. You cannot work from the position or status of someone else. The situation you find yourself in life is never the obstacle to the final liberation. The obstacle is the mind. If you are too old to have sex, then work with meditation, and in your next life you will not waste your youth.

Many bachelors, after hearing the doctrine of sexual transmutation, scuttle feverishly in search of a spouse. Yet, the karma of these individuals may be vastly different than the ideas their minds entertain. It is necessary for some students to remain single for period of time. This may be a year, or it may be ten years. These students must meditate. The Law is always fulfilled. No one who is sincerely working upon themselves is denied the right to enter into the Ninth Sphere (sexual magic). Their Love will appear like a thief in the night, initiated by a spark of sympathy. One must be watchful and serene.

There are Three Factors on the path of self-realization:

1) To die.

2) To be born.

3) To sacrifice for humanity.

Death in this sense is the death of the ego, the "I," the "myself;" death to the habits, the customs, the actions that provide the causes and conditions of suffering in daily life. Birth is that which takes place through sexual transmutation. The third factor is to work on behalf of others.

In the case where one cannot perform sexual magic, then the aspirant must still work with death. This means living the philosophy of momentariness, living instant to instant and transforming the impressions of life, utilizing the methods of self-observation and self-remembering, all founded on the basis of daily meditation. Those who feel as if they cannot progress because they do not possess a husband or wife are ignoring the factor of psychological death. The more one's mind is changed, the more one's life will change. When a person changes for the better, that person attracts better things in life, and as a consequence one of the best things an anxious bachelor can do is comprehend their selfish desires related to having a spouse and working with sexual alchemy.

For those who can perform the sexual act immediately in their work, that is good. It is recommended that short sessions transpire at first. This may be a few minutes, slowly working to up to more lengthy periods. Athletes of sexual yoga can practice for one hour daily. In order for tantric practice to be healthy, one must balance their frequency of amorous union with their frequency of meditation. Without meditation, tantrism degenerates into a thing of the flesh. The Gospel of Philip states that the true amorous union is of the spirit, while the common and defiled marriage is fleshly. This is because without remembrance of God the only thing left is the sensations of the flesh.

Secondly, such a high frequency of chaste sexual union requires that one is not wasting their sexual energy in their activities of the day. Because when someone is identified with any aspect of life, then he or she is wasting energy. Consequently they will find themselves unable to practice sexual yoga at such intensity because the energy will have been wasted.

The student, upon taking up the practice of sexual transmutation, may also unexpectedly begin to expel the sexual energy through dreams. Wet dreams may occur with the accompaniment of an erotic dream, yet many times the dream is so deep that there is no conscious experience or memory of it. Meditation of these moments is essential, in order to remember the dream. The mantra RAOM-GAOM is essential. The mantra RAOM-GAOM helps to penetrate the subconsciousness. When the dream is remembered, the incidents of this dream must be deeply comprehended in order to eliminate the cause of such dreams (lustful psychological aggregates). The physical body also must become attuned to the practice of sexual transmutation because the pathways to retain and return the sexual energy upwards are extremely atrophied in humanity today. This results in the energy, instead of going upwards, goes downwards, because it is the path of least resistance. With practice of the First and Second Factors all of this can be overcome.

In conclusion, we will state that the tantalizing ideas of sexual magic that are inevitably placed in the mind of the aspirant distort the terrible reality of what sexual magic actually is. Those who cannot presently perform the Second Factor must not lament. They must be prudent and work with tenacity against their own ego. They must awaken the consciousness and develop what is called in Buddhism *bodhichitta*, which is the mind of compassion and chastity, because this is necessary for both those who can currently work with sexual magic, and those who currently cannot.

The Third Factor can also be performed by anyone. Yet, while the ego is present, our actions are always corrupted. The true application of the Third Factor, which is to help others, only takes place after we have achieved domination of our own mind. Until then, we are subservient to its whims and its desires, which will distort and sabotage our best intentions. Only the one who knows how to swim can truly help a downing individual. We first need to pull ourselves up out of the water before we can really help others to do the same. Until that time one must of course perform all the help they can, yet, it is only being clarified that the Second and Third Factors only become potent in the individual who is accomplishing the First.

Indecision

> An inhabitant of a two-dimensional world would believe with his two dimensional psychology that all the phenomena occurring in that plane would have their cause and effect, their birth and death only there. Such phenomena would for these beings be identical. All phenomena which originated from the third dimension would be taken by these two-dimensional beings as unique facts of their two-dimensional world; they would not accept being told of a third dimension because for them, only their flat, two-dimensional world would exist. Nevertheless, if these flat beings would resolve to abandon their two-dimensional psychology, in order to deeply comprehend the causes of all the phenomena of their world, they could then depart from it and discover with astonishment a great unknown world, the three-dimensional world. The same thing happens with the question of Love. People believe that Love is only to perpetuate the species. People only believe that Love is vulgarity, carnal pleasure, violent desire, satisfaction, etc. Only the person who can see beyond these animal passions, only the person who renounces this type of animal psychology can discover in other worlds and dimensions the grandeur and majesty of that which is called Love. People sleep profoundly. People live sleeping and dream about Love, but they have not awakened themselves to Love. They sing about Love and believe that Love is that which they dream. When a human being awakens to Love, he makes himself conscious of Love and recognizes that he was dreaming. Then and only then does he discover the true meaning of Love.
>
> – Samael Aun Weor, *The Perfect Matrimony*

Tantra means *thread, loop,* or *continuum*. We can say that tantra is the continuous thread that is weaved upon the *Loom of God*, which is related to the Tarot's Arcanum 24: *The Weaver*. The synthesis of Arcanum 24, 2 + 4, is Arcanum 6: *Indecision (or The Lovers)*. This Arcanum is the choice between the Harlot and Virgin: between Black (Adulterated) Tantra and White (Pure) Tantra. This is related with the Sixth Commandment which states, "Thou Shalt Not Fornicate." Arcanum 6 is related with the birth of the Human Soul, and also with the Son of Man (the incarnation of Christ).

But it happened that after Jesus had risen from the dead he spent eleven years speaking with his disciples. And he taught them only as far as the places of the first ordinance and as far as the places of the First Mystery, which is within the veil which is within the first ordinance, which is the 24th mystery outside and below, these which are in the second space of the First Mystery, which is before all mysteries the Father in the form of a dove. And Jesus said to his disciples: **"I have come forth from that First Mystery which is the last mystery, namely the 24th"**...

– Pistis Sophia, Chapter 1

The Arcana 6 and 24

As we can see, in the *Pistis Sophia* Jesus himself speaks of the Arcanum 24. It is very interesting that scholars do not understand these things. Regardless, those who know, know the first mystery and the last mystery are sexual. This is the Alpha and the Omega, or we could say, *Daath* and *Yesod* (we will discuss this topic in more depth later). Every authentic occultist knows that sexuality is the cornerstone of existence. It is then only by simple corollary to affirm that sex is also the most powerful tool in existence. Existence itself is the fabric weaved by the Loom of God. The Loom of God is formed through the intersection of the Phallus and Cteis. The forces of the universe move like terrible thunders when the Man and Woman become One.

The bohemian tarot has its roots in the same wellspring of wisdom as the Hebraic kabbalah, because both are exponents of the Objective Science of Numbers. Wherever there is Number, there is Science, and numbers find themselves in every authentic religious text. Therefore, the fact that present historians cannot find any link whatsoever between Gnosticism and the Book of Tarot only exemplifies how dark the minds of men have become in this Kali Yuga (dark age). When we illuminate our minds, then all the religious texts become much deeper and richer in their meaning.

It is unfortunate that many traditions that have knowledge of how to handle the sexual energy have degenerated terribly. Some "spiritual" schools are teaching the student to reach orgasm, or to reach the spasm but not to ejaculate, and that this is the way to make use of the energy to awaken the consciousness. Those are adulterations of real tantrism.

Unadulterated tantrism is called White Tantrism, while adulterated tantrism is called Black Tantrism. White Tantrism is also called the Right Hand Path while Black Tantrism is called the Left Hand Path. If we carefully look at the image for Arcanum 6, we see the adept between two women. The woman to his right is the Divine Mother, and to his left, a woman of short hair. Her short hair represents her lack of chastity, and she entices the adept with her nudity. The Divine Mother has a serpent crown, because she is the manifestation of the sacred snake, the Kundalini of Hinduism. The man has fatally crossed his left hand over his right, and although his body faces towards chastity, his head turns backwards.

All authentic mummies have their right hands over their left, this is the true way. This humanity, however, always places their left hand over their right. The left hand represents the venous blood, the poisonous blood (passion). But, remember, the venous blood is transformed into the arterial blood through the transmutation performed in the heart. We must understand the symbolism here: transform the passions of sex into love. In the card however, the adept has placed his passion (left) over his chastity (right), thus, the outcome is fatality.

Look at the plate: the indecisive man is sinking in the waters. He is up to his knees. He has begun to work towards chastity, but he finds himself remembering his past ways; he is turning his head backwards and has forgotten why he left those past actions for new ones. Luckily, atop the card exists a child with an arrow. This is Eros, Cupid, attacking the woman on the left. The woman on the left is the ego. Why does Eros have arrows? The arrows are phallic: they represent scientific chastity, which is the weapon against the ego, and when the ego is annihilated true love reigns. Eros is the Holy Spirit.

Here, also we find that Ero's bow is shaped like a triangle, and, below there is an inverted triangle. That inverted triangle is black, and it represents the three brains, the Three Traitors, the triple aspect of the ego. That triangle needs to become white; it needs to be purified of all desire. When that occurs it can unite with the upper triangle and this is another type of symbolism of the hexagram. The downward triangle represents man, and the upward triangle represents divinity. When they are harmoniously united, then religion has been accomplished.

So, we unite with our inner divinity by uniting with our spouse in chastity. In this way, with healthy eroticism (energy of Eros) we empower our inner Holy Spirit, through the Divine Mother, to eliminate our undesirable defects that have been previously comprehended in meditation. In the Mahamudra (Great Seal) of tantric Buddhism, it is taught that when united with a "sealing partner" (spouse) the grosser elements of the mind are melted (due to the power of sexual union) and allows the tantric practitioners to realize the true essence of the Emptiness.

White Tantrism acts with the sexual energy united in the willpower to transform it into spiritual energy. Black Tantrism acts with the sexual energy united in the desire of sensation, to transform and further empower the ego. There are many methods of Black or Left Hand Tantrism. Some forms simply recommend only short periods of chastity, and that it is necessary to reach orgasm at some regular interval. Although this can be considered Gray Tantrism, it almost always leads to Black Tantrism.

Also popular today are doctrines advocating multiple orgasms, "full body" orgasms, the "three finger lock" technique to achieve orgasm without ejaculation or to achieve retrograde ejaculation into the bladder. Mistaken yogis believe that by achieving retrograde ejaculation, they have accomplished *vajroli*, but this is simply not the case. The most terrible forms of Black Tantrism involve the reabsorption of the ejaculated seminal liquor. They do this in order to assimilate the creative potential of the sexual energy without having to sacrifice the orgasm.

Yet, the outcome is truly terrible because after ejaculation the properties of the semen are modified, and upon reentering the organism through the urethra a violent reaction and subsequent rejection occurs when its transmutation is performed. This rejection damages the connection between the Spirit and the Soul. In turn, the reaction changes the momentum of the creative potential towards the atomic psychological infernos of the practitioner, which fortifies and strengthens the ego. This rejection occurs on the subtle planes, not the physical. Mistaken students interpret this rejection as the activation of their muladhara chakra, which exists at the base of the spine. Their chakras may be activating, but they would be spinning in the wrong (negative) direction.

Every chakra can spin in two ways, from left to right (clockwise) and from right to left (counterclockwise). The Left Hand Path provokes the chakras to spin from the right to the left.

The Right Hand path provokes the chakras to spin from the left to the right. Both types of activity produce psychosomatic results, but one is healthy for the soul while the other is not. It is important to activate our chakras in the positive fashion, moving them from the left to the right.

The foolhardiness of some of these mistaken tantric techniques is made clear when one realizes that such practices are impossible for the feminine sex. It is obvious that these methods are mistaken because a woman has just as much potential to self-realize as a man. If these misguided attempts at vajroli (transmutation) were the true path, then God would be a misogynist. So let us be clear, the true vajroli occurs when the sexual energy is elevated up the spine to the head, without any type of spasm or ejection of sexual energy. Both the man and the woman have the same potential to self-realize.

Remember, the ego is strengthened when it entraps free consciousness. When the ego has entrapped all of the free consciousness, the ego awakens from its psychological sleep. Therefore, to be awakened is a duality. One can awaken through the liberation of desire, or through the concentration of desire. When one awakens through the concentration of desire, then this person gains many negative powers over those who are psychologically asleep. These people are true demons, or Black Magicians.

The path of Black Tantrism is a very easy and quick way to gain psychological power in this world. The reason is because our psyche is already on the brink of being totally entrapped by psychological aggregates. For example, it is difficult to apply our willpower to maintain a daily routine of deep meditation, while it is very easy to apply our willpower to something like watching a television program. From an intellectual standpoint, an aspiring student knows that a routine of mediation is best, yet, he struggles to actually do so. However, if the student's willpower was totally liberated, the inner resistance to any action he wishes to perform would no longer exist.

A Black Magician is someone who is aware of the state of his consciousness and the type of power that can be usurped from it (the consciousness) when he strengthens and concentrates his desire. A Black Magician does not let his desire control him, he lets it *guide* and empower him.

Black doctrines and methods are quite enticing to the modern personality because it flows with the course of humanity. This humanity is sinking into its own inferno of desire. The "I" is desire, and this current culture advocates its deification. Thus, we are indoctrinated into believing that love is nearly synonymous with pleasure.

As we have stated, the battle between love and pleasure is terrible because so much of our willpower is entrapped by desire. It is the Sixth Arcanum, the struggle between love and pleasure, happiness and sensation. The third chapter of the Kalachakra Tantra mentions two types of Kalachakra masters: the upright master is completely chaste and never loses their blissful state of mind through orgasmic release, yet, false teachers have desire for the ephemeral effects of sexual orgasm, and thus they have lost their state of unchanging blissful awareness. We can say the same about Right Hand and Left Hand teachings. If a tantric doctrine advocates orgasm, it is a Left Hand teaching, if it advocates chastity, it is a Right Hand teaching.

Unfortunately in these times, we are tricked by our Three Traitors. We have our Arcanum 6 in the head, the heart, and the sex: 666. Because of this, because we all have the ego which is the mark of the beast, our good intentions are betrayed, and due to the overabundance of Left Hand teachings today, many people fall prey to them. Nearly all of the popular books written today on tantrism, neo-tantrism, sex magic, kundalini yoga, karma sutra, Taoist alchemy, etc., etc. are 100% Left Hand teachings.

The Right Hand Path is one with White Magic and White Tantrism. The Left Hand Path is one with Black Magic and Black Tantrism. Students become confused between these two diametrical systems because both make use of the same principles, the same words, the same symbols, and many times the same appearances. In the opening chapter of this work it was stated that both the Right and Left hand systems hide behind the cross. This is because both use the power of the cross, because everything is within the power of the crossing of elements.

The pentagram was also mentioned in the beginning of this work. Both the Black Magician and the White Magician make use of this symbol, and the naïve fail to understand their subtle differences.

> In symbolism, an inverted figure always signifies a perverted power. The average person does not even suspect the occult properties of emblematic pentacles. On this subject the great Paracelsus has written:
>
> "No doubt many will scoff at the seals, their characters and their uses, which are described in these books, because it seems incredible to them that metals and characters which are dead should have any power and effect. Yet no one has ever proved that the metals and also the characters as we know them are dead, for the salts, sulphur, and quintessences of metals are the highest preservatives of human life and are far superior to all other simples." (Translated from the original German.)
>
> The black magician cannot use the symbols of white magic without bringing down upon himself the forces of white magic, which would be fatal to his schemes. He must therefore distort the hierograms so that they typify the occult fact that he himself is distorting the principles for which the symbols stand.
>
> Black magic is not a fundamental art; it is the misuse of an art. Therefore it has no symbols of its own. It merely takes the emblematic figures of white magic, and by inverting and reversing them signifies that it is left-handed.
>
> A good instance of this practice is found in the pentagram, or five-pointed star, made of five connected lines. This figure is the time-honored symbol of the magical arts, and signifies the five properties of the Great Magical Agent, the five senses of man, the five elements of nature, the five extremities of the human body. By means of the pentagram within his own soul, man not only may master and govern all creatures inferior to himself, but may demand consideration at the hands of those superior to himself.
>
> The pentagram is used extensively in black magic, but when so used its form always differs in one of three ways: The star may be

broken at one point by not permitting the converging lines to touch; it may be inverted by having one point down and two up; or it may be distorted by having the points of varying lengths. When used in black magic, the pentagram is called the "sign of the cloven hoof," or the footprint of the Devil. The star with two points upward is also called the "Goat of Mendes," because the inverted star is the same shape as a goat's head. When the upright star turns and the upper point falls to the bottom, it signifies the fall of the Morning Star.

– Many P. Hall, *The Secret Teachings of All Ages*

Another example of the same elements used in opposite forms is the panca-tattva (five-element) ritual, also called the *Panchamakara*. The elements are referred to the five "M's":

1) Maithuna – sexuality – ether
2) Madya – wine – air
3) Mamsa – meat – fire
4) Matsya – fish – water
5) Mudra – grains – earth

These five elements are related with the pentagram, yet in a strictly feminine form. This is the *shakti* energy, the power of God that is assimilated within our organic machine when we know how to consume the five elements correctly. This ritual is performed in three ways.

Firstly, the exoteric Right Hand (*Dakshina*) yogis practice them in a symbolic sense. Maithuna is meditative union (Samadhi) with divinity; wine is the nectar of the gods (amrita), etc., etc. In this way yogis practice with the five elements in order to master them, yet, the ritual is ultimately incomplete because the ether element can never be mastered without sexual magic. But, again, due to morals of antiquity, few on the yogic path are permitted to receive the esoteric teachings which permit sexual yoga.

Secondly, the esoteric tantric Right Hand adepts perform literal coition (Maithuna) with a yogini wife, drink unfermented wine, and consume a small portions of meat, fish, and grains. In this way they consume the five *tattvas* (elements) which are intelligently used to reach innermost self-realization.

Finally, the Left Hand (*Vamachara*) yogis practice these elements also literally, as a form of ritualistic taboo breaking. Yet, they do so with fornication, drunkenness, and gluttony. This, they state, is a way of showing their non-attachments to all things, and a proof that sprit and body are one. These yogis are very mistaken. They believe that if they do the opposite actions of traditional morals and dogma that they are transcending the attachments to these morals and dogma. Of course this is absurd. One cannot simply do the opposite of the law and reach self-realization, because doing the opposite of a particular moral custom does not mean one has comprehended what that custom is.

The true transcending of inferior laws occurs when one comprehends the nature of these laws. When one comprehends the true nature of a custom, then one simply acts in the correct way, which may or may not be in accord to the traditional morals and customs of any particular locale at any particular time. Some morals and customs are very backwards and degenerate today and there is no need to follow them. Yet, if we simply break every law of the environment with nothing more than a will to oppose tradition, then we are simply inverting our mechanical obedience into mechanical disobedience, which has nothing to do with awakening consciousness.

However, when we observe the two forms of the Right Hand ritual, exoteric and esoteric, we see that the esoteric application is indeed transcending the lesser vows that the exoteric yogis must abide to. In the yogic tradition, the chela (student) is only permitted access to the esoteric teachings when a qualified and empowered guru yogi grants it, and this occurs when the guru sees his chela has comprehended the exoteric tradition and is ready to advance. The eating of meat is forbidden for the exoteric chela because it will provoke lust. Yet, the eating of meat in particular is very useful and even necessary for the esoteric adept who comprehends the powerful nature of the *tejas tattava* (fire element). One who is working on the erotic crucible of sexual alchemy needs the fire element, for it is a great source of power.

Undoubtedly, love is not pleasure. Love is not sensuality, passion nor sentimentality. Love has nothing to do with the orgasm, and although it seems like an obvious statement there are many so claimed Tantric doctrines that state otherwise. Tantric doctrines that speak of so called wonders of the orgasm do nothing but increase the bondage of desire that we have within. Desire is like a fire, and the more fuel you give it (the more you succumb to your desire) the greater the fire becomes. Yet, many students are mislead, because these doctrines state that one must reach orgasm while remembering god, or while having love flow through the body; really, the only thing that is flowing through the body in this moment is not love, but the fornication of that love into fleeting sensations. These sensations are very pleasurable, they "feel" wonderful to the body, but remember, the body is not you, the body is just a vehicle. Protect your vehicle, bathe it, groom it, dress it, but do not become subservient to its lustful appetites. The spirit is strong, but the flesh is weak.

It is obvious that desire is never satisfied, and sexual desire is the most difficult of all desire. To work in the Forge of the Vulcan (God of Fire; volcanoes) is to work with that fire. It is very difficult to work with the fire (Lucifer), but it also reaps glorious rewards. To work with the fire is to work with sexuality, to purify it in the same way that all the impurities of metal are purified by heat.

Of course the sexual act is very pleasurable and there is nothing wrong with that, the problem occurs when *fascination* of that pleasure crystallizes into lust. The sensorial phenomena that register during sex are wonderful things however few people can *transform* the impression of coitus correctly. More often we become very identified with the physical sensations, until all of our sexual energy is removed from us (the orgasm) – thus experiencing a few seconds of intense pleasure. That type of pleasure is of the same quality that a drug addict becomes identified with. People do not like that idea, but it is true. Both the orgasm and narcotics give an overload of sensorial impressions. When this occurs, the vibratory capacity of the physical body is pushed to the limit.

The orgasm occurs at that instant when the sexual energies, whose physical analogue are held within the various glands of the endocrine system, are expelled into the blood stream producing all sorts of seizures, muscle spasms, even a temporary loss of consciousness. It is common to confuse the orgasm as happiness, joy, love, etc. People see the orgasm as something as one the finer things in life, and the extremely mistaken people see it as something that actually uplifts or awakens the consciousness. Really, what happens is a loss of the most subtle and powerful energies of the human machine, the loss of the most expensive resource of the biological organism, the very energy that *intermediates* between divinity and humanity, the very energy that provides the ability of man to *create*. Furthermore, it is an experience that creates more attachment to sensation, more desire.

Drug addicts often believe they are feeling love when they are in actuality just intoxicated with sensation. Nevertheless, they write poems and songs and speak as though they are really in love. They are confusing love with pleasure. The Hippies thought they were experiencing "free love" when they partook in communal orgies, that they were experiencing god by digesting LSD, etc., etc. Their intentions were very good, but they failed to correctly polarize their Dionysian yearnings. It is the same with the so-called "wonders" of the tantric orgasm. In the very end, all that physical pleasure is balanced with psychological pain and disillusionment.

This is not to say that the tantric orgasm is without powerful results. The results are easily and readily developed by those who wish to do so. The tantric orgasm, that is, orgasm combined with directed willpower and imagination, radically empowers the ego to awaken within the consciousness. This brings negative metaphysical experiences and the development of negative tantric powers. Yet, simply because these metaphysical events occur they are mistakenly deemed by these practitioners as positive and enlightening. Of course nothing could be further from the truth. The powers that one can develop by awakening without removing the ego are limited to the regions the ego exists, namely Hell. That is why it is greater to be a beggar in Heaven than a king in Hell. In the end, such edifications of the "I" only mean it is more difficult for its inevitable destruction, which means more suffering for the Essence trapped within that "I."

Let it be deeply comprehended that Man and Woman have the power to create not only physically, but super-physically within the sexual act. The sexual act itself is divine, and when it is not polluted with animal passion, the divine presence of the sexual-creative energy will enflame the consciousness with the intelligence-fire of the Holy Spirit. This is achieved only if the desire for sensual pleasure is refrained, thus "shocking" or modifying the sexual energy into superior frequencies, into types of energy that will ennoble heart and clarify the mind.

Obviously White Tantrism is a frightful and absurd concept to the fornicator, because all he understands is passion, pleasure and sensation. Nevertheless, even if seems impossible, there are things more fine and volatile than sensual pleasures. As a society we do not know this because a transcendental sexual education is lacking today. Substituting for an authentic sexual education is an entirely animalistic and materialistic instruction that merely teaches methods of copulation to circumvent the fear of pregnancy and disease. In this way we remain entirely ignorant of the marvelous powers of the *Ens Seminus*. It is a shame that we do not know of the power of sexual transmutation and we do not understand the mystery of *Jehovah Elohim*. Truly, if the common man knew the power of the *Ens Seminus*, instead of laughing at this doctrine he would be weeping.

There are those who see value in the esoteric philosophy. They are willing to self-observe and change their own psychology, to reach a superior level of being. However, upon mentioning the sexual issue, the sexual problem, they flee like children. These people are simply not willing to sacrifice their desire; really it is that simple. If one truly wishes to understand their desire, they must renounce the orgasm. This is the secret way of every tradition; this is the foundation of change, the raw fuel of transformation. To become celibate upon the physical world is easy, and more importantly, such practice is harmful to the psychology. Celibacy has converted many "holy" men into fanatics and perverts who have abused children, burned wise men at stakes, etc. To transmute the sexual energy is to understand desire, to comprehend desire rather than crave or avert from it, and that is the work of a true man.

Society views the orgasm as "natural," and obviously it is natural for the fornicator to fornicate. Nearly every physical body produced today is through fornication. It is in our blood to fornicate. The nature of a fornicator is within us, but what the esoteric philosophy is concerned with is the development of a superior nature. Therefore understand that if one psychologically develops, their nature is transformed. Inferior natures can be transformed into superior natures, but only through independent willpower.

The nature of God is not the nature of an animal, neither the nature of the intellectual animal. God is not a fornicator, and Jesus stated thus, "Become perfect as your Father in Heaven is perfect." The Immaculate Conception occurs through immaculate sexuality. Remember, nothing is born without sex, and if you are pure in your sex, you will create purity (christic energy), and if you are perverse in your sex, you will create perversity (egoic energy).

If society only could look past their concupiscent minds and the addiction of physical sensation, then it could begin a revolutionary transvaluation. If this occurred, the world would be transformed. To our fornicating society, to give up the orgasm appears to be a terrible and impossible sacrifice. Yet, this is the way. No fornicator, no one who reaches orgasm, can make intelligent use of the most powerful aspect of man. It is very simple. It is impossible to self-realize without the power of the sex. If one is ejecting their sexual energies from their physical organism on a regular basis, then the foundation of their physical and spiritual vitality, over time, regresses and eventually is totally lost.

What is worse, when this potent energy of our sexual system explodes during the spasm, its violent movement degrades the fine and delicate conductors upon which the energy is passing through. There is no doubt that an indulgence in sexual pleasure leads to many hidden effects that science ignores. People grow senile ahead of their time due to fornication. This is lamentable, because few people know these things.

The enactment of lust only creates stronger lust. Desire can only produce its own likeness, and sexual desire only pleases itself through *novelty*. This dangerous combination leads us to become bored, to seek more sensation, and is the reason for the proliferation of sexual degeneration today, all the fascination with internet pornography, sadomasochism, pedophilia, bestiality, all kinds of sexual fetishes, etc. Sexual degeneration is particularly dangerous because it changes the very way the nervous system works. This is how someone develops infrasexuality. The terrible karma of such abuse (besides venereal diseases), is to be born in another life with an imbalanced nervous system resulting in, for example, homosexuality.

Love and desire are absolute opposites. They are two distinct things, like oil and water, that cannot be mixed into one. A moment of love is love, and a moment of desire is desire. When love is present, the temptations of pleasure are nonexistent. When love is absent, only pleasure and pain exist. In other words, when love leaves only Satan remains. When love leaves only Satan remains, and this process takes place within our heart.

Some people are traumatized by the name of Satan. Due to the fanaticism of the past, Satan has been transformed into a truly absurd concept implanted in the minds of believers. Likewise, any logical person absolutely rejects the classical depiction of a man with a pitchfork poking the behinds of heathens. That ridiculous concept is not the Satan that Jesus triumphed over.

Let it be clearly understood that the true Satan, in its final manifestation, is sexual desire. Satan is nothing more than Shaitan, "the Adversary." The advisory of religion is desire and the most potent form of desire is sexual. Satan is very strong and very prominent in our psyche today. He actually does have a trident, and with it he causes us too much pain. His weapon is our three brains acting under desire. When someone acts through desire, pain is the final outcome. It may be weeks, months, or years, or until another life, but everything is balanced with the scale.

Satan gives us pleasure, but only when we tell him to. Satan has to be invited. He will always be faithful to his word; however after pleasure the only thing that remains is pain. There is a limit to pleasure, which is pain. Some, indeed, even experience this limit firsthand. Nevertheless, they are still not satisfied. Desire is never satisfied.

When we swing the pendulum of life to produce pleasure, it will eventually return and give us pain. This is the law of the balance. This is the mechanical nature of life. If today Satan gives us pleasure, then later, Satan gives us pain. Later, he makes us age, he gives us cancer, he gives many men prostate problems. This is what happens when we listen to the Tempting Serpent of Eden. He will give us what we want, and we will be filled with pleasure in eating the apple, but we will also be kicked out of Eden.

A decrepit mind, one in the bondage of desire, destroys the beauty and harmony of love. The intellect caught in the battle of thought destroys any ability of love to manifest. Love is too fine and volatile an energy for the intellect to properly handle. The ego automatically, in an unconscious way, erroneously files away into the memory of the subject all the data it is given in accordance with its subjective likes and dislikes that have formed through its previously stored erroneous data.

There is always an unconscious attempt to have concepts and ideas, no matter how foolish they are, exactly conform to reality. This in combination with the subjective processes of reasoning totally inhibits the fecundation of love. An intellectual person who believes they can find love within their rationality will fail, although few would admit it.

Emotional people place this center of their presence above the intellect, and this is where we find especially passionate people. Passion is not love. Passionate couples are always fighting, always making up, making a big deal about their relationship. They live in fantasy, and cry when times are too harsh continue their fantastic dream.

Love has nothing to do with the personality, nothing to do with likes or dislikes, with sensuality or crude physical attraction. Only within deep contemplation, meditation, can we truly assure ourselves the impulses of our relationship. Many relationships are built on fear of being alone, but the participants of such relationships always believe they are in love. Love and fear are anti-sympathetic, impossible to mix. Relationships built upon anything other than altruism, compassion, charity, kindness, sanctity, etc., are surely ones built upon false claims of love. Nevertheless, although love is delicate thing, it can be grown between any two people who are sincere, no matter how apparently different they are. Obviously this is done by removing, at any cost, all forms of desire. Those who want to know love need to destroy all their desire, every last particle of it.

Man and woman are instinctually pulled together in order to copulate. Obviously Nature wants to sustain itself, but it is not a crime in order to realize the superior possibilities of the sexual energy. There are men and women living at a purely instinctual level of being, and lamentably they will never accept or experience the latent possibilities that the sexual energy is capable of.

Obviously, the outcome of varied modifications of the sexual energy has placed us on the carpet of existence. We were born, a doctor smacked us on the bottom, and we cried in infinite pain for the milk of the maternal breast. The tears of existence are in vain if we do not make use of the energy of creation to transform that very creation itself. There is a more intelligent use of the sexual energy than that of sensual pleasure. In order for the latent possibilities of the sexual energy to unfold within us, here and now, we must transform the sexual energy. That transformed energy empowers the higher purposes of the soul to unfold.

Love has no limit. Love finds itself content. Love finds itself not with fear, not with worry, or thinking, or comparing. Love never finds itself bored. Every moment is full of beauty, harmony, things indescribable, which are felt in the heart... These are things of God. What is love? The great poets always try, but of course when we attempt to describe it, we disfigure it. But Love is always there for those who wish to be with it. Everyone has that right, but it takes work.

Rudimentary Kabbalah

> The teachings of the Zend Avesta are in accordance with the doctrinal principles contained in the Egyptian book of the dead, and contain the Christ-principle. The Illiad of Homer, the Hebrew Bible, the Germanic Edda and the Sibylline Books of the Romans contain the same Christ-principle. All these are sufficient in order to demonstrate that Christ is anterior to Jesus of Nazareth. Christ is not one individual alone. Christ is a cosmic principle that we must assimilate within our own physical, psychic, somatic and spiritual nature [...]
>
> Among the Persians, Christ is Ormuz, Ahura Mazda, terrible enemy of Ahriman (Satan), which we carry within us. Amongst the Hindus, Krishna is Christ; thus, the gospel of Krishna is very similar to that of Jesus of Nazareth. Among the Egyptians, Christ is Osiris and whosoever incarnated him was in fact an Osirified One. Amongst the Chinese, the Cosmic Christ is Fu Hi, who composed the I-Ching (The Book of Laws) and who nominated Dragon Ministers. Among the Greeks, Christ is called Zeus, Jupiter, the Father of the Gods. Among the Aztecs, Christ is Quetzalcoatl, the Mexican Christ. In the Germanic Edda, Baldur is the Christ who was assassinated by Hodur, God of War, with an arrow made from a twig of mistletoe, etc. In like manner, we can cite the Cosmic Christ within thousands of ancient texts and old traditions which hail from millions of years before Jesus. The whole of this invites us to embrace that Christ is a cosmic principle contained within the essential principles of all religions.
>
> – Samael Aun Weor, *The Perfect Matrimony*

Christianity as it is known today is not true Christianity as it was delivered by Master Aberamentho (Jesus). When Christianity was castrated of its sexual nature, what resulted was a perversion. When Jesus was transformed into a weak and effeminate figure the true meaning of the Cross was lost. Jesus Christ is the superman, the authentic mutant, the one who has transcended humanity.

Christianity began to slowly die as the wisdom of the Kabbalah was forgotten. Therefore, what we call "Christianity" is not really as the name implies. The original secrets the first pontiffs of Christianity knew were forgotten, misunderstood, or simply thrown out for a variety of social and political reasons.

The true Christians were driven underground, nevertheless they preserved authentic Gnostic Christian Esotericism by transmitting the doctrine through the parables and secrets of such institutions we call Alchemy, Rosicrucianism, Freemasonry, the Knights Templar, etc. Today, save for extremely rare exceptions, even these organizations are nothing more than shells of their former existence. Lacking the true Gnosis, they have become much like the official "Churches."

Yet, it was to be expected. The evolution and devolution of religion is the reverberation of time itself. Forms of religion die, but the values always remain. We need to comprehend the values of religion, devoid of positive or negative association, because all religions teach the values of the Being. It is necessary to know the Being. The Being does not associate, it does compare or use relativism, it does analyze or have doubt. The Being speaks laconically, and its silence is verbose - it is, it has been, it will always be, the Being.

The mysteries of religion, hidden in parable, are the mysteries of the Being. In the past the esoteric meaning of religion was kept hidden from the public, and known only to the Initiates. This was due to karma, for the development of humanity. Now the teachings are freely given to those who want to know. It is necessary to know the mysteries in order to be received in heaven.

> He answered and said unto them, Because it is given unto you to know the mysteries of the kingdom of heaven, but to them it is not given.
>
> – Matthew 13:11
>
> And he said, Unto you it is given to know the mysteries of the kingdom of God: but to others in parables; that seeing they might not see, and hearing they might not understand.
>
> – Luke 8:10
>
> We speak that we do know, and testify that we have seen; and ye receive not our witness.
>
> – John 3:11

> It is impossible to bring souls into the Light without the Mysteries of the Light-kingdom.
>
> – Jesus, *The Pistis Sophia*

Kabbalah is the foundational basis of the Bible, and truly, every religious text. Anyone who studies the Bible without real kabbalistic knowledge is going to find incipient and contradictory answers, because Kabbalah is the key to the parables of the New and Old Testament. The Kabbalah is misleading because at first sight it appears that anyone can spend some time learning the Tree of Life and eventually they will commit to memory the Kabbalah and all its mysteries. This, especially today, is the common approach people take within and outside of Judaism. However, the true Kabbalah lives outside the rational mind. The student needs to experience the Kabbalah, not theorize or fantasize about it.

Samael Aun Weor states that there are two types of Kabbalists: the Intellectual Kabbalists and the Intuitive Kabbalists. The Intellectual Kabbalist is only able to *interpolate* and *extrapolate* sensory data in attempts to fit the mysteries within that data. The Intellectual Kabbalist lives within the intermediate mind, the mind of belief and the mind of the five senses. Conversely, the Intuitive Kabbalist awakens consciousness. The Intuitive Kabbalist, instead forming theories, charts and diagrams, resolves to live within the mystery itself through the exact science of *meditation*. Only the latter type actually lives the mysteries of the Kabbalah.

The Kabbalah can only be known to the inner mind. Intellectual Kabbalists are like people who hold in their hands a large sum of money without knowing how to make use of it. In other words, an intellectual approach to the Kabbalah is a waste of time. We must use our intellect, but our approach much be based in experience. This is found through the awakening of the consciousness.

It is said that the Kabbalah is the study of numbers, but if simple mathematics could achieve self-realization, obviously the former task would be something mundane, ordinary and common. Authentic kabbalistic mathematical formula is intuitive and beyond what we ordinarily call "thought." Neither does it correspond to what is ordinarily considered mathematics – regardless, it is true mathematics. It is the language of God, the language of dreams, the language of the superior words, the Verb of Gold, the voice of silence, the Pythagorean epistemology. The self-realization of the Being is a kabbalistic mathematical formula that is solved through the awakening of the consciousness.

What is the Tree of Life? The Tree of Life is a glyph that represents the Kabbalah. The Kabbalah is anterior to the symbol known as the Tree of Life. Once we understand this, we will understand more readily that the Kabbalah is found in every authentic religion. Kabbalah means "to receive." Therefore, we are interested in what could be called "kabel regulare." In other words, "to receive that wisdom which facilitates the reunion with our Inner Being." In order to truly understand how the Kabbalah ties in with all religion – how all religion ties together – we must understand *Monistic polytheism*.

> Monotheism always leads to anthropomorphism (idolatry) which by reaction originates materialistic atheism. This is why we prefer polytheism.
>
> We are not afraid to talk about the intelligent principles of the mechanical phenomena of nature, even if people classify us as pagans.
>
> We are partisans of a modern polytheism founded on Psychotronics.
>
> In final synthesis, monotheistic doctrines lead to idolatry. It is preferable to talk about the Intelligent Principles, which never leads to materialism.
>
> Modern monotheism emerged from the abuse of polytheism.
>
> In this Era of Aquarius, in this new phase of the Revolution of the Dialectic, polytheism must be psychologically and transcendentally sketched out. Besides, it must be put forward intelligently; we must set forth wisely with a vital and integral monistic polytheism.
>
> Monistic polytheism is the synthesis of polytheism and monotheism. Diversity is unity.
>
> – Samael Aun Weor, *The Revolution of the Dialectic*

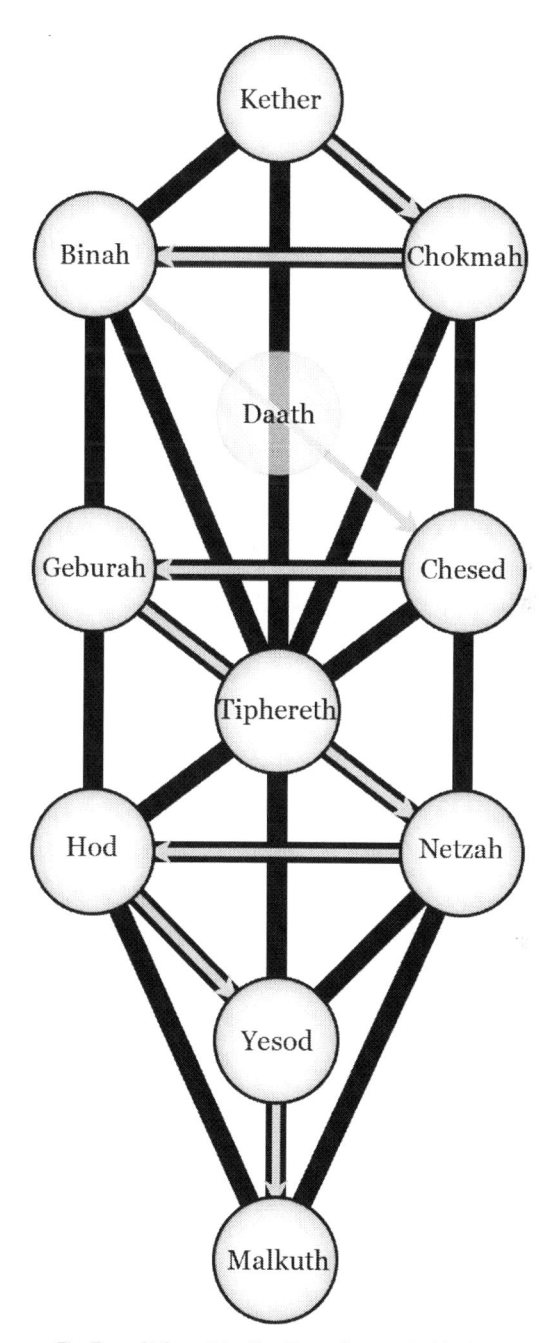

The Tree of Life contains Ten Emanations, or Sephiroth

325

The Tree of Life is a display of monistic polytheism. Monistic polytheism is known in Christianity as the ARMY OF THE VERB, the Angelic Hosts (polytheism) of the Cosmic Christ (monism). Everyone has an individual Inner Being, a Father in Heaven, who is part of the Eternal Common Cosmic Father. Thus, "diversity is unity." Various religions focus upon different aspects of the cosmos, thus they are categorized as one or another "thing." In reality, when religion is integrally understood, we see that the values of religion are immutable. The Gods and Goddesses of a particular religion are simply transformed into the Angels, Buddhas, Divas, etc. of another.

Prince Siddhartha Gautama became the Buddha Shakyamuni, the Awakened One, while sitting in meditation under the Bodhi Tree, "the tree of awakening." The Bodhi Tree is the same tree that is known in Egyptian, Nordic, and Aztec mysteries, and is the same *Olive Tree*, the *Olive Branches*, or the *Tree of Life* that has its existence in the center of Eden. The Garden of Eden is the human body itself.

There are two trees in the Garden of Eden: *The Tree of Life* and the *Tree of Good and Evil*. The synthesis of these trees is found in Buddhism as The Bodhi Tree. In Buddhism we see the positive aspect of this tree, in Christianity, we are familiar with the negative aspect of this tree. Fruits of the Tree of Life give us immortality. When we eat from the forbidden fruit of the Tree of Good and Evil, we are removed from the Garden of Eden, we become ashamed of ourselves, we loose our enlightenment and become full of darkness – we cannot "see" anymore. One form of sight – the inner sight or insight – is replaced with an exaggerated sensual sight. This loss of seeing the inner worlds and the exaggeration of the value of the exterior world leads us to become identified through the processes of fascination.

What is even worse, when we eat from the Tree of Good and Evil is that we can no longer eat from the Tree of Life because we have been removed from The Garden: we loose the gift of immortality. It is at that point when the Wheel of Samara begins and with that, suffering. Through the door of sex humanity left

Eden, which is the perfect, paradisiacal and immortal physical body rooted in the Fourth Dimension, and it is through the door of sex that humanity can return to Eden, to elevate their creative energies to reproduce the perfect, paradisiacal and immortal physical body.

We reenter Eden through the same door we left it: sex. We open that door by meditating under the Bodhi Tree and transmuting the sexual energy (voluptuousness). The Fruits of Eden are sexual because Eden is a sexual euphemism. To eat the fruit is to waste the fruit, to waste the sexual *seed*, or more correctly stated, the *sexual energy*.

The Garden of Eden is our physical body and hence these two trees are inside of us. We study the Tree of Life through the Kabbalah. We study the Tree of Good and Evil through Alchemy. Alchemy is the transmutation of the lead personality into the spirit of gold. Christianity is the most synthetic religion when it is properly understood, and is heavily engrained in Alchemy and Kabbalah. Nevertheless, all other religions carry the symbology and correspondences of these two sciences to their respective degrees.

There are many different ways to organize The Tree of Life. Here we are only going to be very quick moving and present only the most fundamental aspects as it concerns the self-realization of the Being. The glyph itself is composed of Ten Emanations, or sephiroth (plural of sephirah, "jewel"). We are going to begin at the bottom and work our way up, because this is the way we need to work upon it.

> Kether, Chokmah and Binah are the Trimurti of Perfection; they are the divine triangle, the very beloved Father, the very adored Son, and the very wise Holy Spirit.
>
> There is an abyss found after this divine triangle. After this abyss, a second triangle is formed by Chesed, the fourth Sephira that corresponds to the Innermost, or when speaking in Sanskrit, Atman the ineffable one, continuing with Geburah, the might of the Law, the fifth Sephira, which is Buddhi, the Divine Soul, which is feminine. Then follows Tiphereth, the sixth Sephira, the Human Soul which is masculine.

A third triangle comes as an unfoldment and this is represented by Netzach, the mind, the seventh Sephira, continuing with Hod, the eighth Sephira, the Astral Body. Further down is Yesod, the ninth Sephira, the main foundation of sex, the vital depth of the physical organism, the Vital Body or the ethereal vehicle, the Theosophist's Lingam Sarira.

Finally, at the lowest part of the Tree of Life, we find Malkuth, the tenth Sephira, the Physical World, or Physical Body, the body of flesh and bones.

The first triangle, Kether, Chokmah and Binah, is the Logoic. The second triangle, Chesed, Geburah and Tiphereth, is Ethical. The third triangle, Netzach, Hod and Yesod, is Magical. Malkuth, the physical world, is a fallen Sephira.

Three Sephiroth of Form are found in the Pillar of Severity (Binah, Geburah, and Hod).

Three Sephiroth of Energy are found in the Pillar of Mercy (Chokmah, Chesed, and Netzach).

The Pillar of Equilibrium is between these two Pillars, where all of the distinct levels of Consciousness are found (Kether, Tiphereth, Yesod, and Malkuth).

– Samael Aun Weor, The *Initiatic Path in the Arcana of Tarot & Kabbalah*

THE KINGDOM

The Tree of Life represents the different states of Being, and as we climb up the tree we encounter a higher state of Being. Discounting the Klipoth (Hell), Malkuth is the lowest. Malkuth is the fallen sphere.

On the microcosmic tree, that is to say the human analogue of the tree, every sephirah corresponds to a region of the physical body, however, every sephirah also contains macrocosmic meanings as well. Macroscopically, Malkuth represents the physical world, the Kingdom. On the microcosmic tree Malkuth is located at the feet.

When we read that Mary Magdalene anointed Jesus' feet within oil, and dried it with her hair, we must understand that this is sexual, because the foot (Malkuth) of the Cosmic Man is the physical body, and hair represents *chastity*. Recall from your childhood memories the tails of fair maidens locked away in a tower; her long hair is always a testament of her chastity.

Remember the hair is also the key to understanding the story of Samson, who falls asleep after his hair, "his strength," is cut off. Here in the Bible, strength is really sexual strength or chastity. So when Samson loses his hair, he loses his strength. This means that he falls *psychologically asleep* when he begins to profane the sexual force; he fell to the temptations of Delilah.

> His head and his hairs were white like wool, as white as snow; and his eyes were as a flame of fire; And his feet like unto fine brass, as if they burned in a furnace; and his voice as the sound of many waters.
>
> – Revelation 1:14,15

Brass is the outcome of *zinc* and *copper* in the *furnace*. So the feet of God, or, as we can now say, the physical vehicle of God, is a mixture of zinc and copper, which represent the male and female polarities. The furnace in Alchemy always represents the sexual act, or the movement of the sexual fire.

When Adam and Eve left Eden they *fell* into Malkuth. Adam and Eve represent many things, one of which is the Masculine (Adam) and Feminine (Eve) energies within our body. Adam is the Intellect, biologically present as our encephalic fluid. The intellect is a tool for the spirit when it does good and a tool of the demon (ego) when it does evil. When Adam is in the Garden he is doing the will of the spirit. Eve on the other hand is the aspect of sexuality, because it is with her that everything is born and dies; Eve is related to birth, which is sexual, and is biologically present as our sexual fluid. This is why it is Eve who picks the forbidden fruit, because eating it represents fornication, which is within the sphere of Eve.

When Adam and Eve leave the Garden, they bear Cain and Abel. Cain is a worker of the "Earth" which is Malkuth, meaning, *Cain only works with the five physical senses*. Abel was a worker of sheep, which of course has to do with spirituality especially when referenced in the Bible. Cain offered the fruit of the ground to God, the same fruit that Eve ate. But Abel offered the fat of his sheep, and God gave respect to that of Abel, but not of Cain. So Cain, the *animal intellect* that grows stronger through eating the fruit of the ground, kills Abel, the spirit, because he became weak.

The intellect within us has become so strong that it overpowers the voice of the spirit. This is the story of Cain and Abel. Today, the intellect is very strong, but Cain is not Wisdom. Cain-Intellect is the false logic that appears from only looking at the fruits of the earth, the five physical senses, because the intellect cannot see the spirit: Cain is an ignorant intellect.

> And Adam knew Eve his wife; and she conceived, and bare Cain, and said, I have gotten a man from the Lord.
> And she again bare his brother Abel. And Abel was a keeper of sheep, but Cain was a tiller of the ground.
> And in process of time it came to pass, that Cain brought of the fruit of the ground an offering unto the Lord.
> And Abel, he also brought of the firstlings of his flock and of the fat thereof. And the Lord had respect unto Abel and to his offering: But unto Cain and to his offering he had not respect. And Cain was very wroth, and his countenance fell.
> And the Lord said unto Cain, Why art thou wroth? and why is thy countenance fallen? **If thou doest well, shalt thou not be accepted? and if thou doest not well, sin lieth at the door. And unto thee shall be his desire, and thou shalt rule over him.**
> And Cain talked with Abel his brother: and it came to pass, when they were in the field, that Cain rose up against Abel his brother, and slew him.
> And the Lord said unto Cain, Where is Abel thy brother? And he said, I know not: Am I my brother's keeper? And he said, What hast thou done? the voice of thy brother's blood crieth unto me from the ground.
> And now art thou cursed from the earth, which hath opened her mouth to receive thy brother's blood from thy hand; When thou tillest the ground, it shall not henceforth yield unto thee her strength; a fugitive and a vagabond shalt thou be in the earth.
> – Genesis 4:1-12

Cain represents the parts of our psyche which do not understand anything beyond the five physical senses and that which desires sensation. The fruits of the earth are the sexual seeds within man and woman. If you eat and enjoy these fruits (orgasm) rather than transform them, the energy that could of otherwise fecundate the physical organism with divine super-volatile energies are lost. Consequently, the superlative senses of man become atrophied, and in their place is crystallized a false intelligence, the Cain-Intellect. This intellect declares itself to be above and beyond what it does not understand, namely the divine, and paints various sophistic tapestries in order to justify its murdering of Abel, the spirit. It martyrs the spirit to retain its own existence, to remove itself from the God that does not respect him (because he fornicates God's temple, the body). Cain does not understand his own action and does not understand God.

> And the scribe said unto him, Well, Master, thou hast said the truth: for there is one God; and there is none other but he: And to love him with all the heart, and with all the understanding, and with all the soul, and with all the **strength**, and to love his neighbour as himself, is more than all whole burnt offerings and sacrifices.
>
> – Mark 12:28-34

Strength in the Bible means sexual strength and this why we need to love with all our heart, our soul, our mind and our *strength*. This is why when Samson lost his strength he became a fornicator. So, when we *till the ground* (waste the fruit) we will loose our strength, and become vagabonds of the intellect.

Delilah puts Samson to sleep and there she removes the strength of Hercules-Samson. Delilah is Eve, but in this story it is the sinister Eve, the Eve outside of God's Paradise. Samson falls psychologically asleep under the temptations of Delilah and then Samson looses his strength. His strength is within his sex, which is represented by the uncut hair. The story of Deliah-Eve and Samson-Adam plays out within our own heart. Eve is the sexual-regenerative aspect within us, and Adam is the intellect-protective aspect within us.

The Magical or Priestly Triangle

The Magical Triangle is composed of Yesod, Hod, and Netzach. It is called the Magical Triangle because it is here where the three forms of Magic take place: Natural Magic, Hermetic Magic and Sexual Magic. Natural Magic has to do with nature and liturgical ritual, and Hermetic Magic has to do with the mind, both of which are fueled through transformative processes that occur through Sexual Magic.

> There is no doubt that Netzach is where we can find Hermetic Magic, and in Hod we find Natural Magic. Other authors think differently. They believe that Natural Magic is found in Netzach; I have to disagree with them in that matter because when precisely seen, the mind is found to be Mercurial. There are authors that disagree with my concepts. They suppose that the mind is Venusian. I regret to discuss this type of concept because anyone can realize that the mind is Mercurial. Therefore, Hermetic Magic must be identified with Mercury, which is related with the mind. Regarding Natural, Ceremonial or Ritualistic Magic, we can find it in the Astral World, in the astral Body.
> – Samael Aun Weor, *The Initiatic Path in the Arcana of Tarot & Kabbalah*

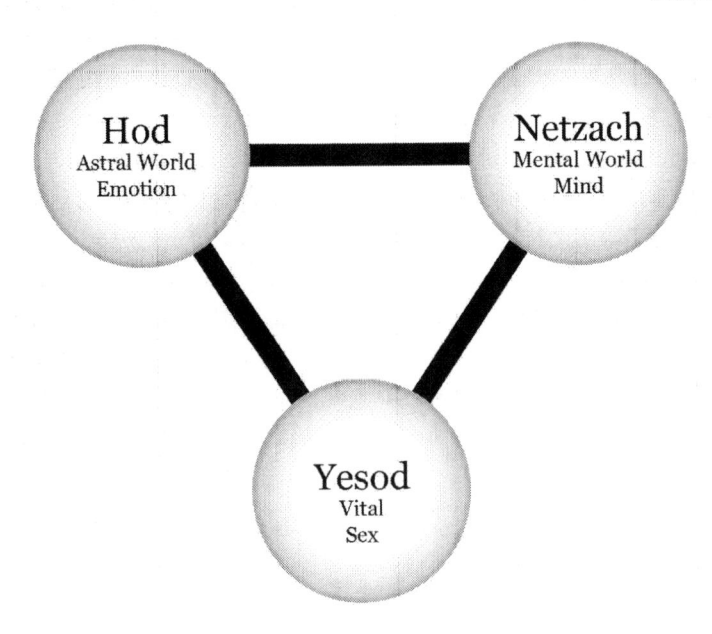

Hod
Astral World
Emotion

Netzach
Mental World
Mind

Yesod
Vital
Sex

Yesod is the vital principle and its translation means "foundation." The vital principle is the tetradimensional aspect of the physical body. Yesod is the World of Eden. It is the principle that keeps the physical body alive (its vitality). Every physical body has a superior aspect to it and this is called the Vital Body. Yesod is the "foundation" of the Tree of Life. Every life begins at Yesod, within the physical body it is found in the reproductive organs of man and woman, because that is where the foundation of all life is. Really, Malkuth must rise into Yesod, because Yesod is the vital basis of the physical world (Malkuth). Eden is the physical body when Malkuth rises into its proper place with Yesod. When this happens, we reenter Eden, our vital basis is perfectly balanced, and we gain eternal life.

Yesod is the Ninth Sephirah; the number nine is then related with Yesod. The Arcanum Nine is sexual, and is related with the nine months of an infant's gestation. Sex is the related with both birth and death because nothing can be born if it is first not dead. Yesod is related with the Moon, Eve, Sexuality.

Hod is related with Natural Magic because it requires superior emotion to facilitate Natural Magic. Hod is very interesting because it is the infamous Astral Body spoken of by the Alchemists. It is related with the *Kamas* of the Orientals. Today it is talked about with much vigor and ignorance. Many mystics today are learning how to come out of the physical body, to have astral projections, claiming to know the mysteries of the universe, etc. The existence of an "astral body" cannot be denied, however, we must admit that most of what is discussed about these matters is all caught up in subjective theory. We need to realize that very ancient wisdom will guide us in these matters; we do not need to listen to people who do not really know anything. For example, there are many books today that speak of ingesting chemicals made in a laboratory that will forcibly remove one from the physical body. This is unnecessary and stupid. We can learn to remove ourselves from the physical body using natural methods, by awakening consciousness.

Samael Aun Weor unveils many keys of astral projection in his books. The Tibetans refer to these practices as Dream Yoga. Therefore, those skeptics that do not believe in the subtle bodies are ignorant. They must simply use the methods previously stated in order to verify the existence of the subtle worlds and the subtle bodies.

> I knew a man in Christ above fourteen years ago, (whether in the body, I cannot tell; or whether out of the body, I cannot tell: God knoweth;) such an one caught up to the third heaven.
>
> – 2 Corinthians 12:2

Many books have been written concerning the kabbalistic "First Heaven" (the Astral World). Initiates of the Theosophical Society speak at length about this Emotional Parallel Universe. As with any sephirothic region, there are sub-planes within the Astral Plane: there are inferior Astral Planes and superior Astral Planes. Some people have the mistaken concept that everything one experiences outside the physical body is objective reality. This is a dangerous misconception and a principle cause of mythomania. Every night we astral project unconsciously and experience many different types of dreams, some of which have no literal meaning. Therefore, we must be careful when we experience different visions and experiences. We have to learn to keep quiet and meditate upon our experiences until the reality is found. Remember, even outside the physical body the ego exists, and that causes our subjectivity. *Objectivity can only be found beyond the mind.*

Netzach is the Mental Body. This is the home of the mind, the basis of logic and reasoning. Logic and reasoning are tools of the mind, they help us in everyday life, but the mind is sly: through its logic and labeling, it believes it contains knowledge. In actuality, the mind itself cannot obtain new knowledge. The mind only deduces knowledge that is given to it by the consciousness. We often believe the mind is gaining knowledge, but is only analyzing knowledge given to it. This is why we begin to identify with the mind, but in reality, it is tricking us. The mind caught within the ego, the "I" is actually tricking itself, our self. All the mind can do is compare attributes of two values that exist upon a relative coordinate. It forms data based upon its own data. In other words, all of its data is relative. The Absolute is unknown to the mind.

We must exchange the dull and depressing processes of reasoning with the beauty of comprehension. There exist logic of an ordinary and common type, but there is also a Logic of the Infinite that opens its vestibule to the esoteric philosopher. This vestibule is profound meditation and sexual transmutation.

> Esoteric Philosophy never believed in the infallibility and totalitarian omnipotence of Aristotle's Logic.
>
> It is necessary to comprehend, it is urgent to know, that Superior Logic existed before the Deductive and Inductive Methods were formulated.
>
> Transcendental Logic is the Intuitive Logic, the Logic of the Infinite, and the Logic of Ecstasy.
>
> – Samael Aun Weor, *The Doomed Aryan Race*

THE ETHICAL TRIANGLE

Situated above the Magical Triangle on the Tree of Life is the Ethical Triangle, composing of Tiphereth, Geburah, and Chesed.

Tiphereth is the home of the authentic Human Soul. It is the Casual Body because it exists in the Causal World, and, oriental theosophy refers to it as Arupic, or *Superior Manas*.

Every sephiroth of a lower order is an unfoldment of a higher order. In other words, the Vital (Yesod), Astral (Hod) and Mental (Netzach) bodies are unfoldments of the Casual Body (Tiphereth). In corollary, the Vital, Astral, and Mental bodies are the soul, but more concretely the Causal body is the soul.

One is not a true Human until they have created the Human Soul. Do we currently possess a soul? No, we do not, and this is stated by Jesus very clearly in the Bible. In patience we shall possess our souls, but only if we are working correctly. What we do have is the Essence, the fraction or seed of a soul. We have the "lunar" aspects of our true soul. We have a Lunar Astral Body, a Lunar Mental Body and a Lunar Causal Body. The term Lunar is an alchemical reference to the mechanical, animal nature of our evolutive history. The lunar vehicles are of an animal quality, and our lunar vehicles are infested with the ego, the crystallization of the untransformed impressions of many lifetimes. We need to destroy the ego, and replace it with the authentic soul, the Solar Bodies.

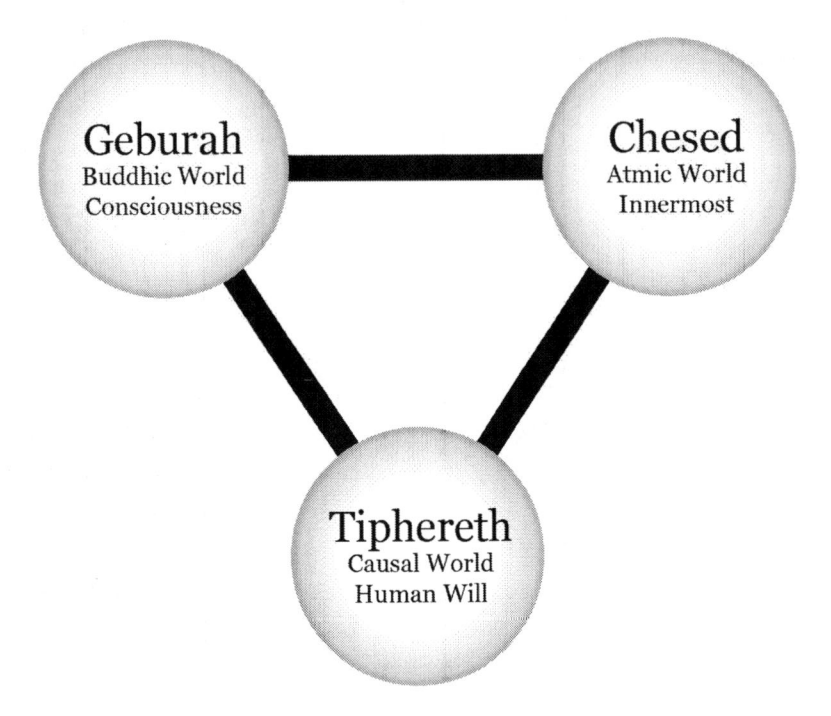

Geburah
Buddhic World
Consciousness

Chesed
Atmic World
Innermost

Tiphereth
Causal World
Human Will

The lunar bodies belong to Nature, they were formed by Nature for the purposes of Nature, and now they will be taken away by Nature because they no longer serve any useful purpose. The lunar bodies are ripe to die in present times. The innocent humanoids of eighteen million years ago have been converted into the cruel and complicated beings that we are today. The lunar bodies, which are now one with the ego, are more or less the crystallization of all our karma throughout innumerable incarnations. The only thing left for the lunar bodies is death. Without death, the inhumanity of this current civilization will continue without end. Those who do not wish to psychologically die by their own will, shall die against their own will because no one can mock the Law of Karma.

Ascending up the Tree of Life is to climb up Jacob's Ladder, to self-realize, to become more conscious. However in order to do this we need to create the Solar Bodies, because the lunar bodies cannot handle the high voltage of God. If Christ were to enter into someone without a soul that person would be instantaneously destroyed. The Solar Bodies are energy, different types of ultra-rarefied matter that must be crystallized using a very special technique. This technique is sexual magic, the Karmamudra of Tibetan Buddhism. It is sexual super dynamics, the positive transmutation of the creative libido into authentic Solar Bodies.

We need to create the soul and to create the soul, we need to be "born again" as it is said in the Bible. To be born again means to create soul. That is why "only those who are born again will see the Kingdom of Heaven." Obviously, we must begin at the foundation to ascend up the Tree of Life. To create soul, to give birth to soul, is exclusively a sexual problem, because Yesod, *foundation*, is sexual.

The term *manas* is Sanskrit for "mind." So the Inferior Manas, or mind, is the Mental World, and the Superior Manas is the Human Soul. The Mind, *manas*, is that which characterizes Man (Manas). With this said, strictly speaking, we are not truly men or women until we have realized the Theosophical "Superior Manas" within us. Right now we only have a *lump of contradictory psychic aggregates* (the ego) within us, leeching off our Essence, leaving it, the most venerable aspect of ourselves, in a hypnotized state. Hence we need to tear off the leeches (kill our egos) so to speak, in order to create an individual mind if we wish to become a true man. The true man is one with a concrete mind, a true individual with a permanent center of consciousness. The Superior Manas, the vehicle of Tiphereth in the Kabbalah, is the Human Soul. Until we have a Human Soul we are not really human, just *intellectual homunculi* – just the seed of a Man. We have to plant the seed in a fecund soil, only then we can grow into a True Man.

Gurdjieff talks about the *hydrogens*. This is not the common hydrogen that chemists are familiar with. In the esoteric philosophy the *occult hydrogens* are studied. Although the students of Gurdjieff know about the sexual hydrogen, they do not know how to make use of the power of the *being-exioehary*. Gurdjieff only publicly taught the "ordinary" use of the sexual function. He only hinted in his discourses the superior use of the sexual function, the sexual transmutation that occurs when the being-exioehary (sexual energy) is transmuted into the "higher being bodies" (Solar Bodies). Sexual Hydrogen TI-12 is the foundation of the crystallization of the solar bodies. Sexual hydrogen is transmuted into the subtle bodies. Sexual hydrogen is known Alchemically as Mercury.

> The Sexual Hydrogen is developed within the human organism according to the musical scale DO-RE-MI-FA-SOL-LA-TI.
>
> The Sexual Hydrogen TI-12 is very abundant in the Semen; this type of Hydrogen crystallizes into new human bodies and when it is wisely transmuted, it takes form within the Astral Body.
>
> By restraining the sexual impulse in order to avoid the ejaculation of semen, the Sexual Hydrogen TI-12 receives a special shock that passes it into another Second Superior Octave. This new octave is processed according to the seven notes of the scale DO-RE-MI-FA-SOL-LA-TI.
>
> An Occultist must never ignore that the transformation of the substances within the human organism is processed according to the Law of Octaves.
>
> The union of the Sexual Hydrogens TI-12 (from a Male and Female and everything that accompanies these two unities) allows us to pass the sexual Hydrogen into another Second Superior Octave whose outcome is the Crystallization of the mentioned Hydrogen into the marvelous form that is the Astral Body. Such Body of Perfection is born of the same material, of the same substance, of the same Matter from which the Physical Body is born. Indeed, this is what the transmutation of Lead into Gold is; in other words, the transmutation of the Physical Body into the Astral Body.
>
> – Samael Aun Weor, *The Doomed Aryan Race*

Beyond Tiphereth is Geburah. In esoteric philosophy we refer to this as the Divine Soul. *That* which awakens within Geburah is

Divine, because Geburah is intuition. Intuition is the facility of the consciousness.

The Buddhic nature, the Awakening, has nothing to do with the Mind; it is beyond the mind. The Buddha does not think; the Buddha is the action of knowledge. Those who attempt to strengthen the mind with data, thought, reasoning, etc., only increase the security of their own intimate prison. Those who wish to strengthen their minds with powers, those who hypnotize others, etc., are committing crimes because free will is a right. That is why these things are Black Magic.

The authentic Human Being

Atman
Chesed
Innermost
King Arthur

The Monad

Buddhi
Geburah
Divine Soul
Guinevere

Manas
Tiphereth
Human Soul
Lancelot

Superlative Consciousness		Objective Mind

The Monad expresses itself through the Atman-Buddhi-Manas.

In meditation we can disconnect from the rational mind (which is entrapped in ego) and temporarily fuse the Essence with the Monad to achieve the *Illuminating Void*. This allows us to see The Reality; it allows us to become Wise. We must stop attempting to strengthen the mind with rigid concepts and unbreakable dogmas of a religious or secular nature. We must let the mind become flexible to flow within the Ocean of the Great Breath of Life. When the mind is silent, then one *is*.

Geburah is the medieval Guinevere, she is the Divine and Feminine Soul. Lancelot always searches for Guinevere because she is the Holy Grail. The Holy Grail (uterus) is the ETERNAL FEMININE; the Lance (phallus) is the ETERNAL MASCULINE. Lancelot is the Human Soul (Tiphereth). The Human Soul is masculine, the Divine Soul is Buddhi, the Feminine (Guinevere). King Arthur is Atman (the Innermost). Trinary, they are the Monad.

The Alchemical Wedding is the supreme joy of finding our Divine Androgynous Nature again. Truly, we are not man, nor woman, but androgynous. We need the Wedding Garments of the Soul to enter heaven, both male and female.

Beyond Geburah is Chesed. Chesed is "Love." Love is our internal Being, and he is God. Our internal Being is the Innermost, the Atman of the Hindus. He is the Father. Really Atman is Father-Mother, it is more correct to call our Innermost "Parent," as the Gnostic Valentinus did. The one who incarnates Chesed becomes *Elohim*, a God-Goddess.

If incarnating the Superior Manas makes one a Human, than the one who incarnates Atman becomes an authentic Human *Being*. Atman is the true Man who has powers over the four elements, the King of Creation.

> In the world of Atman, one has the feeling of being a complete Human Being. Here, the intellectual animal is not a Human Being. The Initiate feels full of immense plenitude. This is the world of the real Human Being in the most objective sense.
>
> His negative part is the physical world. The world of Atman is a positive state. Here we see a city in its real form, because if we look at the table, we see it through many viewpoints, from above, from below from within, from without, and the same occurs when we look at a mountain. Within a kitchen one can see how many atoms cutlery is made with, how many molecules are in the bread or meat that one is about to eat. We do not only perceive solids in an integral from, but moreover, we perceive hypersolids, including

the exact quantity of atoms, that in their conjunction constitute the totality of any given body.

If the student is not prepared, he is deceived, because he finds himself with a world filled with the crudest realism. This is the world of mathematics. Here, one sees the drama of nature; one is a spectator of nature. The world of mathematics is the world of Atman.

The one that thinks is the mind, not the Innermost. The human mind in its actual state of evolution is the animal that we carry within.

The concept of Descartes, *"I think therefore I am"* is completely false, because the true human being is the Innermost and the Innermost does not think because he knows. Atman does not need to think because Atman is omniscient.

— Samael Aun Weor, *The Initiatic Path in the Arcana of Tarot & Kabbalah*

People contrast the Doctrine of the Atman (Hinduism) with the Doctrine of the Anatman (Buddhism). This is simply a different point of view. The Atman is the true self in Hinduism, yet Buddhism teaches that the true self is no-self or anatman. In reality these are the same thing. Buddha taught anatman because the idea of Atman lets one become identified with the idea of a "divine I" that is like our current "I" or self. But the true individuality, the Atman, is nothing like the "I" we live and breathe as. From our point of view, the atman is like anatman.

Everyone has a warrior within. Chesed (Atman) is a warrior, a worker, he must fight against the ego to gain self-realization. The Bhagavad Gita contains the story of Arjuna who is told by Krisha, the Internal Father of each of us has, to go to war against his own kin:

Thus, by Arjuna prayed, (O Bharata!)
Between the hosts that heavenly Charioteer
Drove the bright car, reining its milk-white steeds
Where Bhishma led, and Drona, and their Lords.
"See!" spake he to Arjuna, "where they stand,
Thy kindred of the Kurus:" and the Prince
Marked on each hand the kinsmen of his house,

> Grandsires and sires, uncles and brothers and sons,
> Cousins and sons-in-law and nephews, mixed
> With friends and honoured elders; some this side,
> Some that side ranged: and, seeing those opposed,
> Such kith grown enemies - Arjuna's heart
> Melted with pity, while he uttered this:
> Arjuna. Krishna! as I behold, come here to shed
> Their common blood, yon concourse of our kin,
> My members fail, my tongue dries in my mouth,
> A shudder thrills my body, and my hair
> Bristles with horror; from my weak hand slips
> Gandiv, the goodly bow; a fever burns
> My skin to parching; hardly may I stand;
> The life within me seems to swim and faint;
> Nothing do I foresee save woe and wail!
> It is not good, O Keshav! nought of good
> Can spring from mutual slaughter! Lo, I hate
> Triumph and domination, wealth and ease,
> Thus sadly won! Aho! what victory
> Can bring delight, Govinda! what rich spoils
> Could profit; what rule recompense; what span
> Of life itelf seem sweet, bought with such blood?
>
> – Bhagavad-Gita

That which Arjuna must kill is his own blood: Himself. This is the war on oneself. Arjuna is the Atman, Krishna is the Cosmic Christ. This logic is the key to understanding the parable of Jesus throwing merchants out of the temple. People do not understand that the merchants live in our *internal* temple.

> And they come to Jerusalem: and Jesus went into the temple, and began to cast out them that sold and bought in the temple, and overthrew the tables of the moneychangers, and the seats of them that sold doves; And would not suffer that any man should carry any vessel through the temple.
>
> – Mark 11:15-16

The Supernal Triangle

The uppermost triangle is the Supernal Triangle, consisting of Binah, Chokmah, and Kether.

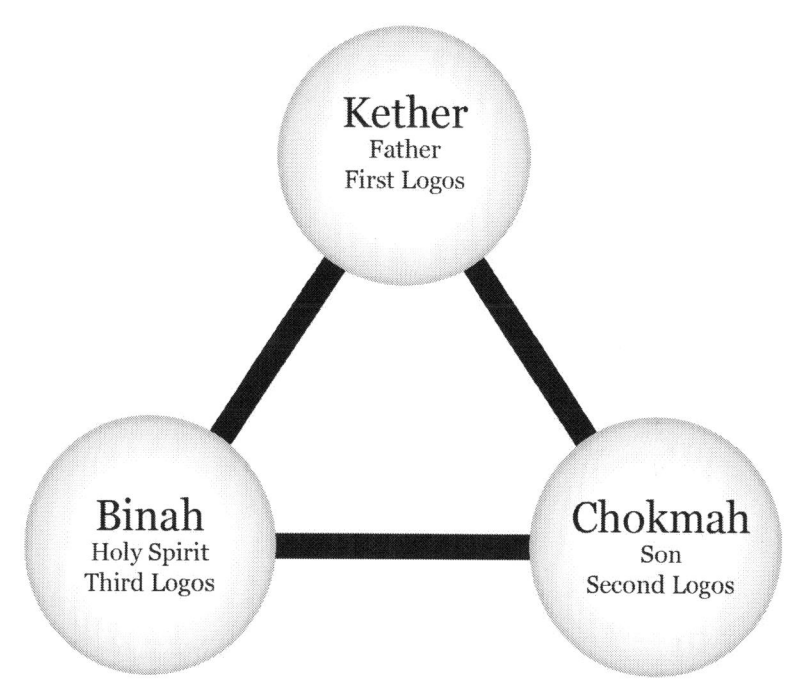

Kether
Father
First Logos

Binah
Holy Spirit
Third Logos

Chokmah
Son
Second Logos

Binah is the Third aspect of the Logos: The Holy Spirit. The Holy Spirit is that force that when represented as a Dove in the Bible impregnated the Virgin Mary. The Holy Spirit is united in a loving embrace with his wife, the Divine Mother, the Kundalini of the Hindus. Every religion has a Divine Virgin: Marah, Mary, Isis, Ram-IO, Tonantzin, Diana, Rhea, Cybele, Adonia, Devi Kundalini Shakti, etc. The Holy Spirit unfolds into the first divine couple, known as Od and Ob in the Kabbalah, Adam and Eve, or Jah and Hava. Father is Jah. His spouse is Havah. From this, Jah-Havah or Iod-Havah, all of creation is born. *Jah-Havah*, or *Jahhavah* is Jehovah. Bibles today incorrectly interpret *Jehovah Elohim*, replacing this descriptive phrase with the ambiguous term God or the Lord God. Jehovah Elohim is Binah.

In the study of Binah once again the sexual topic arrives. Let us now come to the realization that every religion has its foundation in sexuality. Every religion has specific sexual protocols, but for what reason, it is unknown to the world. In these ultramodern times they have been misinterpreted and rejected by society. We now deny the sexuality of religion, we choose to ignore it, and this causes us to become unintelligent in these matters. We are unable to correctly understand religion if we shut the door on the sexual issue.

Binah is the Logos that splits into Shiva and Shakti of the Hindus, Osiris and Isis of the Egyptians, and Joseph and Mary of the Christians. Joseph is Jupiter, or we can say Joseph is IO-Ceph. Ceph, or Cephias is a word meaning "stone."

> And he brought him to Jesus. And when Jesus beheld him, he said, Thou art Simon the son of Jona: thou shalt be called Cephas, which is by interpretation, A stone.
>
> — John 1:42

Jona is Hebrew for "dove," which is of course the Holy Spirit. The symbol of The Stone is throughout the New Testament. It is the Philosopher's Stone of the Alchemists. The Philosopher's Stone is the stone we must build our temple upon so we are not washed away by the high waters of the apocalypse.

> Not every one that saith unto me, Lord, Lord, shall enter into the kingdom of heaven; but he that doeth the will of my Father which is in heaven.
>
> Many will say to me in that day, Lord, Lord, have we not prophesied in thy name? and in thy name have cast out devils? and in thy name done many wonderful works? And then will I profess unto them, I never knew you: depart from me, ye that work iniquity.
>
> Therefore whosoever heareth these sayings of mine, and doeth them, I will liken him unto a wise man, which built his house **upon a rock**: And the rain descended, and the floods came, and the winds blew, and beat upon that house; and it fell not: for it was founded upon a rock.
>
> And every one that heareth these sayings of mine, and doeth them not, shall be likened unto a foolish man, which built his house upon the sand: And the rain descended, and the floods came, and

the winds blew, and beat upon that house; and it fell: and great was the fall of it.

— Matthew 7:21-26

The Philosopher's Stone is the foundation of all creation. It is the foundation, it is *Yesod*. The Cubic Stone of Yesod is the corner stone that the builders rejected. It is the Mason's master stone, Jacob's stone, the Stone Tablets, etc., etc.

> To whom coming, as unto a living stone, disallowed indeed of men, but chosen of God, and precious, Ye also, as lively stones, are built up a spiritual house, an holy priesthood, to offer up spiritual sacrifices, acceptable to God by Jesus Christ.
>
> Wherefore also it is contained in the scripture, Behold, I lay in Sion a chief corner stone, elect, precious: and he that believeth on him shall not be confounded.
>
> Unto you therefore which believe he is precious: but unto them which be disobedient, the **stone which the builders disallowed**, the same is made the head of the corner, And a **stone of stumbling, and a rock of offence**, even to them which stumble at the word, being disobedient: whereunto also they were appointed.

— 1 Peter 2:4

Within Peter, whose name means Stone, we find the passage of the rejected stone of the builders. The stone of stumbling and the rock of offence is the same stone that is used as the cornerstone of our spiritual temple (our soul). The cornerstone is the foundation, the Philosopher's Stone, Yesod, *sexuality*. The cornerstone is sex. Hence it is IO-Ceph, Joseph or Jupiter or IO-Piter, or IO-Peter, which is related to the sex. In this sense Peter, Patar, Jupiter, and Joseph represent the same thing. I-O is the positive-negative, the male-female. Joseph is IO-Ceph. Mary is Ram-IO. Ram-IO-Ceph.

Mary is the Divine Mother. There are many aspects of the Divine Mother. Later we will speak of the *Kundalini* and the *Kundabuffer*, which are the positive and negative aspects of the Alchemical Fire. When we make ill use of the Fire we are crystallizing the Kundabuffer. When we make right use of the Fire we are developing the Kundalini Fire Serpent. The Kundabuffer in

Buddhism is Mara, who is known as the evil god of passion. The Buddha had to overcome his own sexual passion, *Mara*, the ego who uses The Divine Fire, Creator-Destroyer Binah, incorrectly. Mara represents the most sinister, the darkest areas of our infraconsciousness. Mara in the Bible is the Tempting Serpent of Eden in Genesis, and in Revelation it has grown into the Dragon of Darkness.

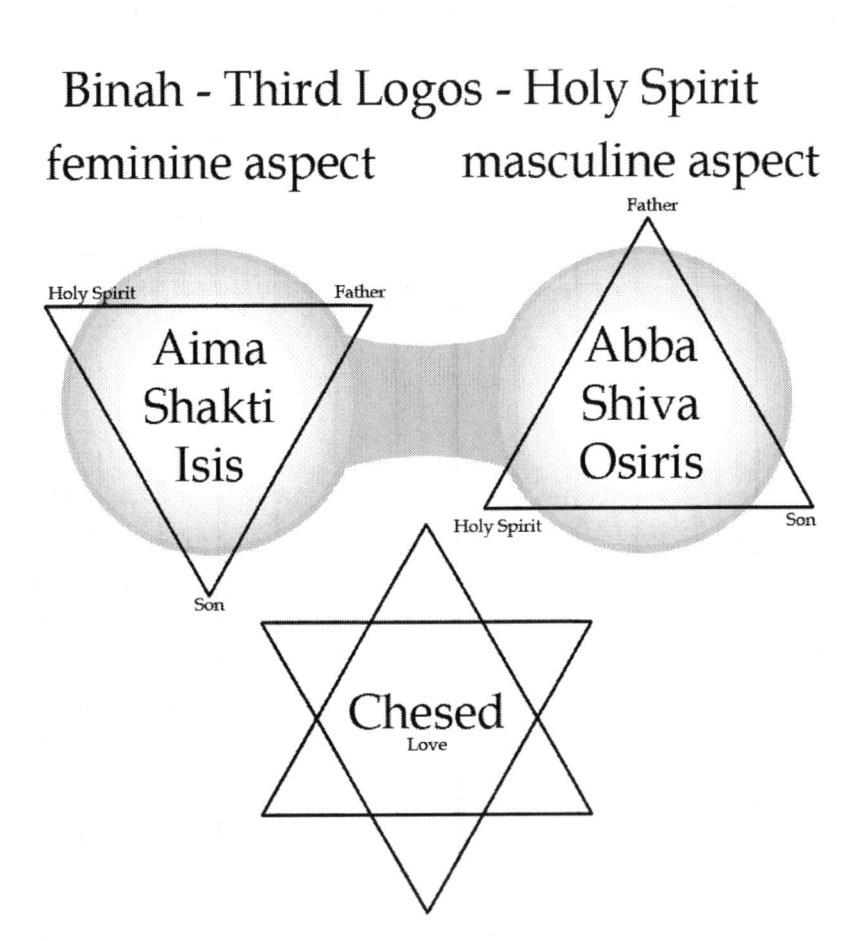

Binah - Third Logos - Holy Spirit
feminine aspect   masculine aspect

Aima Shakti Isis (Holy Spirit / Father / Son)

Abba Shiva Osiris (Father / Son / Holy Spirit)

Chesed — Love

The Holy Spirit unfolds unto the Divine Couple, the masculine and the feminine, each polarity containing the Trinity.

Binah is "intelligence." This means that Binah is the basic intelligence of creation. It is that which guides the animals. It is Binah that directs the chosen sperm to fecundate the egg. It is

Binah that regulates the death and life though the sephira directly below it, Geburah (justice; the action of knowledge). Only Binah has the right to give and take life. Binah gives instinct to the animals. The intellectual animal has Binah working through the metabolism, digestion, breathing, etc. The rational animal has the opportunity to convert instinct into intuition to incarnate "Intelligence." The intelligence of God is sleeping within our sexual center. This is how we give birth to God within ourselves.

Binah is the Holy Reconciliation, the neutral, thus it is sexual. Selling doves is the abuse of Binah: fornicating. The Olive Tree or Olive Branch is a symbol of Binah, sexuality. The rooster is the male sexual aspect. We shall deny the Christ three times before the rooster crows: sexually, emotionally and intellectually.

Sexuality is JEHOVAH ELOHIM: the Holy Spirit. This is irrefutable and indisputable. Those that believe that God is not sexual have a retardation of logic due the conditioning of ignorant norms self-imposed upon society. These people have become victims of the Anti-Christ's (the ego's) morally depredating agenda.

In Chokmah, all the Wisdom of the Word is stored. The physical body of the Cosmic Christ is the Sun. The Christic energy is deposited in the germ of every living creature. Nothing is born without the Christ. Christ is the Light. Christ is the path, the way to the Absolute. This is why Jesus said:

> Thomas saith unto him, Lord, we know not whither thou goest; and how can we know the way? Jesus saith unto him, I am the way, the truth, and the life: no man cometh unto the Father, but by me.
>
> – John 14:5,6

The Cosmic Christ is an impersonal force. Yet, anyone who is prepared can incarnate the Christ and be the host of the Logos in the flesh. If man is a light bulb then Christ would be electricity; electricity is everywhere, but it individualizes in each light. In order to handle the force of this electricity we need to build a higher gauged bulb, in other words, build the Solar Bodies. It is interesting to note that the Wisdom of the Cosmic Christ, The

Second Logs, descends into The Human Soul (Tiphereth), authentically making the WORD flesh. How wonderful it is to know that the LOGOS succeeds in perfecting imperfection! Only Christ can remove all the sins of our psychological world. Without the mercy of Christ, we would already be destroyed by our karma.

Lord Avalokita (Avalokitesvara) is the Cosmic Christ in Tibetan Buddhism. He is the one who perceives the Sound, the Verb, the Logos. The Cosmic Christ in Hinduism in Krishna. The Cosmic Christ of the Aztecs in Quetzalcoatl, the Feathered Serpent. Chokmah is the Holy Denial, the negative; it is the denial of the self, the sacrifice for others, so they can enjoy happiness. Thus, Jesus said, "If any man will come after me, let him deny himself, and take up his cross, and follow me."

Beyond Chokmah is Kether. At the depth of everyone's Being exists the Ancient of Days. He is the Occult of the Occult, the Holiest of Holies. He is the first emanation of our Being, the initiatic principle, the first manifestation of Ain Soph, he is the Being of our Being, he is the root of our Being, our Glorian. He is the One who is manifested, whose Father is the One who is Unmanifested. It is said he has a beard of thirteen knots, which reminds us of the thirteen repentances of Sophia. He is the Holy Affirmation, the unique existence in all of us and exists within everything. He is the Flaming Bush at the top of Mt. Sinai that stated: אהיה אשר אהיה. I AM THE ONE THAT I AM.

THE ABSOLUTE

The Absolute is described by Dion Fortune as "negative existence." This is because beyond Kether, there is a type of existence that the mind cannot comprehend. To the rational mind, the Absolute is a negative existence.

> The Absolute is the Being of all Beings. The Absolute is that which Is, which always has Been, and which always will Be. The Absolute is expressed as Absolute Abstract Movement and Repose. The Absolute is the cause of Spirit and of Matter, but It is neither Spirit nor Matter. The Absolute is beyond the mind; the

mind cannot understand It. Therefore, we have to intuitively understand Its nature.

The Absolute is beyond conditioned life. It is beyond that which is relative. It is the Real Being; It is the Non-Being because It does not keep any concordance with our concepts, but the Absolute is the "Real Being." This is why we do not intellectually comprehend It, because for us the Absolute is like Non-Being; nonetheless, It is the Real Being of the Being.

To Be is better than To Exist, and the reason for the Being to be is to be the Being itself. Our legitimate existence is within the Absolute, which is a Non-Being, a Non-Existence for the human reasoning.

The Absolute is not a God, neither a Divine nor human individual. It would be absurd to give form to That which has no form; it would be nonsense to try to anthropomorphize Space.

Indeed, the Absolute is the Unconditional and Eternal Abstract Space, far beyond Gods and human beings. The Absolute is the Uncreated Light which does not project a shadow in any place during the profound night of the Great Pralaya.

The Absolute is beyond Time, Number, Measurement, and Weight; beyond Casualty, Form, Fire, Light and Darkness. Nonetheless, the Absolute is the Fire and the Uncreated Light.

– Samael Aun Weor, *The Initatic Path in the Arcana of Tarot & Kabbalah*

God as singular is Non-God, the Absolute, the Seity or Aelohim. God as many is Deity or Elohim. Seity is beyond Deity.

There are three aspects of the Absolute: Ain, Ain Soph, and Ain Soph Aur; *Nothingness, Limitless,* and *Limitless Light.*

Ain is the true Absolute Abstract Space, it is the no-thing, the nothing. The Ain Soph are condensation of Ain, the "atoms" of Ain. Within Ain Soph, already a certain type of manifestation has occurred, and it is therefore the beginning and the end of all creation. Everything that exists has come from the Ain Soph and will return to the Ain Soph. The Ain Soph itself is an ocean of Monads. Everyone has an individual Monad or Spirit or God in Heaven. The Monad, the true Being, exists within the Ain's ineffable happiness.

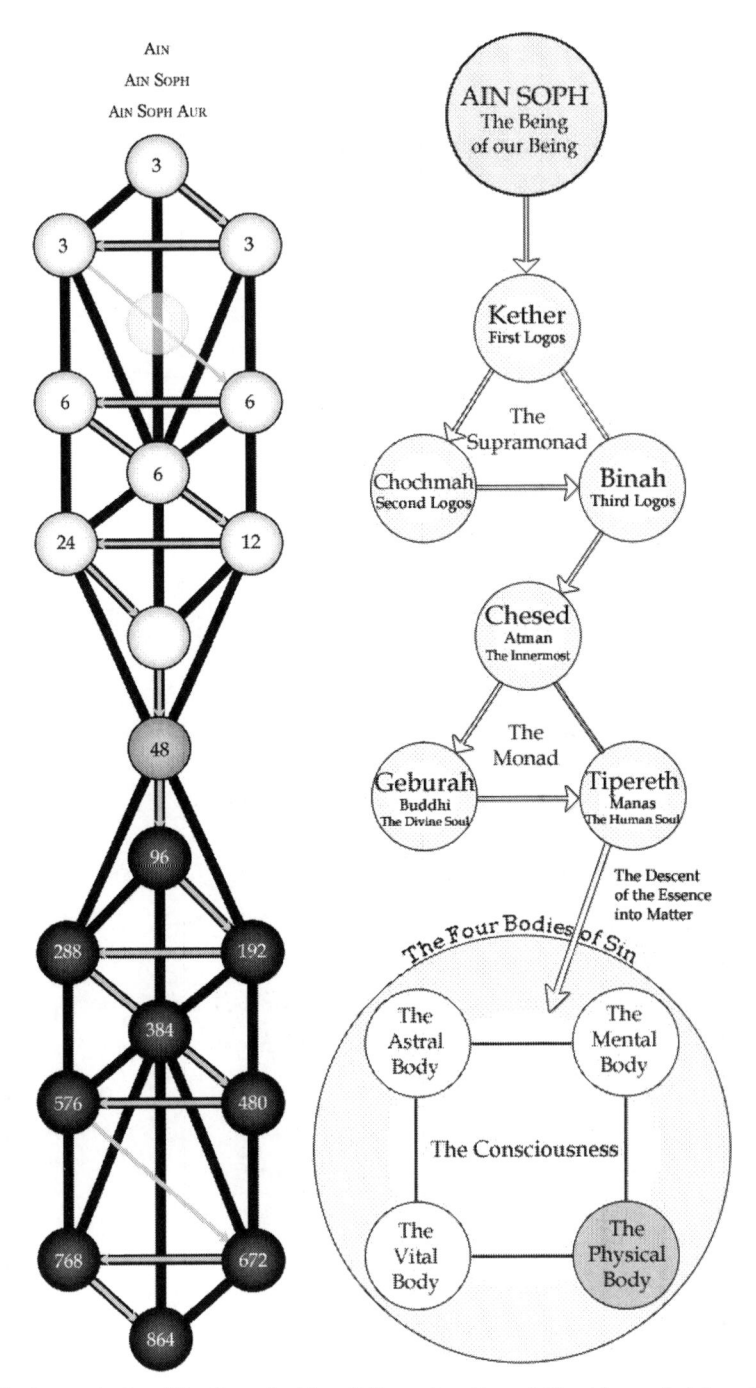

The Descending Ray of Creation as it relates with the number of Laws (left) and the manifestations of the Being (right).

350

Ain
Ain Soph
Ain Soph Aur

Absolute Abstract Space
The Absoulte
12ᴛᴴ Aeon
11ᴛᴴ Aeon

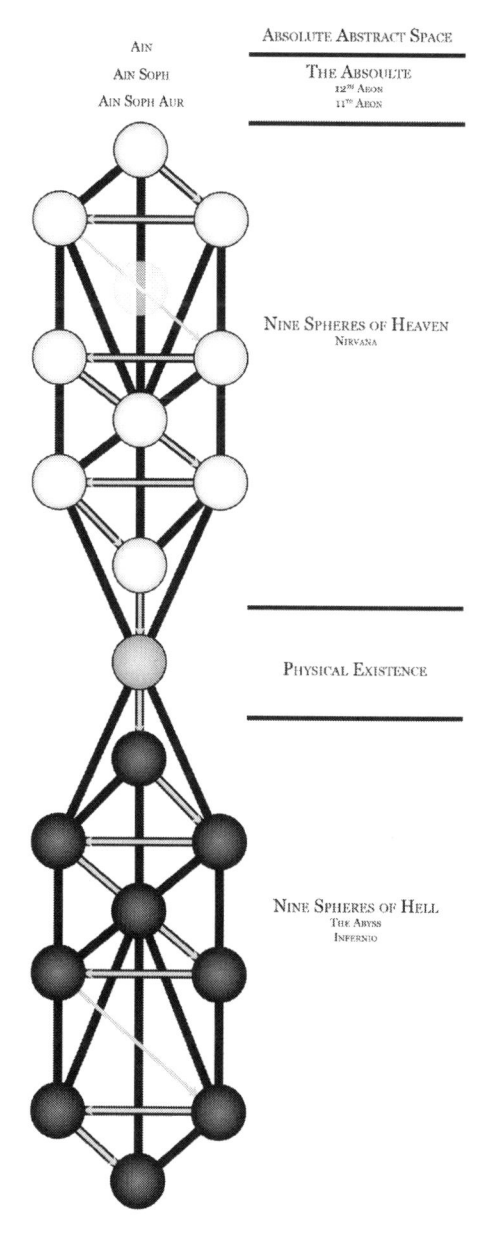

Nine Spheres of Heaven
Nirvana

Physical Existence

Nine Spheres of Hell
The Abyss
Infernio

Heaven, Hell and the Absolute

The Monad itself is happiness. However, true happiness can only exist if one knows what happiness is. Therefore, in order for every Monad to understand happiness, it is sent through a number of transformations that allow itself to understand itself.

The Ain Soph Aur is the Ray of Creation upon which the Monads manifest. The Ain Soph Aur sacrifices itself in order to descend into space, karma, consciousness, energy and matter. All of these things are various transformation of a single Thing. This No-Thing, the Ain Soph, sacrifices into a Thing in order for Monads to self-realize. The Universe is a schoolhouse composed of innumerable monads for the single purpose of becoming aware of happiness.

The Ain Soph Aur expresses itself through the Ten Sephiroth of the Tree of Life. The Ain Soph Aur is the Cosmic Christ, Quetzlcoatl, Okidanok, Vishnu, Kukulcan, etc., etc. It is Christus-Lucifer, the ordered cooperative-antagonism that produces the Universe. Lucifer is not evil; he is merely the one you must fight in order to gain the Light. Lucifer is divine because he is an aspect of God.

The Ain Soph Aur, the Single Law, transforms itself into something more complex, the Logoic World, which contains three laws. Accordingly, the Descending Ray of Creation complicates itself into six, twelve, twenty-four and forty-eight laws as its reaches the physical dimensions (see image). This level of complexity, or density, or the number of laws within each "cosmic unit" or "atom" provides the separation a monad requires in order to understand itself. A viscosity of existence allows the monad to begin with the most elemental forms of being. The great number of laws affords the monad to be under the control of them, which is something necessary in the beginning because the monad is incapable of dominating the principles contained within those laws in a self-conscious fashion. So, the "laws" are handling the monad's existence, they make it possible for it to exist, yet they do so in a mechanical way.

Each law is a relationship enacted upon the "instantaneous-continuum" movement of energy. Therefore, when relationships exist, there is a lot of complication, which removes freedom and happiness from that energy. Regardless, this un-happiness, or non-singularity, is required in order to understand what happiness is. Happiness is only true when one chooses to be happy. One can only choose if they understand what happiness is.

The Logoic world, which only contains three laws, enables a very high level of freedom, and therefore a supreme level of happiness. The causal dimension, which contains six laws, contains less freedom and a lesser degree of happiness is experienced, nevertheless, this is still Nirvana. The laws begin to increase more rapidly through mental, emotional, vital and physical worlds.

Below the physical dimension lies the infradimensions. Here the laws multiply at a horrifying rate. This is Hell, and it is painful because of the large number of laws that exist within these regions. The number of laws that exist within the infradimensions inhibit the evolution of life. This is why Hell is death (devolution) in itself.

Slowly as the inferior laws are understood, the monad yearns to understand superior laws, to gain the ability be self-conscious of happiness within fewer and fewer laws. The Monad works its soul (or Essence of soul if that is the case) to work on himself. It is the Monad that gives the inner sense of urgency, the disquietude of life, the yearning for wanting to know the meaning of life. Through these hunches and impulses the Monad is pushes its soul to find the door of gnosis. Some Monads push their soul very hard to self-realize in one lifetime. Others work their soul in intermediate fashion, which means every other lifetime or for only a part of a life. Other Monads do not wish for realization, or they wish to postpone their realization or their soul is lost in too much karma to be self-realized in this round of Eternity. In these latter cases, the soul develops an atheist personality.

Some Monads are content to self-realize within the Fire, while others wish to self-realize in the Light, which is a much superior work. This is the difference between the Spiral Path, and the Straight Path. The Spiral Path is for the lesser Buddhas, the Straight Path is for the Bodhisattvas with compassionate hearts. Only Bodhisattvas receive Christ in the Light. The lesser Buddhas experience Nirvana, yet the Bodhisattvas that incarnate the Christ experience happiness that is beyond Nirvana.

THE SEPTENARY

The Tree of Life represents Creation itself, the Being. If creation is nothing but a *vibration of energy* then the *harmonious overtones* produced by this energy constitute its organization. The universal septenary nature is due to the Law of Seven. The esoteric philosophy states that it is a principle of the Universe and every creation is ordered in this way. This is the Holy Heptaparaparshinokh.

The seven notes of creation resound themselves everywhere. There are seven colors within the visible spectrum. The number seven wisely orders the Periodic Table of Atomic Elements. Let us not forget, of course, that there are seven days in a week and it is the same number of "days" God created Earth in. Christianity speaks of the Seven Virtues and Seven Deadly Sins. These are the Seven Demons Jesus drove out of Mary Magdalene. In the Kabbalah, the Tree of Life contains 10 Spheres: three are the Logoi, which leaves Seven Spheres of Creation remaining.

Buddha raised Seven Serpents or *Nagas*. The Indian Yogi raises the Fire Serpent up the Seven Magnetic Centers of the body. These Seven Centers, known in Orient as *chakras*, are intimately related with the centers written of in Revelation, when they are referred to as the Seven Churches in Asia.

There are seven Buddhas in every Buddha.
– Buddha Shakyamuni

AIN

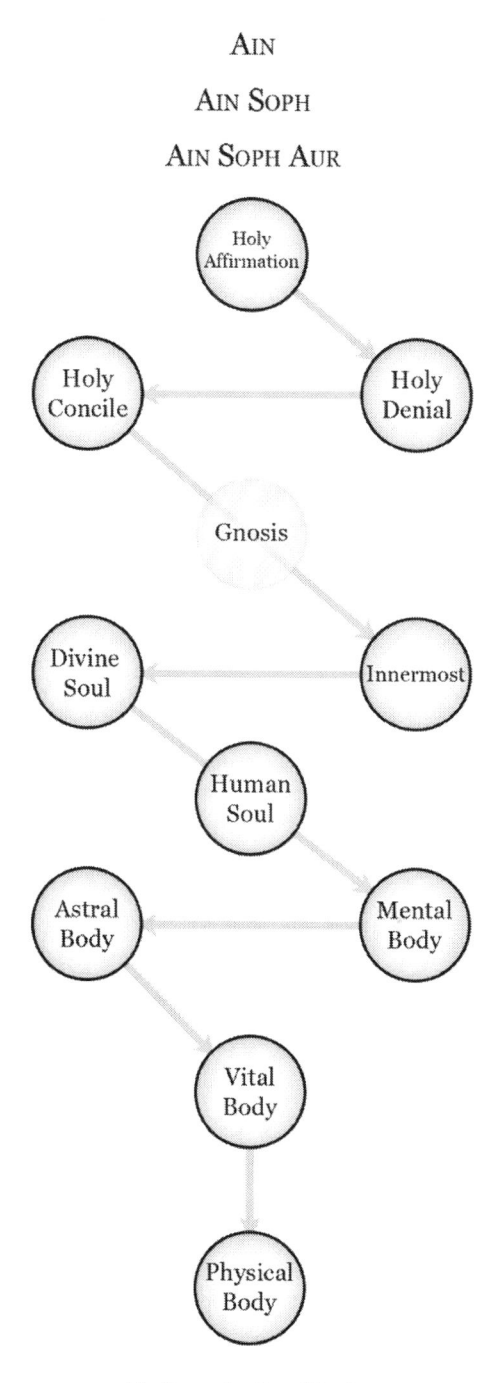

AIN SOPH

AIN SOPH AUR

- Holy Affirmation
- Holy Concile
- Holy Denial
- Gnosis
- Divine Soul
- Innermost
- Human Soul
- Astral Body
- Mental Body
- Vital Body
- Physical Body

The Descending Ray of Creation

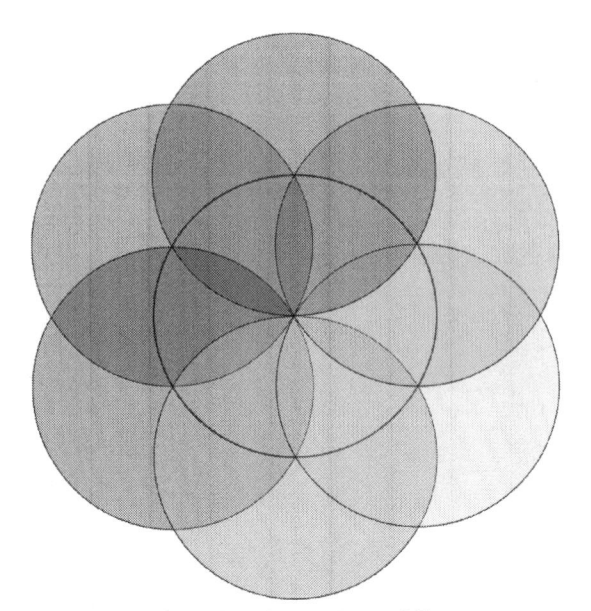

Seven Circles form the Flower of Life.

The Seven Serpents of Buddha

Grace and peace to you from him who is, and who was, and who is to come, and from the **seven fold spirit** before his throne and from Jesus Christ, who is the faithful witness, the firstborn from the dead, and the ruler of the kings of the earth.

– Revelation 1:4,5

On the Lord's Day I was in the Spirit, and I heard behind me a loud voice like a trumpet, which said: "Write on a scroll what you see and send it to the seven churches: to Ephesus, Smyrna, Pergamum, Thyatria, Sardis, Philadelphia, and Laodicea."

– Revelation 1:10, 11

Revelation is book written by Gnostic initiates for Gnostic initiates, for others there is only confusion written in this book. By sending the *Word* to the Seven Churches we illuminate them. We make a living temple by living in them. The word Asia is referring to the Hebrew term *Assiah*, which in the Kabbalah refers to the physical body. In synthesis we must send the Word to the Seven Churches in the body. The Seven Churches are:

1. Church of Ephesus – Sexual glands
2. Church of Smyrma – Prostate region
3. Church of Pergamos – Solar Plexus (stomach)
4. Church of Thyatira – Cardiac (heart)
5. Church of Sardis – Larynx (throat)
6. Church of Philadelphia – Frontal Cortex (brain)
7. Church of Laodicea – Pineal gland

We will state again that these are the same Seven Major Chakras or Magnetic Centers along the spinal medulla spoken of in the Orient. It is urgent that the lower becomes the upper, and the upper, the lower. We have to elevate the lower Yesod towards the upper Yesod (Daath). When the lower Yesod, the sexual function, is elevated to the larynx (Daath) of the cosmic man, his Word has become fructified with the Waters of Life.

The life of Christ is 33 years, the degrees of Esoteric Masonry is 33, meaning we must ascend the 33 vertebrae of the spinal medulla. Three twice is six (3 + 3 = 6). The sixth sphere is Tiphereth, the Son of Man, were the Verb is made flesh. The Sixth

Arcanum is Love. The Fifteenth Arcanum is Lucifer, the mystery of defeating Lucifer is 1 + 5 = 6, Love.

We must connect the sexual glands to the pineal gland through THE DIVINE SEXUAL ELECTRICITY known as the Devi Kundalini Shakti, a force that ascends upon the spine. Esoteric Christianity speaks of this as the Olive Branches upon the Candlestick. The Two Witnesses of the Apocalypse are the Two Olive Branches, a source of everlasting life, known as the Ida and Pingala to the Hindus. They entwine around the *reed, measuring stick,* or spinal medulla to form the Holy Eight, the form of the serpents upon the staffs of Moses and Mercury, the messenger of the Gods.

The creation of the Kosmos Man, or Adam Kadmon, is seven fold, like all creations. It is necessary to understand this. The Hermetic axiom states: *"As above, so below."* This is why the Furnace of Nebuchadnezzar is lit seven times, and why the true Christians walk unharmed within it.

The Law of Seven guides us in understanding the recursive nature of the Cosmos.

The Seven Dimensions of Nature are:
1. Length (number, Malkuth)
2. Height (weight, Malkuth)
3. Width (volume, Malkuth)
4. Time (Yesod)
5. Eternity (Hod and Netzach)
6. Causality (Tiphereth, Geburah, and Chesed)
7. Radical Zero Dimension (Binah, Chochmah, Kether)

The first six are fundamental dimensions; the seventh is the Radical Dimension, that is, the *root of dimension*. Within these Seven Dimensions lay our seven-fold spirit:
1. Physical Body (Malkuth)
2. Vital Body (Yesod)
3. Sidereal (Astral) Body (Hod)
4. Mental Body (Netzach)
5. Casual Body (Tiphereth)

6. Buddhic Body (Geburah)
7. Atmic Body (Chesed)

These seven bodies are the seven-fold nature spoken of in Revelation. The ordinary person only has the Physical and Vital, plus a constitution of lunar, protoplasmic bodies. The solar bodies must be constructed and the lunar bodies must be destroyed.

Alchemy: Liquid Fire, Igneous Water

> For male and female have from of old been regarded as one body, not from any external or visible consideration, but on account of the ardor of that mutual love which naturally draws them together into one; and as the male and female seed jointly represent the principle of propagation, so also the sperm of the matter out of which our Stone is made can be sown and increased. There are in our substance two supplementary kinds of seed, from which our Stone may be prepared and multiplied.
>
> If you are a true lover of our Art, you will carefully weigh and ponder these words, lest, with other sophisticators, you fall into the dangerous pit prepared by the common enemy of man. But whence are you to obtain this seed? This question you may most easily answer by asking yourself another question. What do you want to develop from this seed, and what use do you wish to make of it? There can be no doubt, then that it must be the root, or first substance, of metals, from which all metals derive their origin. It is, therefore, necessary that we should now proceed to speak of the generation of the metals.
>
> – The Twelve Keys of Basil Valentine

Alchemy is a compound word that can be broken down as *Al* and *Chemy*. Al is Allah, or El, the God of Light, and chem is khem or the greek *kimia*, meaning to fuse or cast a metal. Therefore, Alchemy is the Chemistry of God, the fusion of man with divinity.

Many "authorities" on this subject are mistaken. Intellectuals who have no practical alchemical experience state that alchemy is the chemical proto-science that existed prior to the development of the scientific method. This is at best an incomplete definition, because it ignores the true inner essence of alchemical procedure.

Prior to the advancements of what is termed today as the scientific method – one of the many gifts bestowed upon us by the great initiate named Francis Bacon – all the sciences were taught as an inclusive whole. It is natural that the alchemical science bore the laws of chemistry, but this inheritance reflects only a small portion of the complete alchemical discipline.

From *Musaeum hermeticum*, this illustration exemplifies the tantric mystery of DAATH, the cross of opposite triune forces, man and woman, that occurs in the Ninth Sphere (sex).

Alchemy that is practiced today is not concerned with turning literal lead into gold. Therefore chemistry and alchemy serve different purposes: alchemy is a divine science while chemistry is a natural science. Chemistry studies matter while alchemy works to transform it. Chemistry cannot make new life – even an *in vitro* fertilization needs an egg and sperm from parents. Alchemy works with the egg and sperm directly in the Interior Lab.

Therefore only alchemy can create life and it can transform creation itself.

Alchemy is an exact science one uses to transmute the psychological lead into the finest quality gold. The wise men throughout history have known alchemy is foremost a spiritual allegory for a revolutionary psychology that first burns the ego into ashes and later raises the Phoenix, the Christified Soul. From this perspective, we can say that although there are many historical alchemists, not all of them were true alchemists. Some alchemists knew the key, and some of them did not know the key.

A lot is spoken of about alchemy in modern spiritual and esoteric groups. Yet, few know or will accept the true essence of alchemy. In a general sense, the purpose of alchemy is to achieve a transformation of the soul, and there are many practices one can perform to reach this goal, such as self-awareness or meditation. Nevertheless, without the key of alchemy, one is not a true alchemist. What is the key? The key of alchemy is sex, and the work of the Inner Lab takes place within the sexual act itself.

To read the works of Paracelsus, Nicolas Flamel, Basil Valentine, and many others requires the Alchemical Key to extract any true knowledge out of them. These venerable men wrote in deeply symbolic and confusing terms. In this way they kept hidden within their public works the transformations the soul undergoes from beginning to end.

> To each creature God gave its own seed, wherewith to propagate its kind, that in this way there might always be an increase of men and animals, plants and metals. Man was not to be able to produce new seed: he was only permitted to educe new forms of life out of that which already existed. The creating of seed God reserved to Himself For if man could create seed he would be equal to the Creator.

> Know that our seed is produced in the following way. A celestial influence descends from above, by the decree and ordinance of God, and mingles with the proper astral ties. When this union has taken place, the two bring forth a third namely, an earth-like substance, which is the principle of our seed, of its first source, so that it can shew an ancestry, and from which three the elements,

such as water, air, and earth, take their origin. These elements work underground in the form of fire, and there produce what Hermes, and all who have preceded me, call the three first principles, viz., the internal soul, the impalpable spirit, and visible bodies, beyond which we can find no earlier beginning of our Magistery.

In the course of time these three unite, and are changed through the action of fire into a palpable substance, viz., quicksilver, sulphur, and salt. If these three substances be mixed, they are hardened and coagulated into a perfect body, which represents the seed chosen and appointed by the Creator. This is a most important and certain truth. If the metallic soul, the metallic spirit, and the metallic form of body be present, there will also be metallic quicksilver, metallic sulphur, and metallic salt, which together make up the perfect metallic body.

If you cannot perceive what you ought to understand herein, you should not devote yourself to the study of philosophy.

— Basil Valentine

Volumes have been written upon alchemy and the student can go insane attempting to reconcile the labyrinth of symbols alchemy presents. Therefore, let us get straight to the point. There are three principle alchemical elements, which are Mercury (Quicksilver), Sulfur, and Salt. These three elements constitute the Water, the Fire, and the Earth.

The Water is what Paracelsus called the *Ens Seminis* (the sexual energy). The Fire is the Fohat, the Spirit, and the Earth is the body. These elements must be worked in cooperation with each other in order to perform the Magnum Opus, the Great Work.

We must remember that Mercury (Hermes, Water) is the messenger of the Sun God (Christ). Thus, astrologically Hermes is the closest one to the Sun. Here is the sum total wisdom of alchemy: The Mercury (sexual energy) must be transformed into the Sulfur (the spirit) through the medium of the Earth (the physical body).

The Sulfur must fecundate the Mercury to regenerate the Earth. The erotic coals of sexual alchemy, when delicately handled, have the power to burn away the psychological impurities of the aspirant. The alchemist must be very careful to heat the crucible in the furnace, never spilling into the fire a single drop of the Mercury-Water contained therein. Sexual alchemy is a divine practice that is devoid of lust and passion. The orgasm is the loss of the Mercury. To spill the Mercury, the water, is fatal to the Alchemist.

Let us remember that the sexual energy (fire, heat) is always in movement, either regeneratively or degeneratively, thus, the Mercury will fecundate the Sulfur positively (Metallic Spirit) or negatively (Arsenic Sulfur).

The Alchemist knows that the Mercury, the Sulfur and the Salt are always interacting, it is therefore necessary to work these elements. If the Alchemist does not properly work the Mercury, or when it is abused, it becomes Dry Mercury. Dried Mercury is a psychological aggregate. The Dry Mercury in turn produces Arsenic Sulfur, or passionate fire, egoic-fire: desire, lust, etc.

When the Mecury is used intelligently, it passes through three phases:

1. Brute Mercury: Sexual fluid and its related hormones.
2. Essential Mercury: The "metallic" soul of the sperm which is liberated through sexual transmutation.
3. Fecundated Mercury: The metallic soul of the sperm infused with the Sulfur provided by Alchemical Intercourse.

Although it appears preposterous to many, the Bible is an alchemical discourse whose true import is only recognized by those few who comprehend its esoteric knowledge. The Bible begins with the Water (**Gen**esis; Hydro-**gen** and Oxy-**gen**). Water is the source of all creations, which is why in order create, Jehovah Elohim moved over the Genesiac waters.

It is stated in the Bible that Peter walked on the waters. What does it mean to walk on the waters? Practical analysis exuberantly qualifies that to walk on the waters of life is to transform the impressions of life. The impressions, the sensations, must be worked with. Do not throw out or reject the sensations of life. Sensation itself is neither good nor evil. Only the mind is good or evil. We must comprehend our sensations. We have to work with the water (Genesis, creative energy, sexual energy) to walk on the water.

Without comprehension, we fall into the waters. The mind has been stuffed to the brim with false concepts throughout the many lives it has lived. Meditate on the complexity of the mind. One will realize that it is impossible that such an intricate, dense, and complicated labyrinth of an "I" could have been developed in the short number of years accumulated in a single life. The ultra complexity of our own psychology is due to the complication of many lives, not just a single life. Because of our endless convolutions of ego, we contain many concepts in the mind that do not have any reality. The mind we have is full of doubt, uncertainty, criticism, arrogance, fear, pride, etc., etc., but, nowhere in the mind will gnosis be found. Gnosis belongs to the consciousness.

Nevertheless, we must use the mind as the practical instrument that it is. The mind was not constructed to serve doubt, or hate, or pride or lust into the world. The mind is just a tool, a binary operator that attempts to divide the relative Is from the Is Not. The mind labels everything as what it is, and by the absence of a label, what it is not. In the end the mind has nothing more than concepts and labels. Consciousness, on the other hand, acquires knowledge through experience, and it is the only thing that can absolutely discern the Is from the Is Not. The mind works through the consciousness. The fuel of the mind is the consciousness. When the consciousness becomes trapped in the concepts of the mind, the ego is the result.

The waters of life are triumphantly walked upon when the consciousness is in complete equilibrium. When we identify with the impressions of life we fall into the waters. When we fall into the waters of life, then we become a servant of nature and to the external sensory perceptions.

The true King of Creation is that person who nature serves. In order to conquer nature, we must conquer our own interior nature. If we are slaves to our own nature, if we contain the ego, then we remain servants of nature, within and without. Moses was a true magician, a King of Nature. This is how he commanded the waters, this is how he parted the waters.

The water is in synthesis the sexual waters, you know this by now. When Jesus walked on the waters, he told us that we must have willpower over the sexual waters: the ability to command our animal intellect, our animal emotion and our animal sexuality. We can do this by applying our willpower to remain self-aware. Self-awareness is the first step. Always make an effort to be self-aware.

After walking on the waters by Jesus, it was Peter who followed Jesus because it is he who represents the infamous Philosophical Stone.

What is the stone? Hermes, another name for Mercury, is related with the Stone and the Phallus. In ancient Greece pillars called Herms were placed at the crossroads. Atop the pillar was the face of Hermes, and in the center was an erect phallus. They were often accompanied by a pile of stones at its base, placed there by travelers for good luck and fertility. But this custom hides a much more weighty principle than mere fortune and reproduction.

So, here we have the symbols of the cross, the phallus, the stone, the traveler, and Hermes. The stone is the base, the foundation of the Great Work. Of course the stone is sex. The God Mercury is found in the sex. The traveler is the one walking on the path, and the cross, obviously as we know, is the archaic symbol of tantrism, which in the west can be called the Hermetic Art or simply Hermeticism. Hermeticism is the science of Hermes, Mercury, again whose abode lies within sex.

The Stone and Water are really two parts of the same thing. This can be seen in the alchemical treatise called *The Sophic Hydrolith*. This title can be crudely translated as *The Water-Stone of Wisdom*, and with the keys we have unveiled in this chapter, the reader can make sense of this authentic Rosicrucian work. The author obviously knew the secret; he knew that the water and stone are the creative-sexual potential which can regenerate man. It states:

> For as the Philosopher's Stone, which is the Chemical King, has virtue by means of its tincture and its developed perfection to change other imperfect and base metals into pure gold, so our heavenly King and fundamental Corner Stone, Jesus Christ, can alone purify us sinners and imperfect men with His Blessed ruby-coloured Tincture, that is to say, His Blood, from all our natural filth and uncleanness, and perfectly heal the malignant disease of our nature; seeing that there is no salvation but in Him, and that no other name is given under heaven whereby men can obtain happiness and perfection. [...]
>
> Again, if we men would be purified and cleansed of our original sin and the filth of Adam[1] (in whom, through the subtilty of the Cacodæmon,[2] our whole race was corrupted in the very Protoplast[3]), we can obtain perfection and eternal happiness only through the regeneration of water and the Spirit, as the royal chemical substance is regenerated by water and its spirit. In this new and spiritual regeneration, which is performed in baptism through water and the Spirit, we are washed and purified with the Blood of Christ, united to His Body, and clothed with Him as with a garment (Col. iii., Eph. v.). For, as the Philosophical Stone becomes joined to other metals by means of its tincture and enters into an indissoluble union with them, so Christ, our Head, is in constant vital communion with all His members through the ruby tincture of His Blood, and compacts His whole Body into a perfect spiritual building which after God is created in righteousness and true holiness. Now, that regeneration which is wrought in baptism through the operation of the Holy Spirit is really nothing but an inward spiritual renewal of fallen man, by which we become God's friends instead of His enemies, and thus heirs of God and fellow

---

[1] Fornication is the origin of psychological dirtiness, or "uncleanliness" as it is written in the Bible.
[2] "Evil spirit." In other words, the ego.
[3] The lunar bodies are the protoplasmic bodies; they are infected with the ego.

heirs with Christ (i. Cor. ii., Rom. xii., Ephes. ii., Hebr. iii.). For to this end Christ died and rose again, that through this means, namely, through His passion, death, resurrection, and ascension, He might enter the Holy Place made without hands, and prepare for us the way to our everlasting Fatherland. Therefore, we, too, as His brothers and sisters, should follow His passion, and grow like Him in love, humility, and all other virtues, till we are conformed to His glorified body, and until, having lived and died with Him, we also reign with Him, and share His everlasting glory.

But this inward quickening and imitation of Christ, our heavenly King, in our daily lives, is not the outgrowth of our own merit or natural will (for by nature all men are blind, deaf, and dead, as to spiritual things), but is produced solely through the effectual working of the Holy Spirit, who dwells in us through the blessed laver of regeneration. In like manner, the minerals and metals are in themselves gross and dead, and cannot purify or ameliorate themselves, but are purified, renewed, dissolved, and perfected through the agency of the spagyric spirit. Now when we have been incorporated in the Body of our heavenly King, and washed and cleansed of original sin through His purple Tincture, and so rendered capable of bringing forth the first fruits of the Holy Spirit, we are fed up, like little children, and nourished with the pure and health-giving milk of grace, until at length we become living stones, fit for the heavenly building and the highest priesthood, which consists in offering up spiritual sacrifices such as are acceptable to God the Father, through Jesus Christ. For even a Christian, though regenerated through water and the Word, cannot grasp or apprehend all things at once, but must grow gradually, and daily, in the knowledge of God and of Christ.

– The Sophic Hydrolith, Pt. IV

If one were to read this preceding text in accordance with the way modern Christianity is taught, one would think that a man named Jesus is going to save all those who were baptized, as an infant, in the Holy Water of their local Church. But, as we know, *The Sophic Hydrolith* is a work of Alchemy, and it is written for those who know the key.

There exists within each person an intimate Savior, the Christ principle that performs the salvation and regeneration. But, in order for it to take place, we have to work with the Waters of the Holy Spirit. We have to work with tantrism. The Christ principle cannot work within us without cooperation. It is clear that man does not cooperate in the Divine Plan until he has already learned much about good and evil. When one wishes to cooperate with the Sun, that is to say Christ, they inevitably begin the alchemical process. Through alchemy a solid foundation, the Philosophical Stone, for the awakening of consciousness is formed.

> Moreover, brethren, I would not that ye should be ignorant (*without gnosis or direct experience*), how that all our fathers were under the cloud (*a mystery*), and all passed through the sea (*the waters of transmutation*);
>
> And were all baptized unto Moses in the cloud (*the Upper Eden of Daath*) and in the sea (*the Lower Eden of Yesod*);
>
> And did all eat the same spiritual meat (*of direct experience*);
>
> And did all drink the same spiritual drink (*of transmuted waters*): for they drank of that spiritual Rock that followed them: and that Rock (*Yesod*) was Christ (*existing within the sexual seed*).
>
> But with many of them God was not well pleased: for they were overthrown in the wilderness (*of sensual temptation*).
>
> — 1 Corinthians 10: 1-7

This humanity, although it has already suffered too much, still has not comprehended the knowledge of good and evil, and so it continues to reject the Rock. The day when man learns good and evil is the first day he looks for the Rock. Only then, once knowing good and evil, can he go beyond being slave to the sensations of his mortal existence and become the true Icon of God, Paul's *pneumatikon*.

Peter, as we have stated, is the symbol of the stone in the Bible. This is why Jesus names Peter the rock upon which he will build the temple. The Great Arcanum is the dual nature of the *Key of Peter* that Dante speaks of.

> Up the steps my master guided me
> Benevolently, saying: "Ask him now,
> In all humility, to turn the key."
> Falling devoutly at his holy feet,
> In mercy's name I begged to be let in;
> but, first of all, three times I smote my breast.

> Then with the sword he traced upon my brow
> the scares of **seven P's**. "Once entered here,
> be sure you cleanse away these wounds," he said.
> Ashes, or earth when it is dug up dry-
> this was the color of the robe he wore;
> he reached beneath them and drew out **two keys**.
> One key was silver and the other gold;
> first he applied the white one, then the yellow-
> with that the gate responded to my wish.
> **"Whenever either one of these two keys**
> **fails to turn properly inside the lock,**
> **and angel said, "the road ahead stays closed."**
> One is more precious, but the other needs
> wisdom and skill before it will unlock,
> for it is that one which unties the knot.
> **I hold these from Peter**, who advised:
> 'Admit too many, rather than too few,
> If they but cast themselves before your feet.'"
>
> – Purgatory Canto IX

The seven P's remind us of the Seven Sins, the perverted application of the seven virtues. They are upon our head, in other words, our mind, our ego. The ego is the seven headed dragon, the Medusa, that must be beheaded. The wound that must be washed is our own ego.

The key is twofold, meaning Man and Woman. Man is solar, Gold. Woman is Lunar, silver. Peter was crucified, inverted, reminding us that we must descend to the Ninth Sphere. The Ninth Sphere of the Tree of Life is literally sex (birth, Yesod), and the Ninth Sphere of Hell is the sphere of final destruction (of ego). The Key of Peter is the synthesis of death and birth, the movement of opposite extremes. The Key of Peter is the Alchemical Key.

Roger Bacon knew the key. His 1597 manuscript entitled *Mirror of Alchemy*, tells us that the metals fashioned in a mountain's core is due to a consistent and unrevealed heat:

There, through the continual equal heat in the mountain, in long process of time diverse metals are engendered, according to the diversity of the place. And in these Mineral places, you shall find a continual heat. For this cause we are of right to note, that the external mineral mountain is everywhere shut up within itself, and stony: for if the heat might issue out, there should never be engendered any metal. If therefore we intend to immitate nature, we must needs have such a furnace like unto the Mountains, not in greatness, but in continual heat, so that the fire put in, when it ascends, may find no vent: but that the heat may beat upon the vessel being close shut, containing in it the matter of the stone: which vessel must be round, with a small neck, made of glass or some earth, representing the nature or close knitting together of glass: the mouth whereof must be signed or sealed with a covering of the same matter, or with lute. And as in the mines, the heat does not immediately touch the matter of Sulphur and Argent-vive, because the earth of the mountain comes everywhere between: So this fire must not immediately touch the vessel, containing the matter of the aforesaid things in it, but it must be put into another vessel, shut closed in the like manner, that so the temperate heat may touch the matter above and beneath, and where ever it be, more aptly and fitly: whereupon Aristotle says, in the *Light of Lights*, that Mercury is to be concocted in a three-fold vessel, and that the vessel must be of most hard Glass, or (which is better) of Earth possessing the nature of Glass.

– Mirror of Alchemy

Do you see the hidden message? We must imitate the generation of metals as Nature generates the veins of metals in the heart of a mountain. The heat must not be let out, and the Mercury is formulated in a triple receptacle made of Earth. The first, a long and thin vessel must be covered well. The phallus is the vessel. The man must protect himself from the emission of the brute Mercury. This vessel must be placed in another vessel, the vagina. The woman must protect herself from orgasm. The third seal is of the senses. The senses must be closed, meaning, they must not let in the impression of sex too widely, for if they do, then the heat becomes too much, and the Mercury boils out of the vessel.

Let us know conclude this chapter with the complete text of the Emerald Tablet, a deeply kabbalistic and alchemical work by the Thrice Great Hermes Trismesgistus:

It is true, no lie, certain and to be depended upon,

The superior (Eden in Daath, the cosmic chaotic waters) agrees with the inferior (Eden, the sexual waters of Yesod), and the lower (solar fluid in the semen) agrees with the higher (solar fluid, the cosmic waters of Aquarius, Urania-Venus), to effect that one truly wonderful work (of Creation).

As all (created) things owe their existence to the will of the only one (Spirit of God or Ruach Elohim), so all (internal or spiritual) things owe their origin to the one only thing, the most hidden (son of God, the Philosophical Mercury) by the arrangement (or transmutation) of the only (Christonic substance of) God.

The father of that one only thing is the (energy of the) sun (the Prana), its mother is the moon (the Akasa, the superior cosmic waters of Aquarius, Urania-Venus), the wind (the Atmosphere) carries it (as Pranic Light) in its belly; but its nourse is (the sexual organs, whereas) a spirituous (Sanctus dwells within the philosophical stone of the) earth (the sex in the physical body).

That one only thing is (the Semen or the Mercury of Philosophy) the father of all things in the Universe.

Its (Divine Creative) power remains perfect, after it has been united with a spirituous (Sanctus within the Sperm of the philosophical stone of the) earth (the sex in the physical body).

Separate that spirituous (Sanctus or holy fire of the) earth from the dense (fluid of Semen) or crude (Brute Mercury) by means of (sexual transmutation or Sahaja Maithuna with) a gentle heat (without passion), with much attention (by praying to your Inner Goddess).

In great measure (this Holy Fire of Kundalini) ascends from (the sexual waters of Yesod, the sex in the Physical Body) the earth up to (Kether, our Monad in) heaven and (through the Initiation) descends again (as the Son of God), (a) newborn (Son of Man), on the earth (the physical body), and the superior (Supernal Triangle Sephiroth) and the inferior (Ethical and Magical Triangle Sephiroth) are increased in power.

By this (sexual transmutation) wilt thou partake the glory (Hod or Solar Light) of the whole world. And Darkness (or Ignorance) will fly from thee.

This is (Lucifer, the Carrier of Light, the Sexual Potency, the Cherub,) the strength of all powers. With this (White Tantrism) thou wilt be able to overcome all (karmic) things and transmute all what is fine and what is coarse (within your psyche).

In this manner (with the sexual potency) the world was created; the arrangements to follow this road are hidden (within the spermatozoa and the ovum).

For this reason I am called Hermes Trismesgistus, one in essence, but three in aspect. (Because) In this trinity: (Brute Mercury, the Soul of the Mercury and the Mercury fecundated by Sulfur) is hidden the wisdom (Chokmah) of the whole world.

It is ended now, what I have said concerning the effects of the sun (Christ).

– Emerald Tablet

VITRIOL: *"Visitam Interiore Terras Rectificatur Invenias Ocultum Lapidum"*
"Visit the interior of our earth, that by rectifying, you will find the occult stone."

The Two Types of Intoxication

> Dionysian inebriation, Ectasy, Samadhi, obviously is indispensable when one is trying to experience that which is the Truth, the Reality.
>
> Such exaltation is one hundred percent possible by means of the technique of meditation.
>
> Psychedelia is different. This term must be translated as this: psyche = "Soul"; dela = "drug."
>
> By specifying we will state: Psychedelia is the anti-pole of Meditation. The inferno of drugs is within the interior of the planetary organism on which we live, under the very epidermis of the terrestrial crust.
>
> Hallucinatory mushrooms, L.S.D., pills, marijuana, etc., etc., etc., evidently intensify the vibrator capacity of the subjective powers, but it is ostensible that they could never originate the awakening of the Consciousness.
>
> – Samael Aun Weor, *The Three Mountains*

The *American Heritage Dictionary* defines intoxication as "stupefaction or excitement by the action of a chemical substance," and also "exhilaration, excitement, euphoria." However correct this definition is, from the viewpoint of gnosis it is too vague, because in reality there exists two distinct, diametrically opposed states of intoxication. There is an inferior form of intoxication and a superior form of intoxication.

The first type is ordinary drunkenness, as well as the effects of cocaine, heroin, the various forms of *Cannabis sativa*, pharmaceutical drugs, the abuse of caffeine and nicotine, etc., etc. This is what is ordinarily considered intoxication, and it is what everyone today not only has experienced, but, in most cases, seek to experience and to re-experience at a normal frequency.

In this first type of intoxication is included the states of consciousness achieved through the effects of external sensory perceptions, and, the fascination with mental formations. Understanding this we can observe that in actuality, our entire society is intoxicated. Why? Because we can say quite literally that it is inebriated with unquenchable passions, it is delirious with concepts, ideas, theories, beliefs, and dreams that will never find reality, it is dizzy with the desire for wealth, success and the respect of others, it is drunk for power, and distressed with constant fears of death and poverty.

On the busy avenues and at corner of streets, advertisements that play to our sexual desire are found in abundance, and in living rooms, popular television shows are watched that reward arrogance, greed and revenge, that teach us how to be cruel and sarcastic and to make jokes at the expense of others. Religion and politics, which have the potential to truly ennoble and help our daily living, instead are infected with ideologies that appeal to our weaknesses, all the while without making any real positive change in our lives.

Technology, haphazardly considered by many as a modern savior to our modern problems, in the end only gives us more problems... it always provides new things to buy and more money to make. Our technology actually has an enormous capacity to assist our lives, but only in the rarest circumstances is technology advanced under impulse of virtue. Instead, envy, violence, greed, and lust are the primary causes for our technological advancements, and as such our technology ultimately solves nothing.

For example, the widespread proliferation of pornography is aiding the already alarming state of degeneration we are in, and to counter the rising rates of impotence, other forms of (degenerate) science falsely empowers men to force their bodies to have erections, which will only further their problems in the future. What new types of problem will appear tomorrow, caused by our "solutions" of today? The world is dreaming of a society where our materialistic knowledge solves all of our problems. Drunk upon an idea of perfection and lost in the dogma of evolution, we fail to see the reality: that most things in this world are getting worse, not better.

So what about the other type of intoxication? It is this type which is worthy of pursuing, yet it is rather ironic is it that so few attempt to achieve it. It is the quickening spirit, the rapture, the superlative noetic states of awakened consciousness, the mystical ecstasy, samadhi, union with divinity... this, my reader, is the state upon which all people, deep within their hearts, wish to attain, because this is the state of true happiness.

But as a whole we are simply not making the efforts to reach our inalienable right to achieve the intoxicating bliss of *Being*. Millions of ideas which appear to provide an easy path to happiness in reality only serve to keep us sleeping within the machine of nature. Society has a programming, and being the collection of sleeping individuals, it demands its people to accept this programming. There are many types of programs: right wing, left wing, religious, atheist, and everything in-between. Yet, all of them are mechanical, all of them promote a sleeping state of mind, and none of them promote awakened consciousness. It has come to the point where even most forms of religion no longer promote awakening consciousness, but instead simply advocate performing mechanical tasks. Nothing mechanical can awaken consciousness.

So, realize this dear reader: As woeful, or unbelievable it may be, people live and die asleep, and this is all due to the negative type of intoxication. Nevertheless, everyone who lives deeply asleep believes with all their conviction that they are awake and not sleeping. Anyone who believes they are awakened but has never once observed the state of their own mind is living deeply asleep.

Once, during a conversation concerning religious matters, I informed a man of this troubling fact regarding the state psychological sleep that humanity is living in. He disagreed with me by stating, *"That is ridiculous. You are subversively attempting to strike fear within me so that I can become like you and follow your doctrine... you are using a classic fear inducing tactic which disarms the naive so they will totally submit to whatever nonsense you preach to them. Luckily, informed men, like myself, know of dangerous people like you. I will not fall for your trap and as a service to others I will inform them of your misdeeds."* This man possessed what he believed was a formidable theory, yet, he never actually attempted to awaken his consciousness, not even for one moment.

So, within the negative pole of intoxication, we have the psychological type, which is the intoxication of ideas and theories, and the physical type, which occurs through chemical means and sympathizes and aids with the psychological type. Both are obstacles towards happiness.

It should be understood that, in terms of self-development, drinking alcohol is a waste of time. Alcohol dulls the mind in order for it to be subdued from it woes, and it is obvious that consuming alcohol is antithetical to self-observation. To find any success in these studies we require clarity, and a healthy body. It is impossible see anything impartially in the psyche without a clear mind.

If one is serious about cultivating virtue within, then it is better to leave drinking to yesterday. Drinking is an escape from responsibility, right? What else could it possibly be? Why do we want to evade our responsibilities?

Some have a drink to calm the mind down so they can be relieved of worry and tension. Really, it would be better if these people stopped avoiding their self and began to observe, meditate and comprehend their self. To sedate one's self is a form of escapism, which is an earmark of unhappiness. A happy person has no reason to drink, for it would only dull their ability to perceive it.

Why buy or prepare a drink when you can sit within your own mental space and achieve what nothing can buy: clarity of mind. We need to learn to meditate! When a solid foundation of meditative practice is attained, then the negative psychological results of drinking become so clear that one finds themselves thoroughly enjoying sobriety over the so-called "relaxation" caused by alcohol.

Recall all the people that have passed through your life: Who were the most destitute, the most self-destructive, the most depressed and ruinous? It is always the ones who are irresponsible, the ones who cannot seem to *respond* ably to the problems given to them in life. Thus, they are irresponsible.

Of course, we are all irresponsible to one degree or another. Everyone has a different level of being. Those who have regressed to the point that even the average problems of life are insurmountable have become beggars and vagabonds. These are representations of very vulgar forms of irresponsibility.

On the other hand, when we begin to awaken, we begin to increase our ability to respond to life upon ever increasing subtleties. Only then, through enormous effort, do we become responsible in the complete sense of the word. Little by little, by applying willpower, by remaining vigilant in the face of every mental shape, emotional impulse and sensual impression, we gain our rightful state of total responsibility and total happiness. This is a willful, cognizant state of Being.

How can there be *Paramartha* without *Paranishpanna*? How can there be perfect happiness without perfect cognizance?

If we take a look at the world around us, it seems that very few people actually wish to take responsibility of their *entire* life. This must be the root cause of drinking or doing drugs. We desperately want to flee our dull existence, even for just a moment, yet we need to understand that alcohol not only fails to change our world-weariness, it furthermore creates vices and destroys the physical and subtle physiologies.

As it turns out, society just is not interested in these matters. People commonly trade in their birthright, self-realization, for a bottle of wine, dens of fornication, sleepiness, drunkenness and every other vice in life. So, let them drink, let them be "merry," but instead of drinking with them, learn to meditate, learn to become conscious in the moment of now, learn to accept the pleasant impressions and the unpleasant impressions with the same impenetrable serenity. This is the authentic way to enjoy life.

Instead of being noisy, dense, conceited and shameless while full of liquor, or just trying to "blow off some steam," or "unwind," it is a thousand times better to meditate. Neither sleep nor death will rid you of your problems, but awakening to their realities will. Meditation is like a shower for the soul. When you meditate on a daily basis, then one day you realize that without mediation, your state of mind becomes dirty, and then you realize that you have lived most of your life in such mental fogginess, that to live in that state again would be unbearable.

This motivates one to meditate even more. Then, the practice of meditation is no longer difficult, and the brute temptations for sensual pleasure and intoxication slowly fade away, and new, ever more subtle levels of temptation are seen. Layer after layer of the mind becomes ever more apparent, subtle reactions that were once unconscious become self-discovered, the minute impulses previously unknown become obvious, and the outcome of all this is a magnificent type of intoxication of the soul that is totally antithetical to the inferno of alcohol and drugs.

Happiness is consciousness. Really, happiness is a type of supra-sobriety. Happiness occurs when the Essence has the ability to express itself. Remember that the Essence is the seed that must grow into awakened consciousness. The intoxicated human organism looses all consciousness and all ability to respond to the impressions of life. The Essence remains in a latent state when one becomes intoxicated by sensation, alcohol, drugs, etc. Then, what occurs is only what can occur: mechanical reaction, irresponsibility – the inability to consciously respond to the impressions of life.

Some people do not drink and only partake in the use of psychedelics and narcotics. These people believe that through the use of drugs a higher state of mind can be found. Many "hippies" in the 1960's took up this philosophy. However, what became of these people? What kind of higher state of mind relies on drugs? Most people are using drugs just to produce a so-called ecstatic state. Someone may take psychedelic mushrooms and have a vision of Angels and God. However the drug user does not understand what he sees, because drugs do not provide comprehension. Nevertheless, he feels like he now knows god, simply because he had a substantial or unsubstantial vision. Beautiful or macabre visions mean nothing without comprehension.

During the so-called "Summer of Love" in 1967 many runaways arrived at Haight-Ashbury only to find the veracity of a drug infested culture. The harsh reality was total debauchery (with many pimps taking advantage of young women), crime, abject poverty, terrible violence, filthiness, etc., etc. The hippie experiment failed not because their intentions were malignant, but because they confused the delirious inferno of drugs with the awakened state of bliss.

The ego is the cause of all hallucinatory visions. Drugs only help to amplify the negative clairvoyance of the ego. Nothing but auto-psychoanalysis provides true comprehension. Only the self can understand itself.

The drugs that produce a religious or spiritual experience are very easily abused. It is exceedingly rare that anyone ever uses these drugs in a proper format. The indigenous American peoples made use of peyote, but today's seeker should avoid that path. The best thing that can happen by taking this drug is that one experiences things beyond their normal perception, giving the user faith in them. Yet the impulse is so great today for a shortcut to enlightenment that almost without exception all the individuals involved in the drug culture end up abusing the substance and awakening their consciousness negatively.

These false "Shamans" end up taking drugs again and again in order to repeat some experience they crave for. There is only so much a drug can do, and once you have experienced that, why take it again? It is not only a waste of time, but very dangerous to one's psychological equilibrium. The ego can grow and awaken in this state, and the outcome is a negative type of awakening. What is most important to remember in these matters is that drugs are completely unnecessary to achieve positive awakened states of consciousness, and what they can do in a positive fashion is limited while the prowess of meditation literally has no limit.

Intoxication does not end at alcohol and narcotics; it extends itself into all forms of media. There are those, for example, who are very involved with listening to music of their favorite genres, and wherever they go they want to listen to their personal soundtrack. They are stimulated by music in a similar manner an addict is stimulated by his addiction. If confronted, the addict becomes offended, yet, if they attempted to live in silence for even a short period of time a protest would be emerge... perhaps the word "boring" would be used.

There are others who find themselves very interested in matters of sports, they thoroughly enjoy being tugged like a marionette that prances on stage when his team wins, and when the team inevitably loses he finds himself in pain. Tell him to stop being involved in sports and he will not be able to because he is intoxicated with the idea of victory.

There exist people who are intimately involved with their social groups, friends, etc.: they always have someone to complain about, they enjoy gossiping, yet never wish to be thought of in the way that he or she thinks of others. Ask them to express only positive feelings towards their fellows and they will tell you it is impossible, precisely because they are drunk with envy, jealously, pride, etc., etc.

This is because someone who is identified with sensation is acting with their consciousness asleep. The true beauty of life is only perceivable to the awakened consciousness, thus when the consciousness is sleeping, life feels boring without constant stimulation of the senses. As one becomes accustomed to constant stimulation of any category of sensation, the ability to reach infatuation within that particular type of sensual stimulation becomes more difficult to achieve. Thus, a search for both an increase in the frequency and amplitude of the stimulus is searched for. As a corollary, the lack of this stimulus becomes increasingly unbearable, and manifests in what we can call "boredom." Boredom is the outcome of not achieving the desire for sensual stimulation. Obviously, the answer is not in the search for more stimulation but rather in the liberation of consciousness.

> Scratching an itch brings pleasure,
> But more pleasurable than that is not having an itch.
> Likewise, satisfying worldly desires is pleasurable,
> But more pleasurable than that is not having desire.
>
> – Nagarjuna, *Precious Garland*

Beyond external sensations lie the interior states of sentiment and reasoning. Those inclined towards emotional intoxication enjoy themselves through movies, books, video games, gambling, drinking, etc. The intellect is susceptible to the drink of ideas and concepts, ideals, morals and traditions (no matter how absurd they are), and what is worse, some ideas become like a virus that others catch, at which point they proceed to spread the intoxicant yet further. Perverse sexual ideologies, skepticism, dialectic materialism, and atheism are intoxicants of many learned ignoramuses, which is why Samael Aun Weor said, *"Delirium tremens in a drunk alcoholic are an unmistakable symptom, but those intoxicated with theories are easily mistaken for geniuses."*

The psychologically sleeping, intoxicated human organism has no choice but to respond to hate with more hatred, no choice but to get sad when someone insults it, and no choice but to feel proud when someone praises it. That is not happiness, but rather slavery. People are drunk with the idea of freedom, but who actually possesses it?

People enjoy their slavery because it *feels* good. This is a sign of our dependence upon the external sensory perceptions, which itself is an earmark of our state of degeneration. Psychologically speaking, no amount of external sensory perceptions can remove, but instead can only add too, the feelings of being stressed, in fear, anxious, sad, or depressed. Those that feel overburdened by these negative emotions, no matter how much they tell themselves that they should be happy in life, they continue to remain without happiness, precisely because they ignore that their problem is psychological, not sensual or external. They say, "*I know I should be happy, but I find myself in terrible moods even when those around me are treating me well... I don't know why I am depressed...*" We need to change our psychology, and this is only done through self-effort, and with the right tools. Neither the intellect nor drugs are capable of changing us fundamentally. The right tool for self-change is meditation.

> When I had sat thus for some time, I felt myself going out of my body, I saw myself sitting down with the delicate tender leaves of the tree over me. I was facing the east. In front of me was my body and over my head I saw the Star, bright and clear. Then I could feel the vibrations of the Lord Buddha; I beheld Lord Maitreya and Master K.H. I was so happy, calm and at peace. I could still see my body and I was hovering near it. There was such profound calmness both in the air and within myself, the calmness of the bottom of a deep unfathomable lake.... The Presence of the mighty Beings was with me for some time and then They were gone. I was supremely happy, for I had seen. Nothing could ever be the same. I have drunk at the clear and pure waters at the source of the fountain of life and my thirst was appeased.... I have touched compassion which heals all sorrow and suffering; it is not for myself, but for the world. I have stood on the mountain top and gazed at the mighty Beings....
>
> Love in all its glory has intoxicated my heart; my heart can never be closed. I have drunk at the fountain of Joy and eternal Beauty. I am God-intoxicated.
>
> – Krishnamurti

The purpose of this chapter is inform the reader that there are two types of intoxication. Dionysus is often understood of as the God of drinking, but actually it better to state that he is the god of wine. Wine is exclusively thought of as an alcoholic substance, but this is incorrect, for wine is merely an element that causes intoxication. Dionysus is the bearer of a spiritual wine. Therefore, two types of wine exist for two different types of intoxication. Wine inebriates, it leaves behind rationality of the mind, yet one method submerges us into the inferior dimensions and we become animalistic, yet the other exalts us into the superior dimensions where we experience a divine effluence that flows from the heart of our Being out into the universe.

Clearly society understands what it is to be drunk, yet, *Dionysian inebriation* is a total mystery to the normal person. It is, as Krishnamurti stated it, God-intoxication. The true mystery of Dionysus is within the wine. The very first teaching of Jesus was the transubstantiation of water into wine. To drink the wine of Christ is to become God intoxicated. This is accomplished through meditation, through the removal of the false self, through the renouncement of all vices, from the desire to help everyone.

Bacchus (Dionysus) looks at us with the smile of a Buddha and says, *"Brother, drink the solar wine. Brother, sip the divine ambrosia from the chalice of meditation, become intoxicated with compassion, comprehend the mysteries of life and death, reach perfect concentration while in total relaxation. Drink... drink... and you will come to know God."*

Obviously it is possible for everyone to directly experience God. However, it takes sacrifice, and to even begin we must finish with wasting all of our energies. We cannot expect to experience the subtle if we continue to be so gross in our movements. When we fantasize and dream, we are wasting our energy. When we are in any type of emotional tizzy we are wasting useful energy in atomic explosions. It is very normal for us to waste every drop of energy we have within.

When we do not use so much metal energy with absurd dreams and desires, then it is obvious we awake from our physical sleep completely rested. When we are physically awake yet psychologically sleeping, we are wasting enormous amounts of energy. If we understood how much energy we waste everyday, then we would immediately cease our degenerate habits.

Recall that Dionysus was birthed, and then *born again* from the thigh of Zeus, and you will understand that his myth is intimately related with sex. The wine of Dionysus comes from the thigh of Zeus. The water is the semen, the transmutation of water is wine, and the wine rises up the spinal column and fills the chalice, the brain. This is how one becomes god intoxicated. Those involved with spiritual pursuits who fornicate are only fooling themselves; they are like automobiles that have no fuel, thus these individuals become torpid. If you yearn for spiritual progress, then listen to Dionysus: fill your chalice with the sacred wine of light.

The Gods neither smile at exaltation nor cry in front of condemnation. They simply exist, free in their movement and repose. The Gods know freedom! The Gods know happiness!

We urgently need to have direct verifiable experience of spiritual intoxication. It is useless to live in a world of tomorrow: we must change our lives here and now. In order to know, we have to make great sacrifice. It is urgent that the reader develops a routine of meditation, which requires a great deal of patience and willpower. We define ourselves through action. If one is interested in verifying the esoteric philosophy, this one will make great efforts in removing themselves from habits nonconductive towards the awakening of consciousness. It is inevitable that when a student fills his head with too many theories that he has never experienced, he is like a man who builds a house on the sands of a beach. This is how students who appear to be serious end up leaving these studies the moment a contradictory theory appears in his field of intellectual dialogue.

Ten Rules for Meditation

Scientific meditation has ten basic, fundamental rules. Without them, emancipation and liberation from the mortifying shackles of the mind is impossible.

1st Rule: To be completely conscious of the psychological mood in which we are situated, before the arising of any thought.

2nd Rule: Psychoanalysis: To investigate the root and origin of each thought, remembrance, affection, emotion, feeling, resentment, etc. while they emerge from within the mind.

3rd Rule: To serenely observe our own mind; to put perfect attention on all mental forms that appear on the screen of the intellect.

4th Rule: To remember and recall the "Sensation of Contemplation" from moment to moment during the common and current course of daily life.

5th Rule: The intellect must assume a psychological, receptive, integral, uni-total, complete, tranquil, and profound state.

6th Rule: A continuity of purpose, tenacity, firmness, constancy, and insistence must exist in the technique of meditation.

7th Rule: To assist at any time we can in the meditation rooms of the Gnostic Lumisials is commendable.

8th Rule: It is peremptory, urgent, and necessary to convert ourselves into watchers of our own mind during any agitated or revolving activity, to stop at least for an instant to observe it.

9th Rule: It is indispensable and necessary to always practice with closed eyes, with the goal of avoiding the external sensorial perceptions.

10th Rule: Absolute relaxation of the entire body, and the wise combination of meditation with drowsiness.

Beloved reader, the moment has arrived in order to judiciously weigh and analyze these ten scientific rules of meditation.

A: The principle, base, and living foundation of Samadhi (ecstasy), consists of previous introspective knowledge of oneself. To introvert ourselves is indispensable during deepest meditation. We must start to profoundly know the psychological mood that precedes the appearance of any mental form in the intellect. It is urgent to comprehend that all thoughts that emerge from within our mind are always preceded by pain or pleasure, happiness or sadness, like or dislike.

B: Serene Reflection. Examine, estimate, and inquire about the origin, cause, reason, or fundamental motive of every thought, remembrance, image, affection, desire, etc., while they emerge from within the mind. Self-discovery and Self-revelation exist in this second rule.

C: Serene Observation. Pay perfect attention to every mental form that makes its appearance on the screen of the intellect.

D: We must convert ourselves into spies of our own mind by contemplating it in action from instant to instant.

E: The Chitta (mind) is transformed into Vrittis (vibratory waves). The mind is like a pleasant and tranquil lake. When a rock falls into this lake, bubbles emerge from the bottom. All the different thoughts are perturbed buckles upon the surface of the waters.

Let the lake of the mind remain crystalline, without waves, serene, and profound during the meditation.

F: Fickle people who are voluble, versatile, changeable, without firmness, without willpower, will never achieve the Ecstasy, the Satori, the Samadhi.

G: It is obvious that scientific meditation can be practiced individually in an isolated way, as well as in a group of like-minded people.

H: The soul must be liberated from the body, affections, and the mind. It is evident, clear, and obvious that when the soul is emancipated from the intellect, it is radically liberated from the rest.

I: To eliminate external sensorial perceptions during interior profound meditation is urgent, indispensable, and necessary.

J: It is indispensable to relax the body for meditation; no muscle must remain tense. It is urgent to provoke and to regulate drowsiness at will.

It is evident, clear, and unarguable that illumination is the outcome of the wise combination of drowsiness and meditation.

Results

Upon the mysterious threshold of the Temple of Delphi, a Grecian maxim was engraved in the stone that said, Homo Nosce Te Ipsum... "Man, know thyself, and thou will know the universe and it's Gods."

In the final instance, it is obvious, evident, and clear that the study of oneself and serene reflection conclude in the quietude and in the silence of the mind.

When the mind is quiet and in silence, not only in the intellectual level, but in all and each one of the forty-nine subconscious departments, then the Newness emerges. The Essence, the consciousness, is unbottled, and the awakening of the soul, that is to say, the Ecstasy, the Samadhi, the Satori of the Saints occurs.

The mystical experience of Reality transforms us radically. People who have never directly experienced the Truth live like butterflies going from school to school. They have yet to find their center of cosmic gravitation. Therefore, they die as failures, and without having achieved the so longed for realization of the Innermost Self.

The awakening of the consciousness, of the Essence, of the soul or Buddhata, is only possible by liberating, emancipating ourselves from the mental dualism, from the struggle of the antitheses, of the intellectual waves.

Any subconscious, infra-conscious, or unconscious, submerged struggle turns into an impediment for the liberation of the Essence (soul).

Every antithetical battle, as insignificant and unconscious as it might appear, indicates, accuses, aims to obscure points that are ignored, unknown within the atomic infernos of the human being.

To reflect, observe, and know these infra-human aspects, these obscure points of oneself, is indispensable in order to achieve the absolute quietude and silence of the mind.

To experience that which is not of time is only possible while in absence of the "I."

– Samael Aun Weor, *The Gnostic Magic of the Runes*

Comprehension & Elimination

> The Chinese word Mo means "silent" or "serene." Chao means "to reflect or to observe." Mo-Chao, therefore, can be translated as "serene reflection" or "serene observation."
>
> To achieve absolute mental silence in all the levels of the subconsciousness is what is the most difficult, laborious and arduous task.
>
> It is not enough to reach stillness and silence in the mere superficial intellectual level or in a few subconscious departments, because the Essence continues bottled up within the submerged, infraconscious and unconscious dualism.
>
> A blank mind is something exceedingly superficial, hollow and intellectual. What we need is serene reflection if indeed we want to achieve the absolute stillness and silence of the mind.
>
> Nonetheless, it is clear to comprehend that in pure Gnosticism the terms serenity and reflection have much more profound definitions and hence these must be comprehended within their special connotations.
>
> The feeling of serenity transcends that which is normally understood by calm or tranquility; it implies a superlative state, which is beyond reasoning, desires, contradictions and words. Serenity designates a situation which is beyond mundane noise.
>
> Likewise, the meaning of reflection is beyond that which is understood as contemplation of a problem or idea. Now, it does not imply mental activity or contemplative thinking, but rather a kind of clear and reflective objective Consciousness, always enlightened in its own experience.
>
> Therefore, "serene," in this context, is that serenity of non-thinking and "reflection" signifies intense and clear consciousness.
>
> Thus "serene reflection" is clear consciousness within the tranquility of non-thinking.
>
> Perfect serenity reigns when true profound enlightenment is achieved.
>
> — Samael Aun Weor, *The Revolution of the Dialectic*

We must be very clear that what has been denoted in this book as "comprehension" is beyond the duality of the mechanical forms of repression or expression that are commonly invoked by the personality. Many people who wish to change think that it is necessary to learn how to control the "I," but this is a mistaken method. They think if they can learn to express instead of repress certain elements, or repress instead of express, they can modify their lives for the better. All of this is absurd because without knowing what the "I" is, there is no chance for fundamental psychological change. These forms of control only modify the results, not the causes.

Comprehension is not a form of control, it is a method of transformation, a method of not trying to control the "I," but to quite literally destroy the "I." Comprehension is difficult to achieve, because it can only arrive when we neither justify nor condemn our mind. When we are engaging in either of these processes, we are not in psychological equilibrium, and without this equilibrium, self-observation is impossible. Therefore, the death of desire is not found within any type of expressive or repressive thought, but rather in the process of the *comprehension* of the expressive and repressive thoughts.

If you have a problem, or some sort of negative emotion, the solution is not found simply by expressing that emotion, and it is not found in ignoring or repressing it either. When you find yourself thinking too much and causing stress, the solution is *not* to endlessly think about it or to repress it. Simply understand it, and the agitation, the stress, the conflict, dissolves. To understand it, one must observe it, and through observing it, we can transform it. We can transform the impressions of life, the subjective sentiments in our heart, and the absurd ways of thinking that we currently have by awakening our consciousness; this is how we go about bringing comprehension to our selves.

There is profound significance behind each of our psychological defects. To understand this significance requires great auto-observatory efforts combined with humility, and patience. This is not something that happens quickly. Off the top of our head we can find many psychological flaws. It is obvious that, being entirely shallow and unsubstantial, only a superficial change can result through working on self-evident imperfections.

The difference between superficial errors and the true causal defect is that what makes a puddle shining in the daylight different from a great sea at midnight. Our psychological darkness is an entire ocean of titanic depths. To plunge in without losing one's way (falling asleep) is very difficult.

We need to die radically, daily, from moment to moment. A transformation occurs when the consciousness is awakened from moment to moment. The consciousness awakens when we no longer identify with this "I" that feels, and that "I" that thinks, and another that wishes to stay or go... Why do we need an "I" that thinks for us? Why do we need an "I" that feels for us? Who is in control of our mind? What is in control of our emotion? The ego, the "I," Legion, Satan, is what is thinking and feeling for us, and as a consciousness we are identified with the psychological aggregates that entrap us, that think for us, that feel for us... We are hypnotized by our own captors. We feel as if we are those elements, but these elements actually have no intrinsic existence, no *Being*. They are *empty of true existence*, and this is obvious from an intellectual and analytical view, however, we must work very hard to integrate this fact into our moment to moment way of life.

When we view our lives from the vantage point of self-observation then all of these pervasive realities become apparent very quickly. The trick is to remember to observe life without being identified with it. Then thoughts or feelings arise, but they do not become identified with.

The intellect cannot solve these problems – it only changes the appearances and the results, but never resolves the cause – precisely because intellectual understanding is the most superficial level of understanding. The intellect is like a tiny speck of dust in front of the gigantic presence of comprehension. The mind contains 49 levels, and the intellect is merely the first level. Comprehension is the conscious knowledge that reaches to the 49th level.

Likewise, comprehension cannot be found in the memory. The memory is forgetful; to simply commit this or that technique or method into memory is ineffective, because the memory always fails us. Truths that are comprehended are never forgotten. A truth that is comprehended is like a particle of one's Being that has come to know of its own self-nature. In this way, we can say that comprehension is the assimilation of reality within one's self.

Is thinking getting you stressed? Then stop thinking. Are you feeling negativity due to unpleasant manifestations of your neighbors? Then, instead of being negative, be positive. If you unable to do these things, then in the mean time go for a walk in nature, give your spouse a massage, help someone and ask nothing in return, perform charity, listen to beautiful music, etc., etc., and remember that although everything external in your life will pass away, that which is of true value is always within. With a little patience and a little willpower, anything is achievable.

Observation is required to bring forth comprehension. Certain things about our lives begin to become evident when we adopt the habit of continuous self-observation. This provides the impetus for further change. Observation must take place within perfect silence. When the mind is silent it is filled with sweetness. Remember that observation is not judgment; just take inventory of the quality of thoughts, feelings, actions, etc.

Denoted by the sacrifice of our desires, comprehension obviously is the cause and result of a superior and radical transformation. A complete, comprehensive and integral change has its existence beyond the personality and the ego. To change requires effort. Absolute change will not occur from mere ideas and flimsy intentions. Even the best of intentions will produce nothing. Change requires comprehension and comprehension requires meditation. The moment of now is our starting point. To change, one must live a philosophy of momentariness: living moment to moment, instant to instant.

It is common to underestimate our own ignorance and to overestimate our knowledge. Even someone classified as a "Saint," someone who has reached a significant degree of awakened consciousness, still may have many perverse psychological aggregates living within the subconscious darkness. Remember St. Anthony, who was tormented with visions of naked women. He was discovering his own infraconsciousness! If this is the experience of revered saints, then what can be said of us? That same perversity exists within us all; it is only hidden, totally hidden, unperceivable until we begin to awaken.

The ego lives in the psychological darkness and only appears, like a crocodile in muddy waters, for an instant before attacking. This is the "I," this is our own self that we talk and live our lives as. If you wish to catch that "crocodile" you must be able to see it within the instant it makes itself known. This is only possible if we are aware in the moment it occurs. The crocodile is very slimy and if not handled in just the right way will slip from one's grasp. If we remember ourselves an instant too late, we have already become the crocodile, because we have been eaten by the crocodile (identified with the impressions of life). Then the crocodile becomes fat: the impressions of life are incorrectly transformed to further the crystallization of the ego.

In conclusion, the Transformation of Impressions requires one to be with the moment of now, because all change occurs in the moment of now. Change itself is the moment of now. Constantly we are changing for the better or for the worse. Therefore, to wisely make use of the moment of now in order to comprehend the ego is absolutely necessary. To become identified with the impression of now is a total waste of time.

We cannot judge what we do not know, so we must first come to know the ego. Therefore, within a moment, do your best not to condemn or praise. Simply act the best way can at all times, which of course requires an active psychological presence. If the consciousness is not present, then who or what is? If the consciousness is not performing life's duties, then what is the point of living? So do your best to be in the moment.

Now, for example, you find yourself in the moment, yet you are unable to stop thinking, or unable to choose your emotions. Sometimes, perhaps, you feel a deep depression, uncontrollable fear and anxiety, or blood boiling rage. All of this is evidence of that our willpower is trapped in various psychological aggregates. If you find yourself in these conditions - knowing that you are in a negative psychological state - yet cannot seem to do anything about it, do not be discouraged because this is actually a sign of progress: in the past, you would have never each achieved even this level of separation from the ego. With practice, the effort becomes refined and greater success is found.

It may seem impossible to not think, to not feel negatively, but it is possible, you can have the same control over your mind and emotion as you have over your right hand. It took years to become adept to controlling your body, and it will take years to learn to control your subtle vehicles of emotion and thought. Keep trying. Keep ahead. Use the tools, use the mantras, perform the practices, and you will begin to reign over all your vehicles. Listen to the sound of the inner drummer (the Spirit), find your tempo of the inner work and do not miss a beat. This way you will march towards liberation. Little by little you can destroy those shells, those bottles. When the bottles are destroyed, the Genie comes out.

Before retiring to bed, take time to retrospect your day. Within meditation, revisit the day in depth and try to find the moments where you lost your psychological equilibrium. Remember that any moment that you forget your Being - by becoming identified with the impressions of life - constitutes the loss of equilibrium. If you have too many moments like this, then simply review that which you feel most compelled towards. Find the flaw or flaws related with each moment that you focus upon. Meditate on a single psychological flaw until one understands it: perhaps thirty minutes, or one hour, or one week. Every case is different.

If one holds their willpower steady, in order to remember their purpose (meditation), while at the same time leaving their imagination in a void, it is inevitable that "the new" will arrive in a spontaneous fashion. Something new will always fill the void. However, a void is not the same as a mundane blankness or blackness that can appear in the mind. A void is true emptiness, a state of negation: the "blackness" that can mistakenly be imposed upon the mind stuffs it up with the thought of nothing. The difference between the thought of nothing, and nothingness itself is known through practice. Even the expectation of the "new" to arrive is an obstacle for it to appear. The "new" is objective knowledge: knowledge that is totally unabated by subjective elements.

It is easy to misunderstand what imagination is and how it crystallizes upon the canvass of the mind. Imagination does not manifest simply through an image appearing, imagination is any form of creative insight – inner sight. If the meditation is profound, then a clear visual is evident, yet, on other levels of mediation, the insight is more subtle.

It is easy, yet ultimately wrong, to view the process of comprehension, meditation, the workings of imagination, etc., etc., as either being "there," or "not there," "successful" or "unsuccessful." The reality is that everything has a degree, a level, from the most subtle to the most profound.

For example, in the process of mediation, we attempt to be in attention of our own self. It is clear that when this occurs, there is one part that is attentive, and another part that remains inattentive. Therefore, the willpower for attention is neither simply "there," nor "not there," it is both. All of the ongoing processes of the mind are highly fluid, making the mind an ever changing heterogeneous mixture.

So, in mediation, we carefully take that which is inattentive within, and make it attentive, and little by little the mind becomes a homogenous state, a state that is applying all of its capacities towards a single goal. At a steady pace, while holding his willpower balanced and allowing his imagination to perceive a particular defect, the meditator inevitably experiences something:

an insight, a flash of light, a spark of knowledge. This is comprehension on its own level. Understand clearly that this is not thinking, deliberating, day dreaming or anything of that sort. Rather, it is the creative collaborative application of willpower and imagination. When the mind becomes 100% attentive, without any subconscious elements stealing willpower and imagination, then Samadhi occurs.

The willpower is the affirmative or positive principle, while the imagination is the receptive or negating principle. The result is the conciliation, the comprehension. This creative collaborative application can only manifest if the energy to do so is present. How do we ensure its presence? Firstly, by not mechanically wasting the energy of our mind, heart or sex throughout the day. Secondly, by working with the mind in meditation, to temporarily pluck out all of the subconscious elements so that the mind's energy is free to aid in the acquisition of comprehension.

We are like a man who wears 49 layers of clothing, and when we submerge into meditation, we remove one layer at a time. The more layers we remove, the greater degree of liberation that we enjoy. With this liberation, we can investigate our mind more profoundly, and with that, we gain comprehension. With comprehension, we can move to elimination, which will permanently destroy the troublesome "layers of clothing" (the ego). So, understand the difference between temporal liberation, and the final liberation. Temporal liberation occurs according to the depth of any meditation, but the final liberation occurs only when every psychological aggregate has been eliminated.

The flash of insight cited previously is sometimes called clairvoyance, which is just a fancy name for conscious imagination. Conscious imagination is the antipode of dreaming. Through dreaming we see, experience, and can understand to a certain degree our psyche. When we take the same principle but apply it consciously, then the same inherent facilities of the consciousness, now awakened, perceives our psyche with objectivity.

At first, when analyzing an ego, there are just vague images or confusing emotions, or simply nothing. When we can see with the light of our comprehension the true nature of an ego, the vague feelings and hunches have been transformed into precise knowledge. This clarity penetrates into the *significance* of the ego. When we have reached this astounding development, then psychological death is easily accomplished. Before reaching comprehension it is impossible to discern why an element exists in the first place, and therefore, its elimination is something impossible. Even if it were possible, it would be useless because without knowing why a defect exists, upon its removal it would reincarnate itself immediately due to the continued ignorant action which originally produced it.

> Many aspirants to the superior life desperately wish to escape their workplace, to no longer walk around the streets of their village, to take refuge in the forest with the intention of seeking ultimate liberation…
>
> Those wretched people are like silly children who play hooky from school, who do not attend classes, who search for an escape.
>
> To live from instant to instant in a state of alert perception, alert novelty, like the watchman in time of war, is both essential and imperative if we really want to dissolve the pluralized "I."
>
> In human interrelations, in the co-existence with our fellow human beings, there are infinite possibilities for Self-Discovery.
>
> It is well known that in these interrelations the multiple defects we carry hidden in the unknown depths of the subconsciousness always emerge naturally, spontaneously and, if we are vigilant, we see and discover them.
>
> However, it is obvious that Self-Vigilance must always proceed from moment to moment.
>
> A discovered psychological defect must be completely comprehended in the various recesses of the mind.
>
> In depth comprehension is impossible without the practice of meditation.
>
> Any intimate defect is multi-faceted and has diverse links and roots which have to be studied judiciously.
>
> Self-Revelation is possible when there is complete comprehension of the defect that we sincerely want to eliminate.

"Pallas Giustiniani" Athena Nike. She representative the ascending serpentine force.

New Self-Determination springs up from the Consciousness when comprehension is total.

Superlative Analysis is useful if it is combined with deep meditation, then the flame of comprehension appears.

The dissolution of all those psychic aggregates which constitute the ego is hastened if we know how to take maximum advantage of the worst adversities.

Difficult psychological gymnasiums in the home, on the street or at work always offer the best opportunities.

To covet virtues is absurd; it is better to make radical changes.

Control of intimate defects is superficial and condemned to failure.

Deep change is fundamental and it is possible only by wholly comprehending every mistake.

By eliminating the psychic aggregate that constitute the "Me, Myself," the "I," we establish adequate foundations for correct action in our consciousness.

Superficial changes serve no purpose. We urgently need, without postponement, in-depth change.

Comprehension is the first step, elimination is the second.

— Samael Aun Weor, *The Great Rebellion*

Through metaphysical intercourse, the nitrogen and magnesium of ancient alchemists, the polarized astral light undergoes remarkable changes.

Such intimate alterations secretly influence electrochemical relations in the most vital units of our organism in order to transform its structure.

Waldemar says: "*When chemists tell us that all the biocatalysts of an organism appear to be an ordered system of inferior tele-causal factors, which act in accordance with life, in other words in the service of the superior objective of the organism, it is not difficult to conclude that the formation of internal emotions, reflections or impulses, depends on the radio-causal factors of the aura.*

"*Let us take a comparative look,*" says Waldemar, "*At the relationship between the living substance of ions and electrons, and we will be considerably nearer to comprehending the aforementioned.*"

It is clearly evident that at that marvelous instant in the garden of delights, at the exquisite moment when the male organ enters deep in to the woman's vagina, a very exceptional kind of electrical induction takes place.

> It is indubitable, then, that the tele-causal factors of the aura undergoing electric impulses offer surprising possibilities.
>
> In-depth psychological change can emerge in the profundity of the Consciousness if we know how to intelligently make use of the cosmic opportunity presented to us...
>
> We lose such a marvelous opportunity when we intend only to gratify our senses.
>
> – Samael Aun Weor, *The Mystery of the Golden Blossom*

Let it be understood that comprehension can occur without its vital counterpart, elimination. This occurs when we know very well the causes our evil deeds and lustful appetites, yet, simply do not care to remove them. Therefore, elimination is essential.

The subconscious mind is like intricate labyrinth of corridors and, through comprehension we learn the many paths of reasoning, feeling, and acting that the mind operates within. In summary we can say that through our own psychological processes we can become aware of our psychology. This is comprehension. However actual elimination requires something superior to the mind.

Elimination is just that, the elimination of ego. The mind can only label, reduce, deduce and hide from its own error. The true radical elimination cannot come from the mind itself. The mind cannot destroy itself, it can only modify itself. Therefore, the radical and true elimination can only occur through movements of energy that have their source beyond the mind. This is the science of tantrism or alchemy, and it is indispensible in the path of self-realization.

Tantrism is the science of harnessing the resultant energy of the crossing of elements. Bachelors who are chaste have a certain level of energy at their disposal for elimination, and consequently can achieve a certain level of elimination. The level of liberation that is possible for a bachelor is so profound when compared to this humanity's nominal state that some who have achieved it believe themselves to be totally enlightened and liberated. They end up teaching or implying that one is able to achieve total enlightenment without the use of tantrism. Confusion also springs about because many supposedly celibate teachers only practiced tantrism in secrecy, or in previous lives. The outcome of all this are many venerable lineages and traditions that do not teach tantrism either publicly or secretly. Usually, they have good intentions and teach a good doctrine, but they are ultimately incomplete and incorrect.

A true monk or nun is someone that protects their creative-sexual energy. The inferior or initial level promotes sexual abstinence. The superior or esoteric type of monk or nun practices tantrism as a couple. It is axiomatic that couples have the ability to manifest much greater levels of energy than a bachelor.

The creative comprehension of a defect is possible by living moment to moment in a state of alert "novelty-perception," and investigating the various corridors of the mind that open and shut within these moments. To observe, the mind must simply be, without any thought, without any agitation. Through the magnificent technique of self-observation, we find glimpses of psychological imperfections that we never have seen before. Within meditation, when a true sincerity to change is combined with disciplined willpower to achieve it, the most fluid understanding inevitably appears within our heart and the error itself is revealed with outstanding clarity. The Gnostic is filled with joy when he discovers his own imperfections, because then he can eliminate them. The Gnostic wants to shine perfectly in the radiance of his inner Father.

An ego that is understood in depth is like a child. As a child it remains within the psyche yet has little influence upon it. But all children grow, and if left unchecked this child will transform itself into monstrous demon again. So it is at this point that the student aspiring for change must appeal to a power that is superior to the mind in order to reduce particular psychological aggregates to dust. The only thing with this power is the Third Logos.

What is the Third Logos? The Third Logos is the Holy Reconciliation, the Third Principle Force, Binah, the Holy Spirit, Shiva! The Third Logos is at the root of your Being.

The Three Primary Forces are atomic principles upon which all other aspects of the Spirit manifest. Of the three, The Third Force is that which constructs and destructs forms of matter and energy. The Third Force is called Conciliating: it congeals the First (Affirmative) and the Second (Denial) forces. Without the Third, the First and the Second could not exist.

In Christianity, The Third Force is represented as a Man and Woman, Joseph and Mary. The Man we can also call the Holy Spirit. The Woman we can call the Divine Mother, or Kundalini Shakti. As a couple, they give birth to the Intimate Savior. Even if Jesus was born a thousand times in Bethlehem, it would be useless if the Intimate Savior is not born in your heart, by your own inner Iod-Chava: Holy Spirit and Divine Mother. The Savior is born only through tantrism or alchemy. The womb of the Savior is the matter of our bodies. The words "matter" and "Mother" are essentially the same.

Our Divine Mother is a derivate aspect of our own Being. This is the Mother Mary, the Mother Isis, the Eternal Virgin. The Divine Mother loves her child terribly. Even when we continue to turn our back to her, she will always be there because she is our Divine Mother. Without our mother we would truly be lost forever. The Divine Mother is abstract, she has no form, but she can take upon any form to you within your dreams, visions, and meditations.

The Divine Mother carries the Lance or Spear with which we must behead our ego. Athena Nike, the Grecian Virgin, is represented as a warrior and is affiliated with a shield and a snake. Athena's snake is the power of sex, the ascending Kundalini. Athena arms Perseus who goes after Medusa, and he decapitates her fatal serpentine head. Medusa is the representation of the negative aspect of sex.

Perseus by Benvenuto Cellini. He has killed Medusa, representative of the soul conquering the descending serpentine force. Perseus is armed with weapons given to him by Athena.

The myth states that those who gaze into the malignant beauty of Medusa transform into stone. Medusa is the ego one must behead: all of her many vipers (psychological aggregates) must die. Our Essence, the Buddhata, is trapped within the various dispersed egos that in their totality constitute our pseudo-existence. Each ego entraps a percentage of consciousness. Each ego that is beheaded liberates consciousness.

Remember that the ego has terminally infected the Lunar Bodies, a creation given by Nature for evolution. When one is identified with the ego, they are staring into the face of Medusa and do not work upon themselves, and because the intellectual animal is the summit of evolution, the only thing left is devolution.

All the vestments given to us by nature in our evolution are slowly disintegrated in Hell through devolution, eventually returning them to the state of a stone, and then into dust. If the Essence is trapped within the ego, then the Essence goes through Hell, pulled along within the ego. This is why those who stare into the face of Medusa turn to stone. It is better to liberate the Essence through self-will, which is also a painful process, yet it is much less painful, and the wisdom of good and evil is acquired from it.

Reaching Heaven has nothing to do with belief. In the cycles of Time everyone grows up, reaches adulthood and eventually dies, regardless of what they believe. All the matter of nature returns to Nature, every Nature born body is eventually reduced to dust and reused to form other bodies. This is how Nature works.

In the same way, every lunar body grows up, matures and eventually dies, yet unlike the physical body the lunar bodies are born and die in the cycles of Eternity. Even so, they still belong to Nature, and Nature will reduce them to dust regardless of what one believes.

This is why it is necessary to be "born again," to build the chariot that Ezekiel rode to Heaven with, to build the Solar Bodies. These bodies belong to the Monad, the Being, and are developed through individual self-will combined with the sublimation of sexual-creative energy. Therefore, those who disregard sex, those who reject sex, those who abuse sex, are really just identified with their personal Medusa. They work to strengthen her instead of working to destroying her, and they sincerely believe this is the way to Heaven. The crude fact remains, however, that every person who does not remove their ego will turn to stone.

Every entrance into the abode of Medusa is a battle with Medusa. The drama plays itself out with each and every psychological aggregate. When we ask the Divine Mother for the lance, we are in fact begging for the destruction of the *crystallized desire* within us, upon the sublime moments of alchemical copulation. By asking with a solemn heart to eliminate a defect that has been previously comprehended within meditation, the couple takes advantages of the destructive forces of death within the sexual act. The aspirant, while in meditation or during sacred intercourse, can visualize the aggregate that is to be eliminated in whatever fashion is suitable. There are those who visualize, for example, the aggregate in question being consumed by a fire, or being decapitated, etc., etc.

The constructive and destructive forces are present in both tantrism and fornication. In tantrism, the constructive forces crystallize the Solar Bodies, (and potentially a child) while the destructive forces eliminate the ego. In fornication, sexual intercourse with orgasm, the constructive forces crystallize the ego, (and potentially a child) while the destructive forces work to bring physical death into the world. Hence Genesis 2:17, *"you must not eat from the Tree of the Knowledge of Good and Evil, for when you eat of it you will surely die."* Immortality, which occurs after Resurrection, is the consequence of absolute chastity.

Many great yogis and gurus know this secret, the "Great Arcanum." The highest form of yoga is tantric. Very wise Tibetan monks are granted a consort wife. Usually, this would break their vows of chastity, but under these special circumstances, it is allowed because every man needs a woman to complete their self-realization, and every woman needs a man.

> Sexual energy is the finest energy of the infinite cosmos. Sexual energy can convert us into Angels or Demons. The image of truth

is found deposited in sexual energy. The cosmic design of Adam Christ is found deposited in sexual energy.

The Son of Man, the Super-Man, is born out of normal sexuality. The Super-Man could never be born from infrasexual people. The realm of infrasexual people is the abyss. The Greek poet Homer said: *"It is better to be a beggar on earth than a king in the empire of shadows."* This empire is the tenebrous world of the infrasexual ones.

– Samael Aun Weor, *The Perfect Matrimony*

There is an order in the work of self-realization. The one orchestrating the inner-work is the Being. Particular aggregates are brought to the attention of the student through "mysterious" means. The Being provides, through the application or restraint of one's karma, the circumstances that bring into the forefront particular flaws we possess in the psyche. From that point, one has the duty to observe, comprehend, and eliminate that particular flaw. Sometimes we succeed easily, other times we struggle for a long time, and still other circumstances appear in which we totally fail.

Yet, the Being never gives an ordeal too heavy. Failures are due not to our inabilities at an intrinsic level, but rather the failure to realize our intrinsic abilities. When a person takes up the work of self-realization, the Being often provides ordeals that push one to the edge, but the Being never gives his son something truly impossible. The Being wants a perfect soul, free of any impurity, and in order accomplish this He provides intense heat and pressure. The Being is a blacksmith that pounds the impurities out of the iron, but the blacksmith is useless without a forge... Vulcan needs the fire, the sex, in order to temper his sword and give it to Venus. Venus is love.

Vulcan displaying the Sword to his wife, Venus (Love).

Conclusions

Let us now summarize the principle axioms that have been presented in this book:

1. Every religious doctrine contains two fundamental levels. Firstly, the external, base, or exoteric teaching that instructs the public. Secondly, the esoteric or hidden teaching which is historically taught to only to a select group of individuals who were deemed worthy. The esoteric doctrine, *gnosis*, is today being publically delivered, yet the majority of people are not interested.

2. The vehicles (different schools, sects, and teachings) of the esoteric doctrine have waxed and waned throughout the centuries. The pontiffs of strictly exoteric vehicles have regularly persecuted the esoteric vehicles. Nevertheless, a body without a heart is not a living body. The heart of all doctrines is referred to as *gnosis*.

3. The purpose of a soul being born into the body of an intellectual animal (incorrectly referred to as "human being") is to transform instinctive, group-will, into intelligent and true individual will. This humanity is a failure at achieving this goal, and, instead, has developed a powerful current towards the crystallization of animalistic desire. Desire is the outcome of acting under ignorance, and ignorance is the inevitable outcome of enacting intellect without awakened consciousness.

4. It is necessary to awaken the consciousness in order to acquire gnosis, which is knowledge of one's self. Through gnostic development The Doctrine of Many "I's" is experienced, and, as a consequence, provides the realization of the imperative nature to destroy all psychological aggregates, because this is the only way to engender true, individual, human will. Without comprehension, psychological death is impossible.

Meditation is the tool to acquire comprehension. The purpose of meditation is to discover one's self. Forms of meditation are found in every religion.

5. The heart of religious pursuit is sexual in nature. The exoteric forms of religion require total sexual abstinence. The esoteric forms of religion teach how to transmute the sexual energy. Religious forms that undervalue sex, abuse sex, or repress sex, are dead or dying doctrines.

6. Nothing occurs due to belief. Faith is not belief. Faith is direct experience, a testimony of reality. Nothing occurs without a cause, and every cause has a measured effect. Without the Wedding Garments of the Soul, the soul cannot be received in Heaven. The Wedding Garments are fabricated using the "loop of thread" (tantrism).

7. The Being knows itself through his image, which is deposited in the sexual energy of the human soul. By transmuting the sexual energy, the image of God shines within the human soul.

8. Sex has the power to create and destroy not only physically, but psychically and spiritually. Sex is the power of the soul.

9. The Christ Principle finds itself in every school, religion, and tradition. It is only the name of the Principle that changes. The Christ is the Father of all Gods, the Verb, the Word, the Logos, the Light, the Life, the Way, and the Truth.

10. The Being is the Being, and the reason for the Being is to be the Being itself. Nevertheless, without self-cognizance, the happiness of the Being remains incomplete.

Finally, after contemplating all of this, the time has come to retire from the theoretical world and enter into the field of action. I think it is true that this humanity has grown weary from so many theories; today everyone wants to see for themselves.

With the right effort, we can all begin to awaken and with that, enter in the higher modes of life. What is more important than to know how to live without conflict? What is nobler than attempting to achieve the highest possibilities of a human? What is better than acquiring happiness?

Correctly practiced, the ancient teachings presented within are a pedagogy of the soul, a prescription for the alleviation of suffering, but, just as reading a doctor's prescription will do nothing to cure illness, neither will a theoretical reading of this book remedy the sorrows of life.

In the end, it does not matter what one thinks, or does not think. It does not matter what one believes, or does not believe. What matters is that we become conscious, intelligent, creative, and responsible human beings. Everything else in life is of little value.

Peace be with you!

Made in the USA
San Bernardino, CA
12 July 2017